Serving Women

Serving Women
Household Service in Nineteenth-Century America

FAYE E. DUDDEN

WESLEYAN UNIVERSITY PRESS

For Marshall

Copyright © 1983 by Faye E. Dudden
All rights reserved.

Wesleyan University Press
Published by University Press of New England,
Hanover, NH 03755

Manufactured in the United States of America

LIBRARY OF CONGRESS CATALOGING IN PUBLICATION DATA
Dudden, Faye E.
  Serving women.

  Includes bibliographical references and index.
    1. Domestics—United States—History—19th century.
I. Title
HD6072.2.U5D82 1983 305.4'364 83-1263
ISBN 0-8195-5072-8
ISBN 0-8195-6109-6 (pbk.)

5   4   3

Contents

Acknowledgments

I owe a great debt to archivists, curators, and local historians. I would especially like to thank Mary Huth, Karl Kabelac, and Alma Creek of the University of Rochester; Kathleen Majors of the American Antiquarian Society; Mary Smallman of the St. Lawrence County History Center; Mrs. Dorothea Ives of the Town of Salisbury, New York; and the staffs of the State Historical Society of Wisconsin and the Schlesinger Library.

Other scholars contributed generously to my work. Janet Bogdan and William Leach pointed out sources and gave me the benefit of inventive and inquiring critiques. Carol Kammen and Elizabeth Haig directed me to sources I would not otherwise have found. Bettina Berch, Ellen Dwyer, Harvey Green, Dolores Hayden, Karen Kearns, and Michael Sedlak generously shared their unpublished work. Mari Jo Buhle, Robert Bogdan, Alice Kessler-Harris, Sally Gregory Kohlstedt, and Nancy Tomes read the manuscript in different drafts and offered acute criticisms. Although I could not meet all their suggestions, this book is far better for the challenges they posed. Joan Jacobs Brumberg shared her unpublished research, read several different drafts, and never failed to provide a combination of intellectual sophistication and infectious professional enthusiasm. Very considerable thanks are due Christopher Lasch, who as my advisor encouraged this research in its earliest stages. He offered me freedom to pursue the work in my own way, thoughtful criticism on the manuscript at all stages of its development, and, in his own work, unfailing examples of the highest standards of intellectual inquiry.

My experience in public history, especially as part of the Historians-in-Residence program of the New York Historical Resources Center at Cornell University, encouraged me to keep my writing free of scholarly jargon and, I hope, close to the sensibilities of a public that is delighted to learn about a past which includes working people and women. Jeannette Hopkins's editing and Cynthia Wells's copy-editing shaped my prose to clarify my thoughts. Marshall Blake knows too well how much tedium and difficulty my research entailed; this book is for him, with thanks and encouragement in his fight for the rights of another generation of serving women.

Introduction

Annis Hall was born in 1891 in Gouverneur, New York, where her father milked a few cows and farmed the stony soil. When she and her brothers and sisters were young, her mother may have employed a hired girl. Sarah Haynes was born in 1875 in Langley Green, England. The eldest of eleven children of a factory worker, she went to work at age twelve, first as "eyes and ears" to her aunt, who was going deaf and served as head housekeeper in a large household. At twenty-two she came to America and served briefly before her marriage as a "companion" to an elderly lady. Annis Hall Richardson and Sarah Haynes Dudden were my grandmothers. They did not talk about what they had seen of service, and I never thought to ask until it was too late. I have not been able to write the stories my grandmothers never told me. But I have tried, using the tools of the historian, to understand and convey a part of the untold stories of earlier generations of American women, both those who served and those who were served.

In nineteenth-century America, household service was the most common occupation of working women, dwarfing alternatives like needle or factory work, and the experience of being served was part of the common course of middle-class married life. In mid-nineteenth-century American cities, for example, at any given time some 15 to 30 percent of all households included live-in domestic servants. Because American service was overwhelmingly female, it must be understood in terms of the determinants of women's lives, their burdens and privileges as daughters and mothers, workers and consumers, widows and wives. As its title is meant to suggest, this book is not only about the women who served, but also about the significance of the fact they served other women.

As I worked on this research I spoke about it to various groups. Many times I was approached afterwards by members of my audience who had personal stories to tell. "My grandmother . . ." they began. But like me, they often knew little of what must have been significant episodes in the lives of women whom they had otherwise known quite well. As Herbert Gutman has pointed out, much of the history of the American working class is lost to popular memory because one generation cannot or will not tell its painful stories to the next. If upward mobility or success is achieved, that story—the story with the happy ending—is chosen. The selectivity of memory has worked against domestic service not only because it was often painful but also because it was part of female experience and its pains therefore considered private, disconnected, and undignified. Those who employed servants had less urgent reasons to forget their experience, but they have shared a tendency to silence, although the hiring of domestic service was crucial to the practice of sentimental domesticity and the "true womanhood" so central to nineteenth-century middle-class culture.

Historians have rarely and only belatedly considered household service a subject worthy of their note. In 1890 Lucy Maynard Salmon, professor of history at Vassar College, wrote the first scholarly work on American domestic service. A committed Progressive as well as a member of the first generation of trained research historians, Salmon devoted a good part of her book to a statistical study she conducted among Vassar alumnae who employed servants. She offered a historical sketch, a discussion of her survey findings, and proposals for reform that would, she hoped, solve "the servant problem." Salmon's *Domestic Service* (New York:

Macmillan, 1890) stood as the accepted source on the subject until the 1970s when the new social history both reflected and generated new interest in the histories of work and of women. David Katzman's *Seven Days a Week: Women and Domestic Service in Industrializing America* (New York: Oxford University Press, 1978) was the pioneering modern social history of the subject, yet his work shared Salmon's attention to statistical evidence and her assumption that service was an institution of peculiar concern and importance to women. Katzman pushed further, focusing on the period after 1870 and documenting, as of course Salmon could not, the decline of live-in domestic service early in the twentieth century. He directed attention to crucial differences that arose from matters of race and ethnicity, he emphasized the heavy burden of household labor, and he focused attention on the difficult personal relationship between employer and servant. Most recently, in *Americans and Their Servants: Domestic Service in the United States from 1800 to 1920* (Baton Rouge, La., and London: Louisiana State University Press, 1981), Daniel Sutherland provided a sprightly account of service as a homogenous whole from 1800 to 1920. He argued that the diverse servant problems were caused generally by the "belated" or outdated aspects of such work. His extensive research reemphasized the importance of service in nineteenth-century America and reinforced the conclusion that servant problems were of considerable interest to Progressive-era reformers.

This book began out of a concern to understand the realities of "help," or hired girls, and the nature of change in household service from "help" to "domestic." In the popular press of the mid-nineteenth century, Americans commonly said in tones of bitterness and nostalgia: "You can't get good servants anymore." One writer declared in 1841 that old housekeepers complained about nothing more often than the decline of service over the previous twenty or thirty years. "Complaints are incessantly heard," wrote Eliza Leslie, "of the deterioration of servants."[1] Those who spoke of the good old days, however, often referred explicitly to "help." In 1872 Grace Ellis, writing on "Our Household Servants" in *The Galaxy*, referred to "the American 'help' as our grand-mothers knew it," a girl who was "the treasure of the household, beloved by the children and respected by the parents."[2] And in *The American Woman's Home* (1869) Catharine Beecher and Harriet Beecher Stowe pictured a time early in the century when mistress and maid had lived together in a log cabin. Then the rural popula-tion of New England had done all their own work and hired only a few helpers, who lived "in all respects as equals and companions," in a relationship of harmony, dignity, and productivity.[3]

It is easy and of course appropriate to be skeptical of nostalgic remarks like these and to be equally suspicious of accounts like Salmon's that seem to incorporate such nostalgia. Salmon argued that a peculiarly democratic form of service—help or hired girls—took shape at the time of the Revolution and lasted until over-whelmed by the influx of immigrants in the mid-nineteenth cen-tury. She seemed to romanticize antebellum democracy in a style characteristic of Progressive era historians. Modern scholarship has not taken up the question of the hired girl. Because he dealt pri-marily with developments after 1870, Katzman tended to neglect or minimize the significance of help, as did Sutherland, who was committed to viewing service from 1800 to 1920 as an unchang-ing whole. Yet testimony to the existence and the significance of help came from various sources. The first generation of American lexicographers included the term "help" for servants among Amer-icanisms "introduced from the necessity of our situation, in order to express *new ideas*."[4] Antebellum European travelers noticed this distinctive form of American service; indeed, some, like Mrs. Trollope, found in the inadequacies of "help" or hired girls an-other reflection of a chronic "want of refinement" and civilized society in the new nation.[5] Other travelers defended help as ap-propriate to an unpretentious home life, or at least preferable to fawning menials.[6] The reports, although confused, biased, prone to ignore or collapse distinctions, consistently pointed to help as a peculiarly American form of service.[7] David Schob's *Hired Hands and Plowboys: Farm Labor in the Midwest, 1815–1860* (Urbana, Ill.: University of Illinois Press, 1975), has a chapter devoted to the hired girl. Although shaped by the concerns of agricultural history, Schob's research in farm diaries and account books confirmed the hired girl's presence.

I will argue that there were two distinct forms of nineteenth-century household service, help and domestics, which can be fully understood only in terms of the shift from one to the other. The complaints of mid-century about servant problems and the memory of a better past had some truth. The altered usage noticed by Beecher and Stowe was a symptom: "help," or "hired girls," were giving way to "domestics" in language and in fact, reflecting the socioeconomic and ideological transformations of the nineteenth century that recast work roles and family life. As urban industrial capitalist social relations took the place of an older way of life organized around agriculture, handicraft production, and rural customs, American society experienced pervasive changes in the relations between home and production and between worker and marketplace, even in types of work that were not industrialized. The transition from help to domestics in household service was neither a rapid nor a complete transformation, for both types of servant could be found in 1800 and in 1900 as well. Nor do the two types of servants constitute discrete categories into which every individual case can be unerringly sorted. Rather, the help or hired girl and the domestic are models or ideal types, useful not for classificatory neatness but for explanatory power. Their characteristic contrasts elucidate fundamental change in this most common type of women's work, change that varied with the pace and pattern of regional development but everywhere revealed similar direction and substance—everywhere, that is, except the South, where slavery took the place of free service and where even after emancipation service took forms that cannot be understood apart from the heritage of race slavery. Southerners' use of the term "servant" as a euphemism for slave futilely attempted to conceal significant differences. I have largely excluded southern service, slave or free, from this study.[8]

For the sake of examining the contrast between help and domestics, I have identified work behavior that often appeared casual and unsystematic at the time. "Help" denoted less an occupation than an activity and was therefore particularly subject to loose and flexible usage. In practice help were likely to deny the name of servant, while domestics usually had to accept that title. The irregular and laggardly change from one type of service to the other reflected the indirect connections between the private sphere and the larger society. Both types of nineteenth-century servants, help and domestics, performed housework for pay. Servants were increasingly hired on a labor market, but their employers did not behave with the regularity of other employers because they did not compete to realize profits but elected to spend money thus as a matter of preference. Employers consulted changing "needs" that were as much a matter of taste and custom as of budget and technology. Nor did employees, or potential employees, in service always work with the regularity one might expect in a labor market, since so many, especially the farmers' daughters who helped or "worked out," responded as much to personal goals or family constraints as to market demands. Both employers and servants created space for idiosyncratic variety within the two large patterns.

I have examined the social consequences of the transformation of nineteenth-century serving women. The growth and maturation of American industrial capitalism dramatically altered the workplace, even the landscape, and indirectly transformed the home and family life. According to one of the central conceits of nineteenth-century popular thought, the home, woman's special sphere, remained a stable anchor in the increasingly stormy seas of social change. Yet the home and family life *did* change, even though, until recently, historians failed to notice. The change in household service is a way of understanding how the specifics of social change were experienced in women's lives both within and without the home.

As employers demanded longer hours and more stringent work discipline from domestics than they had from help and delegated more of the work to them, they were able to free themselves from a significant part of the burden of household work. In the context of rapid economic development, social identity rested more and more upon proper social observances and effective status competition, while according to the ideology of domesticity middle-class women were to achieve their fulfillment in the elaboration of domestic space and rituals. Since part if not all of their household work was actually performed by domestics, middle-class women were encouraged to use technological advances to raise housekeeping standards, especially those associated with cleanliness. In hiring domestics middle-class women found the means to make domesticity more flexible, accommodating roles of authority and activity rather than passivity and isolation. Supervising domestics could also be interpreted as a form of benevolence, since it was the occasion of considerable contact between women across class lines, and it helped to effect the transition into leisure and consumption since the same domestics who secured a woman some ease also demanded of her a work role similar to that of entrepreneurial men. Supervision of domestics was far from trouble-free, but even its difficulties shaped conventional women's lives and influenced feminist proposals such as cooperative housekeeping. The division of labor struck between employers and domestics may also have made the middle-class family a more effective context for child-rearing than it would become after the decline of live-in service in the twentieth century.

For the young women who worked in service the transition from help to domestics made work more demanding and demeaning, prompting the withdrawal from service of many of the native-born daughters who had been willing to help. The nature of the experience of women in service depended partly on their age, expectations, and family context, and domestic service still offered some attractions to immigrant girls who came from backgrounds of great deprivation and had strong motives to accumulate savings. But wages, hours, and working conditions were not good, and working women's willingness to enter service seems to have reflected above all the lack of alternative employment opportunities. Enduring harsh conditions may have encouraged young women to develop self-reliance but also made it obvious that service was no way to spend a lifetime, and domestic service implicitly taught young women to value marriage and to accept reliance upon male wage earners. Domestic service had drastically different meanings for employer and employee, but it can be understood to have reinforced the acceptance of domestic roles both among the women who served and among those who were served. The contrasting experiences of employer and employee in domestic service illuminate the practical meaning of class in nineteenth-century America, the privileges nourished and the human costs exacted.

One of the privileges of class has been the ability to leave behind documents and thus to enter and to shape the historical record. The major primary sources I consulted for this study were family papers, women's diaries, letters, and reminiscences. These materials, generated largely by middle-class employers, exhibit considerable bias, of course. Still, the historian can, I believe, distinguish between analyzing self-serving remarks and evaluating the record of behavior they contain. When supplemented by the scraps of extant testimony from servants themselves, employer sources can, with care, be used as raw materials for even-handed history. I have attempted to study both sides of the service relationship. Employers left us more records, but they also held more power in the service relationship, so that their intentions and pretensions repay our attention even when we reject their biases.

This study covers a lengthy time span and a wide geographical area. The concerns of social history do not lend themselves to the tidy boundaries historians were once accustomed to find in the study of war and politics. Yet social history has often been pursued by means of quantitative local studies narrowly focused in one area and time. I have great respect for the standards of proof and precision implicit in social science methods, but my own work is different. Because of the nature of the census record of women's occupations, a quantitative local study could not have caught the transition from help to domestics. Nor would a local focus have permitted me to draw upon a sufficient body of primary sources to locate individuals who wrote about the mundane household concerns that most people took for granted or did not commit to paper. I have chosen to pursue this study through widely ranging qualitative sources. My sources span the continent, focusing primarily on New England, the Middle Atlantic states, and the Old Northwest. As noted above, I do not discuss the South directly, and I treat the trans-Mississippi and Far West only occasionally. Such materials have permitted me to discern large patterns of change and to examine a national culture and an emerging labor market that was national, even international in scope. Service was shaped when young women moved to the cities or even across the Atlantic to go into service, and employers fretted about the degree to which their housekeeping arrangements matched those projected in *Godey's*. Of course there was great variety in the experience of service: differences were not merely local but individual, for reasons I have tried to explore. In order to see the large patterns and understand the sources of variety, it has been necessary to see service whole and to accept some of the imprecision this approach implies.

By 1800 household service already had a long and complex history. Helping may have developed through some modification of the traditional European assumption that service was the appropriate occupation of youth, a modification that became necessary in a land in which small proprietorship was easily achieved and egalitarian thought found practical forms. Unfree labor, both slave and indentured, was crucial to colonial development, but the revolutionary era brought the decline of indentured service in all the states as well as the demise of northern slavery, changes that seem to have had as much to do with population changes and economics as with egalitarian thought.[9] It seems likely that in this period the small commercial elite in American cities, seeking an alternative to indentured or enslaved household service, turned to free labor and attempted to imitate European models in creating the earliest forerunners of the domestic, while the rest of the population relied upon the exchange of daughters in helping. But the changing conditions of eighteenth-century service are beyond the scope of this study. Similarly, this book closes with 1890, when Lucy Maynard Salmon inaugurated a period of remarkable concern with, and investigation of, domestic service by Progressive-era reformers. Because I have felt that the work on this latter period by Katzman, Sutherland, and others makes further study unnecessary, I have strayed past the 1890 mark only occasionally, when bits of evidence seemed useful and relevant. I have focused on the uniquely American form of service that had emerged by the nineteenth century and on the story of how and why household service continued to change within that century. The period between 1800 and 1890 permits a view of the emergence of industrial capitalism and urban life, of the women's roles associated with the flowering of the ideology of domesticity, the birth of feminism, and the steady increase in women's work within the paid labor force.

I have been concerned with the service relationship as it was experienced on both sides, with the cultural significance of this work relationship for middle-class and working women, both of whom were, in different ways, consigned to restricted lives. Nineteenth-century household service tells us something about how individuals lived within restrictions, whether resignedly or rebelliously; its story therefore illuminates the slow, difficult, often unseen paths along which women have moved to alter their choices and their world. In ways too often forgotten, nineteenth-century women endured or embraced the narrow sphere allotted to them, tracing out lives whose substance was often shaped by household work, paid or unpaid, done for them or done by them, by their actions and their attitudes when they served or when they were served.

ONE **Hired Girls**

Many mid-nineteenth-century employers of servants looked back on hired girls with wistful nostalgia. Samuel Griswold Goodrich, an author of moralistic tales for children, who was born in 1793, recalled that his boyhood home in Ridgefield, Connecticut had been marked by "perfectly good understanding and good feeling" between masters and servants. The servants had been "treated as friends," "respected and cherished." He thought he knew why service had changed: servants had "lowered their calling by low feelings and low manners." [1]

The perfectly good feelings Goodrich recalled were a figment of his imagination, [2] yet the relationship between help and their employers did in fact involve less friction than would later prevail with domestics. The stresses of helping were eased by the dynamics of production for market rather than for use, and by the open, nonexclusive definitions of family that permitted help to share the dinner table with their employers. Patterns of recruitment, working conditions, and hours all reflected a degree of mutual accommodation that was not without friction but never broke down completely. The helper or hired girl reflected characteristic women's roles and family relations in an American society of small producers.

Household Production

Early in the nineteenth century, women and girls were often hired to assist in producing certain goods for market, especially textiles.

Samuel Griswold Goodrich remembered in his boyhood "the burden of the spinning being done by a neighbor of ours, Sally St. John." Another neighbor, Molly Gregory, daughter of the town carpenter, also helped spin the Goodrichs' wool, singing hymns while at work in their attic.[3] The New England families studied by Nancy Cott frequently hired young women to spin for them. The homespun textiles these young women helped to produce may have clothed the family, but such production also led to participation in trading and marketing networks, since few families possessed resources and capabilities in just the right amounts to meet only their own needs. They commonly paid for certain services, especially spinning, and traded part of the product for the work. Even as early as the seventeenth century in New England, women's production of textiles in the home resulted not in family self-sufficiency but in wives and daughters entering into patterns of local hiring and trade. Late eighteenth-century farm women frequently "changed work," trading certain textile-making skills with others who were experienced in various tasks, including warping looms, making loom harnesses, carding, and—most common of all—spinning. Early in the nineteenth century, homespun entered the market in large amounts, and through its sale women contributed significantly to family income. When they hired help for the process, therefore, they could calculate the profitability of the hiring.[4]

Farm women hired help to work with them in other activities that could be measured against the market. Dairying, from milking the cows to churning butter and making cheese, was women's work, as was keeping chickens and gathering eggs. Many hired girls took on these chores.[5] Farm families carried the produce of this work—firkins of butter and dozens of eggs—into town to sell outright or to exchange for store credit. In the 1790s La Rochefoucauld-Liancourt met young women riding into Philadelphia on horseback with forty-pound weights of butter, cheese, and poultry to sell. Fifty years later Mrs. Houstoun saw farmers and their wives heading into Utica, New York with tubs of butter to exchange for store products.[6] Guri Endresen, living in Harrison, Minnesota in 1866, wrote to her mother in Norway that she milked three cows, and "of these I have sold butter, the summer's product, a little over 230 pounds: I sold this last month [November] and got $66 for it."[7] "Butter and egg money" was no petty matter; for many families it was their only spendable cash because the profits of major field crops went to clear title to the land, to pay taxes, or to finance capital improvements.[8] As was true in textile work, the utility of a helper could be measured against a market return. In 1810 Sarah Connell wrote from Concord, New Hampshire that the "young woman who lives with us . . . soon leaves us, as she is not much acquainted with the business of a dairy."[9]

Hiring help in this way was not a carefree undertaking, but it probably involved less friction than hiring for nonmarket women's work. Work standards could be set at least partly by third parties—by the merchants who determined if the butter was sweet, the cloth even and firm. Women could, in turn, impose those impersonal verdicts upon their help without appearing arbitrary or unreasonable. More important, employers probably found more satisfaction in dealing with such help, even if they were saucy: the transaction either paid or, if not, could be terminated for reasons both parties might consider valid. Their calculation was not exactly a matter of profit and loss, since some part of the product was usually consumed at home. Yet if a woman could realize enough to defray the hired girl's wage and more in marketing the goods, she won for herself an income and a certain degree of independence. She stood on much firmer ground than if she merely expended her husband's income.[10]

The diary of a northern New York farm woman in the 1820s reveals the differing dynamics of hiring help for home production and for other household cares. Phebe Orvis Eastman, born in 1801, lived in Hopkington, New York. An accomplished weaver, she had gone out to weave, taught school, and assisted her uncle and aunt at their tavern before her marriage in 1823. After her marriage she regularly hired girls to spin for her. In August 1827 she recorded matter-of-factly, "Been and hired Ziba Rawley to spin for me." [11] That was that. Ziba Rawley is not mentioned again in the diary, and we see no indications of difficulty, annoyance, or regret. In a similar terse entry Phebe Eastman noted Lucinda Delong's coming to spin for her in the summer of 1829.

Phebe Eastman knew with some precision that such hirings yielded pecuniary rewards. When she was ill one day she wrote, "Wove all day for one yard. Poor encouragement to hire spinning." Her sense of the relative importance of such work is reflected in her repeated frustration on days when she could do "nothing but my chores and attend my Babe." [12] Cooking for large numbers of hired men and caring for the children who arrived at regular intervals did not seem like accomplishments to her; carding, warping, dyeing, and weaving did. She always noted in her diary how many yards she wove. Producing textiles gave her a measure of economic independence. She referred to trading with peddlers and to "settling up" with those for whom she had woven coverlets, just as she in turn settled up with her help.

Hiring help for housework, by contrast, always left her in a nettled mood. She only hired such help when she or one of her family was ill; recognizing that it amounted to an economic drain, she rejected help if she could manage to do so. For example, shortly after her second child was born, when she felt feeble, she wrote, "I do not earn my board seemingly yet it saves one dollar per week by not hiring it done." At another time, when her young daughter was ill, she wrote, "My Babe is troublesome. When I have anyone to help me that makes it unprofitable." [13]

But sometimes Phebe Eastman could not avoid employing help. In December 1827, after her daughter scalded her hands badly, she struggled along for a week and concluded, "Obliged hire a girl, Miss Mary Ann Heath, a good girl." [14] Mary Ann, a neighbor, had worked for the Eastmans before. In July 1826, when Mrs. Eastman had had a two-year-old son and a five-month-old daughter to cope with, Mary Ann had come to spin and to look after the children. She had worked intermittently for Mrs. Eastman that summer and fall, a few days at a time. When Mary Ann's mother died in September 1826, Phebe Eastman was moved by the loss, and the following spring she attended the revival meeting where Mary Ann was baptized. Throughout most of 1827, with the Eastman family in good health, Mary Ann was seldom mentioned in the diary, appearing only occasionally as "visiting" or "spending the night," whether for stints of work or social calls, or perhaps a little of each, it is impossible to tell.

Although Mrs. Eastman felt she could call Mary Ann Heath a "good girl" when she hired her in January 1828, the dynamics of hiring a girl who was "unprofitable," as Mrs. Eastman understood it, soon contributed to friction. Mrs. Eastman was annoyed to discover that Mary Ann was not as skillful at housework as at spinning or minding the children. "I have more to do than I had before I hired a girl," she wrote. Two days later she reported "learning Mary Ann to wash, not tractable." In February she confessed herself "almost tired out and sick of hiring help," and a few days later she dismissed Mary Ann. "I find I can keep my house more decent without a hired girl than with one," she wrote.[15]

Hiring help like Mary Ann Heath had been the product of temporary necessity. The fact that Mary Ann was a local girl known to her employer could not erase the frustrations of one accustomed to hire in order to realize a return on the hiring. When the help was not helpful, it effectively added insult to material injury. Phebe Eastman's difficulties with Mary Ann should serve to part some of the nostalgic clouds surrounding the memories of help, yet at the same time this diary suggests that one particular form of help, such as Ziba Rawley or Lucinda Delong provided, may have been relatively satisfactory.

Most of the opportunities for women to produce for the market in their homes and thereby hire from a position of relative strength began to disappear after 1815, as textile production was taken over by industry. Farm women would continue to produce butter and eggs throughout the century. In 1861 the J. F. Knox family of West Galway, New York hired a girl named Kate to milk a dairy of twenty-five cows, to make cheese, and to do the housework, all for two dollars a week. Ann Diggem worked for the William Thompson family of Salisbury, New York between 1855 and 1857, making cheese and doing housework.[16] Such production became the exception rather than the rule.

Even when they did not produce directly for sale, farm women like Phebe Eastman filled important productive roles. In the 1820s more than three-quarters of the population of the northern United States lived, like the Eastmans, on single-family farms. Women's work was crucial to the farm's survival and success as an economic unit. Phebe's husband, Samuel, probably raised sheep as well as field crops, and he may have done some lumbering and land-clearing on the side.[17] He shot deer for his family to eat in all seasons, caught trout, raised and butchered hogs, and made large quantities of maple sugar. But most of the Eastmans' daily needs depended on Phebe. She made butter and cheese from the cows they kept, and she salted the pork, "tried out" the lard, and made soap by the barrelful. She raised a vegetable garden and gathered wild fruit, including forty-six pounds of blackberries one day in August 1828. She baked and cooked, sewed and laundered the clothing. She even bound the family's shoes herself after an itinerant shoemaker cut them out, and sewed a coat and vest after an itinerant tailor measured and cut the cloth.

The Eastmans had to find a market, if perhaps a small one, for their produce—his corn or wool or lumber, her textiles. They probably needed the money to pay for their newly acquired land, and to build their barn. But they purchased few consumer goods. Over a period of three years, Phebe Eastman mentions purchasing the following items: essence of wintergreen, transparent soap, thread, bedticking, a comb, pins, plaid cloth, a mug, a pair of tumblers, a pound of tea, and some plush for a bonnet. This list is probably incomplete but representative. She often spoke of acquiring those goods by "trading" with peddlers or the storekeeper, a term she evidently meant quite literally in some cases. The work of women like Phebe Eastman, crucial in near-subsistence farming, proved equally vital as farmers began to move into the marketplace, for women's work effectively precluded the need for extensive consumer buying and thus made the enterprise economically viable.[18]

Contemporaries recognized the indispensability of women's work on the farm when they viewed the single or widowed farmer, unsentimentally, as a man in desperate straits.[19] This admission may have meant that, despite the frustrations it often brought, hiring household help when that was economically feasible, was relatively easy to justify. Certainly the agricultural press urged farmers to hire a girl when possible to lighten the load on their wives.[20]

Farm women hired their help in the absence of an impersonal labor market. In rural areas few women participated in wage labor, and there was no formal group of wage workers called domestic servants, only neighbor girls known by name. Almost all women performed housework, and the fact that servants received part of their compensation in the form of room and board helped to blur the line between paid and unpaid housework.[21] So did community patterns of mutual aid, in which women helped one another out without pay in times of need. The hesitation to define hired girls as wage workers was reflected in the term "help" itself, concealing as it did the question of payment. People spoke of "needing a girl," or "hiring a woman," meaning a servant, but the fact of service was left to inference. *Scribner's Monthly* reported in 1871 that in rural areas whenever a woman was heard to use the pronoun "she" without prefix, it could safely be taken to mean her help.[22] Since an economy of small producers did not generate or sustain firm and distinctive groups of service employers or employees, these roles found no fixed designation in the language.

Family Relations

Some women and girls entered into helping roles that substituted for domestic service but were not characterized by monetary relations. The orphaned cousin or the maiden aunt helped—i.e., functioned in lieu of a servant—throughout the nineteenth century. Lucy Larcom took a break from mill work to help a married sister. "My married sisters had families growing up about them," she wrote, "and they liked to have us younger ones come and help take care of their babies. One of them sent for me just when the close air and long days' work were beginning to tell upon my health, and it was decided I had better go." She referred to this sister as having "no domestic help besides mine." [23] Lucy Larcom, with the ability to support herself in mill work, was unusual. Most unattached women would have had more trouble finding work by which they could support themselves, and their informal adoption by other family members would be more permanent, more a matter of necessity.

Such women exchanged their help for a home, but personal friction or family finances could make their position awkward, resented, or crassly calculated. Matty Silver in Edith Wharton's *Ethan Frome* was a poor cousin with "no place to go." She came to Ethan and Zena Frome's house to help without pay. Similarly, Christy Devon, orphaned and taken for granted as a drudge on her uncle's farm, made an appealing heroine in Louisa May Alcott's novel *Work*.

Reality provided the models for fiction. Phebe Eastman had been shuttled between two different sets of aunts and uncles after her mother died when she was an infant. [24] As relatedness became more distant, these arrangements could come to sound thoroughly businesslike. Catharine Maria Sedgwick recalled that after her mother fell ill, "my father employed as housekeeper and general family directress my aunt, the widow of my mother's half-brother." [25]

Although relatives who helped without pay were not really servants, one sort of helper occupied a particularly ambiguous position between servant and nonservant. This was the homeless child, the orphan with no relatives to take her in. Early in the nineteenth century the disposition of orphans still followed patterns established by the Elizabethan poor laws. Orphaned children were commonly bound out at about age ten or twelve to serve until they were eighteen. Boys were bound out to agriculture or trades of all sorts, girls almost always to housewifery—in other words, to helping. Since the girls received only room and board and some sort of premium—a suit of clothes or a small lump sum—at age eighteen, they provided the most inexpensive form of domestic service. In practical terms, girls who were too childish and untaught to be of much help in the first few years soon grew and could be trained to be good help by the time they reached fifteen or so. They then provided cheap and effective service until they turned eighteen. [26] But they were supposed to be at the same time objects of charity and tutelage. Families were to provide them with proper religious instruction and schooling, and in general to save them from lives of disorder and crime by making them a part of a family.

Even when, in the nineteenth century, communities and private charitable organizations began to build asylums to isolate and treat dependents and deviants of various types, including both homeless and delinquent children, the able-bodied orphan who was of sufficient age to be useful continued to be bound out. Asylum and refuge managers proposed only brief periods of confinement for such children, until they were of sufficient age, or, if delinquent, until sufficiently rehabilitated, to be placed. [27]

Most historical work on charity and dependence in the nineteenth century has focused on the history of specific institutions and their clienteles, and it is hard to say, therefore, how many youngsters were bound out. Records of specific charitable societies suggest that they placed only small numbers of girls.[28] Many more children may have been bound out by agreements made directly between employers and living parents who could not raise their children. In Ithaca, New York at about mid-century, the father of a fourteen-year-old girl came to see Mrs. Williams to arrange a transfer from the Riggs family to the Williams family. It was a matter of direct negotiations. Mrs. Riggs had taken Anna as a helper, agreeing to clothe and "school" her three months of the year until she was eighteen.[29]

Women who were involved in charitable work acted as go-betweens. In 1837 Siba Hand Smith wrote to Henrietta Clarke that she had found her a little girl in Rochester: "This I have done through the agency of Mrs. Durand—who truly careth for the poor. The child is about ten years of age."[30] One inquiry received by Amy Kirby Post of Rochester in 1850 made it quite clear that these bindings were arranged by individuals as well as through benevolent agencies. A Mrs. Beatty of Aurora, New York wrote, "Having understood that thee had charge of some benevolent institution, from whence I could obtain a child, I thought I would request thee to have charge of one for me. I would like a girl from 9 to 12 and if thee has not direct management of such a place, thee might possibly find one that would like a home, if so, would thee please write me."[31]

The bound child's ambiguous status is reflected in the language of a letter of inquiry sent in 1834 from Eliza Bacon, the secretary of the Ladies' Orphan Asylum in Utica, New York, to Helen Breese. "We are anxious to know how you like Julia Connors, the little orphan who you took into your employ a short time since and whether you are willing to take the entire charge of her;—in other words, whether you wish she should be bound to your service."[32] Julia is an orphan who must be "taken charge of," yet she is also taken into "employ" or, as Mrs. Bacon plainly states to avoid any confusion, "bound to your service." The terms "girl" and "little girl" stretched to cover this situation. So a Syracuse woman wrote in 1846 that her aunt "would like to get a little girl and asked me to look in the asylum." [33]

Binding out apparently began to decline in the 1830s. With increasing ethnic and religious differences, poor parents became more reluctant to bind their children to families of a different background or faith, and long-term declines in mortality began to reduce the number of orphans with which the population had to cope. [34] Some evidence suggests that the decline in binding out was at least partly due to an increasing tendency to view the bound girl's position as an inappropriate anomaly. In the 1830s the managers of the Boston Female Asylum began to complain that families selfishly wanted only the servant and lost sight of the child. In the same decade the managers of the Salem Female Charitable Society began to bind more girls to strangers and to collect cash wages for their work. [35] Employers were not the only ones who found reason to prefer a wage-work relationship unmixed with pretense to family ties. In *Society in America* (1837) Harriet Martineau reported problems with bound girls. "Under a good mistress," she wrote, "this is an excellent bargain for the girl; but mistresses complain that as soon as the girls become really serviceable, by the time they are fourteen or fifteen, they begin to grow restless, having usually abundance of kind friends to tell them what good wages they might get if they were free." [36]

Thus bound help who were not paid for their work tended, to an even greater degree than unpaid relatives, to muddy the boundaries of household service. Both contributed to the remembered virtues of help by lending plausibility to the belief that the helper was in some sense "part of the family." Sheer economic necessity placed girls in a bound-out situation, and economic motives inspired many of their employers as well. Yet each was supposed to enter into an almost adoptive relationship, on the assumption that performing housework in the home of a stranger could be a quasi-familial rather than a monetary relationship. Such an assumption, dating from the Elizabethan origins of the indenture of pauper children, had seemed realistic in a colonial context in which the family fulfilled many social functions, but its persistence in the nineteenth century also owed something to the conventions of sentimental popular literature.

Probably the most widely circulated image of an ideal servant in the 1830s was a bound girl, Martha, in Catharine Maria Sedgwick's best-selling novel *Home* (1835). Martha works for William and Anne Barclay. Barclay is a printer in New York City, though he, his wife, and Martha are all country-born. Since he is a self-employed craftsman, home and workplace are one, as on the farm. Martha also is an example of ideal country virtues transplanted to city life. She is emphatically a helper: "Servant! we beg Martha's pardon, *help*. Serving most assiduously, she had an antipathy to the word *servant*. Was she not right? *Help* may have a ludicrous and perhaps an alarming sound to unaccustomed ears; but is there a word in the English language more descriptive of the service rendered by a New England domestic; truly a 'republican independent dependent,' and the very best servant." [37] Sedgwick pictures Martha as being taken into the heart of the Barclay family, sharing their hopes and fears and remaining with the family after she is grown. Martha and Mrs. Barclay then combine to take in and raise another orphan, so that Martha becomes a "benefactress" herself and continues an unbroken chain of helpers who work for love rather than money. Sedgwick referred to helping as a new relationship; in fact, it was not new but beginning to decline and in the cities to disappear even as she wrote.

As Carol Lasser has pointed out, the tale of the orphan sent out to service who went on either to marry well or to become a permanent "part of the family" had a long literary run in popular nineteenth-century novels like *The Lamplighter* (1854) and *Redwood* (1824). [38] Louisa May Alcott managed to combine both happy outcomes in her *Eight Cousins* (1874) and its sequel, *Rose in Bloom* (1876). The young heroine, Rose Campbell, "adopts" Phebe, an orphaned kitchen girl, making her first a childish playmate and later an accomplished singer and a polished companion. Phebe eventually marries one of the Campbell cousins, but only after she surmounts family objections to her background by saving the life of the favorite Campbell uncle. Alcott's tales illustrate the literary license often necessary to finesse these stories: Phebe's transit from kitchen to parlor is accomplished offstage, on an extended European tour supposed to have occurred in the interval between the two books.

For writers of sentimental women's fiction like Sedgwick and Alcott, the bound girl provided the means through which middle-class domesticity could extend its all-important influence even to those disqualified by class or family status from enjoying it directly. The bound girl also provided an appealing dramatic persona because she could experience conflict and development in a setting in which many kinds of conflict—for example, that between husband and wife—could not be dealt with. But such writers nostalgically projected the intense emotionalism of emerging middle-class domesticity on to the situation of the bound girl. In fact, the bound girl's position reflected the loose, flexible, and relatively unsentimental definition of family boundaries characteristic of small producers whose homes were necessarily open to hired workers.[39] Mary Ryan has noted that in 1815 in Whitestown, New York several households "sheltered persons with anomalous titles like 'a girl who lives with them,' or 'a girl taken in to bring up.'" Only by later standards of intense domesticity would their presence begin to seem anomalous. As Ryan remarks, the openness of early families—to servants, boarders, kinsmen, neighbors, and church members—could call into question whether they were *private* institutions at all in the current meaning of the term.[40]

Bound helping could encompass a wide range of practical arrangements and emotional possibilities, which accounts for its persistence in an emerging industrial order. Some orphan girls were in effect adopted, for the same reasons of sentiment that prompt modern adoptions. Elizabeth Blackwell, for example, visited Randall's Island to find a seven-year-old orphan named Kitty Barry, who became her daughter, friend, housekeeper, secretary, and companion for life. By contrast, Eliza Farnham recalled her adoption as no more than a maneuver to gain free labor. After her mother died when she was four, she was placed with a western New York farm couple, where her "aunt" beat and abused her.[41]

As the bound girl's situation demonstrates, the notion of family and the notion of help had loosely conceived boundaries. Help were often seen as cantankerous, unreliable, infuriating; help themselves found many of their employers oppressive or obnoxious. But when such difficulties arose, the fact that the boundaries of helping were loosely defined tended to permit personal conflicts to be interpreted as just that—personal conflicts—rather than as examples of a general servant problem.

Phebe Eastman provides one more example of this kind of looseness in definition. In March 1829, carrying a sick baby around and nursing a bad foot herself, she decided to hire another girl. This time she visited her Uncle Brooks and "took home a girl by the name of Margaret Duffy, an Irish girl. Oh God, assist me to train her up in the way she should go thus when she is old she may not depart from it. Aged fifteen." Mrs. Eastman was serious in her resolution to train Margaret; three days later she was "learning Margaret to spool," and at the end of the month she noted "undertaking to learn Margaret to read."[42] Yet just a week later she confessed defeat in these projects, concluding that Margaret would never learn to weave or sew.

Mrs. Eastman was content for a while to let Margaret handle some of the less skilled work at which she seemed competent, such as washing. On at least one occasion she sent Margaret to school with her own children instead of trying to teach the girl herself. Perhaps Margaret was more interested in attending barn raisings, as she did in late April, than in self-improvement. Phebe East-man's opinion of the girl continued to plummet, and by mid-May she concluded, "Margaret is so saucy I can hardly bear her. Have told her if she did not do better I would not keep her." Apparently the warning was ineffective. On May 19 Mrs. Eastman wrote, "The ill treatment I receive from Margaret is worse than hard labour much." On June first she decided to dismiss the girl. Perhaps Margaret had gone elsewhere in the neighborhood with an exaggerated tale of her grievances, for on May 29 Mrs. Eastman had "called over to Mr. Chases and converse[d]. Find Margaret tells lies." [43]

The dismissal evidently spurred Margaret to a furious counter-attack. On June 2 Mrs. Eastman recorded, "Margaret told many lies," and on June 4, "Margaret lies in such a manner that Mr. E. has turned her out of doors." The next day she reflected, "I am astonished to think that any person could do as Margaret has done. I am glad she has left my house." Exactly what Margaret had done we will never know, but she felt as much aggrieved as Mrs. East-man, and on June 10 she returned to the farm to confront her former employer: "Margaret came to tell me I lied once more." [44] That was the end of the story of Margaret Duffy. Through all this bitter feud Phebe Eastman made no general remarks about hired girls or Irish servants, but focused on Margaret, comparing her behavior to what "any person" might do. Although Phebe East-man sometimes delivered herself of a poor opinion of hired girls in general, she also knew her help as individuals and did not readily categorize all her difficulties with them in terms of a generalized servant problem. Hired girls could be unsatisfactory, but Margaret was just Margaret—just outrageous.

Early nineteenth-century helping did in some ways involve less friction than the urban domestic service to which mid-century Americans would compare it, in part, as noted, because of possibilities for profit in hiring help for women's work, in part because of muddy conceptual boundaries of the idea of help, indeed, the idea of the family itself. The helping relationship was not necessarily cordial, but friction could often be interpreted in personal terms rather than in terms of the characteristics of the occupational group.

Recruitment and Hiring

Hired girls enjoyed other advantages over domestics in patterns of recruitment and hiring. A viable family economy close at hand gave them protection and allowed them flexibility. Help tended to enter service casually, temporarily or on a part-time basis. Even though hired for pay, they tended to deny pecuniary motives. Indeed, they often entered service with a sense, excessively protested but plausible nonetheless, that they did so to "oblige" their employer. Those who were neighbors' daughters, like Mary Ann Heath, had homes to return to and were not therefore absolutely dependent upon their wages to survive. In 1815 Hezekiah Niles wrote of women and girls hired to do housework that ". . . if they do not like the usage they receive, [they] will be off in an instant, and leave you to manage as well as you can. They think that the employer is quite as much indebted to them as they are to the employer."[45]

Thomas Low Nichols, born in Orford, New Hampshire in 1815, recalled that in his childhood, "the young lady who assisted in doing the housework . . . considered that she was conferring an obligation as indeed she was."[46] Catharine Sedgwick recalled the difficulty, when she was a young housekeeper in western Massachusetts, of dealing with servants who were "scarcely to be obtained, or, if obtained, coming 'to accommodate you,' and staying only till they could accommodate themselves better."[47] In a thinly fictionalized account of the early years of her marriage to Henry Ward Beecher, Eunice Beecher wrote bitterly of hiring Hoosier help "so conscious of living in a *free country* . . . that all the work they did was felt to be a condescension on their part."[48]

The pretense of "obliging" implied not only that the two parties were known to each other but also that the economic motive was not crucial. Caroline Kirkland, an especially acute observer because she was accustomed to urban domestics in the East, found it hard to hire girls to help her when she set up housekeeping in Michigan in 1835.

I have . . . seen the interior of many a wretched dwelling with almost literally nothing in it but a bed, a chest and a table; children ragged to the last degree, and potatoes the only fare; but never yet saw I one where the daughter was willing to own herself obliged to live out at service. She would "hire out" long enough to buy some article of dress, perhaps, or "because our folks have been sick and want a little money to pay the doctor," or for some such special reason; but never as a regular calling, or with an acknowledgement of inferior station.[49]

Finally Mrs. Kirkland discovered an important strategy: she must just take the girls' helping as a favor. If she in effect agreed to ignore the question of need, all would go well.

Kirkland's observations reflect the way in which the economic situation of poor families directly affected servant recruitment. With land relatively plentiful and cheap in areas like frontier Michigan in the 1830s, the poorest families could usually maintain a family economy that was sufficient if not ample; few would be reduced to pushing their children into selling their labor. A prospective employer might be reduced to urging a girl to enter service by appealing to her sympathy for a case of illness. In a volume of stories based on her Michigan experience, Kirkland pictured herself trying to assist a neighbor who was ill by finding a girl to help her. One mother refused to encourage her daughter "Mirandy" to engage, pointing out, "She needn't live out unless she chooses. She's got a comfortable home and no thanks to anybody."[50] Kirkland cast a scornful eye on the dilapidated "comfortable" cabin. But Mirandy and those like her could indeed regard helping as a temporary choice rather than a regular necessity.

Backed by her own family's economic independence, the hired girl could also refer to republican ideology for language and belief with which to defend herself. Just as her recruitment was optional, so her treatment ought not to be demeaning, or she might readily invoke the tenets of popular democracy. Fanny Wright described one hired girl who responded to perceived abuse with a heated declaration "that this is a free country, that all men are created equal, etc., etc., the whole concluding with a toss of the head and a sudden whisk out of the room." She had witnessed several scenes of this description, she wrote, "and some of my American friends have witnessed many more." [51]

Young women typically went out to help when they were old enough to be useful but still unmarried. Families arranged service patterns to fit in with a major concern of this age group, schooling. In 1824 Sarah Connell Ayer wrote in her diary, "Jane Bailey has come to board with us and assist me between schools." [52] Schob found that many midwestern farm families hired girls to help while they attended school, in which case room and board might be their only pay. Since they had schoolwork to do, the girls' ability to do housework was restricted; one Illinois woman wrote sourly of her new hired girl, "We all know how much such girls can do besides going to school." [53]

Help had other concerns to distract them or draw them out of service altogether. Their own families might need their services, especially if illness struck at home. Mary Ann Heath went home briefly when her mother lay dying. [54] "She had to go cause her mother is ill," wrote Ida Bliss of Westfield, Wisconsin upon the departure of her mother's hired girl. [55] Parental authority did not always offer an excuse for such a summons. Employers reported, "her mother has sent for her," or "her father and mother insist on her coming home." [56] Marriage was the proverbial end to a girl's availability for service. "This [marriage] is what they calculate upon," wrote Hezekiah Niles, "and it is this calculation that makes them 'saucy.'" [57]

Such patterns of sporadic availability meant that an employer was constantly liable to find her help about to leave. Yet the hired girl's availability for hire was no more fitful than the employer's demand for her, with both parties responding to family cues at specific points in their lives. Demand for service was tied to stages in the family cycle. Women with small children felt the most desperate need of help, for reasons that should require no recital here. This time fell during the early years of a marriage, but as daughters grew older, they became available to help their mothers. Ida Bliss, fourteen, filled the place of the departed hired girl in her family. "It seems so funny without Annie, Mamma and I are going to do the work all alone now." [58] Another surge of demand for service followed when the children had grown up and gone, and family income was apt to be higher. [59]

The arrival of a baby usually prompted the hiring of a temporary childbed nurse, who came for a few weeks after the delivery to care for both the mother and the newborn. [60] Some families had to hire wet nurses, another strictly temporary position. [61] Servants hired primarily for child care, referred to as nurses, entered work from which their employer would eventually dismiss them. "My boys have grown too large to require a nurse," Mary Todd Lincoln decided in 1861, and recommended their nurse to an acquaintance. [62] Death in the family was another reason for dismissal of servants. After Mary Stuart Turner's son died at age two, she reluctantly discharged his nurse, "poor Franny." [63]

Families commonly hired temporary help in cases of illness, even when they did not ordinarily employ any service. This pattern appears clearly in Phebe Eastman's diary. The diaries of Jane Bewel Kelly, a farmer's wife in Cottage Grove, Wisconsin, reveals her to be an energetic woman, but with nine of her twelve children still at home and no daughters of an age to help, she found "my health not very good and get so tired I thought I ought to have someone to help me." [64] Even noted opponents of service cited illness as an exception to their strictures on the institution. After condemning the employment of servants as "rotten to the core," William Andrus Alcott added, "If people are sick, it alters the case. Then we often need help."[65]

Birth, death, illness—all these would affect hirings for domestics as well as for help. But the temporary or part-time availability of help could provide appropriate flexibility for sporadic hirings. The custom of watching all night with the seriously ill, whose sickness could take unexpected turns, meant that a hired girl with a home of her own to return to might be desirable, since she was needed for long hours on short notice and then again not at all. Sarah E. Beaulieu, a nineteen-year-old farm girl in Wisconsin wrote in her diary in March 1865 that a neighbor, Daniel Cain, had fallen ill. Sarah and her mother went back and forth to the Cains' to help on a day-to-day basis. On March first, "Ma came saying Mrs. Cain required my services the next day." On the second she "went to Cain's. Daniel seemed better. Did some washing in the afternoon, baked." On the third she was back home, but her mother stayed at the Cains' house and did not return until two days later, when Sarah wrote, "Ma came home and I must go back with her." She did so and sat up all that night watching Daniel, going home after breakfast. Late the following evening she went back and found Daniel "not expected to live."[66] Although Sarah's diary does not mention payment explicitly, it seems safe to assume that she and her mother were paid. Her father and two brothers were in the Union army, having joined up for the sake of the bounty, and Sarah and her mother scraped by as best they could, teaching school occasionally and making and selling hats.

Farm families were more likely to hire help in the summer to cope with the busy season and the hired men. They hired temporary help, often dayworkers, for extra busy occasions like spring and fall housecleanings or harvest time.[67] On November 1, 1827, Phebe Eastman wrote, "Scoured 23 runs of yarn. Washed some. Hired two girls this P.M. for a day or two. Made two bedticks." On November second she "had the house cleaned, not able to do much myself." On the third, the girls were gone.[68] In June 1829 Lucinda Delong came and worked for her for ten days, partly to do some spinning, but probably too because she had "eight men to cook for." Lucy Larcom, born in 1824 in Beverley, Massachusetts, remembered temporary help in her childhood: "There were women who came in occasionally to do the washing, or to help about extra work."[69] When Elizabeth Breese Stevens cleaned house in April 1832 in Batavia, New York, she had "a woman whitewashing" and "two black girls to clean up" besides her usual help.[70] Sometimes married women performed this kind of temporary daywork. Late in the century Sarah Christie Stevens, a Minnesota farm wife, hired Mrs. Vigell, the wife of her husband's hired man, to help with the spring cleaning. The Vigells lived down the road. "Mrs Vigell came up this morning, washed floor of little room, pantry and dining room, cleaned out cellar and whitewashed walls—she is coming again in the morning to wash safe and stain and scrub tables, clean up back room and help move stove."[71]

Help often decided to work or to quit for personal or family reasons: a hired girl went to school, or she was married, or she returned home to help out in illness or emergency there. The decisions of employers and help demonstrate a certain comparability: neither sacrificed the other to petty pecuniary calculation. When this consideration was lacking, tempers might flare. Some employers complained bitterly when they believed their need of help was sacrificed to nothing more substantial than the fact that a girl had saved enough to buy a new dress.[72] Perhaps most situations were less clear-cut. When Eva Beem of Dryden, New York went to help in the Stout family, she used her first pay to buy things she wanted, including new shoes, a shawl, and a bottle of "perfumery." But she also had the money to pay for unexpected essentials, including the dental bills for having ten teeth pulled.[73] If her employers disapproved of Eva's spending style or resented it when she left them after five months' service, Eva was either unaware or unconcerned, for she failed to mention it in her diary. Perhaps hired girls like Eva came from families whose economies were similar to those of the early Lowell mill girls, their fathers independent proprietors yet not among the most wealthy farmers in their towns. The situations of Lowell families meant that their daughters did not work out of absolute economic necessity and could spend or save their earnings for their own purposes.[74]

The comparable orientation to family and personal needs of employer and employed often resulted in a calm acceptance of turnover. This was probably especially likely if the two families knew each other. Jane Bewel Kelley was not greatly distressed when she sent her son Nate "on horseback to see if Julia would work for me but said no."[75] A similar mood is beautifully expressed in a letter from Hannah Kirby Post to her sister in 1824, written from Ledyard, New York: "We have at present a girl by name Catharine Forster whose parents live near us. do not see (as yet) but that she will suit us very well, appears to be an affectionate kind disposition and fond of Mary [their infant daughter]. . . . she thinks of learning the weaver trade in the spring but I suppose we can keep her until the five month [May] provided we do not get tired of each other."[76] In June Catharine was still with them.

Free blacks in service do not seem to have entered into these recruitment and hiring patterns, and were usually denied the title of help. European travelers sometimes remarked that the American idea of help excluded the free blacks who worked as servants. Francis Grund observed that white Americans sometimes hired themselves out as "helps" as a temporary measure, but blacks could not lay claim to that title and remained servants indefinitely. Charles Mackay declared, "The Negro is not a help; he is emphatically a servant."[77] Barred from the egalitarian interpretation of social relations that shaped helping, blacks could not rely on their families' standing in the community for informal protection, as their white counterparts usually could. Even though they nominally had a choice, black families would have been more likely to see their members forced into service not just temporarily but indefinitely, pressed by the kind of poverty that afforded no pretense of obliging.

Economic marginality meant that free blacks had reason to value wealthy and powerful protectors, and early in the century some of them seem to have entered into client relationships with families of the commercial and professional elite. Jess Shorter was a young mulatto who waited on Manasseh Cutler in Washington when Cutler served in the House of Representatives. He returned with Cutler in 1802 to Massachusetts to work for him there. "His polite manner and obliging disposition soon made him quite a favorite with Dr. Cutler and his family. He was sent to school and acquired some learning. In 1808 he married a young colored girl with whom he became acquainted in a neighboring town. A comfortable cottage was built near the parsonage in Hamilton, in which Jess was installed as gardener, and Member, his wife, became the good-natured cook of the family. Here they raised their children, lived happily, and here they died."[78] Black Agrippa and "Mumbet" grew old in the service of Theodore Sedgwick of Stockbridge, Massachusetts, heading a group of half a dozen servants. Like Jess Shorter, they raised their own families in nearby cottages, and like him they won, through faithful service, support until death. Black servants seem to have held similar positions in the William Henry Seward household in Auburn, New York and the home of Judge Daniel Cady in Johnstown, New York.[79] The same expansion of the labor market and market relations in general that would result in the transition from help to domestics probably tended to erode most such client relationships as well. Employers who were more urban, more middle-class, and more mobile would have little need or opportunity to form long-term bonds, nor would they have considered it desirable to be saddled with aging pensioners. Thus, although blacks were excluded from helping and would not participate in the help-to-domestics transition, perhaps the structure of their opportunities in service changed in parallel fashion as most client situations disappeared and black servants were exposed to the market for domestics.

Working Conditions and Hours

The conditions of helping, as of hiring, made for smooth relationships. "Help" was an accurate term, as European travelers often noticed and reported. Farmers' wives like Phebe Eastman offered daily evidence to that effect. "Cleaned the house with Mary Ann's help," she wrote simply.[80] "Lena and I made two cakes, six pies, a pan of fried cakes, and bread," wrote Jane Kelly.[81] In memory this kind of joint hard work took on lyrical dignity, as when John Bigelow, born in 1817 in Malden, New York, recalled his mother and her help making candles and soap, spinning wool and dyeing yarn, and performing all the other housework.[82]

Probably for the women involved such a life seemed more like a daily struggle than a sentimental interlude. In her memoir of life in Illinois in the 1820s, which revolves around her workload, Christiana Holmes Tillson tends to recall her help in light of their varied capabilities. She says, apologizing for her preoccupation, "You may feel that I have attached undue notice to the meals given and the calls on our hospitality, but could you know the labor of bringing from raw materials anything at all presentable for family use, you would understand why the impression was so lasting." One year her husband rode back from Vandalia with a little "Dutch" girl behind him on his horse. Mrs. Tillson thought the poor thing looked about ten years old and sick with "the agy" at that, but she gave her some dinner and sent her to bed, "trusting to the future to see whether I really had 'help,' or more to take care of."[83]

An employer like Phebe Eastman or Christiana Tillson, accustomed to doing the work herself, knew what kinds of results could be reasonably obtained, so that she might brook no slacking but would not demand the impossible. Jane Kelly said she was "so lame and tired" that it was "hard work" to "stir" her hired help.[84] Likewise the employer could adjust the pace to fit conditions, for example, reducing her expectations for washing or ironing when the temperature soared in midsummer. She need not supervise in obnoxious ways, standing over the help, yet she could by her active presence tend to determine the pace of the work. In 1854 the *Ohio Cultivator* explained how work discipline was imposed on the hired girl: "The mistress contrived to have some odd jobs inviting attention, and though she might not have *said* so, yet she looked a kind of reproach against allowing any precious time to run to waste." A working mistress had a certain authority.[85]

Hired girls shared the conditions of the family in which they worked. The girl suffered no indignities of exclusion. She sat down and ate with the family, sharing their table and their food. The travel literature helped to identify the common table as one of the hallmarks of American hired help. Fredrika Bremer reported her meal with a Dutch couple in their log house in Wisconsin: "I sit at table with the men and maid-servants of the family, just as they come in from their work."[86] Because Mrs. Trollope had made this a source of misunderstanding, many travelers took time to explain carefully that while farmers worked and ate with their help, other segments of society did not do so with their servants.[87]

American sources elaborated a similar distinction. Samuel Griswold Goodrich recalled the conventions of rural Connecticut around the turn of the nineteenth century. "In families where all were laborers," he wrote, "all sat at table, servants as well as masters—the food being served before sitting down. In families where the masters and mistresses did not share the labors of the household or the farm, the meals of the domestics were had separate."[88] Catharine Maria Sedgwick, born in 1789, recalled that in Stockbridge, Massachusetts "my father's house was one of the few where the domestics were restricted to the kitchen table."[89] In many areas the common table was the universal practice. One English immigrant wrote to his brother from rural Oneida County, New York in 1829, that here masters and servants ate together "all at one time be they iver so rich," reflecting the fact that "they are all workers."[90] "When dinner time came," wrote one new arrival to Indiana in 1840, "there was my washerwoman sitting down at the table with us."[91] Families like the Eastmans, who lived in a log cabin and dined with hired men and passing peddlers, did not relegate their hired girls to a kitchen table; indeed they probably had only one table.

Eating with the family had considerable significance in the life of a servant. Grace Goddard, who worked as a hired girl in Massachusetts, in writing her aunt "all the particulars" of her situation, mentioned four subjects: her daily schedule of work, attendance at church, her annoyance with her employers' children, and her dining arrangements. "I eat with the family unless [they] have some verry particular company, and they have but a verry little."[92] Hired girls grasped intuitively what anthropologists carefully explain: eating together is one of the most fundamental ways in which human beings form and maintain relationships.[93] Help insisted on eating at the family table as a matter of pride, more so, perhaps, when separate tables for urban domestics became the rule in many areas. In 1895 Mary G. Hungerford recalled, "I can remember visiting, when I was hardly more than a baby, a great-aunt who lived in the western part of New York State, who apologized to my mother for having her two handmaidens sit down to dinner with us, explaining that they were American girls and would never submit to any other usage. I think my surprise must have been manifest in my innocent young features, for one of the 'help' told me snappishly during dinner, that I might stare harder if I put on specs."[94]

Sharing conditions like this made service less obnoxious. It also made the burden of employment sit lightly on the employers. The servant's provisions did not require much cash outlay for farm families who produced so many of their own goods. Even the cash wages of hired girls need not cause a pinch in situations where specie was scarce; at least in the Midwest, farmers often permitted their help to make purchases on their accounts at the local merchants, settling up the balance due at convenient intervals.[95]

With her home close at hand, a hired girl could quit without finding herself utterly homeless. And members of her family could intervene for her. When Mary Todd Lincoln dismissed a girl in her employ in Springfield with sharp words, the girl's uncle came to the house to ask about it.[96] The prospect of dealing with a hired girl's family probably tended to prevent abuses. When Martha Larson's father brought her to work for the Kellys, he wanted to see their organ, and Jane Kelly sat down and "played and sung a tune for him."[97]

If the hired girl fell ill, she might be nursed back to health in the family. Goodrich pointed out, "In health they had the same food; in sickness the same care as the masters and mistresses or their children."[98] Sarah Connell Ayer of Eastport, Maine provides two examples of the assumption that help should be nursed in illness. In 1826 she wrote that "the month past I have had a very sick family. Our hired girl, boy, and the children have all been confined at once with the meazles. . . . They have now all recovered except Lovey, and she is on the mending hand." Lovey Lisenby was the hired girl. The following year Betsey McDonald came to live with the Ayers. When she fell sick for a week at the end of June, she was also nursed in the family.[99] If her own family was nearby, a hired girl might prefer to return home in illness, but women like Sarah Ayer assumed that their help were entitled to care if they wanted and needed it.

The assumption of entitlement, easy enough to sustain when medical care consisted largely of home nursing and hoping for the best, began to disappear in the face of physicians' fees. Account books kept by physicians show that they often treated hired help at the employer's expense, as do farm account books.[100] But other evidence from mid-century suggests that many servants were themselves liable for the physician's bill. [101] As a matter of case law, the servant's legal rights in illness did not include a physician's attendance. Both Kent and Story note this in their commentaries. [102] Later in the century with medical care increasingly a matter of expenditure in a medical market, domestics would find their status sharply differentiated from that of family members. [103]

The question of help's informal rights in illness had a bearing upon reciprocity, since they were expected to take on voluntarily more work when someone in the family fell ill. Facing life's emergencies together could lend grace to an otherwise uneasy relationship. It permitted Caroline Clapp Briggs to perceive and recall real virtues in abrasive help. Mrs. Briggs was born in 1822 in Northampton, Massachusetts, where her father was the town jailer and did a little farming on the side. Her mother was a semiinvalid. She recalled that "the servants in our family were sturdy, self-reliant independent Yankee women who would have scorned to be called servants, but whose faithfulness made up for all grace of manner." They were "often saucy and impertinent, but in sickness they were ready to work all day and nurse all night." Of a helper named Thankful, she wrote, "Her devotion to my mother, whose physical weakness appealed strongly to her pity, though she half despised it, was unbounded, and for years after she left us she would come at any time when there was illness in the family and serve us as faithfully as any child could have done." [104]

Another condition of helping that smoothed its rough edges was the fact that the work was organized more around task than time. Task orientation corresponded to the rhythms of farming, where slack seasons were balanced by hard work in the busy times of planting and harvest. Thankful, helping the Clapp family in Northampton, often worked outdoors in the summer, harvesting broomcorn and taking pride in doing more work in one day than any man. [105] Help had an interest in ordering their work so as to gain time off. Mrs. Briggs recalled of Thankful and the other hired women, "They planned their work after their own fashion, and were invariably dressed neatly, with all work done, by two o'clock in the afternoon. They would have counted it a great hardship not to be able to do that . . . to accomplish their duties within the time they proposed to themselves." [106]

Some travelers noticed this practice. Thomas Grattan wrote of American help, "Engaged to do a certain quantity of work, it is always understood that when it is done they are free to do with themselves what they like." [107] By handling their work expeditiously, help could have their evenings and Sundays off. In the 1830s Michel Chevalier complained, "On Sunday an American would not venture to receive his friends; his servants would not consent to it, and he can hardly secure their services for himself, at their own hour, on that day." [108] Moritz Busch echoed this point: "Sunday belongs completely to the servants, as do the weekday evenings." [109]

Girls often used their time off to go out. Méderic Moreau de Saint-Méry referred to servants "whom nothing can hold in after evening and who often do not return until midnight." [110] Anna Bryant Smith of Portland, Maine complained in her 1807 diary that she had "set up till eleven o'clock waiting for Betsey Delano to come home but had to go to bed and leave her out to my Grief and mortification." [111] In Nathaniel Hawthorne's *American Note-Books* he sketched Nancy, a hired girl who found time for afternoon strolls in her best dress, and who, after milking and supper chores, walked into the village each evening. [112] In Michigan in the 1830s, Caroline Kirkland employed "Jane," who returned from the Fourth of July ball at daylight, changed her dress, and began her round of domestic duties. [113] Martha Larson was so sleepy after one weekend's festivities that Jane Kelly sent her back to bed until noon on Monday morning. [114] Some employers had less patience. In 1853, after Matthias Dunlap's hired girl went to a dance and stayed out all night, returning the next day at noon, Dunlap fired her. [115]

The question of help's taking time off for recreation was a potential source of conflict. But workers had certain customary rights to balance against their employers' wishes. Harriet Martineau suggested conditions of service that should be agreed upon initially by the two parties to forestall conflict. "For instance, the employer stipulates to be informed some hours before, when her domestic intends to go out; and that such going out shall never take place when there is company. In return, she yields all she can to the wishes of her domestic about recreation, receiving the visits of her family, etc." [116] According to Miss Martineau's compromise proposal, help do not have to ask permission to go out but should inform their employer of their intentions.

Help enjoyed receiving company on their evenings off. Caroline Clapp Briggs recalled happy hours spent in the kitchen in her childhood. "It was a great treat of a Sunday evening," she wrote, "to stay with anyone who had a lover, who was sure to come 'courting' on that evening of all others. Then they were dressed in their best and ready for company and . . . no doubt wishing me a hundred miles away." [117] Mary Robbins Post of Westbury, Long Island found herself "sitting up a little later than I wish waiting for our kitchen company to leave." [118] Elizabeth Cady Stanton recalled that in her childhood in Johnstown, New York her nurses would hurry her to bed early, "that they might receive their beaux or make short calls in the neighborhood." [119] When Flora Temple, a girl bound to the Samuel Stoughton family of Gill, Massachusetts, entertained her fiancé, the Stoughtons all went into the big kitchen to leave the pair some privacy in the parlor. [120]

Probably because they were so well known to their employers, help do not seem to have appeared threatening to them even when they fell into sin or crime. Sarah Connell provides a remarkable example of the acceptance of sexual deviance in a helper. In 1810 she wrote a letter in which she discussed libertines, explaining, "I have been led into reflections of this kind, from the situation of a young woman who lives with us." This woman had been seduced under the promise of marriage. To avoid the law which would reward her two hundred dollars for the maintenance of the child, the wretch had married her and then abandoned her, penniless, the morning after the ceremony. "She is obliged to work, for the support of herself and the babe. She calls it Sarah Connell, and I assure you that I am much attached to the dear little girl." [121] The Stoughton family had to deal with a high-spirited girl in Flora Temple, but they tried to find ways to keep her respectable. After Flora spent several days in Greenfield where she "cut up pretty seriously and about ruined her good name," they encouraged her to move her wedding date forward: "This is hastening the time somewhat, but it seems to be best if he cares for her, that he should take her soon." Flora married George Parmenter at the Stoughtons' house, with "quite a little party" after the ceremony. [122]

Even criminal conviction did not necessarily make a former hired girl frightening. Caroline Howard Gilman told the story of a girl whose theft was forgiven and who was taken back into the family. Caroline Clapp Briggs wrote that her favorite gift on her wedding day was a basket of eggs brought by "a colored girl whom my mother had 'brought up.' . . . She had grown into a bad woman, spending most of her time in jail, but . . . with all of us she was gentle and womanly." [123] Employers less sympathetic than Briggs or the Stoughtons or Connell might be angry or disgusted, as Phebe Eastman was when Margaret Duffy told those amazing lies, but they did not seem to be frightened.

Helping was, if not an ideal relationship, not an arena of great conflict. Hiring help to produce for market yielded cash returns, while work for home consumption was both crucial and task-oriented, hence governed by obvious needs and logic. Although money changed hands, helping was not primarily a market transaction. Help were more likely to be treated with personal consideration than domestics would be later, but to construe this as evidence that they were "part of the family" would project values of privacy, exclusivity, and emotional intensity on a household whose definitions and functions were less narrow and more flexible. Rather, the hired girl's treatment reflected her status as a member of another family, one whose independent standing in an economy of small producers was reinforced by republican ideology.

TWO **Domestics**

Beginning in the 1820s and more noticeably in the 1830s, Americans began to hire more servants to work in an explicitly domestic sphere. Abandoning the language of help, they began to call them "domestic servants" or just "domestics." The difference was more than semantic; it reflected altered relationships, in many ways more burdensome to domestics and more problematic, yet more promising, for their employers than the helping relationship had been.

Recruitment and Hiring in an Emerging Labor Market

Changes in women's employment opportunities began to alter the recruitment patterns of service. In the 1820s and '30s a few young women pursued an advanced education in female academies and seminaries and found new opportunities to teach in the expanding system of public education. In the early years of women's entry into higher education, some women still found service a useful stepping-stone. Maria Maynard, born in 1807 in Phillipston, Massachusetts, traveled to Boston, where she worked as a servant for one year and a seamstress for a second year. With the proceeds she entered Ipswich Seminary, newly founded by Zilpah Grant and Mary Lyon, and on graduation took a teaching job in Fulton, New York.[1]

Contemporaries often worried that new opportunities would reduce recruitment into service altogether. When the textile industry began to recruit young women for jobs in the mills, Lucy

Larcom recalled, "We used to see it claimed, in public prints, that it would be better for all us mill girls to be working in families, at domestic service, than to be where we were."[2] By the mid- and late 1840s speed-up and wage cuts made work in the New England textile mills a less desirable and respectable form of employment than Lucy Larcom had found it. But new alternatives, especially in teaching, probably did divert some young women who might otherwise have gone out to help. The girls thus lost to service were those whose family economies afforded them some flexibility, for teaching was so seasonal and sporadic that it did not readily permit continuous self-support. Preparation for teaching also required that a family forgo their daughter's earnings while she was schooled.[3]

For young women from less comfortable backgrounds, the antebellum period looked less like a time of expanding opportunity than one of increasing pressure of sheer economic necessity to enter service. Nancy Cott, who noted many instances of young unmarried women helping with housework for pay in the late eighteenth and early nineteenth century, referred to this practice as "a function of age as much as economic need."[4] But in the antebellum economy many skilled crafts and trades by which a man could formerly have supported a family were being destroyed or downgraded by new mass-production methods. In the growing cities working-class and poor families found themselves cut off from many of the makeshifts available in the countryside—hunting and fishing, gardening, running hogs in the forests, gathering fuel, and the like. Although the urban poor did what they could, running their hogs in the street to eat garbage, for example, they found themselves dependent on money income for the necessities of life—to pay rent, to buy food and fuel. Such families felt active incentives to push their children into the labor market, either to contribute to family income or merely to relieve the family of their upkeep. Girls who went out to service for these reasons did not have a "home of their own" to which they could readily return. Rather than offering a refuge from the need to support themselves, their homes were more apt to call on them for money.

There had always been women whose desperate poverty afforded them no pretense of "obliging" when they did housework for pay—most notably, free blacks. But in the changing economic climate of the 1830s, with the reorganization of industry and burgeoning cities, more young women found themselves without choices. The decline of the small producer affected service indirectly by increasing supply, as daughters were pressed either to make more substantial and continuous contributions to the family economy or to self-support. Gerda Lerner has remarked that the 1830s first saw the lady and the mill girl exemplify the drastically different life courses for women of different classes. In fact, the lady's opposite number was more apt to be the domestic.[5]

Recruitment into service also reflected changes in demand, changes in employers and their hiring practices and aims. Urbanization accelerated in the 1830s, and the sheer scale of city life made it more difficult for employers to find a servant whose family they already knew or to hire through informal personal networks. A more fundamental change was the shifting economic position and style of home life among servant employers. Entrepreneurs, retailers, factory supervisors, and professionals comprised new urban middle classes. In contrast to the farmers and shopkeepers of earlier days, they usually lived in homes separate from the workplace. Paul Johnson has shown that in Rochester, New York in the 1820s and early 1830s much of the city's work was organized into larger units by merchant capitalists, with a corresponding decline in the numbers of workers who lived in their employers' homes. He cites such changes in work and the social relations of work as signaling the formation of the middle class. Similarly, Mary Ryan's study of Oneida County, New York in the same period details "the emergence of a definable middle class." Ryan traces a distinctive middle-class emphasis on privacy and domesticity to "the intensified competition and instability of a rapidly growing marketplace."[6] Household service was obviously not industrialized, yet its terms were recast by the spread of first commercial and then industrial-capitalist social relations among employers as well as servants, as family economies were transformed, classes solidified, and expectations shifted.

The homes of the new urban middle classes were explicitly domestic, private realms. The ideologues of domesticity began in the popular presses to insist that this physical space corresponded to a separate women's sphere, an area of spiritual comfort and compensatory intimacy in what Sarah Josepha Hale called "this bank-note world."[7] Middle-class women welcomed the prospect of more elevated activities than constant domestic drudgery. Having been equipped with some education, they were anxious to devote themselves to church and charitable work, to a newly enlarged view of maternal duties, or even to social life. At the same time the daughters of the middle class seem increasingly to have been withdrawn from housework in favor of expanded education and training in genteel accomplishments during an extended period of girlhood.[8] Servants were to underwrite these new activities of mothers and daughters and to stay at arm's length, no longer sharing a common table. The employers of domestics attached new importance to an undisturbed family table. As Catharine Beecher explained in *Letters to Persons Who Are Engaged in Domestic Service*, the dinner table was the one chance the family had to be together in privacy, to reconvene, as it were, after the husband's daylong absence.[9] Middle-class women needed servants to do the housework for them rather than to help them to do it themselves, and their funds—or rather their husbands' income, for they did not produce for market nor work for pay—allowed them to make choices about the use of their time and effort. They had to hire strangers as domestics in order to do so.

Geographical mobility fostered urban anonymity, as both domestics and employers kept on the move—from country to city, from one city to another, from east to west—at a dizzying pace.

Recent research suggests that transiency was extraordinarily high in nineteenth-century cities, especially among young, unmarried individuals who did not own property. Cheapening transportation widened their horizons. Lydia Maria Child remarked with some alarm on the phenomenon, new in the 1830s, of frivolous traveling by people of modest means, including "domestics all agog for their wages-worth of travelling." [10] Cheap enough to appeal to frivolity, travel was also, and more significantly, a road to a job.

Service itself helped to stir the streams of geographical mobility because its entry requirements were virtually nil, the ability to do housework being considered practically a secondary sex characteristic. Girls and women who needed work knew that they could go to a city, any city, and find work as servants. In Boston in 1831 Mehitable Goddard filled vacancies on her staff with a widow from Hallowell, Maine and a girl of fourteen from Portsmouth, New Hampshire, noting that both of them were newly arrived "strangers" in town. [11] Oliver Wendell Holmes recalled that the family servants in his boyhood home in Cambridge came from rural New England. [12] Such movement reflected economic push as well as pull. In *Society in America* Harriet Martineau reported that the inmigration to Boston, which supplied many domestic servants, resulted when New England farm families fell on hard times as more fertile areas opened up farther west. [13]

Some migrants traveled shorter distances to smaller cities and towns. Eloise Miles Abbott was born in 1821 in Sandy Creek, New York. Before her marriage she pursued what rural work she could find, teaching school in northern New York and "boarding around." But she also moved to Watertown, New York for two years to work as a governess to the five children of N. M. Woodruff, the proprietor of the largest hotel in town. [14] Joseph Kett has suggested that in the antebellum period girls were as likely to leave home for the city as were young men, and a comparison of age-specific sex ratios in some rural and urban areas supports this claim. [15]

Under these circumstances, servants' characteristic restlessness began to look like an acute problem. In 1825 a group of elite families in New York City decided to combat what seemed like a growing servant problem by forming a Society for the Encouragement of Faithful Domestic Servants. (Establishment of similar societies in Boston and Philadelphia followed.) The society's formation was in many ways an indicator of a changing situation. Its very name proclaimed the founders' intention to cease denying the title or condition of service. The founders knew of the existence of a similar organization in London but professed themselves ignorant of its governing principles, declaring they were more concerned with solving their own problems than with emulating a European example. In their first annual report the directors of the New York group, who included wealthy philanthropist and reformer Arthur Tappan, along with other civic-minded men, stated frankly that the servant problems they proposed to tackle originated mainly in servants' "love of incessant change." [16]

In fact, employer demand for domestics, as for help, was subject to great change. Birth, illness, death all visited urban families, providing cause for hirings and firings. Certain aspects of urban middle-class life created powerful new causes for turnover. The practice of hiring extra dayworkers for spring and fall housecleanings was maintained if not expanded, for these households indulged in more elaborate interiors and upheld higher standards of cleanliness. Eliza Leslie offered advice on housecleaning from the standpoint of proper Philadelphia: "Besides the assistance of your own domestics, you will find it necessary to employ at least three other persons: a whitewasher, a scrubber, and a man to take charge of the carpets." [17] Helen Munson Williams of Utica, New York recorded payments in 1854 for daily housecleaning to Mrs. Harvey as well as to her two full-time servants, Nora and Mary. [18] In Milwaukee in the early 1860s, Mariette Chapin engaged the woman who usually did her washing to help with the spring cleaning. [19] Late in the century, Lillian Pettengill encountered one employer who showed herself to be extraordinarily tight-fisted by neglecting to hire the customary extra dayworkers for housecleaning.[20]

In New York City and perhaps elsewhere in New York State, the general custom of a May first moving day encouraged turnover by freeing many servants and places at the same time.[21] The trustees of the New York Society for the Encouragement of Faithful Domestic Servants had occasion to point out the disruptive effects of this practice on servants when they opened a referral service just before May first. They promptly faced a clamor for servants, who, "according to an established custom, had in numbers left their places to obtain higher wages for a few days, in the turmoil of a May movement."[22] The well-to-do left the cities in the summer, heading for healthier, cooler spots and for fashionable watering places. Some left behind a servant to tend the house; others took along a nursemaid to tend their small children, but a significant number of summer layoffs probably occurred.[23]

Employers' abilities to hire domestics tended to expand and contract noticeably with the business cycle. In his investigation of Hamilton, Ontario, Katz found that the acquisition or dismissal of a servant was strongly correlated with economic mobility up or down. In 1850, 30 percent of Hamilton families employed a servant, but in 1860 only 21 percent did so, a drop Katz attributes to the depression of the late 1850s.[24] The family who hired a domestic in good times might have to think of dismissing her when contemplating retrenchments, for she required not only wages but also extra food, fire, and lights, and separate living space in urban areas where the cost of real-estate footage was skyrocketing. In her 1873 novel *Work*, Louisa May Alcott portrayed a heroine who worked as a domestic in households where the husbands struggled in a competitive, speculative marketplace. As Sarah Elbert has pointed out, "There are no faithful family retainers among the female servants in *Work* . . . because the workers' insecurity is part and parcel of their employers' insecure status and anxiety."[25]

The business cycle affected servant recruitment as well as employer demand. In slow times in Boston in the winter of 1830, Mehitable Goddard noted, "Servants are plenty and wages lower —and of course there is a corresponding improvement in the behavior of this class of people. I do not wish them to suffer, for suffering's sake, but I do fear nothing but absolute want will compel them to do their duty—and I believe this winter has been a severe one to those out of employment."[26] As Mrs. Goddard noted, sporadic hirings, layoffs, and turnover worked serious hardships on domestics, who could not readily return, as help could, to their family homes.

Like other workers buffeted by impersonal economic forces, domestic servants learned to make their way in a labor market by calculating their own best interests. No ties to a locale or family acquaintances precluded or muted such calculation, as they might for help. An employer would wake up one morning to discover that the family servant had been—as it seemed—"enticed away" by an offer of higher wages elsewhere. When domestics behaved this way, they roused employers to complain, not only accusing the servant of unfaithfulness but also accusing other employers of piracy. The directors of the New York Society for the Encouragement of Faithful Domestic Servants, who so often announced new trends, referred in 1826 to "this species of *kidnapping* so often practised of late." They declared it "a direct violation of that commandment which says 'Thou shalt not covet,' and . . . a custom which deserves the reprobation of every member of society."[27] In fact, the directors reported, their own scheme of awarding premiums to good and faithful servants met with some resistance from employers who felt reluctant to nominate their domestics for fear they would be "inveigled" away. Mathew Carey claimed that it was often unsafe to speak in praise of one's domestics, "lest they be suborned away."[28]

A domestic who wished to increase her earnings had to think in terms of specializing, and this in turn usually meant changing jobs. Specialty workers—cooks, chambermaids, and the like—

usually earned more than did general servants, and those employers who could hire several specialty workers were of course financially better off than families who had to content themselves with a single maid-of-all-work. As a result the charge of piracy often had a ring of envy in its tone, for lower-middle-class wives who trained inexperienced girls often saw them leave, once trained, for more remunerative work in wealthier homes. Catharine Beecher referred to such losses as "a sore trial."[29] One employer in Springfield, Massachusetts wrote that once she had her servants nicely trained, "some Springfield lady (?) generally shows her appreciation of my merits as housekeeper by kindly relieving me of their services."[30]

Because the employers of domestics fell into a relatively wide range, from wealthy entrepreneurs to their white-collar clerks, domestics who answered the highest bidder for their labor often provoked envy or embarrassment among lower-middle-class employers. One man, looking for a nurse for his grandchild, found himself dealing with a young woman who was so stylishly dressed that he felt awkward. She had just turned down one family in Bond Street because she did not like their looks: "She said she had always received 'eight dollars a month besides presents enough to make up three or four dollars more'!!! . . . Did you ever hear of such a demand from a nurse?"[31] Writing in the *Mother's Magazine* in 1854, a Reverend H. Winslow condemned a habit of "some of the richer families." "It is the practice of giving a *bribe* or *premium* to their servants," he wrote. "They will give exorbitant wages. . . . This is unkind to the less wealthy, as it renders their servants discontented, and often puts it out of their power to procure them on any reasonable terms." Reverend Winslow concluded that the practice of overbidding a less wealthy neighbor for a servant was "about the meanest and unkindest thing I know of."[32]

Inadequate communications and big city anonymity added insult to injury for employers who lost out in the bidding. Prospective servants who decided to take a different place might not be able to write a note nor be willing to take the time and effort to walk across town or spend a fare to soften the blow with an explanation. One New York City housekeeper wrote in 1859 that "servants are the great trial of housekeeping in New York—I have engaged five different girls that never entered my door—simply because after I left them someone offered them more wages." She hired one girl who stayed two days "and coolly informed me a lady that was going into the country would give her eight dollars a month (I was giving six) and she must go."[33] No levels of wealth seem to have been free from this problem; in fact, it may have been more prevalent and more troublesome in the upper ranks. Prominent old families with names like Hone, Auchincloss, and Schermerhorn joined with Astors and Vanderbilts in the New York Society for the Encouragement of Faithful Domestic Servants. It seems likely that by banding together they hoped to put a brake on unseemly and socially divisive bidding against one another.

The cry of piracy and the complaint of "unfaithfulness" reflected the operation of a labor market mediating between employers of differing means and a work force becoming accustomed to mobility and pecuniary calculation. Complaints of piracy, testifying to an unwillingness to accept the market in service, would continue through the century. In the 1870s Eunice Bullard Beecher entitled one of her *Christian Union* columns "Stealing Servants."[34] But a few commentators noted the economic rationality of domestics' behavior. Catharine Beecher stated in her *Treatise on Domestic Economy* (1841) that "it is right for domestics to charge the market-value, and the value is always decided by the scarcity of the article and the amount of demand."[35] As the century progressed, more and more writers professed to accept the invisible hand in the market for domestic servants. E. L. Godkin compared the domestic to mechanics and seamstresses. "Her way of looking at her employer is . . . about the way of looking at him common among all employees."[36] Grace Ellis declared in her 1872 *Galaxy* article that domestic service was or should be "simply a matter of right and business." Servants sell their time and labor for wages; hence it was wrong for an employer to charge the servant with ingratitude in leaving, "when in reality it is simply a matter of dollars and cents, and she has an undoubted right to improve her position." [37] "What is the relation of servant to employer in a democratic country?" asked Beecher and Stowe in *The American Woman's Home.* "Precisely that of a person who for money performs any kind of service for you." [38] Even Charles Loring Brace, who on benevolent and charitable grounds, made a career of placing youngsters in service, argued for a business relationship when he contemplated domestic service in general. "The commercial basis is the basis for it," he declared. "It is a relation which almost necessarily forbids all sentiment; there can be no patriarchal character to it, and seldom even common personal attachment." [39]

As the contradiction between Brace's beliefs and activities suggests, the laissez-faire interpretation of domestic service never sounded fully convincing, even to those who advanced it. Most servant employers continued to consider it a matter of grave complaint that the domestic was a faithless "stranger in the gates." [40] The triumph of domesticity, of a sentimental equation of the hearthstone with the center of the universe and the foundation of society, made it troubling to employ a strange woman to sweep up the ashes from it. The very extension of marketplace relations that made it seem necessary to servant employers to fortify the home as a haven from the world outside also transformed the service employers required to establish order and comfort within. The term "faithless stranger" was a way of giving a name to one's opposite number in a cash nexus, labor market transaction. Every time one of those "faithless strangers" demonstrated that she worked for the highest bidder, the assumption that the home and the world of the marketplace could be kept separate was dealt a blow. The contention of classical economics, that the free operation of a market would yield socially beneficial results, never seemed very convincing when applied to household service, especially not when viewed from the standpoint of a domesticity that tended to be implicitly critical of the marketplace. Commentators who interpreted domestic service in terms of free market economics simply stated a contradiction, for they did not propose to renounce domesticity's vision of the home as a "haven in a heartless world."[41]

Caroline Barrett White and Her Domestics

The experiences of Caroline Barrett White, a matron in mid-century Brookline, Massachusetts, illustrate the patterns of contradiction involved in hiring domestics. In 1851, Caroline Barrett married Francis White, a partner in the Boston tanning firm of Guild and White. The couple set up housekeeping in a rented house in Roxbury in 1855, but three years later they purchased a five-acre estate called "Cliffside" in Brookline. Here the Whites raised three sons and a daughter. In suburban Brookline they could enjoy some rural pleasures; they even hired a man to keep a few animals on their acreage and to cut the hay in the meadows in June. Yet they were only a short ride by private carriage or the horse cars into Boston itself, where they shopped and visited, attended the theater and the opera.[42] During most of their years at Cliffside, Caroline Barrett White employed three servants—a cook, a chambermaid, and, as the children came along, a nurse-maid or governess. She recorded their hirings and firings in her diary often without any mention of their names; they were simply "the cook," "my girl," "my second girl." Sometimes she was able to ask their previous employers for references, but she hired most girls on the strength of no more than their appearance in an interview and the hope that they would "prove good." Again and again she greeted a new employee and reminded herself in her diary that only time would tell: "My new cook, Nancy, came this afternoon. I like her looks and appearance very much—hope she will prove what I need."[43] Thus domestics moved themselves and their possessions out to Brookline, in effect on approval.

Caroline White kept a large and lovely home in the graceful setting of Cliffside. She wanted to shelter the husband and children she adored. When she hired servants she intended to be "suited"; domestics who did not suit, who seemed slow or sloppy, unskilled or disagreeable, promptly received a "walking ticket."[44] Because Mrs. White did not share the work with her servants, there could be no question of altering the distribution of duties to adjust to a particular girl's inaptitudes, as Phebe Eastman had done with her help. She would dismiss domestics for failings that seemed mild enough. "Have got on tolerably well with new help—but do not quite fancy her," she once wrote. "Our girls do not suit us very well and we have told them they may go."[45] Julia Sullivan had worked at the Whites for a full year when Mrs. White asked her to leave. Sometimes she dismissed one servant simply because a better one became available. "Mrs. May called this afternoon," she wrote in her diary, "to say that she knew of a good girl who would be glad of a place and who she thought would suit me better than the one I have—afterwards the girl came to see me—I have not quite decided whether to send Mary away or not."[46]

Some domestics, feeling they had done their best for her, smarted under this regime. In February 1858 Mrs. White hired Mary Bennett, "a pleasant, not young, motherly-looking sort of person," but six weeks later she fired her, having found her "a good-hearted girl,—but not neat enough." Mrs. White noticed that Mary Bennett seemed "to feel that we are unjust to send her away."[47] Caroline White assumed she should pass over hurt feelings and disappointments, continuing to search for the best, the most "skilled" person for the job. She assumed she had the right to change her mind, as she did in September 1872: "Girl came in the morning, and I engaged to *try* her, but about noon another one appeared who was much more prepossessing, and I decided to see the first one and tell her that I had changed my mind—as she was very inexperienced—and have sent word to no. 2 to come if she will." Here she guessed wrong, for she soon pronounced "no. 2" "very unskilled."[48]

Caroline White resented it when domestics proved equally determined to suit themselves and change their minds. Some went elsewhere for higher wages: in October 1867 she lost Hannah, who had been with her almost two years, to her neighbor Mrs. Hooper, "who *outbid* in price of wages."[49] Caroline White knew something of bidding herself, for her means placed her neither at the top nor the bottom of the scale. On one occasion, having hired away Mrs. Amory's cook, she lost out when Mrs. Amory made a counteroffer of higher wages and "large perquisites."[50] Other domestics departed for personal reasons, and this especially annoyed Mrs. White. When a new cook walked out one night after dinner offering no excuse but that she was going home and "could not stay," Mrs. White complained of such "impositions and double-dealings."[51] Caroline White's diary revealed skepticism and resentment when another cook complained of being unwell and left: the girl "expressed the *fear* that she might be sick—and the *wish* to be carried home."[52]

Probably because Brookline was so far to come, Caroline White was often disappointed by domestics who accepted a place with her but never showed up as promised or sent a word of regret. When this happened twice in one week, she broke out of her usually mild diary tone to profess herself thoroughly "indignant." The next day one of the girls actually showed up to explain her delay in arriving. Mrs. White recorded the girl's story of illness in the family as if she believed it was a fabricated excuse: "My cook came out this evening to let me know why she disappointed me—her aunt with whom she is staying is very sick—so she says—and she could not leave her alone—she is coming tomorrow morning."[53] In Caroline White's view, the private or family lives of her domestics amounted to sources of inconvenience, and she relied upon their need for

money to keep them at their places. She expressed relief and pleasure when one cook refused her brother-in-law's request that she
come and nurse her ailing sister: "She says she does not feel it her
place to go and take care of her . . . as she is in need of the
wages." [54]

In 1865 Mrs. White's second girl, Lizzie Blunt, fell ill and gave
notice, saying she thought she could not fulfill the duties of the
place. Indeed, with four children between the ages of three and
nine bounding around Cliffside, keeping the place clean was probably a heavy task for a young woman in the best of health. Mrs.
White regretted the news. "I feel quite tired and used up this
evening—on account of the notice of intention to leave on the part
of Elizabeth Blunt who has been a member of our family so long
[three years] that we are greatly attached to her." But the next day
her regret turned to anger when she received an inquiring call from
a neighbor, Lizzie Blunt's new mistress. The girl had secured a
place where she thought the work would be lighter. Lizzie's move,
perfectly understandable for a girl who had to protect her health
yet needed to earn a living, left Mrs. White feeling betrayed; she
attacked all of domestic service as "a mass of ignorance, falsehood
and deceit." [55]

When Caroline White, who expected to get precisely what she
paid for, fired those who did not suit, she assumed they could take
care of themselves. They were, after all, strangers. Her domestics
in turn behaved the same way, taking or leaving the job as it suited
their purposes; Caroline White was a stranger, too, and they could
assume she would manage somehow without them. Yet Mrs.
White spoke of being "greatly attached" to Lizzie Blunt, and she
regarded Lizzie's quite reasonable decision to change places as a
piece of personal treachery. Mrs. White was not consistent, wanting sometimes a business and other times a personal relationship.
Interchanges involving domestic service, because of its live-in organization and one-to-one relationships, necessarily differed from
the arm's-length transactions increasingly characterizing other

forms of wage labor. There was always the potential for a cordial personal relationship, and sometimes this was achieved. As the case of Lizzie Blunt shows, such human possibilities, even if realized, did not yield an easier relationship; on the contrary, they tended to make eventual succumbing to pecuniary criteria or expediency in hirings and quittings all the more bruising.

Even the most clear-sighted employer could hardly have bridged the gap between the contradictory aspects of domestic service, between the market conditions under which it was hired and the explicitly nonmarket "product" it was organized to yield. Mrs. White's determination to achieve a proper domestic refuge at Cliffside—a realm of order and cleanliness, ease, and even beauty —had the effect of confirming in her domestics the very unfaithfulness she deplored, for they saw clearly enough they were retained solely on the strength of their ability to produce proper results. Caroline White did not grasp the reciprocity or the contradictions implicit in these proceedings. She saw instead an exasperating faithlessness, and she had an explanation for it: the Irish were the source of all her servant problems. "My cook left today and the one I had engaged to take her place has failed to keep her engagement. *Irish fidelity!*" [56] "Mary Whalen, chambergirl, informed me she should leave this eve—she has accordingly gone— this is a specimen of *Irish* kindness and willingness to oblige—She has left me with the four children and no one to assist but the cook." [57] She repeatedly summed up her servant problems by professing herself "heartily sick of the Irish," or "sick of all the race." [58] Despite the fact that she experienced similar difficulties with non-Irish domestics, including Lizzie Blunt, who was English, Mrs. White persistently recurred to the idea that her problems would be solved if only she could find "some good Protestant girls." [59] She spent a good deal of time and energy ransacking the employment offices of Boston for non-Irish servants, in vain. Her husband Frank once joked that the best excuse a suicide could leave behind was "I *kept Irish domestics*." [60]

Since it roughly coincided with the transition from help to domestics, the influx of immigrant women, especially the Irish
"Bridgets," into domestic service seemed to many employers to be
the source of the servant problems of mid-century. Blaming the
Irish avoided the perplexities that arose when commentators tried
to explain the servant problem in terms of free-market economics.
It had the added virtue of absolving employers from any responsibility for the situation.

Ethnicity and Race in the Market for Domestics

When the famine immigration poured into the United States from
Ireland in the late 1840s and early 1850s, it began to look as
though every servant was Irish, at least in the major seaboard cities. The Irish "Biddy" became the stereotype of the servant, and
Biddy jokes celebrated her inadequacies. Biddy answered the door
by yelling through the keyhole; Biddy, accustomed to descend by a
ladder, went down stairs backwards.[61] In fact, Irish immigration
in significant numbers had begun earlier, in the 1820s, and the
early stream helped to encourage and finance the later flood. The
Irish immediately altered servant recruitment patterns. When the
Society for the Encouragement of Faithful Domestic Servants began to run its placement service in New York City in 1825, 60
percent of the applicants were Irish-born.[62]

The prominence of Irish women in American domestic service
reflected the operation of an international labor market. In entering it, Irish women brought expectations and commitments that
led them into service. More young single women were included in
the Irish migrant population than among migrants leaving other
European countries.[63] Facing no language barrier, they could
find ready acceptance as servants, and entering service solved the
problem of finding housing in a strange city where tenement land-
lords practiced price gouging.[64] Irish women left behind family
economies in ruins; their labor market choices seem to have re-

flected a desire to send money home to pay their rent or to pay for
the passage to the United States of another family member. Domestic service, unlike needle or factory work, could yield a cash
surplus that need not be depleted during frequent layoffs.

Irish servant girls who sent money home helped to account
for remittances in staggering amounts. The British Colonial Land
and Emigration Commissioners calculated that remittances from
America transmitted through shipping and banking firms totaled
at least 1,730,000 pounds in the single year 1845.[65] The relatively steady demand for domestic servants actually gave female
immigrants an advantage over their male counterparts in finding
employment. Addressing advice to prospective immigrants, John
Francis Maguire warned in 1868 that girls and women could come
at any season of the year, but men, for whom the counterpart in
unskilled work was outdoor day labor, should not come in the fall
or winter.[66] When Wilson Benson and his wife Jemima arrived
in Canada in 1841, their need for employment led them to separate. She immediately found work as a servant, while he tried one
job after another, plagued by a lack of a saleable skill.[67] Carol
Groneman speculates that Irish families may have chosen to send
daughters rather than sons to the New World precisely because
daughters were more assured of finding employment and more
faithful in sending remittances home.[68]

So powerful was this combination of pushing and pulling factors drawing Irish women into service that it often seemed that
service was their only occupation. A volume called *Advice to Irish
Girls in America, by the Nun of Kenmare* simply assumed that all its
readers would work as servants. The Nun of Kenmare never mentioned any other kind of work but devoted much of her advice to
detailed explanations of proper conduct within service.[69]

Recent community studies document the heavy concentration
of Irish-born girls and women in domestic service. Stuart Blumin
found that in Kingston, New York in 1860, of the 254 Irish-
women of all ages for whom occupations were listed, 240 were

domestic servants.[70] In Hamilton, Ontario, Katz found that in 1851, 47 percent of Irish Catholic girls aged fourteen to sixteen and 61 percent of those aged seventeen to nineteen were servants.[71] Laurence Glasco reported that in Buffalo, New York between half and two-thirds of Irish-born women aged eighteen to twenty-one were servants.[72] Given the high turnover in domestic service, such high proportions in cross-sectional data imply that almost every young Irish woman who came to America spent some time in domestic service.

Had other immigrant women gone to work as domestics as often as the Irish, perhaps employers like Caroline Barrett White would not have been so quick to blame their servant problems on the "Irish race." But other immigrant women did not do so, at least not in large enough numbers to outweigh the Irish. Some recent research suggests that young single German-born women entered service as readily as did their Irish-born counterparts. But because Germans were a much smaller group in most cities and evidently because German servants tended to work for German-speaking employers, such as boarding-house-keepers in working-class neighborhoods, German servants were both too few and too confined to ethnic ghettos to affect the stereotypic view of the Irish as the source of servant problems.[73] Scandinavian women also exhibited a marked propensity for service, but they too were a smaller group and concentrated in particular geographical areas.[74]

Differences in the availability of the different groups helped to make ethnicity the medium through which employers expressed dissatisfaction. As David Katzman has pointed out, employers in Maine claimed to prefer Scandinavian servants, who were scarce, while in Minnesota, where many Scandinavians worked in service, employers considered them inept and untidy.[75] Direct comparison of the factors that propelled some immigrant women into service and kept others out is difficult because data on the composition of the immigrant stream—age, sex and marital status—were not collected as immigrants entered this country.[76] But it does seem clear that different ethnic groups responded differently to the market for women's work, the largest element of which was domestic service. The differing composition of the immigrant stream from different countries itself reflected different judgments about who should come to the New World in order to undertake jobs available here. Labor-market behavior seems to have reflected differences in traditional family roles and culture as well as in attitudes toward or strategies for the process of migration itself.[77]

Whatever the differences between ethnic groups, immigrants in general were often, by the very fact of their migrating, demonstrating severe economic need, need that made them willing to put up with the harsh lot of the domestic.[78] Contemporaries recognized that the immigrants' willingness to enter service in numbers made them indispensable. In her *Treatise on Domestic Economy*, Catharine Beecher noted, "There is such a disproportion between those who wish to hire, and those who are willing to go to domestic service that in the nonslaveholding states were it not for the supply of poverty-stricken foreigners there would not be a domestic for each family who demands one."[79] This steady demand took on institutional forms. When New York State authorities belatedly organized a reception center at Castle Garden in 1855 to protect immigrants from the abuses of "runners," they included a labor bureau where virtually every woman who wanted work was placed as a servant. In 1869, for example, a total of 12,111 women were placed in jobs, 11,673 of whom went to work as domestics.[80]

Race also made a difference in the emerging market for domestics. The flood of immigrants dwarfed free blacks in the ranks of service, so that, even though female black employment was heavily concentrated in domestic service, blacks constituted only a small segment of domestics as a whole. In New York City in 1855, the entire Negro labor force was concentrated in just four occupations—laborers, waiters, laundresses, and domestic servants. Yet blacks constituted only one thousand of the thirty-one thousand domestics in the city.[81] Competition from immigrants may have contributed to or confirmed a distinct pattern among black domestics of living out—that is, living away from their employers' homes. Katzman suggests that this characteristic pattern was southern in origin, dating from the exodus of the freedmen from their former owners' homes upon emancipation.[82] However, a propensity for live-out service had already appeared among free blacks in antebellum Philadelphia.[83] Probably living out did stem in part from the dynamics of emancipation and manumission, as ex-slaves sought to establish their independence in their own homes but found employment opportunities severely restricted.[84] Blacks' tendency to live out may also reflect reaction to the competition of immigrants, especially the Irish.

Historians have noted that immigrants tended to drive blacks out of the skilled trades and much unskilled work during the 1830s and 1840s, thus contributing to a pattern of socioeconomic decline among free blacks in the antebellum North.[85] Some evidence suggests that a similar displacement occurred in service, where it may have been particularly pronounced because co-workers had to eat together and often sleep in the same room, as well as work together. European travelers noted the difficulty or outright impossibility of having black and white servants together on the same staff.[86] As white immigrants put blacks in a distinct minority, the employer who wished to take the line of least resistance would simply hire an all-white staff. Thomas Hamilton observed that in New York in 1833 many families had recently replaced their colored servants with "natives of the Emerald Isle."[87] William Chambers referred to the Irish as having "dispossessed in a great degree the colored race" in service.[88] One Philadelphian witnessed a direct and ugly example of this process when a neighbor discharged an Irish servant and in his place employed a Negro: "Shortly after, his garden was trespassed on, plants and shrubbery destroyed and a paper stuck on one of the trees threatening further injury if he did not send away the Negro."[89] In Louisa May Alcott's novel *Work*, the heroine shows her character when, reduced to taking a job in service, she does not object to working with a black cook, who had been "an insurmountable obstacle to all the Irish ladies who had applied." [90] Since service lay at the bottom of the occupational scale, there was nowhere else for blacks to go, and many of them seem to have turned to live-out service. So long as blacks remained a small minority of servants, this pattern would be easily overlooked. After emancipation and increased migration to the North, black patterns of service would begin to have a significant effect on service as a whole.

The Irish "Biddy"

The Irish domestic, stereotypically referred to as "Biddy," who dominated the labor market at mid-century and therefore drew the blame for servant problems, tended to make an unsatisfactory servant. She carried to extremes what were, in the eyes of employers, the characteristic faults of domestics. Among "faithless strangers" the immigrant woman was most faithless, because so greatly in need of money, and most strange, not just personally but culturally. Like most migrant workers, she tended to think of work instrumentally, and her attitude reinforced her employer's propensity to treat her in the same spirit. The immigrants' motives and qualifications provided a grain of truth for nativist sneers such as that voiced by the editors of *Harper's Weekly* in 1857. They reported that the immigrant women waiting for places at the offices of the New York commissioners of emigration demanded top wages, refusing any offers of less than seven dollars a month, as their relatives in America had written them that they might earn this much. Yet, the editors declared, they were "unwashed and totally ignorant of housewifery." [91] The editors noted with satisfaction that the officials quashed such pretensions, dismissing the women from their offices if they refused to work for whatever wage was offered.

The immigrant woman's heroic struggle to send remittances

home, so admirable in the abstract, resulted in the strenuous effort to maximize earnings that employers resented in practice. The author of *Plain Talk and Friendly Advice to Domestics* considered this ruthless concern a common problem among Irish domestics. She told the story of "Bridget," aged sixteen and just off the boat, who expects to receive six dollars a month because her cousin Margaret gets that, although Margaret has been in America twelve years and is quite expert.[92] "They are ever striving to 'better themselves,' or, in other words, obtain higher wages," one commentator noted.[93] "I believe nothing will bind them but dollars and cents," wrote Elizabeth Sullivan Stuart of her Irish servants.[94]

Most Irish immigrant women had not grown up in households that provided them with useful experience in housework. The very terminology of household equipment was foreign to them. In 1850 Elizabeth Sullivan Stuart took on a "raw" Irish girl who had arrived in Detroit only four days before and who "did not understand the name of an article in the house."[95] Dr. D. W. Cahill explained the situation in a letter to the *Metropolitan Record* in 1860: "Being the daughters of laborers, or needy tradesmen, or persecuted, rack-rented cotters, they are ignorant of the common duties of servants in respectable positions. They can neither wash nor iron clothes. They don't understand the cleaning of glass or silverplate. They cannot make fires expeditiously, or dust carpets, or polish the furniture. Many of them never saw a leg of mutton boiled or roasted. Several of them cannot even prepare their own dinner bacon or pork."[96] Another writer pictured Bridget as wreaking household havoc in a thousand ways, washing her feet in the soup tureen and stirring the fire with the silver gravy ladle.[97]

Such ignorance was more troublesome than it would have been for women accustomed to hiring help. Training a girl was a major disruption for a woman who did not regularly spend her days at housework, since she had to drop her other concerns and descend to the kitchen. Elizabeth Sullivan Stuart explained her method with her raw Irish girl: "By being with her (and I give up the whole of my time to her) I have a servant, and . . . if I succeed in breaking her in, in a little while I shall have some time to *myself*." [98] A writer in *Lippincott's* in 1879 pictured her sacrifices: "Never a pleasant party could I join, because of my pupil—no friendly visitor receive with prompt welcome, because I was a captive below with Biddy. I am to hear the merry voices of my dear ones in the distance and cannot mingle my own with theirs." [99] Caroline Barrett White noted the difficult days she passed instructing new domestics, when the calls and rides of ordinary times had to be suspended. She called it a *"tough business."* [100] Once she wrote that the day held "nothing pleasant while *testing* new domestics—except the evening with Frank." [101] Of course women who did not regularly spend the whole of their days at housework were apt to make poor instructors, either from outright ignorance of the work or of realistic work standards, or simply from a desire to get the girl "broken in" as quickly as possible.

Even the charge that immigrant women were "unwashed" may have contained a grain of truth. Certainly the conditions on immigrant ships may have resulted in just such a state among the newly arrived. More to the point, immigrant women probably brought with them standards of cleanliness that were unacceptable to their employers. Individuals raised in dirt-floored cottages might not have found it easy to adopt standards appropriate for Brussels carpets. Elizabeth Sullivan Stuart, admittedly a martinet on these matters, claimed she had encountered one servant who ordinarily kept her hands so greasy that she found it difficult to turn a doorknob. [102]

The editors of *Harper's* failed to mention one other drawback of hiring Irish immigrant domestics, probably because it seemed so obvious. For many employers, Irish girls made less satisfactory servants because of their religion. Increasing religious differences converted a potential source of reconciliation into grounds for profound conflict between servant and employer. This had been true even when the differences were those between Protestant denominations or between evangelicals and nonevangelicals. In 1837 William Ellery Channing, the Boston Unitarian minister, addressed a letter to the editor of an evangelical newspaper to complain of the objectionable aspects of evangelical religion, including the irregular habits spawned by religious enthusiasm among Boston domestics. "In this city," he wrote, "I have heard complaints of your female members, who are domestics in families, as neglecting the duties and the interests of their employers in their anxiety to attend church meetings." Rather than provoking disagreement, Channing felt, religion should bind servant and employer together with Christian love, "a holier tie than self-interest."[103] While common religious beliefs could provide a salve for the frictions of self-interest, a spirit of denominational competition between servant and employer might prove all the more sharp-edged because honed in the close knowledge each party had of the other's daily lapses in spiritual life. Susan Huntington, a prominent member of the Episcopal church and its benevolent organizations in Boston, found this to be so. On August 20, 1812, she wrote, "One of my domestics treated me in an unbecoming manner, and when I expostulated with her, only continued to justify herself and persist in her rudeness. This circumstance led me to realize, how infinitely important it is that I should ever tread in the precise path of duty, and never turn to the right hand or to the left, lest it should bring a reproach on religion."[104] In hiring Catholic domestics, employers confronted an increasingly heterogeneous society, one in which threatening foreigners could not even be excluded from "sacred" home circles. Some employers simply made servant girls the butt of their nativist hatreds. Mary Grey Duncan asked, "Is Popery having no influence, when, in accordance with its usual treachery, it insinuates female Jesuits—lay sisters—now into this family now into that, in the guise of domestics, to learn family secrets and discover vulnerable characters?"[105] Fretting about Popish treachery when domestics attended mass, employers worried about irreligion when they did not. No wonder some Irish

Catholics found it useful to claim they were Protestants in order to be hired. [106]

The idea that Catholic domestics had been dispatched to spy for the Pope was urged in tracts such as *The Female Jesuit, or, The Spy in the Family* (New York, 1851). "Wherever Catholic domestics are, the views of the family are known to the priest or confessor," declared one nativist editorial. [107] When in 1855 a rumor swept over New England that Irish servants had been instructed to poison the food of their Protestant employers, many domestics lost their places. [108] Even employers who could resist these sensational claims found some reasons to entertain suspicions, especially since servants so often cared for their children. The readers of *The Mother's Magazine and Family Monitor* learned that William Hogan, ex-priest and author of lurid anti-Catholic propaganda, had declared that priests routinely encouraged Catholic servants to carry the small children of the family to them for secret baptism. [109] Hannah Wright Gould of Hudson, New York was no fool, but she allowed such suspicions to cross her mind. In November 1851 she went out to attend a funeral, leaving her infant daughter Lizzie with her Irish nursemaid. Mrs. Gould sat in the Catholic church waiting for the service to begin.

I was wondering if Lizzie was hungry and how long it would be ere the corpse came, when from the other end of the Church where the font is I heard a baby's cry the perfect echo of Lizzie's and Mr. Lamson's voice repeating "renounce the Devil and all his works, all the pomps and vanities of this wicked world?" Then the responses but above loud and clear rose a cry as if Lizzie's own—a staunch denial of the promises given. . . . I was really fidgety—what if it should be Lizzie thought I—what if Winny in her holy Catholic zeal had run down while I was away with Lizzie to the font—that her fond Irish heart may henceforth hope the blessings of the Almighty are with the child. [110]

Mrs. Gould strained her neck in vain, finally relaxing only when the child's screams became too furious to be Lizzie's.

Fears like this led many employers to stipulate "No Irish" when they advertised for domestics. A typical ad declared, "Wanted—at 95 Montgomery Street, A GIRL, to take care of children and do plain sewing. None but Protestants need apply." "Irish" and "Catholic" seemed to be synonymous in common usage.[111]

While the existence of secret baptisms remains questionable, perhaps mothers did have some reason for caution. The Nun of Kenmare in her *Advice to Irish Girls* counseled those who had charge of children to teach them to say "Jesus and Mary" and "short prayers." She held out the hope that Catholic servant girls could convert the Protestant families for whom they worked by their exemplary piety. "I have heard of several families who have been converted to the Catholic faith by the good example of their servants, and the good explanation which they gave of their religion."[112] Mothers who found their children reciting a "Hail Mary" might well prefer Protestant servants.

Fear could be tempered by competition. The editors of one Protestant missionary magazine prodded their readers with the story of "Bridget's Comment." Bridget, a domestic employed by an officer of the denominational foreign missionary board, scoffed at the small sum of money raised by the board: in the same period of time she and her fellow servants had contributed more than twice as much to clear the Catholic church debt. "Give me the Catholics yet!" she was supposed to have exclaimed.[113]

Some advice to employers suggested that they make the best of religious differences by considering their servants as handy objects for missionary work.[114] Such a suggestion was logical enough: the foreign missionary crusade had become a popular preoccupation among middle-class Protestant women, who supported large missionary organizations and read a vast amount of evangelical literature that routinely focused upon the plight of "heathen" women. Yet missionary hopes, like those suggested by the Nun of Kenmare for servants, could only have exacerbated the friction in employer-domestic relations, for Irish Catholics were well accustomed to withstanding efforts to convert them.[115] The advice-givers who urged missionary efforts among servants could seldom cite examples of success. The sensation surrounding the supposed "abduction" of Hannah Corcoran probably testifies to the rareness of her case as well as to nativist fears.[116] Elizabeth Sullivan Stuart, who may have been especially vehement on the subject because her family was, although Irish, staunchly Protestant, assessed the limitations of a missionary policy toward servants in a letter to her daughter. "I think with you that 'Protestant Mistresses have a work to do among the Catholics,' but who is sufficient for these things? Our holiest, wisest Missionaries say tis easier to go to the Heathen than to the Catholics."[117] If, as Ray Allen Billington asserted, "The women of America embraced the No-Popery cause with more enthusiasm than the men,"[118] this may in part account for the sense, prevalent by mid-century, that the servant was not merely a stranger but an alien and threatening stranger.

Blaming the Irish "Biddy" for servant problems reflected her exemplification of the characteristic shortcomings of domestics, for she was forthrightly oriented to cash, and strange not just personally but culturally. In fact the servant problem arose not from Biddy's ethnicity but from a new kind of relationship between employer and employee. Blaming "Biddy" acknowledged the change in patterns of service but obscured many of the determinants of change.

THREE

Changing Patterns of Service

The transition from help to domestics was neither rapid nor complete in the nineteenth century but ragged and unsystematic. Contemporaries often spoke of the change in service, offering, however, explanations that were partial or self-serving. While the census record did not document the transition, early scraps of census data can be seen to reflect it if problems of reporting are kept in mind. Employers blamed the change in service on the emerging intelligence offices. Servants, having increasing problems in collecting their pay, understood that changing employer practices were also involved. The move from country to city was perhaps the most striking change associated with the transition from help to domestics. Defying rigid categorization, individuals moved back and forth between the two roles. They were responding to changing conditions in both supply of and demand for service.

The Contemporary Record

The spreading market in service gave women's service work more formal definition. Once an activity had been transformed into an occupation, its existence was more rapidly recorded. Early nineteenth-century censuses did not pay attention to women's work, but if they had, hired girls would probably not have entered the census record. The census situation required self-identification, but help often emphatically rejected the title of servant, and they were in a position to make their views known, rather than being sequestered below stairs. Their brief and sporadic employment patterns made it less than likely that a census taker would catch them at work. In 1828, for example, Mary Ann Heath worked for Phebe Eastman during January and February, again for a few weeks in late March, and once more in mid-September. A hypothetical census taker, making the rounds in June, as was the custom, would have found Mary Ann at home with her family.

Help's tendency to deny the title of servant could even extend to the question of place of residence, a vital matter from the census taker's point of view. One European traveler early in the nineteenth century recalled his encounter with a hired girl who did not admit to living in her employer's house:

Having called one day at the house of a gentleman of my acquaintance, on knocking at the door, it was opened by a servant-maid, whom I had never before seen, as she had not been long in his family. The following is the dialogue, word for word, which took place on this occasion:

"Is your master at home?"
"I have no master."
"Don't you live here?"
"I *stay* here."
"And who are you then?"
"Why, I am Mr. ———'s help." [1]

A helper who was orphaned or far from home might not be able to stipulate her status in this way, but a neighbor's daughter could and would then simply be enumerated with her own family, not her employer's.

When by mid-century census takers began to take notice of women's occupations, they recorded few servants in rural areas. The 1855 New York State census found one servant to every four families in New York City and Buffalo, yet showed servants to be practically nonexistent in rural areas. Warren County, with a population of 20,000, had just two servants, as did Delaware County with a population twice as large. St. Lawrence County listed just 47 servants in a population of 75,000, including 11,500 farm families. Most rural counties showed similar results.[2] On the basis of this sort of data, students of household service have reasoned that help must have been a minor, even a negligible phenomenon.[3] But this line of reasoning gives inadequate attention to the process of reporting occupations and its peculiar difficulties with respect to women's work.

Throughout the nineteenth century and a good part of the twentieth, the census of occupations was compiled by asking each individual his or her occupation in his or her own words. The census taker translated individual responses into certain established occupational categories, a procedure that generated a count of "gainful workers." Self-identification involved difficulties, as the Census Bureau recognized in the 1930s, when it finally abandoned the "gainful worker" method in favor of the current "labor force" survey methods, in which individuals are queried about their actual employment behavior. The bureau noted, in explaining its change of method, that many individuals failed to identify themselves according to employment they pursued only casually or temporarily. They pointed to students and housewives as two groups most prone to inaccurate self-identification.[4]

As soon as women's occupational statistics were upgraded in the 1870 federal census, it became obvious to those who considered the problem that women might be reluctant to report their employment, especially if it were casual, temporary, or part-time. Given the general presumption that women did not work, they might not even be asked. Urging that women be appointed as census enumerators for the 1880 census, Lillie Devereux Blake predicted, "Women will make more careful returns of the employments of women than appeared in the last census, where work done by women who lived at home but went out as music teachers, dress makers, etc. was almost entirely overlooked."[5]

Some early social statisticians tried to take account of the gray areas in women's employment. The Massachusetts state census of 1875, supervised by Carroll D. Wright, tried to avoid problems by tabulating occupations so as to include every man, woman, and child in the state. The result was a listing of more than 400,000 "domestic servants," the vast majority of whom were housewives.[6] Thereafter the goal of exhaustive occupational listings was abandoned in favor of implicit reliance on workers' self-identification.[7] The resulting data neglect large amounts of unrecorded but remunerative women's work, for example, taking in boarders and lodgers.

The same New York State census of 1855 that showed so few servants in most rural areas contains hints of unenumerated help. A few odd results suggest that some rural enumerators found something to count. For instance, Otsego County, population 50,000, contained nearly 600 servants.[8] With a population only two-thirds the size of St. Lawrence County's, Otsego County had twelve times as many servants. Such results are consistent with the existence of a group of help who refuse to identify themselves as servants and of a few enumerators, as in Otsego County, who take it on themselves to assign the label.

One group of agencies, although working at a later date, seem to have circumvented the problem of self-identification among help. In the 1890s state surveyors, interested in the problems of farmers, asked them who they employed. Forty-eight percent of the Michigan farmers surveyed in 1895 reported that they hired women and girls to help in their homes.[9] In Wisconsin in the same year, 36 percent of the farmers hired "female help" in the summer, and 24 percent did so in the winter. In Ohio in 1893, between 25 and 50 percent of the "reliable" farmers in each township reported they hired women to help.[10] Despite the uncertain sampling methods employed, these surveys do suggest that hired girls were present in substantial numbers in rural economies. They also document the characteristically sporadic work patterns among help. Seventy-eight percent of the hired girls in Michigan had "lost time" during the previous year, but only half of them could attribute their departure from work to either illness or lack of work —most attributed it to "other causes," probably family claims. [11]

Certainly nonquantitative sources frequently testify to the widespread presence of hired girls. Quite ordinary families, like Phebe and Samuel Eastman's, hired help. Sherwood Anderson, who was born in 1876 in Camden, Ohio, the son of a harness maker, recalled that his mother had worked as a hired girl in her childhood and young girlhood, "washing dishes, milking cows, waiting on tables, a kind of half servant." [12] Elizabeth Miller, born in 1848 in West Newbury, Vermont, recalled for Works Progress Administration interviewers a childhood of struggle that nevertheless included hired help: "I was the oldest of six children. Mother was never very well, and when I was about ten, she was taken real sick and had to be abed most of the time. We had help sometimes but I took over and did the work as soon as I could. I learned to wash by scrubbing at the wash tub while the woman who helped was at the table with the family." She herself also "went out to work" and "helped the minister's folks" one spring. [13] Unlike later historians, Lucy Maynard Salmon did not have to rely upon census data; she insisted upon the significance of help as an early form of service because she had seen it firsthand. Born in 1853, she had grown up in a home in Fulton, New York where the neighbor's daughter helped and ate with the family. [14] One upstate New York farm wife detailed a lifetime of hard work and "doing without" and concluded with the admission, which she evidently considered a mild boast, "all this time I had a hired girl only a year and a half." She had married in 1861, bore eight children, and raised five to adulthood. She helped make hundreds of pounds of maple sugar each year, kept sheep and spun and wove the wool, milked four to eight cows, churned the butter, did her own washing, and furnished her house with rag rugs of her own making. She raked hay, husked corn, dug potatoes, stacked cordwood, pulled flax, spun and wove her own linens and towels. Yet even in a life like this, there were times—probably when children were small or during illness—when the family hired help.[15]

As soon as working women began to appear in census data, domestics, in contrast to help, cut a bold figure in sheer numbers. The problems implicit in self-reporting were apparently eliminated, as the domestic was likely to be reported upon by her employer. Systematic national data on women's occupations in the nineteenth century begin with the federal census of 1870, when for the first time census marshals were told to record the occupation of each person, male or female, regardless of age or marital status. Recognizing the significance of the 1870 data, most surveyors of women's work have focused their attention on trends from then forward. It has been possible to trace changes after 1870, as service began to decline in relative significance in the market for women's work and as—especially in the twentieth century—black women played an increasingly important role.[16]

For the period before 1870, the census record on domestics is fragmentary, but it testifies to their large numbers in urban areas. Original city censuses and local studies provide an accounting of domestics in Boston in 1845; Buffalo and Providence in 1855; Hamilton, Ontario in 1851 and 1861; and Milwaukee in 1850 and 1860.[17] The cities of Boston and Providence counted servants at the time their censuses were taken, recognizing that the omission of such a large group would leave a gap in the data. The table of occupations in the 1855 Providence census would have lost its largest occupational group if the 2,240 "servants and waiters" had been excluded. Such early city censuses confirm what the federal census would document amply in 1870 and thereafter: domestic service was by far the largest single occupation for women, dwarfing alternatives like factory or needle work. In Hamilton, for example, 72 percent of employed women were domestics in 1851, 59 percent ten years later.[18] Some of the same censuses documented the importance of domestic service among young women of particular ethnic groups, including its near universality among young Irish women.

Census takers also recognized the importance of servant hiring and prepared tables entitled "Number of Domestics," breaking them down by ward of residence and place of birth of the head of household.[19] Full-time live-in domestics were present in 17 percent of Boston families in 1845, in about 19 percent of Providence and Buffalo families in 1855.[20] In Hamilton, domestics lived with 30 percent of all families in 1851, 21 percent in 1861.[21] The city censuses confirm the importance of ethnicity in servant hiring. In Providence, 25 percent of native-born families employed servants, but less than 2 percent of the foreign-born did so.[22] Among native-born Buffalo households, fully 40 percent included full-time live-in domestics.[23] In Philadelphia in 1880, 16 percent of native-born white families included live-in servants, while only 9 percent of German and 5 percent of Irish families did so.[24] Census data also document the expected effects of class, as measured by occupation, on the likelihood of hiring servants. Kathleen Conzens found that among native-born families in Milwaukee in 1860, 85 to 88 percent of households headed by professionals, proprietors, managers, or officials employed domestics. So did more than half of clerical and sales workers, and of petty proprietors, managers, and officials. Among skilled workers the proportion employing domestics fell to just 16 percent.[25]

Some estimated data for the early period deserve to be looked at skeptically. For example, Oscar Handlin attempted to estimate the number of domestics in Boston from the 1850 manuscript census, despite the fact that women's occupations were not recorded in that census.[26] And Stanley Lebergott's bold estimates of the numbers of servants nationwide between 1800 and 1850 have little basis other than the extension of a simple curve.[27] Fragmentary though it is, this evidence from mid-century certainly seems sufficient to demonstrate that domestic service was a large institution and that the experience of service, while still looming large in the lives of women, was divided in a way that helping had not been. Some women—ethnic and working-class daughters—were quite likely to work as domestics, while other women—middle-class native-born wives—were quite likely to hire domestics. Women experienced one side or the other of the service relationship, but not both sides.

The Intelligence Office

The new patterns of labor-market recruitment and hiring that distinguished the domestic from the hired girl were exemplified in the operation of "intelligence offices," employment agencies specializing in supplying servants. The intelligence office was both symbol and evidence of the fact that the service relation had increasingly been confined within an impersonal cash nexus.

The term "intelligence office" is obscure but apparently American, for in Britain such agencies were called "registry offices." Intelligence offices existed in New York City, at least, by the first years of the nineteenth century.[28] An employer who needed a servant was accustomed first to make personal inquiries among family and friends. For help, these methods had sufficed, but for domestics, they did not. Some prospective employers placed want ads in the newspapers or answered ads placed by domestics in search of work. But ads were an inconvenience. Placing an ad meant interviewing a stream of girls in one's own home. When her ad appeared, Susan Brown Forbes, of Boston, saw nine applicants the first day and several more the next.[29] Answering a domestic's ad meant a tedious journey to areas of the city that were far from elegant or even safe. Equipped with her own carriage, Nettie Fowler McCormick of Chicago once spent an entire week "looking for those who have advertised."[30] And ads could not canvass the supply of servants. Many prospective domestics placed no ads because they had no homes in which to receive mail or visitors, or because they were illiterate and could not prepare an ad at all. They might try going door to door or even stopping strangers in the streets to ask if their services were wanted, but such measures were far from effective.[31] Thus, the intelligence office.

Intelligence offices seem to have thrived, although it is difficult to find a contemporary who had a good word to say for them. Some specialized in providing certain types of domestics—black, Irish, "American," or the like. Their proprietors, often women—some operating out of their own kitchens—were petty entrepreneurs in a low-overhead and vaguely disreputable business. Virginia Penny, who visited several of these offices in the 1850s and 1860s, reported that they charged each prospective employer or employee between fifty cents and one dollar. This fee entitled her to the "privileges of the office" for two or three months. The prospective servant usually had to wait in the office for an employer to choose her. Proprietors reported different means of obtaining or checking on the domestic's "character"—that is, her recommendation from a previous employer.[32] Offices often combined job placement with other services aimed both at householders and at workers. Titus' Servants and Real Estate Agency in New York City boasted an especially wide range: "Servants of all kinds. Men and women for day work. Orders received for white washing and wall coloring. Letters written at short notice. No servants sent from this office without good references. First class colored help can be procured by giving notice. All orders promptly executed. Orders received for carpet shaking."[33]

Intelligence offices had little reason to exercise scrupulous care in matching servants and places. After all, if the domestic provided proved unsatisfactory or unfaithful and was dismissed, they would thereby have another chance to collect a fee. Offices were not above shady practices, such as encouraging servants to misrepresent their qualifications and skills. They would advertise jobs with high wages that on application proved to have been "just filled" or would collect fees in return for the names and addresses of prospective employers that they had simply copied from the help wanted ads.[34] By the standards of business practice in an age of wildcat banks, watered stock, and adulterated foodstuffs none of these activities was extraordinarily duplicitous. Yet employers reacted to intelligence offices with an indignation rarely encountered in remarks by these genteel ladies and gentlemen on other subjects.

Sidney George Fisher, who with his wife, Bet, patronized "Mrs. Bourke's intelligence" in Philadelphia in 1870, fumed at the ordeal. "It is a most disgusting business, this of running to intelligence offices, and unfit for a lady. Bet always meets ladies elegantly dressed in one room waiting to choose, and a crowd of hideous Irish monsters in another waiting to be chosen. Out of the lot it is rare to be able to select one fit to enter a decent house."[35] The journalist Mary Abigail Dodge visited two intelligence offices in Boston at about the same time. She found the first run by a woman who was "delicate and refined in appearance," the second by "a florid, flourishing woman not awkward in expressing her mind freely." In both establishments she was horrified by the assembled servants. She saw "coarse, ignorant, unintelligent, unhelpful faces; such stolid indifference, such unshrinking self-assertion; such rude, brawny, worthless womanhood!" She said she was "shocked to find suddenly springing up in my heart a sort of hate and hostility toward them. A distaste for republican and individual liberty, a longing for an absolute monarchy came over me."[36]

In a short story in *Godey's* in 1868, the heroine, Mrs. Young-bride, dismisses her cook, Biddy, for slovenliness and incompetence, and Biddy reports to "the office" in search of another place. The proprietors place Mrs. Y's name on their books, but Mrs. Y is determined to free herself from an institution she regards as the source of her bondage. "A great institution is the 'office' . . . the custom other places is here reversed, and the servant is the mistress. She sits enthroned, waiting to receive the homage of dependent and tributary housekeepers. The nominal head of the establishment is tolerated only as the advocate and pleader for the unfortunate employers, who come here desiring humbly the gracious condescension of the kitchen queens." [37] Servants who receive Mrs. Y's name from the office walk to her house to apply for work only to find that Mrs. Y, with "grim satisfaction," slams the door in their faces or refuses to answer the doorbell. To the author, this display of bad manners was a personal triumph. [38] Elizabeth Ellet agreed. "The low character of servants heard of at common intelligence offices has caused such places to be held in small esteem, for their recommendations can in no case be depended on." [39]

Caroline Barrett White found this was true. On July 2, 1860, she stopped at three intelligence offices in Boston looking for a Protestant girl, without satisfaction. The proprietor of an office under Pine Street Church promised her husband he would send out a "first-rate" Protestant girl who would be "all right." The girl never showed up. When Caroline White went back into Boston she discovered no one had been sent, and she agreed reluctantly to take an Irish Catholic. [40]

In an atmosphere of hostility and casual misrepresentation, employers believed intelligence offices capable of all sorts of malfeasance. In May 1857 the editors of *Harper's Weekly* reported widespread rumors of the offices forming "combinations to keep up wages beyond their legitimate level." [41] Caroline Dall reported the "open secret" that "in all our largest cities, the marts of vice are stocked from these places." Even if this were not true, she claimed, the intelligence offices would be grossly abusive because "kept by ignorant or inexperienced persons who often lose sight of the interests of both the employer and the employed in their own pecuniary loss or gain." [42]

The directors of the New York Society for the Encouragement of Faithful Domestic Servants said in 1825 that "the vitiated character of the Intelligence Offices, generally, was quite proverbial; and an Office, where masters and servants might find their interests equally consulted, was yet a desideratum." [43] They set up an office where servants' references would be scrupulously checked. The domestics would benefit by the substitution of benevolence for the profit motive, since they would pay no fees and would be encouraged to enter regular savings at interest in a savings bank. The society's plan of action reflected the belief that the offices were to some extent responsible for servants' "unfaithfulness."

The New York Society's office was only the first in a long line of benevolent intelligence offices, none of which ever drove the for-profit offices from the field. But the logic of the project was perennially appealing. The abuses of the intelligence offices were real enough, and ladies eager to alleviate urban poverty found themselves drawn into attempts to find work for women and girls. Like Abigail May Alcott, who was an agent for the South End Friendly Society in Boston from 1849 to 1850, they discovered a resource in their own domestic service requirements and proposed to solve, in effect, two thorny problems at once. Mrs. Alcott set up a room where the poor might come for food, clothing, and fuel, but soon found that almsgiving was "the least expedient way of relieving want." She began to place some of the women and girls as servants. "I announced that from three to six o'clock P.M. I should furnish help for families. . . . Immediately I had applications from every part of the City as well as neighboring towns."[44] When the society's funds ran low, she charged a small fee to both servants and families, realizing enough to pay the rent and keep the relief operation solvent. After her association with the South End group, Mrs. Alcott ran her own intelligence office for a while.

Other small-scale informal operations tried to cope with the need. In Malden, Massachusetts in 1864, the wife of a black minister helped to place black girls in service positions.[45] In 1852 Rev. J. C. Guldin, a clergyman of the Reformed German churches in New York City made a practice of finding places for German girls in "good Protestant families."[46] Caroline Dall urged ministers, overseers of the poor, and committees of "educated women" to carry on such work.[47]

When Sarah Josepha Hale, as editor of *Godey's* during the slump of 1858, conceived a scheme to help industrious women in the eastern cities who had been thrown out of work by the "dreadful revulsions" of business, nothing seemed more logical than to transport these women to the West, where they were wanted as servants. The Industrial Women's Aid Association would collect five dollars in advance on wages from families in the West and pay the girls' passages with it. The association was to be, as Hale put it, "a gratuitous intelligence office." [48] Hale soon washed her hands of the whole project. "We cannot flatter ourselves that the benefits we have rendered others have been at all in proportion to the trouble and expense and annoyances we have had to undergo," she declared. Many of the applicants were unfit, and few city women were eager to take the low wages offered in rural areas; the fare was to be deducted from their wages, and they might find themselves virtually marooned if the work were unsatisfactory. A few enjoyed a free train ride west, absconding before they reached their appointed destinations. Meanwhile, so many prospective employers applied, specifying "all the virtues," that most had to be refused and their fees refunded, with resulting inconvenience and annoyance to Hale's subscribers.

Hale did not consider the idea discredited. On the contrary, she urged a nationwide system of "Homes for Domestic Training" in every city where immigrant girls could learn to do housework. Trusty agents could find places for them in the West and see that they got there. [49] The appeal of displacing the intelligence office and the difficulty of doing so suggested similar institutional schemes. In New York City in 1853, a group of benevolent ladies organized a Christian Home for the Female Servant on the corner of Sixth Avenue and 36th Street. They offered temporary housing, free if the girl could not pay; evening school; and religious services. Most important, the home offered free placement in service positions, charging its fees only to employers. New York City had twenty-six intelligence offices at the time. The charitable journal *The Five Points Monthly Record* explained why the ladies organizing the home saw those "mere mercenary establishments" as their point of attack: "They serve to lighten the inconvenience of changing servants frequently, and as plainly aggravate the same evil a hundredfold, besides training the girls to proficiency in the worst faults of their class."[50] The ladies understood that the servant problem involved the domestic's status as a faithless stranger.

No class of persons exists in this country, to whom the name of *stranger* with all its painfullest associations so truly belongs. Aliens to our race, our soil, our institutions and our faith, they are also thrown into a position of antagonism in interest and feeling. . . . They enter into no truly humane and social relation with our families, of which they never are members, but only uncomfortable appendages, tolerated because we cannot do without them . . . the utmost duration of this heartless and mercenary connection being probably not longer than six months.[51]

Such a situation, they urged, "exacts from our sympathies and self-interest alike, a peculiar regard."

In effect, reformers proposed to attack the entire servant problem by attacking the one point at which the labor market for service took on an institutional form. They planned to replace entrepreneurial operations with benevolent institutions, believing that benevolent institutions could harmonize the interests of servant and employer and rationalize the market for servants, both by enforcing skill standards and by encouraging more young women to enter service. To blame the intelligence office for servant problems had the advantage of stimulating practical measures with the promise of amelioration. Of course blaming the intelligence office for servant problems was similar to blaming the Irish: each was a confusion, a mistaking of a part of the difficulty for the whole. Very few employers detected the fallacies in this scheme. One of these was Herman Melville. In his novel *The Confidence Man*

(1857), Melville included the intelligence office as a symbol of the perils of a cash-nexus society, along with patent medicines, bogus charities, land fraud schemes, and other snares for the unwary.

A "man from Missouri," approached on board the riverboat *Fidèle* by an agent of the "Philosophical Intelligence Office," exclaims, "As for Intelligence Offices, I've lived in the East, and know 'em. Swindling concerns kept by low-born cynics, under a fawning exterior wreaking their cynic malice upon mankind."[52] Yet the man from Missouri finds that cynicism is no defense; he succumbs to the agent's appeal and advances three dollars on the promise that a boy will be sent to him.[53] The agent is, of course, one of the several guises in which the confidence man appears. In giving this intelligence office the label "philosophical," Melville pointed out that claims to high-minded benevolence may easily be advanced for purposes of profit or self-promotion. Indeed, the hallmark of the confidence man was his habitual protestation of disinterest and benevolence. Unlike the ladies of the Christian Home for the Female Servant, Melville doubted that sympathy and self-interest could combine so smoothly.

In Melville's view the confidence man cannot be a solitary malefactor, for he often depends upon the greedy or at least unreasonable hopes of those whom he swindles; his "suckers" expect to get something for nothing or to make use of others. The man from Missouri, for example, is an overbearing fellow whose behavior as an employer is suggested by his contention that machines make the best workers. Only machines, he declares, "faithfully attend to their business. Disinterested too; no board, no wages; yet doing good all their lives long; shining examples that virtue is its own reward—the only practical Christians I know." Doing good is reduced to commodity production. "What a difference," he exclaims, "in a moral point of view, between a corn-husker and a boy! Sir, a corn-husker, for its patient continuance in well-doing, might not unfitly go to heaven. Do you suppose a boy will?"[54] The intelligence office agent is deceitful, and the boy he supplies will undoubtedly be unreliable, but the man from Missouri will get what he deserves. Melville saw in the intelligence office only the characteristic mutual deceit and ill-treatment prevailing between employers and workers, entrepreneurs and customers, men and their fellow men; he would not permit one side to lay all the blame on the other. The "intelligence" office, providing not intelligence but cynical trickery, symbolized the sacrifice of human relations, home comforts, even a reasonable correspondence between work and fact, in a marketplace society.

The Problem of Payment

For employers the intelligence office symbolized the new cash-nexus relationships of service. It furnished a lightning rod for employers' resentment of the operation of the labor market in service. But the office was merely a middleman for antagonistic relations between employer and domestic. Domestics learned to fear not only the office but also unscrupulous employers, who taught them to cultivate a protective self-reliance that hired girls had not needed. Louisa May Alcott's experience in service illustrates the difficulties of securing payment in service work in a labor market. "What *shall* I do?" she wondered at age eighteen. She had tried teaching and hated it, tried sewing, but it paid too little. "I was ready to work, eager to be independent." [55] In working as a city missionary her mother encountered one "Reverend Josephus R." who was seeking a "companion" to do "the lighter work" around his household. Conquering her qualms, Louisa decided to take the position. Abba Alcott asked Reverend R., as a kind of afterthought, about wages for her daughter. He replied: "My dear madam, in a case like this let us not use such words as those. Anything you may think proper we shall gladly give. The labor is very light, for there are but three of us and our habits are of the simplest sort . . . money is little to us." Mrs. Alcott did not press him further.

Louisa quickly found the work far from light, as the clergyman idled and scolded about a dirty and dilapidated old house, demanding fancy cooking and plenty of cosseting. She shoveled snow, scrubbed floors, made fires, and sifted ashes "like a true Cinderella." She stayed a month, as agreed, and was implored to stay longer and break in a new girl. Two prospects came but each fled after a day or two, "condemning the place as a very hard one and calling me a fool to stand it another hour." After seven weeks she decided to depart, whether there was a replacement on hand or not. She set off down the road on a bleak March afternoon, clutching the small pocketbook her employer had given her. "Unable to resist the desire to see what my earnings were, I opened the purse and beheld *four dollars*. I have had a good many bitter minutes in my life; but one of the bitterest came to me as I stood there in the windy road, with the sixpenny pocket-book open before me, and looked from my poor chapped, grimy, chill-blained hands to the paltry sum that was considered reward enough for all the hard and humble labor they had done."[56] Her first impulse was to return and fling the money at his feet, but she went home to tell her tale "and leave my parents to avenge my wrongs," preferring to drop a veil over that "harrowing scene": "I will merely mention that the four dollars went back and the Reverend Josephus never heard the last of it in that neighborhood." She had been denied fair wages because, naive and trusting, she had relied on vague assurances rather than a firmly agreed-upon wage.

Alcott declared that she learned from this experience how to treat servants with sympathy and justice. A hired girl would probably have appealed to her parents, just as Alcott did, but a domestic would doubtless have seen no recourse and kept the pathetic sum. A domestic, with no parents to protect her, at least none who could affect the reputation of a minister in his own circle, would have had no hope of direct redress. Employers bristled when prospective domestics questioned them closely about the work and the pay. But domestics who left before they could be replaced, who, as

Caroline Barrett White said, felt no inclination to "oblige," had been schooled by scoundrels like the Reverend Josephus. They had learned how to look out for their own interests.

Domestics seem to have had a more difficult time collecting their wages than help had had. Without the informal pressure of a servant's family and community, even a firm wage figure was no more than a verbal agreement between two parties, one far more powerful than the other. In her novel *Live and Let Live; or, Domestic Service Illustrated*, Catharine Sedgwick described several employers who abused their power, disregarding verbal agreements or interpreting them to their own liking. "Mrs. Broadson" engaged two domestics for a single place, as "insurance," and when both showed up, she dismissed one. She took advantage of a Polish waiter who did not speak English well enough to know his rights, and she tried to pay no wages at all to any domestic who failed to work through the entire first month. Sedgwick assured her readers that this last maneuver was common enough.[57]

Some scattered evidence suggests that domestics tried to protect themselves against such abuses by one of the only means open to them—by demanding payment more regularly and more frequently than help had to do. Had Louisa May Alcott demanded a week's pay at the end of her first week, she would have discovered that the Rev. Josephus meant it when he said, "Money is little to us." Help's wages were usually quoted by the week, but farmers' account books show that hired girls let their wages accumulate. A girl might be advanced enough to finance some needed small purchases and receive a lump sum for the balance at the end of the year or the end of her term of employment.[58] After Mary Ann Heath finished work for Phebe Eastman in February 1828, Mrs. Eastman noted that she "settled with my hired girl, her account eleven dollars."[59] A farmer in Salisbury, New York in the 1850s, William Thompson, recorded in his diary large lump-sum payments when he settled with Ann Diggem, equal to a year's wages less a few advances for shoes, shoe repairs, and the like, also duly recorded in the diary.[60] Even hired girls who were eager to spend their earnings trusted their employers to hold their pay for several weeks or even months.[61]

In the 1860s Anthony Trollope remarked on a tendency he perceived among Americans to run up bad debts to their servants. In England, he wrote, there was a presumption that "failure to pay one's washerwoman was the mark of lowest insolvency, quite apart from the inability to pay a merchant"; but in America the washerwoman and the merchant were "about equal game."[62] In 1855 the managers of the charitable Rosine Association of Philadelphia reported receiving complaints from domestics who had been denied their wages. A Philadelphia alderman told them of receiving "frequent applications from women who had been domestics in families, to institute suits for the recovery of wages from their employers."[63]

Even employers who did not use the impersonality of the labor market to evade their obligations altogether discovered they could press certain advantages in the matter of wages. In 1855 the anonymous author of *Plain Talk and Friendly Advice to Domestics*, a New England matron, reported that the ladies of a town "will sometimes make a rule among themselves that they will not pay to exceed $6 a month to any girl, and call any lady to account who transcends this."[64] An 1895 report detailed a similar combination to restrain wages: "In one or two of the largest cities small clubs have been formed among married women whose means permit large establishments. . . . A scale of prices is fixed for the domestics employed in their houses, and the rates decided upon are those which prevailed five years ago."[65]

Turnabout was fair play, some domestics reasoned. Caroline Barrett White encountered one servant who demanded a full week's pay when she was dismissed after having worked for only a few days. Declaring that she would not leave until she received the full amount, she accosted Mr. White and created a lively scene in the kitchen. "She refused point blank to budge," the diary recounted, "and tried to intimidate him by all sorts of threats. . . . she *yelled* and *shrieked* and acted like a maniac, but finally started off without being forcibly ejected." [66] Another suspicious cook refused to leave when told that she was dismissed and that her employer's husband would pay her at his office: "She said she would not go a step after it, but would stay another week and do nothing." She resisted a deduction from her wages for breakage, again threatening she would not leave "until every cent was given." [67] A Staten Island woman reported "quite a scene" when a cook who had been employed for a fortnight was dismissed. The family summoned a police officer who remained until she packed and left "(although she tried to brow-beat *him* down). . . . Oh her language was dreadful." [68]

The changing circumstances of service eventually suggested to benevolent groups a strategy that, unlike efforts to displace the intelligence office, more frankly recognized the antagonistic relations between employers and domestics and proposed to strengthen the domestics' hand in that unequal contest. In 1877 a group of elite Boston women formed the Women's Educational and Industrial Union to "open up avenues of industry for women," and to "aid, strengthen, and elevate each other." They established a reading room and began a series of evening classes. One of the earliest acts of the union was the formation of a Protective Committee in 1878 to act on complaints about "the injustice done to working women in withholding their hardly [*sic*] earned wages." [69] Year after year the Protective Committee was preoccupied with cases of domestics who had been defrauded of their wages. Reports by Kate Gannett Wells, chair of the committee, detailed stories like that of "one honest, happy-go-lucky domestic" owed ninety-two dollars by her employers: "Each day she trusted it would be paid, each week her mistress needed her help, each month the children cried when she talked of going, and she stayed on, believing. Now she has to suffer the penalty of her own good will, for the employer has nothing."[70] When one employer died before paying a domestic $350 she was owed, the executors of the estate maintained that she had worked for her board only. The committee provided her free legal advice and representation. Most cases were less dramatic, and Wells expressed exasperation "when two angry women dispute about half a dollar." "We appreciate the value of fifty cents to a working girl," she stated, "but why should there be any doubt as to the sum for which she was engaged?"[71] Eventually, in 1885, the union developed an employment bureau to handle domestic servants; their primary approach to servant problems, however, continued to be the contractual approach of the Protective Committee, which urged regular payment and written agreement on terms of employment. The union distributed a circular giving the main points of law on subjects applicable to domestics, such as the week's trial for satisfactory work, giving notice, liability for breakage, and the like. Without the union and similar organizations—like the Legal Aid Society of New York—the letter of the law was often irrelevant.[72] The domestic could incur a larger sum in legal fees than she could hope to recover.

In *Popular Science* Oliver Lyman blandly explained that, although it was illegal for an employer to deduct the value of breakage from a servant's wages without specific prior agreement, employers could and did do so. "As a matter of practice and advisability," he wrote, "the illegal method of deduction, although it overrides the servant's rights, is better for her, as it saves her the expense of a lawsuit merely for a principle."[73] Such a remark illustrates the ease with which most employers blinked at injustice on wages: it would have been "better for her" to be subject to no illegal deductions at all. Kate Gannett Wells urged domestics to adopt one of the few means of self-defense available—simply to leave if they were not paid promptly and in full. After several years on the

Protective Committee, she said of her experience: "It is difficult for a well-bred woman to realize how constantly girls are cheated." [74]

From Country to City

In Eliza Farrar's book *The Young Lady's Friend*, a chapter on "Treatment of Domestics and Work-Women" warned young ladies to understand their domestics. She noted, for example, that some domestics, brought up in the country, had worked only in houses where bells were not used and would resent being summoned so impersonally. Rural employers did not need such advice, she said:

I am aware that there is a large class of readers to whom the foregoing observations on the treatment of domestics will not apply. Persons living in the interior of the country, on farms or in villages, where the population is thinly scattered over the land, generally share in all the labors of their household and will be under no temptation to commit many errors pointed out in this chapter. When the only assistance they receive is from a person who is treated as an equal, and sits at the same table with the family, there will be no room for much of the inconsiderateness here mentioned. [75]

The author of *Plain Talk and Friendly Advice to Domestics* remarked, in her sketch of an independent Yankee helper named "Mehitable," that "city housekeepers would hardly comprehend such a case, although it is common enough all over New England." There was no such thing as a servant in the rural vocabulary, she explained, and no objection to "working out." [76]

Urbanization itself was not the only cause of the change from help to domestics, but it permitted and encouraged the full realization and free operation of the labor market for service. As a town grew into a small city impersonal market institutions like the intelligence office became necessary. In 1885, when the population of Cortland, New York reached about 8,000, the passenger agent for the New York Central Railroad added an intelligence office to his railway ticket business.[77] Urban anonymity made possible expediential hirings and firings, even shady practices like nonpayment, dealings that were simply not possible in small towns where everyone knew everyone else's business and where the social relations and values of a small producer economy endured. In such settings employers may have wanted domestics, but they often had to deal with girls who wanted to be help and whose family economies placed them in a strong bargaining position.

In 1874, when Maud Nathan was twelve years old, her father suffered business reverses, sold his seat on the New York Stock Exchange, and moved from New York City to Green Bay, Wisconsin as general passenger agent for the railroad in Green Bay. "One of my mother's greatest trials," Maud Nathan wrote later, "was her difficulty in securing servants. The only ones available were the daughters of well-to-do farmers who would condescend to be 'helpers,' but resented being called servants. They expected to be treated as members of the family circle and to sit with the family at meal time. This condition my mother, with her New York traditions and southern background, refused to comply with."[78] When Mrs. Nathan found that the consequence of her refusal would be a cookless kitchen, she compromised, permitting the girl to eat in the dining room but only after she had served the family.

In Elmira, New York in 1847, Miriam Berry Whitcher, wife of a local clergyman, dismissed her helper Martha, explaining, "I feel discouraged when I think of *Hired girls*, and all the trouble we shall probably have in that respect. I do not think I could ever endure all that I did while Martha lived with us. I never want another one who expects to be *company* for me." Mrs. Whitcher, an educated woman, had no patience with small-town female concerns. She wanted a servant who had no ideas of equality and would not presume to sit at her table. Finally she found a candidate who could not demand treatment as help: Jane, a young black woman.[79]

In North Adams, Massachusetts Marianne Finch, an English visitor, encountered one servant who was clearly a hired girl, for she asked Miss Finch if it were true that in England they called hired girls "servants" and did not eat with them. At another house she met a woman who set up a separate table for her domestics; one girl left the house in a matter of hours after discovering that there was no place for her at the family table.[80]

Mary Hardy Williams of Ithaca, New York was familiar and comfortable with urban life and its style of service. Her husband was a well-to-do and prominent man who made his money in lumber, banking, and railroads and served as a state senator and a charter trustee of Cornell University. She drew on her urban connections to recruit domestics from larger labor markets. Having thirteen children, she employed a large staff, including immigrant women and free blacks, and treated them as domestics. Yet she also hired local girls whose backgrounds, attitudes, and reasons for entering and leaving service were more characteristic of help. Girls from Searsburg and Troupsburg, Danby and Dryden worked for Mrs. Williams for a while and then went home to attend school or to help their parents.[81]

In Detroit in 1850, Elizabeth Sullivan Stuart did not have to make the compromises characteristic of Ithaca, North Adams, Elmira, or Green Bay. She could demand domestics and make her demands stick. She described her methods of dealing with a servant who had the temerity to imply that her employer might take on part of the work: "I would have paid her passage and told her that the intelligence man had sent a wrong person—you wanted a girl to do your work and not a fancy article—I suppose she was to eat at table with you—how absurd."[82] Mrs. Stuart's assumption of labor-market relations was crystallized in her reference to another servant as "that miserable $7-a-monther."[83] Discontented with the service her domestics provided, she tended to blame their Irish ancestry, rejoicing, for example, when her daughter was able to hire "a *woman*, and not a headlong, Irish, heedless animal."[84] Yet she held no brief for hired girls. Urban anonymity, like the ethnicity of the Irish or the race of blacks, permitted and, in effect, encouraged employers like Mrs. Stuart to make servant hiring a simple exchange of cash for work.

James Russell Lowell wrote in 1846, "I love our Yankee word [help], teaching, as it does, the true relation and its being equally binding on master and servant."[85] He had not noticed its eclipse. As late as 1890 William Dean Howells objected, "They are not our servants, they are our helpers."[86] But others, despite difficulties with domestics, saw help as outmoded, troublesome, and inappropriate to genteel life. In 1857 the editors of *Harper's Weekly* remarked, "The old New England notion that the word servant was degrading, and that a separate servants' table was a thing not to be thought of, has died out in this meridian long since and it is well so."[87] A writer in *The Ladies' Repository* in 1870 found Irish and German servants satisfactory, but, as for hired girls, "everyone knows they are too thoroughly American to live with."[88]

Harriet Beecher Stowe's *The Chimney Corner* dismissed hired girls as "half-and-half people," "so sensitive, so exacting in their demands, so hard to please, that we have come to the firm determination that . . . whoever we are to depend on must come with *bona-fide* willingness to take the position of a servant."[89] "Vexatious trials must be those country 'helps,'" wrote an employer from Troy, New York in 1846; "one must have great patience to endure their liberty-loving airs."[90] Another, who had a "dreadful" time finding a servant in Cleveland in 1883, rejected a hired girl: "At last one offered who is very nice and pretty, but would only answer for the country as she sits at the same table."[91] "Girls in the city will not go into the country to live," wrote one rural employer in 1844, "and the girls living about here have such topping notions that one is better off without them."[92]

In an exchange of letters in *Arthur's Home Magazine* in 1863, a correspondent from Carroll County, Illinois portrayed hired help as the rule throughout the West. A number of sharply critical replies from other western women pointed out that, whatever might be the situation in Carroll County, their own areas supported thoroughly refined society with proper domestic servants to match. One "lady correspondent" who conceded that "hired help" prevailed "in the country and in small towns" protested that in the western cities and larger towns servants were "like the domestics of the East." The editor could only conclude diplomatically that conditions were "local" and "transitory." [93]

In a case described in Mary Hardy Williams's correspondence, an urban domestic was able to adopt work patterns characteristic of help. A friend wrote to Mrs. Williams from Dryden, New York about an Irish girl named Catharine Kane who was looking for work in service after some years "in the City of New York." She had come to Dryden "a short time since to visit her Mother and friends. They desire to have her obtain a place near them and not return to the East. Her wages has [sic] been five dollars a month but she does not expect that here, she would like one dollar a week." [94] Catharine Kane arrived only to find that her mother had acquired several cows and would not "consent to have her engage to work so near home. The *Old Lady* says if she remains in the country, she must help her milk and churn next summer." [95] In New York City Catharine had been a self-supporting domestic for years, but back in the country, she found her labor needed at home. Perhaps Catharine did not find this prospect altogether attractive, for she was reported to be thinking of returning to "the East" in the spring. If she did stay in Dryden, she could have worked as a temporary helper during the winter months, when the work of milking and churning tapered off. Catharine Kane's case illustrated the influence of a girl's family economy on her participation in service.

Lizzie Wilson Goodenough's experiences show the effects of differing employer demand. She was born in 1844 in Brattleboro, Vermont and orphaned at sixteen, working thereafter as a servant in and around Brattleboro, where her only relative, a brother, lived. In 1865 Lizzie worked in two households; in one she was a hired girl, and in the other a domestic. She began the year helping the Howes, farmers who lived out of town. Lizzie and Mrs. Howe often worked together. "We have been washing this forenoon," was a common entry in Lizzie's diary for a Monday.[96] Lizzie often shared the ironing with a daughter, Celia. The precise mix of sharing the work apparently varied considerably, but Lizzie never seems to have felt herself unfairly exploited. After she finished her work, she had time for her own sewing. On January 31, 1865, for example, she had the washing done, the beds made, and had swept up by ten o'clock. Then she began work on her brown alpaca. Some days she could even say, "Have not been doing much today. Have sewed some, crocheted some, and knit a little this afternoon."[97]

Lizzie counted herself as one of the family at the table, noting once that there were only four "of us" to eat supper.[98] She and the Howes exchanged favors casually; Mrs. Howe brought braid for Lizzie's dress from Brattleboro, and Lizzie in turn did some sewing for Mrs. Howe. "We have had quite a knitting circle this afternoon. Mrs. Howe, Celia, Sarah, Melissa and myself have all been knitting."[99] Lizzie received callers at the farm, paid visits, and periodically spent time with her brother and his family. She evidently liked the Howes, for she would continue to see Mrs. Howe and Celia socially years after she had ceased to work for them.

Despite these advantages, Lizzie left the Howes in the spring of 1865 and, after spending a few weeks at her brother's house, took a job in Brattleboro with the Tripp family. Perhaps she was attracted by higher wages, for she turned down other offers. "George Clarke was down here to hire me this forenoon. Could not see going there, as he said he had been hireing a girl for 1 and 5 a week. Told him there was no use in talking."[100] At the Tripps she would make $2.50 a week. Perhaps she thought town life would give her more opportunities for socializing; certainly she saw the parade and fireworks on the Fourth of July and every circus that passed through town. Assuming the expected role of a domestic in this town household, she did most of the work by herself, especially the washing, which she dreaded in hot weather. She noted working with Mrs. Tripp only on unusual occasions or for fancy work—

making cake or currant jelly, or dressing fish when Mr. Tripp and the boys went fishing. Even though she was in town, she often felt lonesome.

Lizzie began to dream of different kinds of work. One Saturday morning she wrote, "How I wish I was sewing for a living but instead of that I must go to baking this morning in the hot and hateful old kitchen but it shant last always there is other work that I can do besides housework."[101] In 1866 she turned to her skill with a needle as an escape from service. She sewed vests to custom order for a local merchant while boarding with families in town. Because her diaries begin to lag, we cannot follow Lizzie Wilson's working life for a period of years. She returned to service in 1869, eventually returning to the Howes, and worked until her marriage late that year to Henry Goodenough, a laborer who later established himself on a farm. Her 1874 diary reveals that as Lizzie Wilson Goodenough, then caring for two small children, she would occasionally hire help herself for a few days or weeks at a time. In July, seven months pregnant, she wrote, "Have got to stop work or go under. Have hired Ellen to come up and help me."[102]

As the experiences of Catharine Kane and Lizzie Wilson Goodenough suggest, the differences between help and domestics were not simply a matter of setting, of urban versus rural, even though contemporaries often noticed changes in service in terms of an urban-rural contrast. Nor were they characteristics of individuals, permitting an easy labeling of women as one or the other, but rather they formed patterns of behavior into which women entered according to the economic situation in which they and their families found themselves, patterns that were shaped and reshaped to meet their employers' demands.

This is reflected in Clara Loring Bogart's novel *Emily: A Tale of the Empire State*.[103] Mrs. Bogart's rather stilted tale was meant as a temperance tract rather than as a comment on women's work. The story is set in the mid-nineteenth century in upstate New York, where the heroine, Emily Allen, is a farmer's daughter. When a neighbor, Mrs. Lanning, falls ill, her daughter Elsie cannot manage alone and tells her father that perhaps her friend Emily Allen would come to help. "Does she ever work out?" asks Mr. Lanning. "No," says Elsie, "but perhaps she would come for a few weeks to help me just to accommodate."

This accommodation is arranged between the parents. At first Emily's mother objects, but Mr. Lanning assures her that the work will not be too hard: the boys will bring in the wood and water and do the churning. "He also represented his daughter's urgent need of assistance, and offered liberal wages for a few weeks' work, promising to procure other help as soon as he could get time." Emily's stint as a helper, a few weeks spent among friends and neighbors and an amusing set of hired men, passes pleasantly enough.

But Emily's father, never very prosperous, soon falls on harder times. One night Mrs. Allen asks, "Emily, how would you like to work out this winter? At doing housework I mean." She explains that Mrs. Watson, one of her cousin's neighbors in the city, is in need of a girl and the cousin has asked if Emily might be interested. There are only three in the Watson family and they send the washing out, so the work cannot be too hard. What kind of people are they? Emily asks, and her mother answers, "They are rather stylish people, I think, and I am afraid their hired girl would be considered a mere servant, to be kept in the kitchen as much as possible."

"I like to do housework very well," Emily responds, "but I don't quite like the idea of being somebody's servant." Still, the wages of $2.50 a week are an inducement, since they are far more than she could earn around home. And, Emily reflects, since she doesn't know enough to teach school, she has no other way to earn money. She leaves her family at the farmhouse gate, going off on her own for the first time to the city. Mrs. Watson proves to be a disorderly sort who hates housework, is given to reading novels and spoiling her young son, and is stinting in her praise lest the girl be encouraged to "undue familiarity." Emily fights loneliness, and indignation, too, at having to eat alone in the kitchen after waiting on the family in the dining room. Fortunately her evangelical piety sustains her and fortifies her for the greater trials to come, when her suitor will prove unequal to the temptations of alcohol.

Emily Allen, who was both helper and domestic, knew the one to be a harder job than the other. There was a certain romance in the portrayal of the Lannings but also a realistic appreciation of job mobility, of how an individual could move back and forth between the two conditions of help and domestic. As the labor market for domestics became established in the cities, girls and women could, by moving between country and city, in effect select the kind of service preferred, weighing family needs and resources against local ties and pecuniary rewards. In consequence of the higher wages offered to urban domestics, the opening of other kinds of factory and shop work to women, and the lower age of marriage among women in frontier areas, help was harder and harder to find. "Help cannot be had in the farm house, for love nor money," wrote a matron in Fore's Bend, Minnesota in 1880, "Our young people are all rushing to town." [104] Abigail Scott Duniway described "hired help" as "unattainable" in Oregon in the 1860s because girls married young. [105] An early twentieth-century report by the U.S. Department of Agriculture noted that hired girls were scarce in Colorado because "most girls in the Rocky Mountain tier of states marry before they are twenty." [106]

Sally Rice was seventeen when she left her parents' farm in Somerset, Vermont in 1838 to "work out" as a hired girl in Union Village, just over the New York border. She wrote home, eager to reassure her parents that her health was good and to tell how she had purchased a bonnet, shoes, and eight yards of calico. [107] A year later she wrote again, after a visit home, that she was glad to return to her friends at Union Village: "I can have a home here as long as I will stay and am steady. They are very anxious that I should live with them as long as I work out anywhere." Her parents must have urged her to stay home or to marry a young man from Somerset, but she now viewed her hometown as a "desert."

As for marrying and settling in that wilderness I won't. . . . I am most nineteen years old. I must of course have something of my own before many more years have passed over my head. And where is that something coming from if I go home and earn nothing. What can we get off that rocky farm only two or three cows. It would be another thing if you kept nine or ten cows and could raise corn to sell. . . . It would surely be cheper for you to hire a girl one that would be contented to stay in the desert than for me to come home and live in trouble all the time.[108]

She urged her parents to move off their stony little farm.

Sally Rice went on to work as a hired girl in Millbury, Massachusetts but then in a few years tried working in a textile mill at Masonville, Connecticut, as a deliberate experiment: "I well knew that if I could not make more in the mill than I can doing housework I should not stay." She found it noisy and confining in the mill, but she calculated its benefits: "I do not wear out my clothes and shoes as I do when I do housework." If she could clear two dollars per week over her room and board costs, she thought that better than doing housework for nine shillings. On the other hand, the factory was located in a swampy hollow, and after only a few months, she found it affected her health. "It was killing me to work in it," she wrote, and went back to housework in Massachusetts.[109] Leaving home did not trouble Sally Rice, who first helped and then moved in the larger market for women's labor. Jane Emeline Jacobs, who worked in a factory in Lawrence, Massachusetts, also found her health unequal to the task. Still, in her home in Sutton, Vermont, "a girl cannot get more than a dollar a week doing housework," she wrote in 1854. She considered going to the city as a domestic for higher wages, but then wrote to her aunt in the Oregon country. "I have heard that a girl could get thirty dollars per month, but I suppose clothing is dear there." She thought she might come along if "Uncle Nelson's folks went west." [110] Records do not tell us if she went, but she too weighed the limited rewards of helping against other forms of work that meant leaving home. Because American agriculture continued to be dominated by small family farms, some farm daughters, not feeling constrained to respond to the pecuniary incentives of urban or factory work that would have required their moving away from home, continued to act as hired girls in rural areas right through the end of the century.

The daughters of industrial wage-earners or impoverished European peasants, pressured by circumstances either to contribute to a family wage economy or to remove themselves as burdens through self-supporting employment, presented themselves in the labor market without the implicit backing of a self-sufficient family economy. They were therefore vulnerable as domestics to abuses in the intelligence offices and problems in collecting their pay. Along with supply, demand changed as urban middle-class employers of household workers began to require longer hours and stricter work discipline, hiring and firing in an instrumental, impersonal fashion. Such employers were probably influenced by the example of employer practices in the economy at large, where fewer and fewer workers lived with their employers and where the expansion of the industrial economy implied precisely this antagonistic differentiation between capitalist and worker, employer and employee. Domestics' employers did not behave as consistently as did other employers, whose very existence as bosses depended upon the realization of profit and, therefore, upon the use of workers to that end. Changing demand for household service also stemmed from new visions of women's roles, which were reshaping middle-class domestic life and family relations. Varying influences, direct and indirect, changed service sporadically and unsystematically; help persisted in some areas and homes long after domestics had become prevalent in others, and mixed patterns often prevailed.

FOUR The Elaboration of Needs and the Division of Household Labor

The nature of the demand for household-service work, as well as its purposes and organization, lacked the uniformities common to wage work that produced profits, yet certain rough patterns emerged. When not devoted to marketable products like textiles, household work shared with help seems to have been directed toward meeting rather minimally the tasks of daily necessity. Work was done by hand.

The household regime of Phebe Eastman may have been typical of life of women who employed help at the turn of the nineteenth century. Mrs. Eastman kept the home fires burning. She or her hired girl had to haul the wood to the fireplace, tend the fire regularly, sweep up and haul the ashes away. Fireplace heating was dirty as well as inefficient; a poorly constructed chimney could smoke or carry ashes out over the room in a downdraft. Tinderboxes were so difficult to use that most families kept a fire going on the hearth year in and year out.[1] In order to light her home, Phebe Eastman turned her hand to candle making, a tedious piece of work. If she used a lamp, it was a guttering, open-flame variety, prone to smoke and foul odors, and requiring regular trimming and filling.[2]

Like heating, cooking chores centered around the fireplace. Open-fire cooking involved maneuvering iron cranes, spits, and heavy cast-iron pots, and perhaps stoking a brick oven for baking. A woman had to tend the fire closely, stoop frequently, and haul fuel and ashes. Cooking utensils turned black with soot, and so often did the hands and the clothing of the cook.[3] Stoked for cooking, the fireplace threw off plenty of heat: a boon in winter, it made cooking in warm weather a sweaty ordeal.

At the turn of the nineteenth century, the high cost of transportation and limited means of preservation made American cooking quite seasonal and often monotonous. Foreigners were amazed at the effects of the severe American climate on food spoilage. Isaac Weld reported that during the summer meat became tainted in a day, that poultry should not be killed until four hours before wanted, and that milk "turned" one to two hours after being taken from the cow.[4] Although the refrigerator was patented in 1803, its use spread slowly until the late 1820s, when new methods of ice cutting began to bring down the cost of ice. For families like the Eastmans fresh meat was available only at butchering time; otherwise they ate it cured or pickled. Butchering-time brought hard work; Phebe Eastman made head cheese and "tried out" hundreds of pounds of lard. Milk that could be cooled only in a springhouse or cellar tended to sour readily; cream rapidly grew tainted and butter rancid. Mrs. Eastman worked to keep up with the yield of six cows, making her own cheese as well as butter. Women preserved fruit in the form of jellies and jams, made cucumbers into pickles and cabbage into sauerkraut. They dried what fruits and vegetables they could and stored others in root cellars. The work of preservation was extensive and preparation, though simple, was tedious. Early cookbooks were brief.[5] Mrs. Eastman did not refer to menus or specific recipes; she just "baked" or "boiled a dinner."

When Mrs. Eastman cleaned her house, all the water had to be hauled by hand. Phebe Eastman wrote of "trying to clear the logs of our house from dust and webs" and concluded, "A log house is a dirty thing."[6] She also scalded the logs and the bedsteads to kill insects. Undeterred by screens or insecticides, flies invaded houses in warm weather and covered everything with flyspecks; they were joined by mosquitoes, cockroaches, moths, and often bedbugs. One woman, recalling Ohio in 1830, said that "the difference between those who were naturally clean and orderly and those who were not was perhaps more marked in those days than it is now. It was easy, for instance, since we had no screens, to let the flies spoil everything. My mother just wouldn't have it so." She recalled that her sister placed rounded covers over every dish on her table.[7] On occasion Mrs. Eastman "washed floors" or "scoured all I could" and then hung up pine boughs, probably to discourage insects and freshen the air.[8] Like hanging pine boughs, the use of white-wash, common in spring and fall housecleanings, involved not removing dirt but covering it up. There are hints in Mrs. Eastman's diary that her home was, while tidy, not particularly clean. She was energetic and hard-working, and she tried to get quickly through her "chores"—washing, cooking, and sewing—so that she could spare a few minutes for her craft, weaving.

The entry "washed" in Phebe Eastman's diary meant that she had done a laundry, a major daylong effort that began with stoking large fires to heat the water. Using hard well water complicated the task: one woman recalled that she had to spend half of every wash-day softening the water by adding lye, boiling, stirring, and skim-ming.[9] Hauling water, hand-wringing wet clothes, and lifting and carrying tubs to empty them made washing hard physical labor. Phebe Eastman, like most women at the turn of the nine-teenth century, also made her own soap, using lye prepared from wood ashes and grease saved from cooking.[10] Mrs. Eastman did not mention ironing in her diary; she may have considered this encompassed in the general term "washing," or she may have dis-pensed with it.

Phebe Eastman not only sewed virtually all her family's clothing but also wove the fabric for most of it. She cared for the children and nursed anyone in the family in illness. She eventually bore eleven children and raised nine of them to maturity. She seems to have expected to delegate to hired girls only two types of work, spinning and looking after the children. Other kinds of work she shared with her help, working with the girl as an "assistant" unless prostrated by ill health. Together they performed the handwork needed to extract family necessities from raw materials. Given the sporadic availability of help and the low level of household technology, however, women like Mrs. Eastman could not hope to delegate any significant portion of their household duties.

The change from help to domestics was prompted by, and in turn furthered, the elaboration of employers' "needs," needs that rose on the tides of changing tastes and family budgets. The functions of domestics reflected the double nature of the middle-class home itself: still the scene of mundane, repetitive, and rather primitive housework, but at the same time increasingly conceived of as a refuge from the world of work. Where home and work-place were one, as in an artisan's shop or on the family farm, there could be little opportunity for concern with appearances before visitors, since such concern would tend to impede the essential business of work. But with home and work-place separated, the temptation arose to try to appear to best advantage before others. So too the value of home life changed for family members when they no longer spent the day in close proximity; the home became the place where intimate family relations were renewed, often quite deliberately, during the few hours available after the day's work was done. The nature of woman's role in the home changed, as she inherited command of this private sphere, finding in its ordering her own work, indeed her "profession." Such changes in the economy and in the ideology of home life made service more problematic, for they implied a set of new needs that required domestics rather than help and increased the burden of work for domestics beyond what had been expected of help.

Status and Domestics

In the nineteenth century, as per capita production increased and with it the American standard of living, the demand for servants rose.[11] But because the rewards of growth were unequally distributed, both among individuals and across a dizzying business cycle, economic rewards were often sought and savored in a spirit of competitive anxiety. The antebellum period saw a remarkable growth in the size of the largest American fortunes. By the 1840s entrepreneurs in banking, real estate, manufacturing, and railroads had begun to amass wealth on a scale that dwarfed old money based on land or commerce.[12] The new barons of transport and industry enjoyed their fortunes in highly visible urban settings, just as the cities themselves entered into a period of dramatic growth. While their eyes were dazzled by the glittering new "millionaires," even more modest middle-class businessmen, retailers, supervisors, clerks, professionals, and the like, enjoyed increasing buying power. Changes in production and distribution helped to make consumer goods like clothing, fuel, housing, and home furnishings more affordable. And retailers, advertisers, and publishers began to develop a lucrative partnership based on the realization that a literate public with buying power beyond bare necessity might be actively persuaded to buy.[13] Many individuals found their ideas of the necessary and their appetites for the desirable expanding. Although the power to satisfy these new wants varied greatly, a shift in standards tended to permeate society from top to bottom.[14]

J. A. Banks has argued that in nineteenth-century England middle-class families used their rising standards of living for the sort of "ostentatious display" that required more and more domestic service. Increases in middle-class incomes were usually followed by disproportionate increases in expenditure on servants.[15] Although Banks's evidence, composed of scattered household budgets, is more suggestive than convincing, some part of the increasing American demand for domestics clearly reflected a new concern for status. As Raymond Williams has pointed out, the very notion of "status"—i.e., social stratification based on consumption patterns or styles of life—was born or invented in the nineteenth century. [16]

American society had no formally fixed, hereditary wealth, no aristocracy; it had only money, older and newer, and in the quickening pace of the nineteenth-century economy, old and new money, possession and acquisition, fell into distinctive patterns. Families who had had money and the social status it could buy for some time found no need to advertise their position. Parvenus, by contrast, spent their new money as conspicuously as possible precisely to demonstrate that they possessed it and thereby gain recognition and admission into the society of old money. Nineteenth-century men about town referred to these two groups as "nobs" and "swells," so distinctive did they appear in the context of rapid economic change and the growth of huge new fortunes. [17]

The "nobs" characteristically resisted the "swells," conveniently forgetting their own forebears and adopting the pose that social status should depend upon hereditary position or even upon virtue. Yet the nobs eventually succumbed to the sheer pecuniary magnitude of the swells' social campaigns: Mrs. Astor eventually accepted an invitation to Mrs. Vanderbilt's fancy dress ball. "Always in America," as Mills put it, "society based on descent has been either by-passed or bought-out by the new and vulgar rich." [18] Thus, American pursuit of status in high society revolved in cycles of resistance and absorption, as dollars translated into proper decorum and social observances. Contemporary sources indicate that this upper level status struggle was well under way in major American cities in the 1840s and 1850s, although it would reach crescendo in the seventies and eighties that helped give that age the name "gilded." In the forties, Anna Cora Mowatt's play *Fashion* parodied the parvenu. Liveried servants began to appear in the streets of New York. By the fifties, New York high society was formal enough to recognize itself under the title "the upper ten thousand," and some "upper tens" hopefully researched their coats of arms in the *American Handbook of Heraldry*.[19]

The status struggle often seemed to disappear at its highest levels, since those at the peaks could afford to cultivate an indifference to it. The diarist Sidney George Fisher reflects the mood of composure that old money could sometimes achieve in the face of the status struggle. Fisher, a member of the first circles in Philadelphia, was annoyed by the nouveau riche and slightly puzzled by the hectic pursuit of great wealth. Fisher could not summon up much interest in making more money, although his very indifference led him to financial embarrassments. He took note of the bidding up of consumption standards. In 1850 he wrote, "I remember when $3000 was considered a comfortable and genteel income for a family, and $6000 thought very rich, now $6000 is very moderate, and $10,000 is necessary for elegance and anything like style."[20] Fisher remained unmoved by such changes.

In general, however, the openness of the American social situation made for a persistent note of shrillness, principally from the swells but also from the nobs who attempted to outdistance their pursuers.[21] European travelers often puzzled over the fact that, for all their democratic ideals, Americans included so many snobs and social climbers among their number.[22] Ward McAllister, who served as high society's "Autocrat of Dining Rooms" in the seventies and eighties, left a hilariously affected memoir, *Society As I Have Known It*, which illustrates the terms of status pursuit. In an account of a picnic at his country place at Newport in the 1850s, McAllister wrote, "I felt that it would never do to have a gathering of the brightest and cleverest people in the country at my place with the pastures empty, neither a cow nor a sheep. . . . I at once hired an entire flock of Southdown sheep, and two yoke of cattle and several cows from the neighboring farm for half a day, to be turned into my pasture lots, to give the place an animated look."[23] He devotes great attention to appearances, to beauty, but a version of beauty that is tamed and reduced to matters of purchasable decor. He dilates on the niceties of giving dinner parties, warning against the "fatal mistake" of allowing two white or brown sauces to follow each other in succession or permitting truffles to appear twice in the menu.[24] In this manner status leaders zestfully decreed constant subtle shifts to confound their pursuers. The pursuit of status, although closely dependent upon disposable income, could seem to take on a life of its own, separate from, and indeed opposed to, the dreary economic facts of life. Fashion and the fashionables, McAllister announced, prevent the country from falling into a humdrum rut, saving Americans from "becoming merely a money-making and money-saving people, with nothing to brighten up and enliven life."[25]

Status pursuit flourished also in humbler middle-class precincts. The middle class was inclined to disapprove of a game they could not hope to win, yet as surely as the well-to-do expanded their standard of living, middle-class standards edged upward. In Kingston, New York in 1851, when Judge James C. Forsythe held a party to open his new home, a local diarist wrote, "The Judge's new house is a splendid affair throwing all others in Kingston in the shade." (Kingston had at that time a population of about one thousand souls.) The diarist remarked on the delicately carved marbles, the rich mirrors, paintings, and furniture. He wrote of an evening of music, champagne, and oysters.[26] The guests watched their manners and personal appearance. Returning the invitation, to maintain social exchange, they had to make their own homes presentable. Doubtless the Judge's party prompted some Kingstonians to consult advice literature on dress, etiquette, and decor. This literature aimed precisely to extend and interpret genteel standards to those whose background and experience did not provide them with the requisite knowledge.

Like the Kingston residents who saw that night that they had been put "in the shade," members of the lower middle class probably hoped not so much to win status as to avoid losing it, to avoid

looking dowdy or ridiculous or pathetic. The anonymous author of
Six Hundred Dollars a Year explained how she stretched the salary
of her husband, a factory supervisor, by exercising careful economy
and making wax flowers to sell. "Humble as was our position in
the great world," she said, "we had a certain status to maintain.
We must live in a respectable house, we must dress genteelly at
least, and keep a servant too."[27] She calculated that they could
spare $1.50 per week, or $78.00 per year, for a servant's wages. At
this level, status concerns took on a mood of neither composure nor
zest, but one of grim calculation and anxiety. Developments in
publishing in the 1830s facilitated the spread of standards of urban
gentility. Mechanized presses and more rapid transportation encouraged the establishment of a large and diverse group of national
magazines and newspapers, including many devoted to women's
interests. Magazines like *Godey's Lady's Book* spoke to a national
audience with advice on etiquette and domestic life, projecting the
standards of respectability. In *The Gilded Age*, Twain and Warner
pictured *Godey's* circulating in Obedstown, East Tennessee, where
it "was regarded as the perfection of polite literature by some of the
ablest critics in the place."[28] The transportation revolution also
helped to spread genteel standards, as proper matrons moved west
or wide-eyed girls visited relations in the big city. "I notice everything and am very particular," wrote Caroline Cowles Richards,
altering her deployment of the teacup after a visit to her aunt in
New York City in 1863.[29] In her New York novels, Harriet
Beecher Stowe assessed one psychological mechanism that eased
the spread of higher standards. The spendthrift in the family, Aunt
Maria, is always able to represent herself as sensible and sober,
thanks to the spectacle of "those Elmores": "We must keep in sight
of them. All I ask is to be *decent*. I never expect to run into the
extremes those Elmores do."[30]

Status pursuit and status maintenance at every level depended
upon the ability to hire domestics. Nobs shaped their composure
in lives cushioned from childhood by service in abundance. In

Philadelphia, Sidney George Fisher, with his wife and one child, kept four servants and when contemplating retrenchment he reflected that, as his wife had argued, "It is impossible to get along with less . . . impossible for a *lady*."[31] Swells found domestics equally indispensable, since high-priced domestics could establish in their homes the style and magnificence appropriate to their new positions. To set standards they had not themselves grown up with, many imported British butlers and housekeepers. Judge Forsythe needed domestics to clean his carpets and to polish his mirrors and marbles. To show off his new home and possessions to the rest of Kingston, thus converting mere possession into social achievement, the Judge also needed domestics taking coats at the door and handing around the champagne and oysters. For the author of *$600 a Year*, hiring a domestic took on an urgent necessity; it was a matter of setting herself off from those below who were just not "respectable." Leonore Davidoff refers to this minimal but crucial function of domestics when she terms them "deference-givers."[32] Was it possible for a lady—"a woman of education, cultivation and refinement"—to "do her own work?" Yes, Harriet Beecher Stowe once argued, but she protested too much, insisting such a lady could have as much free time for reading and embroidery as ladies who hired service. And she had to concede that "ladies who did their own work" were not satisfied: their "sense of gentility" and self-respect were troubled.[33]

Nineteenth-century satirists who burlesqued the age of nob and swell did not neglect the domestic. Miriam Berry Whitcher amused the readers of *Neal's Saturday Gazette* and *Godey's Lady's Book* between 1846 and 1849 with tales of "Aunt Magwire" and the "Widow Bedott." Aunt Magwire was the soul of common sense but her sister "Silly" Bedott was an avid social climber whose pretensions were given added absurdity by her remarkable dialect. Having exhausted all possibilities for remarriage in Wiggletown, the Widow Bedott declares its residents "a perfect set o' Goffs and Randals" and sets out to make new conquests in the more elite circles in Scrabble Hill. After managing to ensnare an eligible widower, the Elder Sniffles, in marriage, she informs her new husband that he must fix up his house. Mr. Sniffles ventures to say he considers it quite comfortable. "Comfortable! Who cares for comfort when gintility's consarned! *I* don't." She outlines her plans. "You'd ought to higher the ruff up and put on some wings, and build a piazzer in front with four great pillars to't . . . and have it all painted white, with green winder blinds. *That* would look something *like*, and then I shouldent feel ashamed to have ginteel company come to see me, as I dew now." The new Mrs. Sniffles's ideas of "gintility" extend to a grand program of acquisition, from new "sofys and fashionable cheers" and "mantelry ornaments" in the parlor to new hats adorned with plenty of "artifishels." [34]

More important, a new role is assigned to Sal, the girl who had been brought up by the first Mrs. Sniffles "as if she was her own daughter." The new Mrs. Sniffles keeps the girl toiling in the kitchen while she receives company in the parlor and declares her intentions to convert the girl from help to domestic: "I rather guess I'll larn that critter to know her place, afore I've ben here much longer. She haint never had no instruction about what belongs to her sittiwation. . . . I mean to show her the difference betwixt genteel folks and them that's born to be underlin's." [35]

Another satirist, Ann Sophia Stephens, who wrote *High Life in New York*, took on the persona of the naive but natively shrewd "Jonathan Slick." Visiting cousins in New York City, Jonathan finds their elegant manners "stuck up." He is puzzled at having to ring a bell rather than knock and momentarily nonplussed by the butler who answers the door and asks him what he wants: Jonathan tells him, "None of your business," and pushes inside. Back home in Connecticut Jonathan "keeps company" with Judy White, his mother's "hired gal." [36] Both Stephens and Whitcher understood that help could not be useful in the pursuit of status, and they portrayed contrasts in service to ridicule the elaborated needs of the new urban middle class.

The Work Behind the Status Struggle

One who employs a servant achieves a superior status that is to some extent intrinsic to the relationship and independent of the servant's duties or the texture of day-to-day operations or relations. Authors of nineteenth-century etiquette books understood this and warned their readers to avoid the subject of servants in conversation, as not only boring but as too blatant an effort to advertise the fact of command: [37] "It is not polite for married ladies to talk, in the presence of gentlemen, of the difficulty they have in procuring domestics, and how good-for-nothing they are when procured." One etiquette book referred to complaints of servants in conversation as "evidence of deficient breeding." [38] More subtle methods of stating the same case were apparently acceptable: the Potter Palmer house in Chicago was built without exterior locks or doorknobs. [39] Domestics functioned in specific ways to secure and protect their employers' status and thereby took on a task unknown to help. Although status is essentially relational, sociability had to be managed in the context of private homes. Social participants therefore needed a reliable set of signs, rules, and go-betweens. They found them in cards, calling etiquette, and domestics. [40] Although domestics were buffers, transmitters, or menial facilitators, as social nonparticipants they commanded no notice or regard in themselves.

Social participants paid and received calls, the basic social units, like currency, and some employed cards to assist in calling and as proxies for actual calls. [41] Because no telephone warned that a caller was about to make her appearance, the servant who answered the door performed a crucial role. If the mistress preferred to see no visitors at all, she could tell the servant to say that she was "engaged" or "not at home." She could, with the servant's help, select her visitors. Scrutinizing and relaying cards or merely remembering names and faces, the servant could weed out the undesirables. And if the caller was welcome, the servant could show her into the parlor to wait for a few moments while her employer arranged her best appearance. [42]

The formal call was intended to be brief, but the card made possible an even more convenient form of social exchange. By receiving a card at the door, registering the equivalent of a call, the servant permitted her employer to maintain a wide set of genteel acquaintances without the burdensome necessity of talking to them regularly. These acquaintances would be available, as acknowledged social equals, for occasional large parties or for purposes of marriage prospecting. [43] Humorists who poked fun at these polite hypocrisies incidentally highlighted the domestic's role:

Caller: "You are sure Mr. Blowton is not at home?"
The New Servant: "Well I ought to be. He told me so when I took your card up, and said if you would call sometime when he was out he would be glad to see you." [44]

Observance varied with social position. The use of cards seems to have been confined to the more affluent in urban areas. So did a convention for managing a large social life, the "day," a regular time when one would be at home to receive one's intimates. The author of *Six Hundred Dollars a Year* did not employ cards, nor did Alcott's March girls, but they both paid and received calls, those minimal transactions of gentility for which one needed a domestic.

The woman without a domestic had no choice but to be home to all who chose to present themselves, unless she resorted to the shabby expedient of refusing to answer the door. She might well be caught in the midst of housework. When Caroline Barrett White first moved into Cliffside in 1858, she lost all her servants but one and had to do much of the work of getting settled by herself: "Mr. and Mrs. May and a Mrs. Carter called today about noon, just as I was in the midst of dirt and dust—my hair all disheveled—a much soiled morning dress on etc. and the house was in keeping with its mistress—but it cannot be helped. I showed them about with as good a grace as I could, but felt sorry that their first impression of our new home should be so unfavorable."[45]

Calling etiquette contrasted with informal practices on the frontier or in rural areas, where, in the absence of public accommodations, custom required a welcome for all comers at all hours. Some residents of isolated areas seemed to feel, like Phebe Eastman, that any visitor provided a welcome break in a lonely and grinding work routine. European travelers' accounts provide an unending chronicle of meals and beds served up in the nearest cabin or farmhouse discovered along the road as darkness fell.[46] Cabin or farmhouse architecture and life in a small community made it impracticable to be falsely "not at home." Help made inadequate social gatekeepers because they refused to behave as social ciphers.[47] One Boston housekeeper employed several transplanted rural helpers who became the butt of humor when they refused to be invisible and persisted in speaking to guests, asking rude questions and the like.[48]

The memoirs of women who had left middle-class homes in the East for the frontier often emphasized the irksomeness of being unable to control one's social life and subject to continual intrusions by people whom they did not care to see.[49] In the cities, calling practices reflected class differences. Davidoff has noted that nothing so divided the life-styles of the nineteenth-century English middle and working classes as calling and visiting, because the middle classes could accept or reject social interaction, while the working classes were expected to be instantly available to their "betters."[50] In the United States, intruding uninvited on poor people in their homes—"friendly visiting"—became the recommended form of charity after mid-century.

Middle-class women were probably well aware that having domestics permitted them to control their social lives, to be seen when and how they wished. In a short story in *The Ladies Wreath* in 1848, several small-town ladies debate whether or not to call upon Dr. Morris's new bride, who is being frugal by keeping no servant.

"We might surprise her in *dishabille*, or even in the kitchen, which would be rather awkward, you must confess," says one fashionable miss. The author means to condemn the idea that employing domestics is a prerequisite to respectable social life, but she admits that such opinion is "too generally entertained to attract observation." [51]

Employers who might have been reluctant to acknowledge directly the status functions of their domestics revealed those purposes when they complained about servant problems. They were annoyed when the housework was done poorly but furious when a domestic embarrassed them in front of guests. Employers with little to spend on domestics often hired untrained girls and found much to complain of, and the advice literature addressed them with improving or consoling words.

Beginning with the apparently simple business of answering the door, the domestic was to be both discreet and alert, protecting the home from interlopers, salesmen and even thieves, yet giving a courteous welcome to desired guests. She could easily bungle the job. In one short story in *Godey's* of 1855 an inexperienced Irish maid allows an "entry thief" to rob the parlor on the pretext of waiting there for the mistress to appear; after that experience the maid becomes so suspicious that she insults a family friend who pays a call and innocently attempts to be seated in the parlor. In Harriet Beecher Stowe's short story "The Trials of a Housekeeper," an inexperienced servant answers the door and shows strangers who have come to make their first call right down into the kitchen where they discover her mistress struggling to spit a greasy roast. These domestics' blunders were carried to such extremes that a good-humored laugh ensued. [52]

In the Proctor family of Utica, the chambermaid was told to "learn the appearances of agents and peddlers" and to excuse her mistress to them. She was to admit those with cards and also those with a "name and an errand," humbler local residents who did not qualify as social intimates but could look to this powerful family for informal help and local leadership. In order to sort out callers and behave appropriately to each, the chambermaid would have to become an authority on the social hierarchy in this small city. Her employer was keeping watch for any "deficiencies" or "want of thought."[53]

Lack of discretion in the front hall reflected directly upon the domestic's employers. In *The House of Mirth*, Lily Bart's mother sneered at her cousins who, although wealthy, chose to live "like pigs." Mrs. Bart's disgust stemmed in part from the fact that her cousins employed "slatternly" parlormaids who said "I'll go and see" to visitors "at an hour when all right-minded persons are conventionally if not actually out." Etiquette authority Robert Tomes needed only one look at a servant who opened the door in soapsuds to the elbows to pass judgment on the family.[54] The *Ladies' Book of Etiquette* spoke sharply about domestics who answered the door tardily or held it open a crack as if afraid the visitor wished to enter for the purpose of murder. The employer must train them, "as they come here from the lowest ranks of English and Irish peasantry, with as much idea of politeness as the pig domesticated in the cabin of the latter."[55]

The front door drama was only the first in a series of scenes before guests in which the domestic reflected creditably upon her employers by being inconspicuous, deft, and deferential. She needed to manage her presence properly in front or back, up- or downstairs areas. By midcentury changing domestic architecture reflected the sense that domestics should inhabit areas of the home where all the work was to be performed, while the family lived in other areas designed for display, comfort, intimacy, even study, but not for housework. More and more, architects designed and families built houses with basement kitchens and separate flights of back stairs. The fashionable brownstone provides a good example of housing designed for domestics, with its kitchen in the basement, an uninhabited company parlor on the first floor, family living and dining rooms on the second floor, and bedrooms above.

On each floor precious space is sacrificed to not one but two sets of stairs. Halls provided settings for greetings and formal inter-change, as well as transition spaces or buffer zones in which domes-tics could perform their go-between roles. The terminology of dramatic performance is appropriate to the formal behavior domes-tics were supposed to maintain in front-stage settings.[56]

The domestic might commit faux pas not only by her actions but also in her dress or manner. When Helen Munson Williams wrote herself a memo entitled, "Things about which I wish to have an understanding and agreement before engaging a second girl," she thought of appearance first, before duties, hours, or wages: "She must keep herself always neat and tidy in her person and never go to the door, or wait on the table with disarranged hair or in any but a *clean and smooth white apron*." She decided to provide the girl with three fresh aprons a week; "If more are required she must wash them herself."[57]

Certainly employers wanted their domestics to avoid a sloppy or "slatternly" appearance. But they grew even more indignant over excess in the other direction, exclaiming, for example, about a chambermaid "dressed in silk, with artificial roses in her hair."[58] According to employers, domestics were notoriously inclined to extravagance in clothing, ignoring repeated advice designed to convince them of the merits of "good, inexpensive calico."[59] "Now there is no point where domestics so often show their want of good education and good taste as in the choice of their dress," wrote Catharine Beecher. "Everyone knows that the income of a domestic is very small, and that they are daily employed in work that soils a dress." When, therefore, domestics appeared in dresses suitable only for "persons who have wealth and employments that do not soil dresses," everyone would judge them "deficient in good taste and a sense of propriety."[60] Excluded from sharing meals, domes-tics could nevertheless reject the role of social cipher and advance silent, visual claims to human notice and consideration by wearing fine clothing, on duty and off. Sir Charles Lyell was startled to learn that two female traveling companions in his hotel were domestics on vacation, for their appearance had not betrayed their occupation.[61] No employer wanted to attract catty remarks like Frances Seward's when she saw the governor's wife "in a very shabby cloak and hat" quite overshadowed by her waiting maid: "The maid was the better dressed of the two."[62] Late in the century some well-to-do employers who offered higher wages were able to insist on a version of livery, usually just a cap and apron, but middle-class employers had to compromise: "Do not be too censorious about bonnets and hoops," wrote one author, explaining how to have good servants.[63]

Employers considered it poor form if a domestic spoke without being spoken to. It was embarrassing if she was impertinent or interjected remarks into her employers' conversation. Nor should she betray her presence when out of the room: "Shrieks of laughter from the kitchen, singing and calling through the halls, stamp a house at once as belonging to the vulgar and uncultivated."[64] Elizabeth Sullivan Stuart was so infuriated when she and her guests were exposed to her neighbor's noisy servants on a side porch just under the window that she spent eighty-five dollars to erect a fence and add shutters.[65]

A cook might produce a culinary fiasco when guests came to dinner. On one occasion Elizabeth Cady Stanton's cook got drunk and spoiled most of the dishes on the menu for dinner guests Charles Sumner, John Greenleaf Whittier, and Joshua Leavitt. Stanton and her husband sought to cover the defects by "brilliant conversation." Stanton wrote that she feared being hung for "breaking the pate of some stupid Hibernian for burning my meat or pudding on some company occasion."[66] Employers insisted that meals should be served promptly at the specified hour, despite the difficulties of timing meals produced on recalcitrant cook-stoves.[67] Sarah Josepha Hale insisted that the cook allow fifteen to twenty minutes extra before the dinner hour: overcooked food was preferable to delay.[68]

In the dining room itself, etiquette authorities stipulated an increasingly elaborate style of service and equipment, requiring considerable serving skill. Domestic advice manuals provided extensive instructions on everything from "crumbing" the cloth to managing the finger bowls. When Eliza Leslie began to describe how to set the table and serve the meals, she shifted without explanation from addressing the employer to addressing the domestic, writing, for instance, "If there is soup, set the tureen by the mistress of the house." [69] With the introduction of service *à la Russe*, the hostess was left with almost nothing to do. The domestics were now to ladle the soup and even carve the roast. [70] One social arbiter described the benefits of this system: "Dish after dish comes round as if by magic and nothing remains but to eat and be happy." [71]

Among Mrs. Astor's "four hundred" this happy effect was probably achieved; here high-priced trained butlers and footmen could even, on occasion, manage a set of decorative live swans cruising in a long pool in the center of the table, not to speak of the food itself. [72] In more modest homes, the "waitress" was only the second girl, or even the single servant, scrambling back and forth in an attempt to be both cook and serving girl. A hostess would watch in apprehension lest she serve from the wrong side or in the wrong order, too fast or too slowly, forget the spoons or dump the gravy on a guest's gown. "Give your orders before dinner," one etiquette book commanded, "and through the meal never speak to the servants." [73] Many authorities were frankly pessimistic. "In this country of untrained servants," Elizabeth Smith Miller wrote, "most ladies have but little pleasure in giving dinners, as there must be a constant undercurrent of anxiety about the table and the service. This anxiety begins with the soup and ends only with the coffee." [74]

Indeed, the need to appear properly before guests sometimes converted domestics' daily routines into drill sessions. Eliza Leslie advised families to insist on formal service at table even when they were home alone; otherwise the domestic might forget the proper routine and err in front of guests.[75] *The Mother's Magazine* told its readers, "It is a great point to live always in the same manner as regards style, to have the cloth laid as carefully alone as when there is company. When this is the case, no wife feels afraid of her husband bringing in an unexpected guest, and it is gratifying to a husband to find a guest of this kind received quietly."[76] With matters of appearance embedded in the practices and standards of daily life, their arbitrary nature tended to become invisible except to outsiders. An Indian chief visiting Philadelphia early in the century observed a servant girl engaged in the daily routine of polishing the brasswork in a fireplace. "How foolish these white people are!" he remarked to his companions. "Thus to labor and toil about things which can answer no good purpose; certainly these white people must be fools!"[77] Domestics, themselves so often strangers to their employers' culture, doubtless entertained similar opinions.

Domestics saw and often resented their use in status competition. They knew that guests meant more work, with no extra pay.[78] Employers charged that unscrupulous domestics habitually chose the moments before guests arrived to demand privileges and concessions, or, failing that, to leave without notice precisely so as to embarrass them. One observer wrote that the servant girl thus "avenges herself on her servitude by being the terror of our social life."[79] Julia Ward Howe composed a verse about the situation ("real trouble") when the cook left on dinner-party day.[80]

Domestics performing before guests could not help but buttress or sabotage their employers' status claims. Although largely inexperienced and ill-paid, they nevertheless shouldered a heavy responsibility. The peculiar rancor of complaints in the mid nineteenth century stemmed in part from the status functions of domestics. Their employers hoped to buy not just labor but that rare commodity, the admiration of others.

The elaboration of needs and the pursuit of status were not accomplished without a good deal of unease. Enjoying the rewards of economic growth posed considerable difficulties for nineteenth-century Americans. Daniel T. Rodgers has shown that after mid-century the work ethic became an increasingly ritualistic and unexamined formulation, continuing to command the allegiance of Americans even while the economic context in which it had made sense was transformed.[81] Reassurance, evasion, and rhetorical exorcism of the problems of growing luxury and lost simplicity provided major themes for midcentury popular culture. Henry Ward Beecher won enormous popularity in part because he offered successful Americans a solution to the pressing moral dilemma of wealth, reassuring them that comfort and gentility were compatible with Christian virtue since their "elegances and luxuries" would spur the less fortunate to hard-working emulation.[82]

Simultaneously loving and fearing luxury, individuals tended to fasten upon particularly flagrant symbols to exorcise their anxieties. The "Monster Bank" was one of these symbols, Marvin Meyers suggests, and "the fashionable woman," so roundly condemned and yet so flourishing, seems to have been another.[83] This tendency was exacerbated by the obscurity of the fundamental changes afoot in the maturing American economy, with its unaccountable cycles of boom and bust, its abstract problems of banking and currency and tariff. The particulars of consumption, by contrast, were visible, palpable, easily grasped.

Middle-class women who performed no remunerative work and hired domestics to do the housework found themselves particularly at hazard in the ideological tensions resulting from rising living standards. The domestic, an evidence of the ability to pay and a means to secure her employer's ease, often seemed an obvious anomaly. The domestic's role in status maintenance was especially difficult to reconcile with traditional republican values, but amid the general hand wringing about luxury, only a few enthusiasts launched a frontal attack on service. William Andrus Alcott, a cousin of Bronson Alcott and a follower of Sylvester Graham, in *The Young Wife* (1837), argued that keeping servants was unnecessary, costly, destructive of family privacy, bad for the children, and highly antirepublican. But his case depended on the premise that a normal middle-class way of life involved great waste of women's time and effort. Alcott urged women to serve their families a simple, easily prepared Grahamite diet of whole grains, fruits, and vegetables, with no meats, seasonings, desserts, coffee, or tea. He opposed serving hot food and recommended eating only one type of food at a sitting. He praised the dinner table graced only by cold boiled potatoes, with no butter and no beverage but water.[84] Naturally these prescriptions had limited appeal. Reviewers predictably scoffed at his views on servants as "visionary schemes."[85]

Commentators agreed that the domestic was a ready symbol and a real symptom of the dangers of luxury and idleness, but they did not question the legitimate need for some household service. In 1841, Mrs. A. J. Graves remarked that the increasing number of servants in the country was an obvious indicator of the "extravagance and ostentation everywhere prevailing." She guessed, in alarm, that the United States actually had more servants in proportion to its population than England did. Yet she made it clear that household service was not in itself objectionable: "It is by no means intended to be implied that the mistress of a family can be its sole manual laborer."[86] In *The Frugal Housewife*, Lydia Maria Child spoke of the need to prevent "vanity, extravagance and idleness" among young women, which she assumed was in part the product of improper reliance upon domestics, yet she did not propose a wholly servantless home.[87] Child, the partisan of frugality and usefulness, tried to distinguish between a woman's legitimate hiring of assistance and her immoral purchasing of leisure.

Child and others of like mind were aided in making this distinction by the fact that housework continued to be so greatly burdensome throughout the century. The most notable critic of the status functions of service, Thorstein Veblen, underestimated the continuing substantive component of housework. In *The Theory of the Leisure Class* (1899), Veblen argued that servants were no longer needed for useful work but only for status seeking, either in conspicuous consumption or in ostentatious leisure: "The apparatus of living has grown so elaborate and cumbrous in the way of dwellings, furniture, bric-a-brac, wardrobe and meals," he wrote, "that the consumers of these things cannot make way with them in the required manner without help."[88] Veblen maintained servants demonstrated that their employers were powerful enough not only to do nothing themselves but also to stand the cost of hiring attendants to perform empty ceremony and thus display what he called "vicarious leisure."

Although Veblen then qualified his point nearly to extinction, he insisted that the essential characteristic of the servant's life was the uselessness that demonstrated status. He pointed to an important function of domestics, one that distinguished them decisively from help, but he erred in insisting that status pursuit and maintenance were the only real purposes for hiring otherwise useless and idle domestics. Veblen was committed to a complete satirical reversal—discovering a "leisure class" in a society verbally dedicated to the work ethic, "barbarianism" in the citadels of high culture, and the like. Otherwise he might have observed that the activities of domestics reflected a remarkably effective compromise between status and display on the one hand, and mundane necessities on the other, a combination that left servants not in idleness but busier than ever. Home life and housework offered a ready field for elaboration and the concerns of status and decor precisely because they were still so firmly occupied by necessitous cares.

New Conveniences and Higher Standards

The burden of housework and thus the work of the servant was determined, as Veblen did imply, not only by tastes and budgets but also by technology. Tastes and budgets tended to permit and encourage the expansion of housework in the pursuit of status; technological change tended to reduce its burdensome nature.

Still, technology's effect was neither so sweeping nor so liberating as Veblen supposed. The first historians who addressed the changing nature of household work, the historians of technology, told a story of progress with nineteenth-century technological advances reducing housework, easing servant problems, and laying the basis for the eventual displacement of domestics by more efficiently designed houses and mechanical conveniences.[89] More recent students of household work, especially those concerned with the twentieth century, when time spent on housework did not notably decline, have concluded that there is not necessarily a simple inverse relationship between the acquisition of household technology or the commercialization of household work on the one hand and the total burden of household labor on the other. Technological aids to housework may be of only marginal assistance, may require maintenance work themselves, or may be applied to purposes not of work reduction but of meeting heightened standards of cookery or cleanliness.[90] In the 1830s the women of the new urban middle class began to hire domestics and to shape with them a new division of household labor. The relative scarcity of "good" domestic service made nineteenth-century American employers eager to acquire household technology. But, given the context of a status struggle, the existence of some service workers, and the ideology of domesticity, technological advances were predictably employed to raise housekeeping standards rather than, for example, to expand leisure time. Industrialization and technological changes in areas of heating, lighting, cleaning, cooking, and sewing gradually did lift some of the heavy burden from the shoulders of women like Phebe Eastman, yet even by the late nineteenth century, housework had not become much easier. Rising standards of household care were promulgated in the advice literature of domesticity, where women learned the proper employment of the domestic in a division of labor that assigned her to menial work so that her employer could take on the tasks of judgment, direction, and sentiment. Both would be kept busy.

Advice literature indicates that the work associated with heating fell to the domestic. "Light the fire," she was told, "clean the fender, fire irons and hearth; take up the ashes, sweep the carpet, shake the hearth-rug and lay it down again."[91] The first labor-saving innovation in nineteenth-century home heating was the introduction of coal, which began to be widely distributed by the 1820s. It threw out a stronger, steadier heat than wood, yielding more warmth with less attention. One contemporary recalled that, after a new coal grate was installed in the dining room, "The water *never froze* on the sideboard the whole winter!"[92] During the 1830s and 1840s, more and more families began to acquire newly developed airtight stoves for home heating. Such stoves worked more efficiently than any fireplace, with less heat loss up the chimney and with dampers to control the speed of combustion, and their rapid adoption reflected fuel economy as well as convenience. By the 1850s such stoves were in common use.[93] The introduction of friction matches in the 1830s probably saved as much work as coal stoves, for "locofocos," or lucifer matches, eliminated the need for constant vigilance to keep a fire of some sort going. Around mid-century a few wealthy families installed coal-fired central furnaces to heat their homes. In 1855 Henry Ward Beecher put one into his new house in Brooklyn Heights.[94] When *Little Women* sold well in 1868, Louisa May Alcott used some of the money to install conveniences, including a furnace, in her parents' Concord home.[95] The furnace saved work, since the fuel and ashes remained in the cellar and there was only one fire to demand attention.[96] But families wealthy enough to afford a furnace probably did not have labor saving in mind; their domestics tended the furnace and also lit occasional wood fires in the old open fireplaces when their employers wanted to enjoy the charm of a flickering fire. According to the advice literature, the waitress or second girl commonly tended the furnace, although the wealthiest homes employed a furnaceman or outdoor man.[97]

From the 1830s onward, the design of lamps and the production of lamp oils steadily improved. Lamps required less physical labor than candlemaking, but they still demanded a great deal of time and attention, since carelessness could be fatal. One alternative, gas lighting, grew rapidly from the thirties through the fifties. Gas was cleaner and easier to use than oil lamps, and gas lighting became common in middle-class homes in urban areas.[98] One woman wrote with evident pleasure that her new house was "lighted with gas and warmed with a furnace, so that in that way much labor is saved."[99] Even this preferred fuel gave off so much smoke and odor that many Victorian homes had ceiling vents to carry off the fumes. In the late 1850s, kerosene appeared and in the next decade quickly captured the market for lamp oil. It burned brighter and longer than other oils and with less odor, but it was also highly explosive. The user could not safely blow out a kerosene lamp, for example, nor allow the fuel reservoir to drop to less than half full.[100] Despite technological advances, nineteenth-century illumination required careful use to avoid fire or explosion. According to Catharine Beecher in her *Treatise on Domestic Economy*, the care of lamps required so much discretion that, rather than trust it to domestics, many ladies "choose to do this work themselves."[101] Improvements in the technology of heating and lighting lessened women's work within the home, but a considerable burden remained, especially the menial work of fuel and ash carrying assigned to domestics.

The industrialization of textile production early in the nineteenth century largely eliminated a part of women's work in the home that had been divided with their help. This may not have been a welcome change to skilled weavers like Phebe Eastman, for it removed a source of craftsmanlike pride and independent income. In the nineteenth century the commercial production of ready-to-wear clothing grew rapidly, although by 1880 only about two-fifths of men's clothing was ready-to-wear, and women's clothing lagged far behind. Only in 1860 did the ladies' garment industry become large enough to merit notice in the federal census, and it was concentrated in a few nonfitted items like cloaks and crinolines. Well into the twentieth century women continued to sew most of their own clothing at home or to have it sewn by dressmakers. [102]

The woman who did not do her own sewing hired custom work done by a seamstress or dressmaker. In rural areas the seamstress sometimes lived in for a few days or weeks while she did the work. [103] In the cities a fashionable dressmaker was often a *house*, the employer of a large corps of seamstresses, rather than an individual. A few domestic servants did plain sewing for their mistresses, but it was secondary to their other duties as chambermaids or children's nurses. [104] Although needlework was notoriously inexpensive to hire, middle-class women were often reluctant to do so, since this work, for those who had to choose an area in which to economize, was cleaner, less strenuous, and more genteel than cooking or washing. [105] Dress was well suited to express status claims, and nineteenth-century women employed the benefits of technological advance, most notably the sewing machine, to enhance standards of appearance and follow fashion, which became ever more elaborate, even fantastic, after mid-century. [106] Rising standards of dress did not, however, affect the division of labor between employer and domestic, since women pursued fashion with their own needles or sewing machines or those of ill-paid seamstresses.

Throughout the nineteenth century care of the sick remained within the home as one of women's responsibilities. Anyone who could summon the means or the energy stayed out of hospitals, for they were charitable institutions populated by the destitute. [107] Like most domestic advice-givers, Catharine Beecher included extensive chapters on caring for the sick in her *Receipt-Book*. Beecher saw no need to declare women's responsibilities in this area; she simply took them for granted. [108] Family letters and diaries of the period reveal the enormous burdens in time, effort, and emotion that home nursing of the seriously or terminally ill placed upon women.[109] This work derived little benefit from technological or institutional change until late in the century when the transition from home to hospital care began. In 1900 the *New York Times* would praise hospitals for affording "great relief to the family from physical as well as mental strain," noting how often home care had resulted in "the breakdown of some member of the family from overwork and anxiety."[110] Insofar as standards for home care rose, they probably tended to encourage the hiring of trained private-duty nurses rather than increasing the work of domestics or re-modeling the division of labor between employers and domestics. Both home sewing and care of the sick, by absorbing women's energies in work they tended to prefer not to delegate to domestics, made it seem all the more necessary to employ servants for work that could be passed on, especially cleaning and cooking.

Cookstoves first appeared in cities in the 1820s, and more and more families purchased them in the next two decades.[111] The cookstove, with its removable ash boxes, and soot trays, and its dampers to control the draft, was cleaner and easier to tend than a fireplace. Many models included a waterback, a built-in tank able to keep large amounts of hot water on hand. However, the cook still had to regulate cooking temperatures without a thermostat or thermometer, by sticking her hand into the oven and counting until she had to withdraw it: a count of twenty was good for roasting meats, while ten was too hot. Employers complained that domestics who knew nothing about the management of stoves were either tardy with meals or else burned the food, when they could manage to get the fire going at all.[112] The cook had to haul fuel in and ashes out, and she had to spend time blacking the stove to prevent rust. When the cookstove first appeared, women welcomed it with enthusiasm.[113] By 1873, when Caroline Corbin wrote, it looked more like the symbol of household drudgery: "The thoughtful housekeeper knows full well what is the black beast of her despair. It is the kitchen stove. There it stands, sullen, immovable, inexorable . . ."[114]

Like the fireplace, the cookstove threw off large amounts of heat and therefore encouraged establishing a kitchen separated from the rest of the house. The high cost of urban real estate meant that many city kitchens were situated in the basement throughout this period, while country houses often included a wing for a kitchen or even an additional "summer kitchen." [115] Separating the kitchen from the rest of the house allowed it to be close to the wood room or coalbin but increased the steps necessary to serve a meal, answer the door, or attend to anything else while working in the kitchen. Some architects and domestic reformers attacked the basement kitchen, citing the extra labor for women in constantly climbing stairs. [116] Yet a centrally located kitchen was impractical as long as women cooked with wood or coal. The heat produced, useful in one season, was sure to be offensive in another. [117] In any case, the separation of the kitchen from the rest of the house reflected a concern with appearances and the presence of servant staffing, both of which made labor saving a secondary concern.

In the 1830s food supply patterns, and therefore cooking, began to change, thanks to refrigeration and railroads. By 1838 the New York *Mirror* could remark that although it was only a few years since the refrigerator had come into common use, it was now considered an "article of necessity" as much as a carpet or a dining table. [118] Initially, refrigerators were relatively costly, but prices soon began to fall, and housekeepers learned to contrive home-made substitutes. [119] Refrigeration permitted year-round slaughtering and successful storage of milk. In 1839 refrigerators were introduced into the public markets of New York City. [120] In the home, refrigeration permitted the cook to store supplies and leftovers, although it involved some additional work: supplying fresh ice, emptying drip pans, and washing out the refrigerator regularly.

At the same time the network of railroads began to bring the cook more produce, including fresh milk on the milk trains and fresh fruits and vegetables from the truck farms that grew up near many large cities. With the construction of the Erie Railroad in 1842–43, New York City residents could for the first time buy other than "swill" milk—milk produced by stabled cows fed on brewery wastes. The price of milk in New York dropped while consumption increased markedly. The building of the railroad also stimulated truck farming in Rockland County.[121]

More than technical changes were at work in convincing Americans to relish what the railroads could provide. The Grahamite dietary reformers, by helping to dispel lingering public prejudice against fresh produce as a cause of disease, made cooks more willing to use fresh fruits and vegetables. By mid-century Americans had decided that tomatoes were good to eat and lost the suspicions that had made them refer to watermelons as "cholera-bombs."[122] In the 1860s railroad cars packed with ice rolled over the widening rail network to bring out-of-season fruits and vegetables to the major cities. By the 1870s, middle-class advice literature could scold parents who denied their children proper diet in a land "where the whole year round, fresh luscious fruit of some kind is always plenty and cheap."[123]

The railroads and refrigeration facilities brought more raw materials but few finished products to the kitchen. They did not lessen preparation work. Nearly all bread, for example, was still baked at home. Only the poor or what some thought to be the "shiftless" purchased baker's bread, an object of general suspicion. Catharine Beecher advised, "Baker's bread is often made of musty, sour or other bad flour, which is made to look light, and the bad taste removed, by unhealthy drugs. . . . The only safe method is to have all bread made in the family, and to take all needful care that it shall be uniformly good."[124] She went on to explain how to monitor the cook's performance. As late as 1909, only fourteen percent of the flour consumed in America was made into breadstuffs or cake outside the home.[125] This home baking of yeast breads was time-consuming and difficult, since the yeast solution itself was homemade, the flours not yet standardized, and

the oven temperatures variable. Commercial canning, which began to expand in the 1870s, had little effect for some time on
family diet or the household workload.[126] The only significant
mechanical help a cook commanded for any of this work was her
cookstove. A wide variety of patent kitchen gadgets testified to
persistent hopes of labor saving, but Mary Virginia Terhune's 1871
list of labor-saving devices every woman should have in her
kitchen—including a raisin-seeder, egg beater, syllabub churn,
apple-corer, potato-peeler, and farina kettle—testified to the limitations rather than to the powers of mechanical aids.[127]

Throughout the century American cooking seems to have become more elaborate and refined, thereby requiring more achievement from the cook. The combination of a mechanized publishing industry and universal literacy meant that, beginning in the
1820s, advice literature played a part in this change, as American
cookbooks offered an increasing variety of recipes. Increased elaboration also reflected the imitation of European styles and manners, especially of French cuisine, then in its most heroic period. In
1844 Nathaniel Willis commented on the rage for French cuisine
in New York City.[128]

By the 1870s fashionable cooking schools in the major eastern
cities taught housekeepers the mysteries of anchovies and caviar,
and well-known chefs like "professor" Pierre Blot passed on advice
in the columns of fashionable ladies' magazines.[129] Ladies learned
how to choose foods, compose menus, recognize and stipulate
quality, even to prepare some haute cuisine themselves so that they
could intelligently "go into the kitchen every morning to make
arrangements with the cook."[130] Edith Wharton recalled that her
mother, a member of one of New York's most elite families, inter-
larded the pages of her favorite cookbooks with hand-written recipes, for "to know about good cooking was a part of every young
wife's equipment." But the actual work was done by the family
cooks.[131] This culinary enthusiasm reflected the status struggle,
for French cuisine, with its intricate sauces and rare ingredients,

could readily express claims to social superiority. It seems clear that the spread of haute cuisine among the most privileged households, and moderate imitations in lesser precincts, brought with it new notions of refinement and enjoyment that developed a life of their own. Refined tastes implied more care and effort devoted to cookery.

Rising standards for American cooking probably also stemmed from economic developments, as improvements in transportation and communication broke down rural isolation, exposing more and more people to what good food—or at least better food—might be. Traveling in Virginia in the 1830s by stagecoach, Harriet Martineau stopped at a house where everything on the table—bread, coffee, butter, eggs, ham, and steak—was so sour and rancid that none of the passengers could eat a thing. Yet everyone maintained a polite silence, and later one of her fellow passengers explained to Martineau that the road was newly opened and the people "have probably no idea that there is better food than they set before us." [132] American cookery already reflected plentitude, if not refinement, since all food, especially meat, was so cheap that cooks were tempted to multiply dishes. [133] Nineteenth-century European travelers were astonished at the meals for which American hotels became famous: beef, pork, poultry, fish, and shellfish all served at once in an ill-assorted but impressive profusion. [134]

Home cooking seems to have followed similar patterns. In 1846 Catharine Beecher suggested this menu for the young housekeeper giving her first dinner party: soup, fish, boiled ham, boiled turkey with oyster sauce, roast duck, scalloped oysters, potatoes, parsnips, celery, pudding, pastry, fruit, and coffee. Beecher praised this menu for its simplicity, appropriate to those of "moderate" means, "inexperienced in cooking" and entertaining. Two domestics, she said, would be needed to serve the meal in the dining room and two others to cook and serve in the kitchen. [135] Thus the natural bounty of the American environment tended to encourage profusion at the table, while the influence of foreign example and expertise lent a concern for more careful preparation and artful combination. These changes did not operate with equal force in every kitchen, but both developments tended to increase the work of preparation, serving, and cleaning up, simultaneously introducing a new range of cares in planning and choosing.

Evidence suggests that middle-class wives employed cooks if they could but began to take on themselves the chore of marketing in this period. Many early travelers had commented that husbands, not wives, went to the open-air meat and produce markets in the cities. Mrs. Trollope wrote, "It is the custom for the gentlemen to go to market at Cincinnati, the smartest men in the place, and those of the 'highest standing' do not scruple to leave their beds with the sun, six days in the week, and, prepared with a mighty basket, to sally forth in search of meat, butter, eggs and vegetables." [136] Harriet Martineau, Michel Chevalier, and Carl David Arfwedson witnessed similar practices in the 1830s. [137] In Beecher's *Receipt-Book*, the section on marketing, concerned solely with the selection of meats, did not include an assertion that marketing was the duty of women, a claim she advanced on so many other subjects. Mention of marketing was notably absent from Beecher's sections on the providing of family stores and the systematic daily and weekly arrangement of time and work. [138]

By the 1850s the responsibility for marketing seems to have begun to shift. One writer complained that men had enough to do without the imposition of this inappropriate women's work: "It might be supposed," he said, that husbands had quite enough to do to attend to their own duties, "without the additional burden of what properly belongs to their wives. Going to market, dealing with the grocer." [139] By the 1870s Eunice Beecher insisted that every lady should know how to do her own marketing and should teach her daughters to do likewise. [140] "A servant's judgment is seldom trustworthy, and the husband *may forget*," she wrote. Even if he should not forget, the husband cannot be expected to "understand his wife's business as well as she does herself." [141] In *The Bazar*

Book of the Household (1875), Robert Tomes declared that a husband who went to market and ordered groceries compensated for his wife's dereliction of duty.[142] The New York Cooking School's ladies' classes taught marketing skills, such as how to tell if fish were fresh.[143]

Why did women begin to do the marketing? Thomas Farrington DeVoe's account of the New York City markets refers to the spread in the 1840s of "meat shops," which drove many of the public markets out of business. These neighborhood shops eliminated the need to venture into the crowded and dirty markets where livestock arrived on the hoof to be slaughtered and where all sorts of disreputable characters congregated.[144] In the 1860s several major cities began to require removal or prevent construction of foul-smelling slaughterhouses within their boundaries, and refrigerator cars began to be the cities' main source of meat, with slaughtering done at the great midwestern packing centers.[145] The elaboration of the distinction between wholesale and retail trade facilitated by refrigeration, rapid transport, and the desire to clean up the cities' sanitary conditions meant that retailers could be more respectable and accessible to ladies. In 1880 a report on the public markets of Cincinnati stated that "they could be entirely abolished with very little inconvenience to anyone," mostly because "'daily markets,' as they are called, are abundant all over the city where everything needed in families in the way of meats and vegetables, as well as groceries, is kept for sale."[146] Expanding variety in supply and increasing elaboration in cooking probably helped to make marketing women's work, by necessitating more careful choices, rather than the errand work of picking up whatever was available or in season.[147] The rise in cooking standards thus led to a new division of labor between the cook and her employer, actual preparation assigned to the one, planning and marketing to the other.

Standards of cleanliness seem to have undergone a remarkable rise at the expense of the domestic's labor. Improved methods of heating and lighting still spread coal dust, ashes, and grime through the house, especially in winter months. The growing cities offered peculiar housekeeping trials in the days when pigs ran in unpaved streets, sewage and surface drainage systems were incomplete or nonexistent, and home chimneys and smoky factories darkened the skies.[148] Not until the 1870s did window screens begin to appear as luxury items, offering some defense against insects.[149] Midcentury housekeepers continued to undertake massive spring and fall housecleanings to fight the grime produced by heating, lighting, and insects. These routines seem to have loomed large in the lives of ordinary women, who wrote about them in their diaries and letters in tones of accomplishment or relief.[150] The work required about a week of concentrated effort, for which time women often hired temporary dayworkers to help not only with cleaning but also with renovation.

The municipal waterworks constructed during this period made considerable difference in the ease of cleaning. Before the development of these water systems, city dwellers had depended upon neighborhood or private wells. Because the water was hauled by hand or purchased from a water cart, it was used sparingly. Much of it was too hard to readily dissolve soap. The new waterworks, developed in most of the major cities by the 1850s, piped soft running water right into the house. Largely middle-class areas received the water directly and in ample supply.[151] In areas beyond the reach of the water systems, women continued to pump and haul well or cistern water.

The job of keeping the house clean grew more burdensome as machine-made upholstery, drapery fabrics, carpeting, and heavily carved furniture crowded the Victorian parlor. The mass-marketing of these goods increased maintenance chores in the home: protecting rugs against moths and whipping the dust out of furniture would have been unnecessary had rag rugs and unupholstered furniture prevailed.[152] The housekeeper expected not merely to furnish but also to decorate. Currier and Ives tapped a vast market in the 1840s with their "Colored Engravings for the People." Inexpensive "lithos" and "chromos" both reflected and encouraged the belief that even quite modest homes could provide uplifting aesthetic environments.[153]

Rising standards of cleanliness coupled with lagging technical capabilities seem to have resulted in the widespread custom of keeping order in the parlor by not using the room. The "neat housekeeper" always felt nervous when father, husband, son, or brother entered the best parlor: "She knows he will throw all the blinds and windows wide open the first thing, invoking a cloud of dust, and destroying at one breath the labor of precious hours."[154] Of course the very fact of a separate parlor in middle-class homes represented an advance in standards of household appearance over those prevailing in a cabin like Phebe Eastman's, where one or two rooms served for all living and working, and cleaning often focused on sweeping and on efforts to restrain the insect population. Countering the taunts of pundits, defenders of the uninhabited parlor cited the savings in labor they achieved. After an unaccustomed stint of housework, the popular writer Mary Abigail Dodge exclaimed, "My only wonder is that women who perform their own housework do not shut up their houses altogether and live in the barn-chamber!"[155]

In the eighteenth century to call a housekeeper "notable" meant she was efficient and effective, but by the mid nineteenth century this term, and its synonym, "famous," had come to denote a woman who made the home a miserable place by her relentless pursuit of unattainable spotlessness. Warnings in print treated her rampages as a common problem: "All of us have met these painful people," one author wrote. "They live in slavery and to a hard taskmaster, for this is not a clean world."[156] The notable housekeeper tended to complain about her domestics, she continued, but caused her own problems through being overly severe.[157]

An editorial in *Harper's Bazar* in 1874 attacked the old custom of spring and fall housecleanings and announced higher year-round standards for the late nineteenth century. "A dwelling in the hands of an efficient housekeeper . . . ought never to be allowed at any time to become such a receptacle of filth as to require those Herculean labors." [158] Authoritative advice such as this played an important role in raising standards. Often it upheld standards that fell only a step short of "famous" levels. An essay on "The Moral Influence of Good Housekeeping"—a common theme in domesticity and a way of looking at housework that logically tended to raise standards—warned readers not to be the "slaves of order" yet went on to insist upon "rigid system in your household arrangements." [159] Another writer advised, "The charm of housekeeping is in the order, economy and taste displayed in attention to little things, and these little things have a wonderful influence. A dirty kitchen and bad cooking have driven many a one from home, to seek comfort and happiness somewhere else." [160] By associating cleanliness and order in housekeeping with moral values and family stability, the experts tended to make extremity a form of pragmatic virtue. They subjected their readers to a barrage of rules and standards seldom couched in tone of reassurance or moderation. Jane Cunningham Croly praised one woman who kept her house in the "shining purity of heaven," in "exquisite order and cleanliness"; she termed soap and water "adorable," worth more for purification for body and soul than "bushels of sermons." [161]

Famous housekeepers were the butt of jokes and complaints, but they sometimes occupied important positions of social authority. In the domestic advice column written by Eunice Beecher, wife of Henry Ward Beecher, for the *Christian Union* in the 1870s, Mrs. Beecher championed notable standards. She worried about the March winds that penetrated the tightest house and made it necessary to dust and wash windows several times a day. She recommended liberal use of "sheet tidies" and "pillow tidies," furniture whips, brushes, brooms, and clean linen. She commanded the cook: "All utensils should be examined thoroughly rinsed with hot water and wiped dry each time you taken them out for use, if only to remove what dust may settle on them while in the closet." [162] Such maniacal standards of cleanliness did not go unchallenged. One reader complained, "Please, Mr. Editors, can't Mrs. Beecher be persuaded to write less dreadful housekeeping rules?" Perhaps, the reader wrote, servants in the East would tolerate it, but "Western help and indeed Western housekeepers" could never meet such standards "unless time was no more and we had all eternity to do it in." [163] Mrs. Beecher retorted that cleanliness was next to godliness, and that anything worth doing was worth doing well. Her correspondent had indicated how domestics, because more subject to their employers' will than help, were implicated in rising standards. Mrs. Beecher chalked up a similar complaint by another reader to the woman's indolence, but her advice consistently assumed two or three domestics could be deployed against the many "sickening," "foul," and inexcusable forms of dirt and disorder.

Another group of authorities, the hygiene and public health reformers, provided another important boost to standards of household cleanliness in this period. The water cure movement of the 1840s and 1850s helped to make bathing more popular. Catharine Beecher urged daily bathing to prevent the build-up of poisons on the skin. She herself frequented water cure establishments and helped to popularize the association between personal cleanliness and good health. When William Andrus Alcott wrote *Ways of Living on Small Means*, he exempted the concerns of cleanliness from cutbacks: "I think that no person I have ever seen spends too much time in attending to personal cleanliness, nor even to having clean garments. Either the mistress of the family—the wife or mother—should wash much and often, or get somebody to do it." Alcott, who held aloof from rising standards in other areas, was an extremist in this one. [164] At least one observer in the late 1860s noticed that standards of cleanliness of apparel were rising; men wore clean shirts three times a week or even every day. [165]

Laundry work remained a heavy task, in spite of a better water supply and the development of improved laundry equipment. Many versions of a hand-cranked mechanical washing machine were invented in this period, but they seem to have been of little value in saving labor. Probably most women continued to use the traditional rub-and-boil methods in a once-a-week session, as recommended in the advice literature.[166] The hand-cranked wringer, which saved hand-wringing the wet clothes, was widely adopted. Another improvement that spread quickly was the "fixed" tub or sink, which did not require lifting and carrying to empty.[167] In 1873 Eunice Beecher summed up the changes of the previous twenty years in the best-equipped households: where before tubs had to be carried, water pumped by hand, and every article wrung out by hand, now, she wrote, we have hot and cold running water, wringers, and tub sets with built-in drains.[168] By 1875 women were more likely to purchase soap, although fast-dissolving soap powders remained unknown, and laundry soap in bars had to be scraped and boiled into soft soap.[169] Some urban women avoided the labors of soap making without resort to purchase by exchanging their grease for soap with itinerant "soap-fat" merchants. In a letter to her sister Julia Ward Howe recalled her dealings with a soap-fat merchant who gave her thirty-four pounds of good soap for her kitchen grease.[170]

The advice literature recognized ironing as a separate day's work in itself, usually reserved for the day after wash day. Clothes required sprinkling and then ironing with flatirons heated to the proper temperature, this ascertained by guess or experience. Ironing was an especially unpleasant job in hot weather. The only mechanical aids developed in this period were the mangle, for pressing flat items between rollers, and the soapstone iron, which retained heat longer, but neither of these came into general use.[171] Catharine Beecher listed an impressive array of implements necessary for ordinary ironing, including at least three flatirons for each person ironing, a bosom-board to iron shirts, a skirt-board, and a fluting iron.[172] The billowing yardage of women's clothing in this period, together with prevailing fashions for ruffles and tucks, helped to make both washing and ironing more demanding.

Commercial laundries appeared in the 1850s after the patenting of a washing machine on the modern principle of a rotating perforated drum, but since this equipment had to be driven by steam power, it was limited to a few large plants in major cities.[173] Laundry work was the most onerous part of housework, and housekeepers were eager to delegate it to a domestic or a laundress. In general, the single maid-of-all-work did the laundry, leaving her mistress to cook or clean for the day. When two domestics were employed, the cook did the laundry, perhaps aided by the second girl. A laundress hired by the day might come to the house and do the work or simply come and fetch the dirty clothes to do them at her own home.[174]

Employers sometimes put the laundry out to a laundress to placate their other servants. Elizabeth Sullivan Stuart feared she would lose her cook after the arrival of several relatives for a long visit. She had hired the cook when she had a small family but now felt compelled to raise her wages and, "as if this was not sufficient inducement," put all the shirts out to be washed at five shillings a day.[175] Some advice writers assumed that domestics would do a laundry of "towels, dusters, servants' clothes, etc.," while the good clothes of the family would be put out to a laundress.[176] Families who hired no other domestic service turned first to a laundress. George Martin was a carpenter in Rochester, New York when his wife nearly died of childbed fever after delivering their fifth child. "I hired a woman to do the washing every week all the time and still do," he wrote, "but Betsey has never regained her health yet."[177]

With the expansion of municipal water systems, baths and water closets began to appear in middle-class homes, making personal cleanliness easier to attain. Political struggles were necessary to put through these municipal improvements basic to greater

cleanliness in housing, clothing, and person. They involved strenuous campaigns by public health reformers who sought to associate
dirt with deadly disease in the public mind. Measures taken
against cholera and other municipal health threats had similar
effects.[178] But without knowledge of the causes of specific diseases, all kinds of dirt and impurities tended to be condemned
equally. Nineteenth-century women learned from authorities of
one sort or another that bad ventilation in their homes—and even
dust on their floors—caused disease. Beecher and Stowe, who
compared some homes to the Black Hole of Calcutta, warned that
unventilated sleeping rooms caused scrofula and consumption.
Robert Tomes casually remarked on the dangers of household dust,
as if every informed person knew of it.[179] Even some of the new
household conveniences were accused of spreading pestilence or at
least requiring more housewifely vigilance. Indoor plumbing, for
example, was said to release deadly sewer gas into the home.[180]
With such a view of disease causation, it was easy to argue and then
to assume that women were quite literally responsible for the
health or illness of their families through their standards of housekeeping. The notion was reflected in the title of Catharine Beecher's *Miss Beecher's Housekeeper and Healthkeeper*.[181] Since, as Regina
Morantz has pointed out, health reformers aimed to secure social
importance and an active life for women by defining their domestic
activities as a kind of medical science, there was no necessary limit
to their tendency to raise cleanliness standards.[182] The experts,
whether in hygiene or in domestic science, often seemed to advance new standards as a claim to power but heeding their advice
would have proved a burdensome obligation without the ability to
delegate significant amounts of household labor to domestics.

An elaboration and refinement of the private sphere flowed from
the century's status struggle and from the tenets of middle-class
domesticity. The gains of technology and commercialization were
consistently applied to higher standards of cookery, cleanliness,

dress, and social observance. In the new division of labor that resulted, domestics were to shoulder the burden of menial work, leaving their employers free to attend to the concerns of direction, decor, propriety, culture, and sentiment. "If I could get Margaret back I would like it," wrote one Iowa employer, "because I could devote more time to music and reading." When her domestic was ill, she wrote, "the cooking and all the housework devolved upon me."[183]

The employment of domestics not only permitted this division of labor but also itself encouraged the raising of standards because live-in domestic service was hired in large, indivisible units. The first domestic hired might be unable to perform all the work of a family, but the second or third might find it hard to keep busy. Indeed, according to the claims of status, a proper appearance at the front door required domestics who bore no visible signs of engagement in onerous household duties. Employers, loathe to permit their domestics free time once all tasks were done, felt tempted or obliged to invent new tasks to fill the hours but not dirty the apron. They could most easily do so by refining cleanliness standards. "If you get thro' the work of any day before the time allowed," one employer commanded, "stand in different lights to see if any mark can be found on windows or mirrors that a cloth can remove, rub your finger along between the blinds, on the lower ledges of the door panels or the baseboard, on the rungs of chairs."[184]

The standards of elite homes demanded painfully difficult emulation by more modest families. The woman who could afford to employ only one domestic was caught in awkward compromises; unwilling to share household drudgery with her domestic, she was also unable to delegate that work as fully as the advice literature tended to suppose. Even with technological advances, there was still more menial work than one domestic could assume completely. Elizabeth Ellet was unusually frank among experts in recognizing this problem. Where two or more domestics were kept, she declared, the employer and the home should always be *"mis à quatre épingles*, or, in other words, in such order that a visit from royalty itself would scarcely create any bustle." [185] But the employer of the single domestic would face difficulties. "With all the activity and good will in the world, it is physically impossible that a girl can be in two places at once; and yet she may be just performing some nice operation in cookery while a visitor may be knocking at the door, and her mistress ringing impatiently to have something done towards tidying herself or the apartment." How could this be managed? Only "by the mistress bestirring herself and aiding in smoothing the difficulty." [186] How this would work in practice remained unclear, for Ellet stipulated it was absolutely necessary for the employer of a single servant to require "a regular plan of proceedings," yet illustrated her point by a case demanding improvisation.

"Maggie and I get along splendidly," one employer wrote. "She takes care of all the back part of the house upstairs and down, cleans the lamps and does all the cleaning I want done in here and takes the baby whenever I want her to." [187] The author of *Six Hundred Dollars a Year* detailed her penny-pinching methods but boasted that she had a good servant, Jane, "who was able to do the whole work of my house, excepting only such trifling portions as I chose to do myself." The author rose at six, aired and dusted the parlor and in winter raked the fire and stoked it with coal. Then, "refreshed and invigorated by this stirring exercise, I was ready to begin my day's employment, be it sewing or fancy work." She had to admit that the arrival of her first baby began to overtax this tidy arrangement. [188] Things did not run so smoothly when girls were less energetic and efficient than Maggie and Jane. The dilemma of the nineteenth-century housekeeper with one domestic, pursuing household standards that really lay beyond her reach, anticipated the woes of the twentieth-century housewife attempting to meet by herself household standards forged with the aid of live-in domestic service in the previous century—a pursuit made plausible in both instances by the significant but still inadequate assistance of mechanical conveniences.

The Division of Middle-Class Mothering

The employer who delegated menial housework to her domestics turned to social life, direction, and decor, and above all to motherhood. The ideology of domesticity insisted on motherhood as her paramount task, and by 1835 child care had been defined as the mother's vocation, one that required time, self-denial, conscious effort, and almost constant attention.[189] In an age that produced "manuals for all things," advisors to mothers firmly asserted their ability to mold any offspring into either a wretch or another George Washington. Phebe Eastman's diary almost never mentioned child care, but it had become a major preoccupation by the adulthood of Ellen Birdseye Wheaton, wife of a dry-goods and hardware merchant. She fretted in 1851 that spending her time sewing or any such "confinement of my energies" was "really unjust to [the children] and I won't be guilty of it anymore."[190] Despite the long-term decline in the birth rate during the nineteenth century, mothers seem to have experienced little if any lightening of their child-rearing responsibilities.

Mid-nineteenth-century mothers began to fret about the bad effects domestics might have upon their children.[191] They were apt to expose children to excessive heat or drafts, or push the baby buggy too fast, or administer opiates or punishment for crying. They were notoriously supposed to impart fears and superstitions to young children, probably because, forbidden to discipline children directly, they resorted to threats of ghosts and bogeymen.[192] They could even impart "viciousness of mind, of manners, and of morals."[193] "I am confident that mothers are not sufficiently careful," Lydia Huntley Sigourney declared, "with regard to the conversation of domestics or other uneducated persons who, in their absence, may undertake to amuse their children." [194] "Select not to nurse thy darling one that may taint his innocence," said another advice-giver. [195] When the Philadelphia Society for the Encouragement of Faithful Domestic Servants addressed the public in 1829, one of the three purposes it announced was "to guard the infant minds of children." [196] One grandmother expressed relief when her son and daughter-in-law dismissed their children's nurse: "Another year of Kitty Neal would have remedilessly ruined them." She referred to an acquaintance who felt that "her children have (in principles) been sadly injured by servants." [197] Should a mother then dismiss her domestics? On the contrary, the demands of child care often seemed like the most compelling justification for hiring domestics.

Mrs. Sigourney wrote that a mother should "provide herself with competent assistance, in the sphere of manual labor, that she may be enabled to become the constant directress of her children and be happy in their companionship." [198] She told the story of a young mother who felt she could not afford to hire domestic assistance and so did all the work herself while her children became wild and unruly. "She was an educated woman and a Christian. Her children should have reaped the advantage of her internal wealth, as soon as their unfolding minds cast forth the first beams of intelligence. But she led the life of a galley-slave, and their heritage was in proportion." Mrs. Sigourney went on to invoke "the modern system of division of labor" to justify hiring domestics. [199]

Rising standards for both housekeeping and child care were implicit in the cult of domesticity. Domestics could bridge the gap between these two often incompatible aims. Domestics could create an environment that was warm, clean, and attractive, without the strain and aggravation that often arose when parents tried to achieve these things unaided. This could prevent parents' learning to resent the disorderly ways of young children. Domestics also participated directly in child care, for despite the advice literature's worries about delegating the sacred offices of motherhood, the economy and practical appeal of this service was compelling. Young girls who served as nurses drew low pay even among servants, and they could exempt parents from the trying aspects of child care or simply from its confining continuity. Advice to mothers that they should always feed, bathe, and dress their own children, for example, suggests by omission that diaper changing could be left to the nurse.[200] Nurses who slept in the same room with infants—a common arrangement—assured parents of an uninterrupted night's sleep.[201] The single maid-of-all-work may have had little time for child care per se, yet her presence in the home provided ever-ready baby-sitting, permitting parents to retain their freedom to come and go. Among families who hired no full-time service, a laundress could provide important assistance simply by taking on the job of washing diapers.

Childbed nurses helped to ease women into their roles as mothers, shielding them from the shock of complete postpartum responsibility and initiating them into child-care methods. Caroline Barrett White's first child was born on May 27, 1856. We do not know just what her service arrangements were, but they certainly made it possible for her to slip into the responsibilities of mothering gradually, for on June 12 she wrote, "My baby has been good as a kitty for the two nights I have taken care of him."[202] Her second son was born on September 4, 1858. Mrs. Jones of Cambridge did such a thorough job as childbed nurse that on September 29, Caroline White confessed, "I hardly feel that he is mine yet, I have had so little care of him—but when Mrs. Jones goes I shall probably *realize* that he's mine."[203] Elizabeth Cady Stanton had her own ideas about child care and contested with her childbed nurse after her first child was born about matters of feeding and clothing. Stanton finally succeeded in convincing the old woman that some of her "book-learning" ideas might be correct, but experience indicates that an exclusive reliance on advice books usually makes for an anxious and stressful initiation into motherhood.[204]

Of course there were drawbacks to the division of child care. Sometimes a woman realized that a nurse had usurped her place in the infant's affections. Nettie Fowler McCormick traveled extensively with her husband when their daughter Anita was small. In April 1868, when the child was nearly two, Mrs. McCormick went to her bed late one night to arrange the bedclothes. The child murmured in her sleep, not "mama," but the name of her nurse. [205]

For the children, despite all their parents' worries, domestics must have proved a decisively positive factor. With the separation of the home from the workplace and the consequent departure of the father for most of the day, domestics provided important opportunities for adult contact and companionship for children. The "sacred privacy" of the home might otherwise have spelled loneliness and boredom. Children who grew up with domestics lived in a more populous domestic world, one more like the world at large, and they found more actors to mimic as they learned their own parts. Mary Hardy Williams recorded her small son George imitating the cook's colloquies with his Aunt Jane: "Georgie goes to the hall door, and opening it as she used to, he comes to me with 'Miss Hardy, what will *oo* have for dinner?'" When Georgie recalled his baby brother who had died, he pictured a scene with a servant: "Mama, Ann used to say 'Babie open your little mouth,' and then Ann used to put bread and milk in his mouth with a spoon, so." [206] Domestics could often provide more opportunities than their parents for children to join with them in the interesting bits of work through which children learn the satisfactions of accomplishment. Elizabeth Breese Stevens described her son Charley running about upstairs and down to see their servant Joanah, helping Joanah cut up pumpkins or apples, or scour candlesticks. [207]

Domestics could be a source of information about aspects of adult life that parents alone might have been incapable of conveying. They regularly introduced young children to the facts of class and race. On a visit to relatives, Frances Seward wrote to her husband about their young Henry. "I am afraid his manners and morals will not improve much while he is here—he came out of the kitchen today and said his Ma was a nigger which appears to be the mode of addressing poor little Mary by the hired girls." She recalled that she herself had learned the significance of this word from her father on an occasion provided by an old family servant named Peter. "I shall always remember the first and last time that I ever used this term in speaking to Peter when I was a little child. Pa reproved me very severely and I honour him for it." [208]

Robert Coles has suggested that servants in wealthy households teach young children about the existence of people less fortunate than themselves and cause them to assume that they are entitled to make use of those less fortunate. In effect, servants reconcile the young to their privileges. [209] Nineteenth-century diaries often reflect the assumption of privilege that Coles calls a sense of "entitlement." Sidney George Fisher assumed that one way or another he would be served, and servant problems once made him reflect that slavery was "not without its merits." [210] He tended to recall childhood events surrounded by a halo of service: of his brother's birth he recalled "my being taken by Mrs. Cavender to see him and how he looked." [211]

Nineteenth-century memoirs sometimes suggest that servants could provide children with more decisive influences, even with profound advantages. During many pages of childhood recollections Elizabeth Cady Stanton in her *Eighty Years and More*, seldom mentions her mother. But she recalls the servants vividly, especially a black man named Peter. Because the Cady children were considered safe in his care, Peter could take them all over Johnstown with no other supervision. He liked to go to the courthouse and hear the cases being argued, and young Elizabeth spent hours there, listening to the language of the law and learning to feel perfectly at ease in public places. Stanton cites Peter as an important influence in her life, recalling, "He was the only being, visible or invisible, of whom we had no fear." [212] Edith Wharton's memoir portrays her mother as distant, even cold, but she freely credits her nurse "Doyley," Hannah Doyle, with the sort of warmth and stability most children attach to their parents: "I pity all children who have not had a Doyley—a nurse who has always been there, who is as established as the sky and as warm as the sun, who understands everything." [213]

James Brossard's study of autobiographies and interviews to determine the effects of servants on child development revealed that a few children did acquire deep fears from servants' threats or superstitions, but many others turned to servants for the benefits of companionship and for another window on adult life. A few were fortunate to find in servants "mitigators of the harshness of family life," and some even found "mother surrogates." [214]

Heinz Kohut has cited the presence of servants as a "psychotropic social factor" acting within family life to affect changing personality patterns. [215] He suggests that servants in the home can "counteract the influence of narcissistic deprivation" through their emotional involvement with children, and he speculates that the presence of servants in the home, although compatible with traditional psychological problems like hysteria or obsessional neurosis, tended to minimize or forestall the more serious narcissistic disorders or "self pathology" so often seen today. If this is so, the presence of domestics provided a significant advantage for nineteenth-century middle-class families in rearing their children, and the long-term decline of service may be associated with "the narcissistic personality of our time." [216]

The diary kept by Hannah Wright Gould of Hudson, New York in the years of her daughter Elizabeth's infancy illustrates some of the ways in which domestics could provide supplementary parenting, making life easier for both parent and child. Mrs. Kilbourne, the childbed nurse, arrived four days after little "Lizzie" Gould was born in September 1851 and stayed about a month. Probably because of Mrs. Kilbourne's presence, Mrs. Gould's diary entries betray little of the anxiety or sense of inadequacy common to women learning to care for their first-born. After Mrs. Kilbourne left, Hannah Gould found her pipe on the stove and, putting away the little piece of clay, recalled the time she had imagined her absent husband drowned in Long Island Sound and could not sleep. Mrs. Kilbourne sat up and smoked to keep her company, telling stories of anxious moments in her own past.

Mrs. Kilbourne was succeeded by Winny, a young Irish girl. No more than a teenager herself, Winny lavished attention and affection on Lizzie. Often Mrs. Gould's diary entries record Winny's delight in the child. It is almost as if she were learning by watching Winny to experience and express her own love. Although Mrs. Gould also had three stepchildren, Lizzie suffered no neglect; on the contrary, she shared the attentions of two adoring women. One morning Mrs. Gould emerged from the bedroom to find that, apparently as usual, Winny and Lizzie were long since up and occupied. "Winny was trotting Lizzie by the stove, and declaring Lizzie had just been telling her 'Sure, if she only had her little rubbers here, she would walk into town with her little Winny' . . . and Lizzie was looking up as if charmed by Winny's tongue. . . . all this talk seems to delight Lizzie exceedingly. She crows back answers that Winny interprets marvelously to her liking." [217] When two-month-old Lizzie went on her first sleigh ride, her reactions were muted, but Winny provided plenty of delight and color: "Winny laughed and talked, enjoying the ride very much—wished to know which was east, and told which way the snow came in 'auld Ireland.'" [218] Similarly, Lizzie was still too young to appreciate that occasion beloved of parents, baby's first Christmas, but Winny could provide a reflected charm. On December 9, Mrs. Gould wrote, "'Sure and will Santa Claus want to kiss Lizzie when he comes?' asked Winny this evening anxiously, as she trotted Lizzie to the old tune, and listened to our talk of Santa Claus and the reindeer. . . . 'Will he expect to kiss Lizzie? I would not let him if I were you, maybe it will freight her, put her to bed and go yourself before he comes.' And then a little while after she asked if Santa Claus ever travelled through Ireland for she had never heard of such a person. And he lives in her memory as St. Patrick or perhaps more surely as Mr. Gould himself." [219] Mrs. Gould's literary bent, evident in her graceful prose, benefited from domestic service, for the diary bespeaks time, even leisureliness, in the days of the mother of a young infant.

In a more serious situation, Lizzie's mother woke in the middle of the night to find that Lizzie had the croup. Her husband was away, the fire was out, the kettle frozen, and the mercury at eighteen below. "I had to break through ice an inch thick—I then rushed to the front door—the stars were all out cold and desolate—the air seemed frozen as the ground, and I was bare foot on my way to Case's when Winny pulled me back, begged me to go to Lizzie, and ran herself bare footed and just as she left the bed." Winny waked the neighbor, Case, and he harnessed his horse and drove off for the doctor. "We wrapt Lizzie up every five minutes for six hours in a warm cloth wrung from mustard water—put onions to her feet, and Winny sat with her on her lap all the while. She said no one should hold Lizzie but herself—she would hold her till she died and then leave the house right away. She could not live here without Lizzie." [220] Lizzie did not die: the mustard water and the onions and the love were efficacious. Winny left the Goulds after about a year, apparently drawn away by a family obligation. Mrs. Gould went with her in the train as far as Newburgh. "Winny had Lizzie's type taken on my lap and many a time she took it out in the cars and sobbed aloud over it." [221]

The status struggle and the tenets of domesticity entailed elaborate new needs and created more work within the home, vitiating the effect of advances in household technology and requiring domestics to whom large chunks of housework could be delegated. In this new division of labor, only child care was likely to occasion a degree of harmony between employer and domestic.

FIVE **A Woman's Business: Supervision**

According to the ideology of domesticity, women's private influence acted as a balance wheel to the disorderly and stressful competition of market society. Domesticity thus conceived, depended upon extending women's activities far beyond the ambit of housework narrowly conceived—the mundanities of food, clothing, and shelter. As one conventional formulation put it, "The true sphere of a wife and mother is not merely that of a ministering servant to the physical wants and necessities of her family; it is to be the enlightened instructor and guide of awakening minds, her husband's counsellor, the guardian and purifier of the morals of her household." [1] Domesticity's new view of women's roles, while implicitly assigning the domestic to drudge work, called employers to "higher" tasks and to supervision.

These developments were crucial to domesticity's flexibility and hence to its durable appeal. The hiring and supervision of domestics permitted women's role within the family—and therefore the relationship between the family and the larger world—to bend to accommodate individual preferences, changing realities, and considerable discrepancy between theory and practice. In theory promising women a gratifying measure of spiritual and social power, domesticity prescribed that every woman find fulfillment as wife, mother, and housekeeper. In practice this was a narrow set of choices, and domesticity often involved little more than a humdrum life in an isolated setting. A woman who could hire domestics had some ability to pick and choose between those activities she would perform and those she might delegate. Mothers, for example, could and did delegate much of child care to servants but generally escaped censure so long as they did not contest the principle of motherhood's sacred responsibilities. And domestics provided handy scapegoats when domestic life fell short of its lofty goals.

Hiring domestics eased the adoption of a new relationship between the economy and the home, the home increasingly became a locale of consumption. Families with domestics could acquire the products associated with rising standards of living without experiencing the burdensome necessity of caring for the incoming tide of furniture, carpeting, and clothing. Supervision permitted both middle-class and affluent women to forge an accommodation between the work ethic and leisure, to enjoy a measure of luxury and self-indulgence while retaining the moral authority essential to true womanhood. Because domestics were often considered incompetent, supervision was required. The total delegation of housework and the embrace of pure leisure were therefore precluded. Those who supervised domestics often found it a role that offered flattering parallels to the work of entrepreneurial or managerial men. Supervising domestics even seemed to offer a promising field for "missionary" work within the home, because it involved contact between women across class lines. Emphasizing supervision made domesticity more flexible, less isolating, more rewarding.

A Flexible Balance Between Work and Leisure

The authors of domestic advice literature and of women's didactic fiction, including Catharine Beecher, Lydia Huntley Sigourney, Catharine Maria Sedgwick, Sarah Josepha Hale, Elizabeth Ellet, and Eliza Farrar, habitually assumed that their readers hired and supervised domestics.[2] The ideal wife and mother was to be neither a solitary drudge nor a useless butterfly but an active, competent supervisor. They cited as reasons for instructing their readers in the mundane details of housework the housekeeper's need to do her own work in the frequent intervals between domestics' departures and new hirings and the need to train inexperienced servants. Catharine Sedgwick explained, "Circumstances peculiar to our domestic life make it imperative upon American mothers to qualify their daughters to superintend their domestics, and to prepare the future housewife for the exigencies that await her; as emergencies constantly occur where the lady must perform the primitive offices of woman, or her family must be comfortless."[3]

The advice-givers regularly counseled women to achieve through supervision a middle ground between idleness and drudgery. The Reverend Jesse Peck warned readers of *The Ladies' Repository* in 1858, "Two extremes are to be avoided. They are excessive toil and total neglect of domestic labor." The proper way, he explained, was to "be yourself a practical housekeeper; understand every particular of kitchen labor; give it your personal attention, and occasionally if not regularly do some parts of it with your own hands."[4] Another author complained of the two extremes: on the one hand, "The life seems merged and lost in mere mechanical drudgery," while on the other, "the home duties are ignored altogether," and the mother "goes down to the frivolous, vapid social world."[5] Elizabeth Ellet expressed equal scorn for "ultra-housewifery" and for young ladies "brought up wholly without reference to home duties."[6] *Harper's Bazar* spoke with contempt of the "woman of quality" who spent half her day dabbling in soapsuds but stipulated, "The higher culture and aims in life for which we are contending render women not indifferent to or incapable of household duty." They concluded that women should supervise the work of their servants, rather than doing the work themselves.[7]

Caroline Barrett White lived an unharried, pleasant life in Brookline, Massachusetts, a life with time for visiting and travel, reading and the theater. Even when her four children were small, the sunny, placid months and years flowed by easily with many small happinesses secured by her staff of three domestics. Mrs. White made preserves and cleaned house in occasional stints, plunged into housework capably when she found herself short-handed, and, when staff left, trained new domestics, but her principal daily occupation was to make sure that the servants did their work. She would refer to her husband, Frank, as busy with alterations about the grounds and to herself as occupied with spring housecleaning, although hired workers actually performed both these tasks while she and her husband supervised.

Mrs. White did not consider herself idle nor exempt from household cares. In 1874 she inscribed on the flyleaf of the fourteenth volume of her diary two brief notes that framed her attitudes toward her life. One was a quotation from "Mrs. Stowe": "Household cares are a drudgery only when unpervaded by sentiment. When they are an offering of love, a ministry of care and devotion to the beloved—every detail has its interest." The second was a note to herself: "A reason why the rich or those who are not compelled by necessity, should bear their part in the world's toil—this is such a weary *work a day* world to the great majority of people, that the *example* of those who work from choice, and not necessity, is salutary in its influence on those who *must labor*—as it assures them of sympathy from a class who will be *honored*, much as we may talk of the equality of mankind—and gives an air of *respectability* to *necessary work*."[8] She lived, as she saw it, at the intersection of two relationships: one of sentiment—a ministry of care to husband and children—and one of work—of salutary influence upon and example to domestics.

When Henry Ward Beecher was the center of the most notorious scandal of the nineteenth century, his wife, Eunice Bullard Beecher, was described by the press as a "shrew" who made her husband's life "hell on earth." Her own writings reveal a jealous and resentful woman given to manipulative bouts of hypochondria.[9] Eunice and Henry Ward Beecher dealt with their unhappy

partnership by maintaining proper appearances and seeking com-
pensations elsewhere. Mrs. Beecher found security and revenge in
creating a domestic world of perfect order and ruthless neatness in
which she was undisputed ruler. In the name of preventing a thousand tiny incursions of dirt and clutter, she insisted that husband
and children meet her standards. Her standards required her also to
assemble and then tyrannize over a staff of domestics. In her household advice columns, she recommended hiring domestics in the
largest possible numbers and providing for their strictest treatment.[10] She warned that domestics might be guilty of such
crimes as using dishtowels for potholders, or failing to close the
kitchen door, not to mention forging recommendations and filch-
ing supplies. She suggested hiring girls just off the ship at Castle
Garden, but wrote sourly that "not one in a hundred" of all the
Irish could ever be trained to be "neat, energetic, faithful and
truthtelling." New girls in her house were "inevitably" sloppy
when they dusted: "Wherever there is any elaborate carving, intricate molding, or dainty piece of statuary, requiring extra care, the
dust has settled, and lies unmolested in ugly masses, defacing or
concealing all the beauty."[11]

Catchpenny wisdom in the nineteenth century warned against
thwarted women who would take out their frustrations in petty
tyrannizing over servants. Josiah Gilbert Holland's *Letters to the
Joneses*, a set of twenty-four letters to a fictitious family warning
them of a catalogue of moral derelictions, included one to "Mrs.
Jessy Bell Jones," who bullied her servants. "Every nature which
has any force in it will assert itself somewhere," the author admon-
ished: "If you, Mrs. Jessy Bell Jones . . . possessed a recognized
value out of your house, or in your parlor beyond other women of
your set or class, I think you would be content—that your servants
would get along well enough, and that you would get along well
enough with them."[12] The author of an article on servants in
Godey's of 1864 advanced a similar theory about women who bully

their servants, concluding, "The weaker, as well as the stronger, sex love power and love the manifestations of it."[13]

On the strength of her husband's considerable income, Eunice Beecher managed to carry her tyrannical supervision to astounding lengths. Her *Law of the Household* reveals how thoroughly home life had been converted for her to the management of servants, a management with markedly expansionist tendencies. The "law of the household"—the entire contents of the book—turns out to be a listing of her domestics and their duties, a staff of baronial proportions: housekeeper, secretary, superintendent, butler, second man, third man, housemaid, chef, chef's assistant, first chambermaid, second chambermaid, lady's maid, handyman/engineer, night watchman, laundress, and laundress's assistants. "The following pages," she declared, "will give you my schedule of work"; in fact, they detailed the servants' schedules of work.[14]

In her introduction, addressed to "My Dear Children," Mrs. Beecher passed on her system, professing the hope that it would make life easier for readers, despite the improbability of their being able to reproduce this kind of staffing. She recalls the day when she first understood her life's work. As she and Henry stood watching the workmen building their house, she had wished aloud that her servants would work as efficiently as these laborers. Her husband replied, "Do you see that man standing by the gate? He isn't doing anything but watching; he's the boss." "That night," she wrote, "I saw the vision of woman's emancipation through system. Why shouldn't a woman conduct her household as a business, prepare herself for it as a man prepared for his life work—in other words, make a business of housekeeping, and learn as much as she can of it before marriage."[15]

Occasionally a woman was able to transfer the supervisory skills developed in the home to larger fields of entrepreneurial activity. Nettie Fowler McCormick honed her administrative talents on a staff of five or six domestics and then, after her husband's death, transferred her attention to the McCormick Harvesting Machine

Company and became its virtual if not actual president through her son, Cyrus, Jr.[16]

Authors of popular fiction for women contrasted their heroines with two stock characters: the idle, heartless social butterfly, absorbed in mere pleasure seeking, and the hardbitten, joyless woman who considered life an endless round of housework and made her family miserable.[17] Harriet Beecher Stowe employed versions of these two stock characters, Marie St. Clair and Miss Ophelia, in *Uncle Tom's Cabin*.

Stowe elaborated her vision of the balanced middle way in her New York novels, *My Wife and I* and *We and Our Neighbors*, published in the early 1870s. Ann Douglas has discussed these enormously popular novels as reflections of sentimental culture, describing the heroine, Eva Van Arsdel, as a "parasite," a consumer with no "faculty," or practical ability, completely reliant upon her Irish cook to do all the real work of domesticity.[18] Stowe, in fact, explicitly distances Eva from the fashionable world where she has grown up. After Eva makes a love match with a journalist who has no fortune and her father goes bankrupt, she bids her fashionable dressmaker goodbye, and she and her new husband set up housekeeping in an old house in a distinctly unfashionable street with only one servant. Eva embraces this life. She is weary of vapid high society and eager to create a happy home: "Though a city girl and a child of wealth and fashion, she had what Yankee matrons are pleased to denominate 'faculty,' which is, being interpreted, a genius for home life."[19] Indeed, the dictates of fashion take a terrible beating in these novels in the person of "Aunt Maria Wouvermans," a pompous old spokeswoman for maximum expenditure and worldly concerns, who is, like the character modeled after Victoria Woodhull, "Audacia Dangyereyes," both a figure of fun and a symbol of dangerous extremism in women's roles. Eva is a "manager"—a term Stowe insists on—not because, as Douglas asserts, she "stretches her presumably limited budget," although this is certainly true, but because she knows how to be a tactful supervisor. Eva uses her domestic servant to free herself for those uplifting activities, primarily church and charitable work, Stowe considers to be the essential pursuits of womanhood.

Sarah Josepha Hale also testified to the importance of domestic supervision for successful domesticity in her 1845 novel *Keeping House and House Keeping: A Story of Domestic Life*. Hale's heroine, Mrs. Harley, begins the novel as a vain and frivolous young bride who refuses to concern herself with her domestic duties and hires more and more servants despite her husband's warning of their financial ruin. She defends her wish to hire a housekeeper: "What time could I get to sew or read or prepare for company or receive any, if I made myself the slave you wish?" It is, of course, the domestics who "enslave" her, for they are dishonest or incompetent, and she is too ignorant of domestic work to detect their peculations or correct their errors.

When her fashionable party is a failure, Mrs. Harley begins to suspect, "There is no pleasure in the kind of life I lead," and Mr. Harley, who has all along been urging a more rational household regime, invites wise old Aunt Ruth to come and stay with them. She dismisses the incompetent servants, sets the house in order, and slowly begins to teach Mrs. Harley her duties, expatiating on "the folly of entrusting to others the duties which a wise Providence designed as a wholesome discipline to ourselves, the slavery it engenders, the weakness it fosters, and the debasing influence it exerts upon the immortal mind, which can only strengthen itself by vigorous exertion." [20] Aunt Ruth points out Mrs. Harley's fundamental error: "My dear, you confound all good management with labour; this is not correct."

Mrs. Harley turns to Bible reading, breaks off her connections with haughty fashionables like "Mrs. Gerrish," and nurses her little Johnny through scarlet fever. With her new style of active and intelligent management, Mrs. Harley is a changed woman. She is able to reduce her staff from three to two, one of whom is a girl taken "to bring up." Hale writes, "She now, prompted by pleasure as well as by duty, gave all necessary attention to her affairs, and succeeded so well, simply with the assistance of Dorcas and Marianne, that Mr. Harley said his expenses would not exceed his income." [21] In the happy conclusion Mrs. Harley is seen dressed with "elegant simplicity," retaining the most sensible among her fashionable friends, and presiding over "delightful little parties, which were characterized by liberality without useless profusion."

In this book the content of domesticity depends upon matters of servant management—ordering material and labor. The choice of action in the novel suggests that servant management could also provide a lightning rod or a diversion for marital conflicts that might have been much less easy to "manage." Servant problems are, it seems, the only sources of Mrs. Harley's derelictions of motherly duty and conflicts with her husband. Hale's conclusion, with its visions of "elegant simplicity" and "liberality without profusion," suggests that the notion of a middle ground in domestic life tended to collapse into the desire to have the best of both worlds, to enjoy the moral superiority of diligence and the palpable delights of acquisition and display. The great appeal of managing domestics was that it promised to combine the two.

Entrepreneurial and Benevolent Models

Women's supervisory activities in the household imitated those of entrepreneurial men: hiring and firing, instructing and driving. As she described her staff, Eunice Beecher sounded like a businessman who had built a small shop into a good-sized concern. The character of servant supervision was such that system, order, professionalism, even "women's emancipation"—Eunice Beecher, who typically scorned feminist goals, chose this term—could all be found within it. Even the contradiction between feminist goals and conventional female roles became harder to detect when household supervision provided satisfactions similar to those of men's work in the public sphere, and feminists themselves needed domestics to gain time to engage in feminist agitation. The flexibility of domesticity in practice helps to explain the appeal of conventional women's roles, an appeal that may be difficult to perceive in the blank prescriptions of the "cult of true womanhood." [22] The home could come to resemble the realm to which it proposed to stand in contrast, the male business world.

The authors of *Ann Connover*, a tract prepared for servants by the American Sunday School Union, mixed Biblical injunctions with business analogies in urging servants to be contented with their places. When pious Aunt Jane advises the heroine, Ann, to be satisfied with her station, she notes that this world is like a "large manufactory" in which each person has some particular thing to do: "All persons are God's workpeople. They are like factory people." [23] For those who would assume the role of supervisor in this scheme of things, the advice-givers recommended a posture appropriate to command: "Decision of character is most necessary to be acquired by the mistress of a household. In the daily routine of life she should calmly and judiciously decide upon her course of action, and afterward maintain her position gently but firmly." [24] She must have "a system of supervision" and stick to it with firmness and regularity. [25] Other writers recommended specific policies proven in business practice. Abby Sage Richardson counseled housewives to deal with the servant problem by dismissing all incompetents and strictly enforcing the requirement of letters of recommendation. Housewives, she declared, must deal with each other "as men of business do, in recommending and dismissing." [26]

To compare favorably with men who were supervisors in the business world, women needed both practical knowledge and rational habits of mind: they must know how to do all the work of their own concern and be able as well to combine and rationally coordinate its components with forethought, even "science." The author of "Maids of All Work" in *Godey's* recommended that with system, good habits, and forethought "the domestic mill" would function smoothly. [27] Another writer compared the housekeeper to the man who, in the midst of a busy train station, calmly oils the wheels of the cars, but, she asserted, the housekeeper served as engineer and conductor as well.[28] An "educated housekeeper" writing in *The Ladies' Repository* judged the housekeeper's role more demanding than that of many male entrepreneurs: "There's more room for science and thought, and skill in managing a household properly than you'll ever find in your dry-goods store, with a bank and a grist-mill thrown in."[29] Others agreed: "The woman who is able to systematize and carry on the work of an ordinary family illustrates higher sagacity than is called for by seven-eighths of the tasks done by men."[30] Individual women took the advice to heart and wrote in their diaries of "getting a system of housekeeping established," of having "the wheels of the household machinery to keep in motion," and of the need for "tact, judgment, skill, prudence [and] energy."[31]

Their husbands' experiences in supervising clerks taught women that they needed to be familiar with the work in order to supervise properly. "Does Mr. Million, downtown," asked one author, "set his clerks afloat in his warehouses, and tell them to do their work, while he reads the last essay on political economy, or smokes his cigar at Delmonico's?"[32] Mrs. Hughes, fictional housekeeper of *The Biddy Club*, learned the same lesson in a conversation with her husband one evening, when he referred to a new clerk who, although ignorant, would soon be valuable because Mr. Hughes could teach him everything. "I have had practical knowledge of it all," he boasted, suggesting that housekeepers might solve their servant problems if only they could say the same.[33]

One fictional husband reminded his wife she could not shirk her supervisory duties within the home: "I cannot thus delegate my business duties to anyone; without my governing mind and constant attention, everything would soon be in disorder, and an utter failure, instead of prosperity would be the result."[34] Citing this story, Nancy Cott has written, "Ironically, the rhetoric that intended to distinguish 'home' and 'woman' from 'the world' and

'man' tended to make the two spheres analogous and comparable."[35] This comparability was rooted not in mere rhetoric but
in activity, in women's supervision of their servants.

So common were tidy proposals about supervision that one
writer burlesqued their simplicity. In a short story in *Godey's*, a
pompous "Mr. Brown" tells his wife, who complains of servant
problems, to do as he does in business: "Establish a certain rule,
and see that it is obeyed. That's my plan and I have no trouble. An
employee of mine knows that it is as much as his place is worth to
go contrary to rule." "Order among intelligent clerks may be easily
enough attained," Mrs. Brown retorts, "but I'd like to see the
order you would maintain with a parcel of subordinates like our
Biddy to deal with." As it turns out, her point is quite correct: in
the conclusion of the story Biddy responds to Mr. Brown's shouted
orders by flinging the roast on the floor at his feet, splattering him
with gravy.[36]

Popular literature suggested that the supervision of domestics
could be shaped to benevolent as well as entrepreneurial models.
Catharine Maria Sedgwick elaborated this view in her 1837 novel
Live and Let Live; or, Domestic Service Illustrated. There Sedgwick
showed that the proper supervision of servants not only permits the
housekeeper and her family to enjoy a happy, well-served home life
but also yields the opportunity to apply improving benevolence to
the domestic and through her to all the poor. Lucy Lee, the heroine, goes out to service at age fourteen because her father is a hope-
less drunkard. Lucy's peripatetic life enabled Sedgwick to portray a
series of situations that exemplify domestic error and domestic
ideal. Mrs. Broadson, Mrs. Ardley, and Mrs. Hartell are all idle
fashionables, ignorant of the work their houses require and hence
inconsiderate, alternating between exploitative demands and a cra-
ven tolerance of servant incompetence. Mrs. Lovett and Mrs. Hyde
provide two ideal types of employers at different income levels.

Mrs. Lovett, the wife of a baker, is a warm-hearted woman who treats Lucy as a helper; Lucy will marry her son Charles in the happy conclusion. But Mrs. Hyde absorbs most of Sedgwick's attention as the ideal supervisor of domestics. She is wealthy and has a large staff but is knowledgeable and considerate to all. She looks on her domestics' high turnover and ineptitude as calling her to their teaching and improvement: "She knew there must be changes," Sedgwick explains, "and one of her objects was to qualify those she employed for the happier condition that probably awaited them—to be the masters and mistresses of independent homes." [37] Indeed, the entire Hyde household resembles a charitable institution. Lucy exclaims, "There is not one, even down to Gracie, that is not teaching some poor ignorant creature something. Did you ever see anything prettier than Gracie teaching English to those little German children, that they have saved from destruction as it were? If every family were like this, there would be an end to poverty and misery." [38] Mrs. Hyde's charity takes the form not of largesse but of moral and practical teaching. Lucy, declaring that Mrs. Hyde has "qualified me to take charge of a family of my own," elucidates: "Some think the rich can only be generous in giving; what a mistake! Mrs. Hyde does not give the half that Mrs. Ardley does in presents or in charity, but she gives her time, she imparts her knowledge, she infuses her spirit, and oh! none but those who live with her know how faithfully she tries to lay the foundation of religion." [39]

Sedgwick's title is inaccurate: her subject is really "Live Properly and Show Others How," and she believes that supervising domestics within the home provides the means to do so. The young servant, properly taught, will become the anchor of a virtuous home life for her own husband and children, and thus the poor can be "saved from destruction." In *We and Our Neighbors*, Stowe's heroine, Eva Van Arsdel Henderson, similarly pursues benevolence after marriage through her supervisory role. Her domestic's headstrong daughter, Maggie, has "fallen." Eva reclaims Maggie from her evil ways and sets about her rehabilitation by providing the girl a place in service in the Henderson household, alongside her mother.[40]

A fragment in the papers of Helen Munson Williams testifies how strongly Sedgwick's ideas struck an answering chord among middle-class women. This handwritten piece, dating from about midcentury, proposes that twelve matrons form a committee to carry out a plan for "home missionary work." The plan calls for each family to take a fifteen-year-old girl from a "respectable" home "to lodge, board, clothe and instruct in the business of housekeeping, including cooking and laundry work, for two years in return for her services without wages." At the end of two years she will be rewarded with a diploma and the ability to earn wages—i.e., work as a domestic. Mrs. Williams listed the "Objects to be Attained" in this project:

To make domestic service respectable and respected.

To restore the right relationship between classes, and to bring them nearer to each other in the ways appointed by God and nature.

To fit women by having them trained in domestic service to become good wives, mothers, housekeepers and homemakers, and so to offer the greatest safeguard against the influence of saloons and the growth of intemperance among men.

To draw women out of the paths of temptation by restoring them to their proper sphere, leaving the shop and the factory to be supplied by the men who are now standing idle.[41]

Home life itself could be viewed as a social mission because it was the locale for the most direct contact between women across class lines.[42] Precisely because of all its frustrating inadequacies, domestic service provided a vast arena in which to do good. Sometimes women showed considerable naiveté about the mundane realities of recruitment and hiring. Mrs. Williams's plan, for example, would certainly have failed if it were tried, since inexperienced fifteen-year-olds could find paid service positions without going through an unpaid two-year training program. But the potential for missionary work in the home affected institutional efforts to help the poor, as is evident, for example, in the history of the Home for the Friendless in Rochester. In the 1840s a group of benevolent ladies organized the home to "afford temporary aid and protection to respectable but homeless and friendless girls seeking employment," thus protecting them from "the snares and temptations of the city." What did the ladies propose to do for "the friendless"? Find them jobs as servants, "situations in worthy and Christian families."[43] Nineteenth-century female charitable and benevolent groups consistently regarded domestic supervision as a model and a resource. Efforts to rescue prostitutes supposed that repentant women would be placed in domestic service, as were female orphans and juvenile delinquents. Efforts to alleviate female poverty often gave rise to charitable versions of the intelligence office.

Despite the pretension to missionary work, supervising domestics mainly involved teaching secular practical skills, like the punctuality and early rising that Mrs. Hyde emphasized in Sedgwick's *Live and Let Live*. Confrontations with Irish domestics, who combined a stout Catholicism with a distinct lack of practical skills, probably tended to confirm the focus on secular goals. In *The American Woman's Home* (1869), Beecher and Stowe recommended that women look on their domestics as calling them to "the duties of missionaries" in the home, but they specifically disavowed actual conversion efforts: "In speaking of the office of the American mistress as being a missionary one, we are far from recommending any controversial interference with the religious faith of our servants." They called instead for "the manifestation of a friendly and benevolent interest in their comfort and improvement," incuding teaching them how to read, how to make and care for their clothing, and how to perform all their household duties properly.[44] The improving influence women proposed to exert over their domestics increasingly amounted to instilling in them the characteristics of good workers—skill, docility, punctuality. When one fictional housekeeper declared, "I've done with missionary work," another, the heroine of the piece, responded that "God has not given up requiring such work of us. We must never lose sight of the fact that if we do our whole duty by our servants, we shall educate them." The subject under discussion was whether or not employers should compel their domestics to learn to use new kitchen gadgets and conveniences.[45]

Anna O. Williams of Buffalo, New York needed a servant in March 1864. "A poor little fatherless and motherless presented herself in a cold dripping state without any home and entirely friendless. I had not the heart to turn her off, although she looked so ill I did not know but I was taking fever or smallpox into the bosom of my family." The girl bathed, went to bed, and awoke the next morning refreshed and well and ready to work: "She has been brought up in the orphan asylum of the Sisters of Mercy and is in many respects well-trained. Can do all my upstairs work better than any large girl I ever had although only thirteen."[46] Susan Brown Forbes of Boston and Springfield, Massachusetts patiently practiced benevolence toward her domestics, asking only that they show themselves willing to work hard. When Annie Ladd started work for her in April 1865 the girl was lonely: "I went down this AM and found her crying before breakfast." Mrs. Forbes comforted the girl, got the breakfast started, and made it a point to invite Annie to come with her and Alex to a "missionary concert" the next evening.[47] When another servant, Ann Dury, fell ill, Susan Forbes made inquiries in person until she could secure a place for the girl at City Hospital. Young Mary Parker's wild habits made her an unsatisfactory domestic, but Mrs. Forbes put up with Mary's sauciness and penchant for disappearing without notice, reproving but not dismissing her and worrying that Mary might have gone "where she ought not to be" or was "going to ruin." At one point Mary flounced off to work elsewhere, but returned to Mrs. Forbes, confessing that she was "homesick."[48] Mrs. Forbes was active in the founding of an orphan asylum called "The Home for Little Wanderers," and she encouraged her laundress to surrender her children to the home.[49] She arranged for a minister to preside when her domestic Katy Sears was married, and a year later Katy reappeared "in miserable health, to tell of her husband's abuses" and ask Mrs. Forbes and the minister to intervene with him.[50] Clearly Susan Forbes won the genuine trust and loyalty of some of the women and girls who entered her kitchen, but her benevolent activities were trimmed to the necessity of shaping good workers: when Annie Ladd was "not equal to the work," she had to go. Similarly, Mrs. Forbes's eagerness to find a hospital bed for Ann Dury probably reflected not only pity for the girl's condition but also a desire to be freed from the burden of her care.

A fragment in the Proctor family papers entitled "Being A Cook—An Autobiography" suggests the power servant supervision could have over the imagination. After laboriously inventing a plausible means by which a woman of education and genteel sensibility could enter this kind of work, the narrative died. The handwriting and the style show that it was written by one of the Proctor sisters; evidently this was the only subject that ever prompted an excursion into fiction by these otherwise practical women. Elizabeth Sullivan Stuart even dreamed about supervision. In the dream her departed husband appeared to her: "He put his hand on my shoulder, looked very solemn, and said, 'Betsy you suffer yourself to be too much troubled about servants, do not let these things trouble you.'"[51]

The Problems of Supervision in Practice

Supervising—the separation of head and hand—was not a particularly common feature of the world of work in the mid nineteenth century, a world still composed largely of small farms and shops. The development of the supervisory function, a step crucial to industrialization, was not easily accomplished. The success of the

Boston Manufacturing Company, for example, was due less to technical than to managerial breakthroughs, specifically the formation of a managerial function bridging the gap between the capital and marketing capabilities of the merchant stockholders and the technical skills of mechanics and machinists.[52] Again and again success in the early textile industry depended upon finding an individual who was sufficiently "practical" to understand the work and therefore to command the workers and yet would remain loyal to the interests of the ownership. Men like Patrick Tracy Jackson, Paul Moody, and Kirk Boott, through filling such roles, earned a place in American business history. The persistent danger, once ownership and skill were no longer united in the person of the independent craftsman, was that the owners "no longer possessed the knowledge to match their responsibilities."[53] Managers and supervisors were hired to know how to perform, and thereby control, work in which they did not participate.

Once management had established itself, the possession of knowledge and therefore control of work continued to be a point of contention between supervisors and their workers. Skilled workers sometimes enjoyed a considerable degree of authority and control, but most important decisions rested with foremen who had worked their way up from the ranks. They had the power to hire and fire, to determine methods, tools, and work pace. The "foreman's empire" became less and less satisfactory as firms grew larger and larger. Shop-floor conflict tended to increase because the foreman's control was arbitrary and abusive, shaped by favoritism and prejudice. The foreman's supervisory power was weakened in the worker's eyes "since the boss's authority was clearly being used for personal gain rather than because production demanded it."[54] By the turn of the century, big business was ready to try new methods of supervisory control, including Frederick Taylor's scientific management. Scientific management aimed for the separation of head and hand in order to achieve complete control over the knowledge, and therefore the standards and the pace, of work. Engineers and formally trained supervisors would take the place of foremen, chosen for practical experience. By taking control of the knowledge of the work, subdividing it, and hiring cheaper, less skilled workers, profits would be increased. Once the work was subdivided, scientific managers would also take control of the pace of the work so as to increase output. In the industrial workplace scientific management sparked concerted worker resistance that limited its effectiveness, but management had seized a powerful means of control in the separation of knowledge from execution and would pursue this method in the twentieth century.[55] Within the home, supervision resulted in patterns of contest for control that were similar to and in some cases anticipated those in industry.

In recommending to middle-class women the role of domestic supervisor, the advice-givers insured a market for their own expertise, since the housekeeper needed to be able to teach and direct operations she herself did not regularly perform, had perhaps never performed. Systematic study and recourse to expert advice seemed called for, and from Catharine Beecher on, those who spoke for the study of domestic economy could justify it in part by reference to the poor quality of domestics.[56] The domestic advice literature consistently interpreted mastery of household skills as an intellectual accomplishment, best pursued with the help of intellectual aids such as reference books—their own products—and crash courses. Beecher and Stowe cited the image of a teacher: "The first business of a housekeeper in America is that of a teacher. She can have a good table only by having practical knowledge and tact in imparting it. If she understands her business practically and experimentally, her eye detects at once a weak spot; it requires only a little tact, some patience, some clearness in giving directions; and all comes right."[57] The terms in this passage—"practically and experimentally"—add the language of science to that of mere practice. The authors suggested that a housekeeper should make her own bread for a month, after which time she would understand the process and could cease to do any more than teach it. Such speedy mastery was supposed to be possible for educated women. "A well-trained mind, accustomed to reflect, analyze, and generalize, has an advantage over uncultured minds even of double experience. Poor as your cook is, she now knows more of her business than you do. After a very brief period of attention and experiment, you will not only know more than she does, but you will convince her that you do, which is quite as much to the purpose." [58]

Good cooking is, of course, less an intellectual accomplishment than a craft, and a few weeks will seldom suffice to make a good cook. Much unavoidably depends upon experience. "I am learning Bridget Cousin Mary's girl to make bread," one woman wrote to her mother, adding, "I am very glad I know how myself." Another boasted, "My winter's experience makes me a pretty good manager." [59] A passage from Catharine Beecher's *Domestic Receipt-Book* suggests some of the difficulties in putting supervision into practice. Beecher insists that making good bread is essential to family life and a positive duty of every woman. "The last grand essential to good bread is *good care*. Unless the cook can be fully trusted, the mistress of a family *must* take this care upon *herself*." The reader might suppose that Beecher is recommending that the employer make the bread herself. But no: "She must, if needful, stand by and see that the bread is wet right, that the yeast is good, that the bread is put where it is warm enough, that it does not rise too long, so as to lose its sweetness (which is often the case before it begins to sour), that it is moulded aright, that the oven is at the right heat, and that it is taken out at the right time, and then that it is put in the right place, and not set flat on to a greasy table, or painted shelf, to imbibe a bad taste." [60] Here was a recipe for conflict. The cook was supposed to endure her employer officiously hovering over her, giving minute instructions but not actually working. Few domestics wanting a job would be apt to claim total ignorance of their work and hence perfect readiness to be taught. Thus the seemingly innocuous proposal to "teach" the servant could involve in practice an intense surveillance designed to detect errors, much like the minute supervision characteristic of scientific management.

Since the "product" in housework was ill-defined and differed from one employer to the next, "errors," in any case, might be merely differences in taste and habit. Help could become aware of differences in style or method by working alongside their employers, but domestics might find their employers' versions decreed in the irritating manner proposed by Beecher and enforced as not merely preferred but correct. One employer referred to a domestic as "very wasteful and will throw a whole loaf of bread into the swill pail if she is not watched"; another was scandalized to find her cook sweetening pies with handfuls of sugar rather than using a measuring spoon.[61] But stale bread might be thrown out in one household and destined for bread pudding in another, while experienced cooks can season by pinch or handful without waste or error. The domestic advice literature proposed promulgating standards in all things, but frankly conceded that enforcement would be difficult. In her *Treatise* Beecher remarked, "Few domestics will make a bed properly without much attention from the mistress of the family. The following directions should be given to those who do this work."[62] She warned that domestics were apt to wash dishes poorly and provided a set of standards.[63] To soften the effect of this barrage of supervision, Beecher and Stowe could only recommend tact: forewarn, they suggested, rather than scold or find fault.[64] However tactfully she might go about it, the employer was requiring the domestic to meet a set of standards that were abstract and often unrealistic, derived not from the employer's own experience but from the advice of experts.

Possibilities for conflict were reinforced by the fact that the employer's ability to set standards was held to be a crucial part of her role. When the bread failed to rise or when the sauce curdled, both cook and housekeeper might be honestly at a loss to explain why. But the housekeeper, having heard from experts like Beecher and

Stowe that she should know, and moreover that she should convince her cook that she knew, might be tempted to bluff and bluster. Mary Virginia Terhune, who wrote the best-selling *Common Sense in the Household*, admitted in her autobiography that she had one resolve from which she never swerved: "If my cook did not understand her business, and I understood it even less, I would not confess it."[65] An article entitled "How I Kept House by Proxy" in *Scribner's Monthly* told of the author's experiences with a superb Chinese cook, Chek Sau, during a residence in Bangkok. When later she heard complaints from other employers about him, she was baffled. Chek Sau explained that he would not be instructed by those who knew little or nothing of the art he had mastered: "I am always willing to be told *what* to do, but never *how* to execute the order, especially when, in that department, I happen to know far more than my teachers." The author's great virtue as an employer had been the youthful inexperience that made her happy to leave the cook to his own devices. The significance of her title is that, in doing so, she felt she had only been housekeeping by proxy.[66] Ignorant housekeepers were like the industrial directors who "no longer possessed the knowledge to match their responsibilities," but they would be convinced to change their ways not by the disciplining hand of business losses but by the harrying advice of experts in domestic economy.

Since she so often worked out of her employer's sight, the domestic seemed to require new, more formal methods of supervision. One of these methods was the inspection tour. Catharine Beecher recommended that every room, drawer, and closet be examined monthly. Mary Hooker Cornelius recommended a daily inspection tour, and Elizabeth Strong Worthington's model housekeeper arranged to be "in and about the kitchen a certain time each day."[67] Architectural separation had some of the same effects as the increasing size of industrial firms, making direct and literal "oversight" more difficult. One writer in 1879 referred to "long flights of stairs" having made it practically impossible for a woman to spend much time teaching her cook.[68] Formal written instructions seemed like a promising substitute. Beecher suggested drawing up a monthly bill of fare for the cook, and she cited with approval one family in which the mistress wrote instructions for each of three domestics on a large card suspended in the kitchen. The papers of the Proctor family of Utica contain examples of such instructions in small notebooks. One note told the cook, "All her departments will be daily visited by one of the family." Another concluded, "In the preceding arrangement of work, the greatest thought and care has been taken to give each maid on each day only what she can do well."[69]

Lack of direct oversight often imparted an air of deception to domestics' faults and an air of meanness to employers' efforts to detect them. Some employers resorted to shabby tricks like leaving pins under the carpet to see if the girl swept there. Others complained that they found "hidden filth" in the kitchen cabinets after a domestic's departure.[70] Help had perhaps been slovenly as often as domestics, but in the nature of their situation they could not conceal it and so appear to compound the fault with dishonesty.

The possibility that their domestics were dishonest became a nagging fear for many employers. Whenever anything in the house was lost or misplaced, suspicion fell upon domestics; employers could in effect presume a domestic guilty unless proven innocent, at least to the extent of firing her and denying her a recommendation.[71] One employer warned another, when recommending two domestics, that she had "missed money lately" although she had "no reason to suspect these girls."[72] Early in the century, Fanny Wright encountered one young woman with the sensibilities of a helper, who quit a position when she discovered that her new employer had locked away all the plate and silver spoons: "I could not stay in a house where a doubt seemed to be cast on my honesty," she said."[73]

Employers worried not only about plate and spoons but also about bread and butter. Architectural separation of one part of the

house from another seemed to place extra pressure on the trust-
worthiness of domestics, since they so regularly had to admit and
deal with tradesmen and delivery boys. Rachel Williams Proctor's
instructions to her cook emphasized keeping the rear door bolted at
all times and not letting the butcher's and grocer's men go alone
into the cellar, where the stores and refrigerators were kept.[74] Domestics also dispensed charity at the back door, and so fell under
another cloud of suspicion.[75] Jokes about Biddy pictured her "entertaining legions of 'cousins' on her employer's victuals; loading
her mother, in the guise of an old beggarwoman, with pillaged
food at the basement entrance."[76] Many servants came from traditions of relatively free-handed charity or mutual assistance
among the poor. A well-to-do Irish farmer's servant might distribute food daily to dozens of paupers who came to the farmhouse
door, but an old-country style of generosity could get an Irish
domestic into trouble in the United States. One fictional servant
voiced disgust with mistresses who thought you a thief "if ye give
a starving childer a little sugar or tea for its mamma."[77]

Suspicious employers locked up the provision cabinets. "It is
sometimes the case that the constant change of domestics, and the
liability thus to have dishonest ones, makes it needful to keep
stores under lock and key," Catharine Beecher said but noted that
the practice might cause resentment. "This measure is often very
offensive to those who are hired, as it is regarded by them as an
evidence both of *closeness* and *suspicion* of their honesty." She advised
employers to explain that locked provisions would prevent suspicion from falling upon honest domestics.[78] "We have generally
not had very trusty girls," one employer wrote, "and have got in
the habit of overlooking closely."[79] Later in the century such procedures seemed more routine, less in need of excuse, and Eunice
Beecher went so far as to recommend patent locks, since servants
might use skeleton keys on ordinary ones.[80]

The most common and pervasive means of extending supervision involved transforming servants' work discipline from task to

time. Rather than having a certain amount of work to do, as help had, domestics were expected to be at work constantly unless explicitly "off." An employer need not wait to evaluate results; she could tell at a glance at any odd moment if the domestic were diligently occupied with the work supposed to be done at that hour. This change in domestic work discipline involved a significant lengthening of the hours of work for domestics as compared with help.

Late nineteenth-century social investigators discovered that domestics not only worked longer hours than any other women workers but also spent the remainder of their time effectively on call. Only when they left the house on their two half-holidays each week were they really free of the job. On the days when they had their customary one afternoon and evening off each week—usually Thursday and Sunday—they typically had to do seven or eight hours of work before they could leave the house. Many individuals could testify to being deprived of their holidays when it suited their employer and to getting up at four or five in the morning and working until late evening.[81]

Long hours and lack of personal time would figure prominently when Progressive-era investigators asked working women about the comparative disadvantages of service. They complained that Sunday, far from being a day of rest, was apt to be extra busy, with large family dinners and company and with the domestic trying to hurry through it all in order to get some time off. They spoke bitterly of having no time in the evenings to call their own, even to do necessary personal sewing. When Ida Jackson, factory inspector for the state of Wisconsin, asked factory girls about the disadvantages of service, the most frequent complaint was "this very practical question of freedom after working hours, of regular and unrestricted periods of leisure."[82]

The social habits of urban employers tended to stretch out the work day: the main meal of the day having been moved from midday to evening to accommodate a husband's separate workplace, it might already be late evening by the time a girl served and cleaned up.[83] Evening social occasions, reflecting the demands of urban commerce for a full day's attention from the men, required that domestics answer the door, watch children while the mother went out, or sit up and wait for the family's return. Employers could argue that the city streets were no fit place for young women to while away their evening hours, but this was to some extent a rationalization. The fact that domestics did not help but carried the main burden of the housework alone made it hard to do without them even for a few hours; often no one else could put together a presentable meal.

A few reports from the 1840s and 1850s suggest that employers of domestics enforced changes in work discipline and hours against some resistance by servants accustomed to the practices of helping. Mrs. A. J. Graves remarked that in the cities girls often wanted to engage to do specific work and then get their time off; her report carried the implication that employers rejected such notions. Catharine Beecher bluntly advised domestics to abandon their ideas: they must accept the fact that most employers wanted to "hire *the time*" of the domestic rather than certain tasks.[84] One writer in *Godey's* suggested making this supposedly tactful statement to newly hired domestics: "I cannot tell you exactly what I require. I wish you to do whatever work I arrange for you as best suits my convenience and not your own; and you must trust my judgment."[85] Such a regime was a long way from the mixture of work and leisure enjoyed by help: time off in the evenings had shifted from an acknowledged right to a privilege that must be specially begged and life thus converted into an endless work session, broken only by infrequent holidays. "It is not strange that girls dislike housework," Kate Gannett Wells declared, "when they know that no matter how well they have done their work, they must ask leave to go out in the evening, and must be home at a fixed early hour."[86]

The author of *Plain Talk and Friendly Advice to Domestics* (1855) testified to the fact that these restrictions on their time rankled domestics, even while she argued that they should not. She presented a fictional sketch of the servants of a large town talking together in which Elizabeth, the troublemaker in the group, harps on the issue of time off.

Elizabeth: . . . we won't be giving the mistress the fashion of asking leave when we want to go out. Soon as the work is done we'll fling on our things and go.

Susy: But what if she should have company, or be going herself?

Elizabeth: Divil take her! She's no business to be having a houseful of company every ither night, or be wanting to go out nather. I want my liberty, and like to stay at home no better than her ladyship, and sure its me that's been at work all day, and not herself.[87]

Elizabeth wants a real day off for socializing: "Girls, its Sundays we are to have to ourselves. Sure six days is enough to work, and the seventh that belongs to us. Faith! it is so pleasant to wake up Sunday morning, and hurry off to Jem O'Doolie's at the crossroads. Isn't it the six miles' walk we enjoy? Isn't it a glorious time we have, eating and drinking, and telling all that's happened during the week back, and isn't it here that we finish off the evening, and have a shindy wid the boys, arrah!"[88] If, at this distance, the appeal of Elizabeth's words seems to rise above the author's intentions to the contrary, we need only consult the chapter heading to remind ourselves that such attitudes toward leisure as a right were considered "evil counsels." *Harper's Bazar* noted the hardness of the domestic's lot in terms that were frank but thoroughly unsympathetic: "A servant's work, it is said, is never done potentially if ever actually; she is liable to be rung up at all hours; her very meals are not secure from interruption, and even her sleep is not sacred. All this sounds very dreadful, but it really only comes to this, that a servant who is engaged to answer the bell is expected to come when it rings."[89] No longer hired to do certain work, domestics were engaged to "answer the bell," the same symbol of work discipline that tolled in the factory. When domestic supervision imitated the factory's, by being geared to time rather than task, it created a nearly impossible work situation, for the domestic's time was completely at her employer's command. All of life threatened to become one endless workday. In the name of perfecting control over servants' behavior and thus "improving" them, employer supervision tended to eliminate the time and the space for domestics' private lives. No wonder domestics responded with the sauciness, resistance, and high turnover of which employers so often complained.

The scientific management that proved relatively successful in industry was less successful in the home. Few households offered possibilities for increased division of labor since the number of domestics was small and relatively fixed, and domestics were already among the lowest-paid unskilled workers. Because the work could not be subdivided, it was not really possible for employers to appropriate the knowledge involved in the work. The cook would learn to cook, not just, for example, to peel potatoes; thus she would be equipped, like Chek Sau, to contest supervisory control. Uncontested control of work and workplace would prove difficult enough for industrial managers to achieve, although they could rely on leisure time as an ally, since it provided workers a chance to recuperate from heightened work discipline. The fact that domestics lived in, supervision controlling them twenty-four hours a day, assured that their resistance would be fierce and unending. For domestics, leisure became a bone of contention in its own right. Finally, it was not possible for women to solve their supervisory problems as capitalists solved theirs, by recruiting a professional corps of managers. In industry managers might justify their salaries through increases in productivity, but in the home "upper servants" were just one more expense, not to mention a threat to the housekeeper's claim to the work ethic. Supervisory expertise therefore had to be achieved rather than delegated.

Despite all its frustrations, household supervision provided middle-class women a challenging field for activity and social authority, probably helping to prepare middle-class women for the domination of nineteenth-century charitable activities through their voluntary benevolent groups and for the significant roles they played in founding the so-called helping professions during the Progressive era.[90] Unlike supervision in male-dominated industry, where the profit motive made the pretense to benevolence more difficult to sustain, domestic supervision required exacting approved, "improved" behavior from lower-class individuals not for profit but for a combination of the supervisor's convenience and the worker's own "good." It therefore anticipated the style and the aims of social work in the welfare state.

Supervision's Problems Addressed: Cooperative Housekeeping

The problems of domestic supervision could teach feminist lessons. Although middle-class women liked to compare their supervisory roles to those of male entrepreneurs and managers, their situation bore more similarity to the foreman's. Some exercised power arbitrarily because they were less concerned with output than with personal aggrandizement. And just as a foreman could be overruled by owners or upper management, so women had to answer to husbands when dinners were late or buttons popped off. One fictional husband cursed the cook and his own wife at the same time: "She [the cook] is a fool, and I always knew it. Nobody but a simpleton would ever have engaged such a girl!"[91] Theodore Tilton badgered his wife about her household arrangements and expenses and put her in the impossible position of trying to get her domestics to meet his erratic demands. At one meal he said he wanted no more coffee or tea or pastry on the table, and at the next meal he angrily demanded a cup of coffee and a piece of pie. He ordered breakfast for eight o'clock and appeared at ten, angry because his beefsteak was by then dried out.[92] Faced with these frustrating realities, many middle-class women lent their attention to a proposal that built upon the conditions of domestic supervision in order to transform them, cooperative housekeeping.

Cooperative housekeeping began in the late 1860s as the brainstorm of Melusina Fay Peirce, wife of Harvard philosopher Charles Sanders Peirce.[93] "Zena" Peirce unveiled cooperative housekeeping in a series of five articles in the *Atlantic Monthly* in 1868 and 1869, and major metropolitan newspapers here and abroad reported on and discussed her proposals.[94] Several groups hastened to try her plan for centralizing most housework—including cooking, laundry, and sewing—in cooperative workrooms. Peirce herself organized the original Cambridge Cooperative Housekeeping Society, composed largely of the wives of Harvard faculty and other Cambridge luminaries.[95] After her Cambridge experiment failed due to what she later called "husband-power," Peirce traveled in Europe, spreading her ideas and gathering new inspiration from European experiments in socialist cooperation.

Mary Livermore, editor of the *Woman's Journal*, helped to make sure the cooperative housekeeping idea was not forgotten. On the subject of "modern housekeeping," *The Woman's Journal* wondered in 1870, "Where is Mrs. Peirce's 'Cooperative Housekeeping,' which was so big a star of hope in the horizon of distressed housekeepers, a year or more ago?" Whatever fate had befallen the first group, the editors declared, "We still have faith in the plan and believe it practicable."[96] Mary Peabody Mann's committee on cooperative kitchens led the New England Women's Club into an extensive discussion and debate on the subject. A speaker at the First Women's Congress in 1873 urged that cooking and laundry be banished from the home, and Peirce herself addressed the Fourth Women's Congress in 1876 on cooperative housekeeping.[97]

The idea enjoyed a renewed vogue in the 1880s, thanks to the publication of Peirce's *Cooperative Housekeeping* in 1884 and the vision of a society with no housework offered by Edward Bellamy in *Looking Backward* (1888). Late in life, Melusina Fay Peirce would complain, with some justice, that Bellamy and Charlotte Perkins Gilman had stolen her ideas. In tracing the cooperative housekeeping idea, Dolores Hayden has shown that Gilman stood heir to a long tradition of proposals to move housework out of the home.[98] Hayden also shows that cooperative housekeeping was no sectarian enthusiasm limited to a few feminists or socialists. Everywhere women looked they saw the promise and the power of organization, whether in industry, in apartment hotels, or in the Civil War's Sanitary Commission, and many concluded that the reorganization of household work after such models might solve their problems more directly than the ballot. In 1869 *Arthur's Home Magazine* ran a notice reprinted from the *Brooklyn Union* of cooperative housekeeping's main principles, terming them "practicable" proposals in an area where reform was "imperatively demanded."[99] In 1871 an editorial on women's work in *Harper's Bazar* reviewed the difficulties of women with complex households and inept servants, and declared without prelude, apparently confident the reader would understand the reference: "For ourselves, we are free to say that the surest help out of the darkness which we see is in the adoption of the Cambridge plan of associated kitchens."[100] When the New York *Daily Tribune* reviewed Peirce's book in 1884, the editors commended her "sensible suggestions," likely to be "at no distant day the basis of a domestic reform."[101] Even writers who did not favor cooperative housekeeping knew of the scheme and often felt obliged to define their objections to it. Between 1869 and the 1920s, women in dozens of American cities and towns organized functioning cooperative housekeeping associations.[102]

As Peirce explained the idea in her original *Atlantic* articles, the matrons of perhaps three dozen families in a neighborhood would unite to form an association. The association would provide them and their families with food—both supplies and cooked meals—and clothing—both sewing and laundry—out of a central kitchen and workroom. The cooperative matrons would each purchase a share in the cooperative for one hundred dollars to provide start-up capital and then buy all their family needs from the cooperative at retail prices. In Rochdale fashion, they would accumulate dividends or profits on every expenditure. The central kitchen, store, and laundry would save them "all the expense and house-room of separate cooking and washing conveniences, all the waste of ignorant and unprincipled servants and sewing women, all the dust, steam and smell from the kitchen, and all the fatigue and worry of mind occasioned by having the thousand details of an elaborate modern housekeeping and dress to remember and provide for." [103]

Association members who were particularly inclined toward household management could be employed as the managers of the workrooms, for which they would receive salaries comparable to those of managers in industry. They would supervise the work performed by the association's employees—former cooks, laundresses, and seamstresses. These workers would enjoy the benefits of an eight-hour day and a healthful environment. Such division and organization of labor, together with economies of scale, would ensure higher standards at lower costs. Instead of a cook in every family, half of them incompetent, a few of the best cooks would prepare delightful meals for all the cooperators under the aegis of the gourmet authority Professor Blot. Meals would be delivered hot and ready to serve to the several blocks covered by the association.

The chief virtue of cooperation lay not so much in better and cheaper housekeeping results as in reordering the roles of women. Those among the cooperators who wished to do so could find well-paid, respectable work as directresses and supervisors, realizing in fact the entrepreneurial tendencies of domestic supervision. Others would be freed from domestic duties to devote themselves to self-cultivation and accomplishment. Peirce speculated at length on this, predicting that the release of so many educated women whose talents were buried under home duties would bring wonderful results in art, music, literature, medicine, architecture, and the law. This reorganization of labor could even make the struggle for suffrage unnecessary: by taking control of what Peirce called the distributive sector of the economy, women would achieve real power, so that their own women's congresses would be respected and effective.[104]

As Peirce proposed it, cooperative housekeeping's justification lay in the choices it would open for educated middle class women; its method in adjusting their supervisory relationship with their domestics. By changing the locale and organization of most housework, domestics could be in effect changed into or exchanged for ordinary wageworkers. The benevolent impulse in domestic supervision would be more fully realized, for these workers would be better off than most working women, enjoying an eight-hour day, for example. Since little work would remain in the home, service there could be reduced in most cases to hiring a live-out cleaning woman for a few hours each week. The workers in a cooperative would also be more subject to rational work discipline than domestics. In an important passage Peirce emphasized how cooperative housekeeping would "almost entirely blot out from our domestic life the SERVANT ELEMENT!"

Those outrageous little kingdoms of insubordination, ignorance, lying, waste, sloth, carelessness and dirt, that we unhappy housequeens have to subdue afresh every day, and every day more unsuccessfully, will all be merged as the good-for-nothing little German states are being swallowed by Prussia into a thoroughly organized, well-balanced despotism, whose every department is arranged, down to its minutiae, with the most scrupulous exactness, and where lynx-eyed matrons and officers have nothing else to do but to note that each servant does exactly the right thing at the right moment, and knows the place for everything and puts everything in its place.[105]

As the tone of this passage makes clear, much of the appeal of cooperative housekeeping lay in its promise to transform the supervision of domestics into a more thorough, systematic, and profitable form of control over the same workers. Peirce speculated that cooperative housekeeping might extend to all levels of society, but she assured her *Atlantic* readers that "the amount of the admission fee, like the pew rent of our churches, will decide the character of each cooperative association." [106] She did not explain how the division of labor in the central workroom would be arranged among women who ordinarily did all of their own housework. Would one or two of a group of working-class women or farm wives attempt to assume a "lynx-eyed" despotism over fellow cooperators? [107]

In a letter to George Eliot in 1869, Peirce emphasized the central role of the employer-servant relationship in her conception. She told Eliot of her *Atlantic* articles and of the Cambridge group just getting under way: "Such is the disorganization of the old relationship of mistress and servant in this country, that there are already eight towns where women are waiting only to see us get fairly started here, to attempt the same thing themselves." [108] Mary Livermore and *The Woman's Journal* read cooperative housekeeping in the same way, as a direct outgrowth of servant supervision and problems with it. The *Woman's Journal* declared that the hope for cooperative housekeeping lay with "the present Bridgets of the kitchen": "Only let them persist for a few years longer in their unreasonable exactions, in their unthrift and unteachable ignorance, in their despotic domination, and in carrying elements of barbarism into the houses where they are employed, and light will come out of this darkness. The evil will cure itself, for it will become so sore that cooperative housekeeping, in some form or many forms, will be a necessity." [109] Domestics themselves understood that cooperative housekeeping was aimed at them. In 1890 a well-financed cooperative housekeeping association failed in Evanston, Illinois when the servants of the cooperators formed a league and went on strike. They understood that, as Hayden puts it, cooperative housekeeping "meant a 'speed-up' for some, and a layoff for others." [110] The rationale for the program of cooperative housekeeping was based squarely on the comparability of male and female supervision. Peirce proposed to perfect that comparability in order to make women's supervision yield profit and power, while continuing its distinctly benevolent style. It was precisely the question of the degree to which cooperative housekeeping could or should emulate a capitalist or entrepreneurial model that would furnish the main point of debate among its many and diverse adherents over several decades.

In her original proposals of 1869, Peirce displayed considerable ambivalence about the capitalist, as opposed to the supervisory, aspects of cooperative housekeeping. Despite the obvious influence of socialist ideas and experiments on her proposals, she tended to use the term *cooperative* as synonymous with conglomeration, often expressing envy of and enthusiasm for capitalist accomplishments.[111] Others who considered her proposals quickly realized that raising sufficient capital would be a critical problem for cooperators. As early as 1870, *The Woman's Journal* noted that cooperative kitchens would require "expensive machinery, steam apparatus, ranges, ovens, wagons for transporting meals to and fro"; hence, "the improvement must be initiated by men . . . not because of any inferiority of capacity in women but because women have not the capital to set in operation such a system."[112] By 1876 Peirce herself had concluded that the fatal flaw in her original plan lay in the fact that matrons did not have independent incomes, so could not contribute needed start-up capital without the approval of their husbands. She told the Fourth Women's Congress that cooperating women must therefore limit themselves at first to a store on the strict Rochdale model, with no salaries for managers. The cooperators would have to begin from benevolent motives alone and work without pay until they could accumulate, through their Rochdale dividends, the capital needed to undertake the more ambitious parts of cooperation.[113] Peirce's European trip seemed to stimulate her concern for working-class women, and she revised her cooperative housekeeping proposal further to stipulate that the employees of the cooperative association be required to become shareholders as well.[114] She now saw gender differences as more fundamental than class differences and attempted to redraw her scheme to lessen dependence upon middle-class husbands and build opportunities for working-class women, including former servants. Hayden shows that one wing of the material feminist tradition carried on in this vein, pressing for collectivized housework as part of a socialist reordering of society in general or working to apply it to meet the pressing needs of working women.[115]

Other partisans of cooperation saw little reason to wait until women had accumulated their own capital; like *The Woman's Journal*, they urged turning to male capitalists. At the 1876 Women's Congress Anna Garlin Spencer, disagreeing with Peirce, took this side of the question. Speaking on "The Organization of Household Labor," she declared, "Cooperative housekeeping schemes which have been presented to the public require large money capital and the highest kind of associate action for their realization; hence the practical difficulty in their way." She proposed to encourage individual entrepreneurs to make "a definite business" of each component of housework.[116]

In the 1890s Helen Stuart Campbell would reject the idea of cooperation but call for the organization of housework through "combination in a business sense and with business methods."[117] It remained for Charlotte Perkins Gilman to develop and publicize this vision most thoroughly. In her novel *What Diantha Did*, Gilman would picture a shrewd businesswoman and a benevolent female capitalist combining to organize housework into an industry. The heroine, Diantha Bell, explicitly dismisses "that often-repeated foredoomed failure called cooperative housekeeping"; her own operation is a business, returning ten percent on investment to her wealthy backer.[118] Eventually many women who were frustrated by middle-class domesticity "redefined cooperative housekeeping in favor of social housekeeping" and attacked the problems of supervision as home economists or social workers, developing programs to recruit and train working women to be more efficient domestic servants and good citizens.[119]

If the proposals of cooperative housekeeping demonstrate how much servant supervision made nineteenth-century middle-class women's roles comparable to those of the men of their class, its difficulties turned precisely on the limited but decisive points of difference. Cooperative housekeeping failed because most employers failed to rally to a proposal for radical change. As Hayden points out, cooperative housekeeping experimenters found that it "did not pay," since economies of scale could seldom outweigh the cheapness of unpaid and ill-paid women's household labor. The enthusiasts of cooperative housekeeping tended to be most interested in the possibility of escaping household duties altogether; thus their personal dedication flagged in the face of a laborious effort to begin the experiment without needed capital. Those who continued to believe in reorganizing household service work began to think that housework should be adapted to the organizational principle of the economy at large, the profit motive. Placing their faith in a capitalist reorganization of household work, they withdrew from utopian experiments, but capitalists proved to be less than eager to organize household work into industries. Probably because service work involves inherent limits to productivity and hence relatively low profit margins, entrepreneurs preferred to substitute commodities for services wherever possible. Technical innovations of the late nineteenth and early twentieth century, most notably the small electric motor, lent themselves to profit possibilities in selling goods, not services. Entrepreneurs manufactured washing machines, for example, rather than organizing the laundry industry.[120]

Women's persistent enthusiasm for cooperative housekeeping testified to the way in which the organization of the middle-class household could shape feminist goals as well as the ideology of domesticity. The division of labor between a housekeeper-supervisor and her domestics suggested the possibility of a further reorganization of the household in which housework would be collectivized and supervision perfected in the interest of freeing women. The disappearance of live-in domestic service from the middle-class home in the twentieth century seems to have made it more difficult to imagine ways in which household labor might be reorganized collectively outside the home, now that household work and personal life are collapsed into one undifferentiated woman's "role."

In the 1960s a few radicals would experiment with communal living, but recent feminists' solutions to the dilemmas of private household work have tended to revolve around demands that men begin to share household burdens, while day care, fast food, and household conveniences reduce the workload to be divided. Much of contemporary feminism is unabashedly upper-middle-class in its reliance on the paid household labor of poorer women. The cleaning women typical of twentieth-century service do not hold jobs that are "good" by any objective standard, but they are involved in less onerous service than were nineteenth-century domestics. Living out, they are hired for specific hours, and they often perform their work without direct supervision, while the employer is at work or otherwise out of the house. They may also receive vacation pay and Social Security like other workers. Much of the conflict characteristic of nineteenth-century relations between employers and domestics has disappeared.

SIX

A "Girl's" Life and Work

Young women decided whether to help or "work out" by weighing family obligations against school and work opportunities and pecuniary considerations. Eva Beem, for example, was twenty-seven, unmarried, and living at home with her sisters in 1871. Anxious to earn some spending money of her own, she tried sewing and selling patent gadgets, but she did not need to go in search of opportunities in household service. "There was a man up here to hire a girl," she wrote in January 1871, after her sister Nancy had agreed to work for George Ward that summer for two dollars a week. Eva did not take the first job offered: "I stoped [*sic*] into Mr. Minneahs and he wanted to kill me for eighteen shillings a week." Making a better bargain with Mr. and Mrs. Stout for three dollars a week, she went to work for them in April and stayed until September. As she was leaving, a Mrs. Adams "came and brought Mrs. Stout's new hired girl." [1] The job could have continued, but Eva had made her purchases and was growing restless. Helping did not require leaving school; in fact, helping made it possible for some girls to attend school when they would otherwise have found it too expensive or too far from home. Elizabeth Miller, born in 1848 in West Newbury, Vermont, had an offer to go to her uncle's home and attend school there, but her mother was ill: "I've got to stay with Mother. She needs me." [2] Some girls, Sally Rice, for example, found in helping grounds on which to elude or reject family preferences and to begin considering alternative forms of work.

But in general the sporadic and temporary nature of helping seems to have accurately reflected its function; it was not the prime concern of the young women who moved in and out of it casually while holding family, friends, school, and beaux as their priorities.

Helping cannot have been leisurely for hired girls who had to keep pace with hard-working employers like Phebe Eastman or Jane Bewel Kelly. But it was similar to their work at home and its human context made it varied. The hired girls in the Rundlett family became the companions of the Rundletts' daughter Belle. One hot July day in 1867, Belle wrote, "Terry the hired girl and I went a strawberying in the fare woods in the afternoon. . . . we got a good many." When Belle's mother was away, she and Anna Gorman, another hired girl, seemed to enjoy running the household: "Got up early. Anna mopped and we had a fine time."[3] Grace Goddard, a hired girl in Massachusetts in 1848, wrote of her relationship with the children of the Shedd family: "I could not wish a better place if it were not for the little plagues."[4] Like any kind of acquaintanceship, helping could stir conflict or conviviality. A girl who helped got out of the house, got to know some people outside the family, and earned some spending money. If she went far enough, she might attend a different church or meet young men whom she would not have met at home. But this interlude was largely a variant upon helping her own mother and a prelude to her own work as wife and mother and indeed hirer of help. Working as a domestic, by contrast, was a distinctively harsh formative experience.

"A Hard and Lonely Life"

A woman needed robust good health to be a domestic. Employers who hired older women felt obliged to assert that they were "strong" or of "good constitution."[5] Many former domestics would cite physical exhaustion as their reason for quitting. One maid quit because she was just tired: "She said she had been doing housework for several years, and she always noticed that after a girl had kept at it long she broke down, and then she was no use to herself or anyone else." [6] When the New York *Express* deplored the fact that women would remain in the wretchedness of needlework rather than take up the "light work and kind appreciation" to be found in domestic service, Parker Pillsbury responded declaratively: "The work is never 'comparatively light' in genteel households. Never." [7] The wretchedness of needlewomen, Mathew Carey pointed out, was a consequence of the fact that many women who were too ill or feeble or old to do the heavy work of service tried to earn what little they could by sewing. [8] One employer referred to a girl who "had got quite overworked in the large family (one of my neighbors) where she had lived three years." She was reported to be "resting a few weeks" before she could take another position. [9] In 1848 Jane Aiken of Auburn, New York informed a prospective employer that she was engaged to work for a Mrs. Rathburn, but she held out a possibility: "She should be able to tell in the course of a week whether she should be able to do the work—I believe the family is large and they keep but one girl." [10] Even Lillian Pettengill, the Mount Holyoke graduate who would investigate service at the turn of the twentieth century and praise it as "heathful" work, had to admit that when she worked as a domestic her hands became so tired and sore that she could scarcely move them in the mornings. [11]

Domestics not only worked hard but had to accept severe limitations in their daily lives. Choices about food had narrowed since the domestic did not eat at the same table with her employer and thus had lost the ability to communicate her likes and dislikes informally. Although she ate separately, she did not enjoy the privileges of privacy. Her food was chosen for her. If she worked for employers influenced by dietary reformers, she might find coffee and tea forbidden or restricted. [12] The Irish Catholic domestics who worked for Rachel Proctor were permitted eggs but not fish on fast days. Mrs. Proctor also forbade them cabbages and onions, remarking that it was "disagreeable" to be waited on by those who had been eating onions.[13] Some employers provided a separate menu for their servants but one that was less elaborate than the family's own, perhaps even miserly. Domestics had to prepare and serve delicacies they could not share. In most households the domestic would eat the remains of the family meal, which might be cold and perhaps inadequate for a hearty appetite. When some domestics over-indulged in leftover pies and cakes, their employers, indignant over this unconscionable excess, forbade all desserts.[14] Domestics' mealtimes were seldom a time for relaxation since they were never free from the threat of interruption.

Nor did domestics enjoy space they could call their own. Some slept in "windowless garrets," unheated in winter and stifling in summer; others worked for employers who provided no separate room at all and expected them to sleep on a cot in the kitchen.[15] One woman recalled a servants' room over the kitchen, "hot and close in summer, and cold in winter," where there were four beds for five girls and just two bureaus and one washstand for all.[16] The maid in the Hooker family in Rochester was luckier than most when she found an iron bedstead in a freshly painted room.[17]

Employers even tried to control their domestics' clothing and appearance. Anastasia Dowling, a domestic in Buffalo in 1870, did not allow her occupation to hamper her desire to dress well; on the contrary, she triumphantly wrote home to Ireland to assure her friends that in America "There is no end to fassions."[18] A few of the wealthiest employers affected European-style liveries and uniforms, but many could do no more than fret or scold about clothing that looked impractical or presumptuous. Some employers did manage to stipulate that their domestics wear a cap and apron, or cotton dresses at work. Chambermaids in the Proctor household had to wear black dresses in the evenings, with white collar, cuffs, and apron. The cook did not have to wear black but did have to don an apron should she have occasion to answer the door.[19] The domestics of one fictional housekeeper were required to wear calico gowns—because woolen ones absorbed perspiration and became "unpleasant"—and caps—because covering the hair was "hygienic." They might crimp their hair but not wear curl-papers in the kitchen or at work. And they were instructed to take a bath twice a week and to wear separate night clothes, not their underclothing, to bed.[20]

Given the limitations on the strictly physical side of life, domestics had every reason to fasten upon emotional ties and human contact. Naturally their employers preferred domestics who were "the very quiet kind, never wanting to leave the place unless it is very necessary."[21] But young girls, many of them separated for the first time from family lives of dense sociability, found the isolation of domestic service extremely painful.[22] Of course, domestics who were thrown together might keep one another company. One young girl described the scene in her grandmother's kitchen: three servants sat around the table, each with a candle, and one read aloud while the other two sewed.[23] It is probably significant that the two middle-class women who worked as domestics and wrote about it, Louisa May Alcott in *Work* and Lillian Pettengill in *Toilers of the Home*, emphasized how important it was to work alongside sympathizing fellow servants, captured for their readers in the characters of Hepsey and Freida. Like working women in other settings, domestics tried to find work where relatives or friends were already established, both to ease the process of finding or starting at a new place and to make the work pass more pleasantly.[24] But this was harder to arrange in service than in larger shops or factories. Helen Campbell's 1887 investigation of poverty quoted a native-born chambermaid who complained of having to associate with a cook and waitress who were "just common, uneducated Irish." "I had to room with one and stand the personal habits of both."[25] In 1860, two of Caroline Barrett White's domestics were "at swords point" and did not speak except to bicker and taunt each other. Hannah Wright Gould found the English and Irish on her staff "fighting about the Queen of England and the

Pope of Rome!" As often happened, she had to dismiss one of them to restore the peace.[26]

Most domestics toiled alone, and isolation was greatest for the maid-of-all-work who shouldered the heaviest workload at the lowest pay. Three-quarters of the domestics in Providence in 1855 worked in single-servant households, as had 45 percent in Boston in 1845.[27] Isolation was especially hard on immigrants. One girl of seventeen had been in America five months and still could claim "no friends excepting one aunt." There must have been many who felt like the girl who worked for Almira Porter in 1840: she was "terrible homesick and means to go back to 'sweet Ireland' as soon as she earns the means."[28] Girls in this position strove to maintain ties with home. Johannah, working for the Graves family in Syracuse in 1849, yearned to go down to the depot to meet briefly with a Mrs. Daly, "her old friend, who has news from Ireland for her." She had to wait until Saturday to do so, and then could go only if her employer could "spare" her.[29] Many young women thought service in the country "too dull," but going out of the city was reportedly a real "bugbear" for "most Irish girls," because of the lack of opportunity for sociability.[30] Isolation was even more total for German girls who did not speak English; hence their preference for working for German-speaking employers, or at least for working together in pairs or for staying in metropolitan areas with German-speaking communities. Two young German women, cousins, arrived in New York City in 1852. One was an orphan, and the other had lost her father and left her mother behind in Germany. They searched for the brother of one, but they found he had gone to Canada, and they lacked the means to follow him there. They were receptive when the Reverend J. C. Guldin offered to place them in service: they had been in service "at home" and were recommended by pious persons who knew them there. But the girls backed out when they discovered that Rev. Guldin wanted to send them to a rural area among people who spoke no German.[31]

"The girls usually like to be where they can easily get together," wrote one employer from Ithaca, New York, explaining why girls preferred to be downtown rather than on the Cornell "hill."[32] Harriet Prescott Spofford noted that the Irish girls of a neighborhood would regularly gather in one or another kitchen for an evening's visit. Many employers would forbid such groups in their homes, assuming the refreshments would be furnished out of their larder, and even employers like Spofford, who permitted such gatherings, disliked them. Spofford resented being unable to go into her own kitchen in the evening without seeing half a dozen strange faces frowning at the interruption, seeming critical and ready to gossip, "making you an exile from your own hearth."[33] The cellar of a brownstone was apt to be small and dank, a poor spot in which to receive friends, and in close urban settings the neighbors might object if domestics sat on the back or side porch. Employers expected to detect no evidence of entertaining—no noise drifting upstairs, certainly not the use of any tea or bread and butter to serve the guests. "That Carrie Collins bears a rather hard name—for wildness and using provisions. I will tell you when she lived with Miss Conrad she had another with her like-minded and they moved pretty fast. They used to have oyster suppers and use Miss C's bread and butter."[34] Socializing was in itself suspect: one employer referred to her domestic as a doubtful case on the grounds that "she seems young and loves society."[35] Another domestic who "had a good deal of company" was told "the folly of it" by her employer and "seemed to be determined to reform."[36] Elizabeth Sullivan Stuart declared flatly that she would not keep a girl who wished to give or go to parties.[37]

Because entertaining within the employer's walls was subject to so many strictures, domestics sought to get out when they could. Children's nurses had an excuse for a daily outing, which might include the opportunity to meet and gossip with other domestics. Others had to wait to "rush abroad at the first opportunity and stay till the last moment."[38] In the nineteenth-century "walking city," where most people traveled less than a mile from home to workplace, domestics might find themselves far from family or friends in an unfamiliar neighborhood.[39] Some employers were wise enough to grant their domestics a week or two of vacation, for visiting. One domestic took two weeks off when her brother was married.[40] Others were able to leave only in cases of family emergency, and naturally they were tempted to slip away without leave or to overstay what was supposed to be only a brief visit.[41] Mary, who cooked for the Wheaton family, was told she could not be spared on Saturday, but when Mrs. Wheaton was out of the house Mary slipped off to see her family, leaving a promise to return on Monday. She did not return until Tuesday evening, when Mrs. Wheaton would have fired her if there had not been guests arriving.[42] Susan Brown Forbes did fire Kate Quinn after she "went out PM and again this eve without leave"; it was nine o'clock at night when Kate was sent on her way.[43]

Employers were simply unwilling to permit extended absences, so domestics promised short ones, often reconsidering once they were away, as did the girl who "asked to go up and see her sister and did not come back."[44] Often they had their reasons; girls frequently quit to get a place nearer their relations.[45] But they judged correctly that employers would have been unsympathetic to a frank explanation. Martha Jarvis, who worked for Susan Brown Forbes in Springfield, went off on a boatride one Sunday afternoon in June 1867 and did not return. Mrs. Forbes concluded it was "all planned ahead," as indeed it probably was, for Martha's husband was coming out of jail.[46] Domestics like Martha knew that employers fumed about "exactions" on their time for visiting relatives, and they preferred to avoid scenes or browbeating by offering acceptable stories. Illness was a good story, though overworked. "Margaret was to return to me in three weeks when she left me," wrote Clara Dodge of Burlington, Iowa, "but her family have all been sick and she has not as yet come back."[47] When Maggie Sullivan complained of feeling ill and left the Forbes household to see a doctor, Mrs. Forbes solicitously told her not to hurry, but she grew angry after sitting up until eleven o'clock. Maggie did not return until late the next day, saying that the doctor had found her "near" fever and forbidden her to work. Mrs. Forbes concluded Maggie had actually been frightened by her purchase of several bushels of peaches and plums for a stint of canning and had secured "some other place in town."[48]

Employers did not always approve of their domestics' leisure time activities. Irish domestics came from a background in which liquor was an ordinary part of conviviality, and the confinement and the hard work of service made it tempting to nip surreptitiously in the kitchen or to go "on a spree" during time off.[49] "The greatest curse of servants is that love of drink," wrote Nettie Fowler McCormick. "I have no end of trials with our servants." Few could manage the tolerant tone of Susan Hooker, who wrote of her domestic, "Once in a while she drinks but otherwise she is a splendid girl."[50] In a letter home to County Donegal, a young girl who had just entered service in Iowa in 1889 delivered her opinion of prohibition: "This country is not as good as it was, they are not aloud to sell no more liquor in the state of Iowa."[51] Kate Carey had to testify to a checkered employment record because she had so often been dismissed for drinking. Had one employer dismissed her for lying? "No. Nothing but 'toxicated. I told her I wasn't 'tight' and I was 'tight.'"[52]

Through the long days and weeks of work domestics could look forward to holidays. The Fourth of July was a favorite holiday. Kitty Graves's Johannah and another domestic were reported eager for the day in 1849, "making great calculations on the fun they will have."[53] But servants could not always count on gaining time off from employers absorbed in their own holiday plans. Mary Adams, who looked after Nettie Fowler McCormick's children, yearned to be with her parents and brothers and sisters on New Year's Eve, 1862, "but denied that is contented," or so Mrs. Mc-Cormick thought.[54] For Caroline Barrett White's cook, Thanksgiving was not a holiday but a lot of extra work and she was probably treated to a dressing down the years she burned the plum pudding and spoiled the oysters.[55] Domestics claimed Christmas most insistently of all, sometimes overstaying the stingy time allotments granted by their employers.[56] Caroline Barrett White once referred to her servants as "spending the holiday away from home," but in fact they had gone home.[57] One year Caroline Barrett White was prevailed upon to allow her domestics St. Patrick's Day off.[58] But many domestics had to work through holidays, perhaps consoling themselves with thoughts of a family celebration too far away to visit. Irish girls sent the bulk of all their remittances back to Ireland at Christmas and Easter.[59]

If domestics did get out of the house on festive days, it might well have been to go to church, to mass on Christmas or to a church picnic on the Fourth of July.[60] Irish and German Catholics in service were accustomed to the traditions of "Tridentine" Catholicism, emphasizing the observance of sacraments, devotional practices, and confession. Church law required them to attend mass on Sunday and other special feast days, and those who were absent without a strong reason committed a mortal sin.[61] Maggie, who worked for Susan Hooker in Rochester and took her religion seriously, in February 1869 "changed her seat" from St. Mary's to St. Bridget's Church, and in April she was greatly fatigued, having "fasted so much during Lent she could hardly stand up."[62] It was difficult for most Catholic domestics to maintain these observances. Some got up long before daylight to attend mass and still be home in time to cook breakfast.[63] Others were able to obtain time off for their religion: one domestic was described as a "strict Catholic" who "wants most all of the Sundays to go to her Church." Domestics who worked for Rachel Proctor could leave the house on a Saturday night to go to confession, but only for a short time and only for that purpose.[64]

Some employers were hostile to Catholicism, but they were apt to find their domestics stood firm on this point. Historians of immigration have agreed that the Catholic church actually gained participation and prestige because it was one of the few institutions that followed migrants across the Atlantic.[65] Even if they had not previously been notably pious, domestics had especially strong reasons to honor the religious observances that spoke to them of home. Other ethnic customs may have been similarly reinforced. Lonely and far from her loved ones, "Irish Katy" sat up all night at her cousin's wake. She had to walk five miles back to her employer's house before breakfast, and though the snow lay thick on the ground, she did not complain.[66] German Protestant girls were reported unwilling to go into the country "away from their meetings," for "though they were Protestants, they could not understand [the] language enough to hear preaching."[67]

Vulnerable Workers

The harshness of life in service meant that it was often the occupation of last resort, gathering in those who struggled to find ways to support themselves along the fringes of destitution or dependency. As one of the very few forms of women's work that permitted unskilled women to be continuously self-supporting, domestic service enlisted women who were entirely on their own, whose family economies had been broken or destroyed. Such young women faced a labor market that provided them little or no choice: for women who could not be teachers, in areas where there were no factory jobs, domestic service was practically the only alternative.

Service recruited some women who were mentally or physically handicapped. One turn of the century probation officer referred to a young woman of "limited intelligence" as lacking "mind enough" to do factory work: "housework is all there is for her."[68] A Pennsylvania employer referred to her domestic's only fault as "lack of intelligence."[69] Eliza Woodson Farnham encountered a one-handed maid and a one-eyed cook in frontier Illinois.[70] Mary Dean's article in an 1877 issue of *Lippincott's* was no soberly factual account, but she probably spoke accurately in referring to some hired girls who were so "slow" that they could not tell time and always forgot to put on the kettle.[71] Evidence on these points is elusive: reticence or propriety seems to have prevented the explicit mention of physical handicaps, while employers were so apt to complain of the stupidity of servants as to make it difficult to detect anything unusual. It does seem likely that the transition from help to domestics would have made service more difficult, if not impossible, for handicapped women. A servant who cannot tell time may be useful as a helper, with her employer there to tell her when to put the kettle on, but as a domestic she will be fired for being late with the meals. Mary Heaton Vorse, a labor journalist, sketched a fictional employer who looked over one shy young applicant and declared, "She looks stupid."[72] Demanding punctuality, perhaps depending on written instructions, the employers of domestics had little patience with those who were "lacking in the upper story."[73] One referred to her girl as "a shocking dunce"; another exploded, "Her *dullness* is so provoking!"[74] Emphasis on proper appearances before guests caused employers to reject women who were sloppy or ill-kempt, not to speak of those with outright physical handicaps. Physical disabilities made it especially difficult to keep up with the stringent work discipline domestics faced; a woman with one arm applied for work with Susan Brown Forbes but concluded she could not manage all the work.[75]

Service also enrolled some women who were, apparently, mentally disturbed. A girl who was "a queer piece" but "smart in her way" might make an acceptable servant. But what was an employer to do with a girl who wrote anonymous letters, spread "Paris green" on the neighbors' steps, and tried to burn down the woodshed?[76] She would certainly have sent a hired girl home, but what of a domestic who might not have a family to go to? In August 1853 Ellen Birdseye Wheaton's second girl, Eliza, swallowed bedbug poison, "either thro' anger, fear, or spite," after a severe scolding from the cook, lay desperately ill for two weeks, and finally died. Mrs. Wheaton had pitied the girl, who was an orphan and would, she knew, find it difficult to get another place, and so she had kept Eliza on, although aware that the girl "never . . . had much intellect" and was "not a suitable person to have in my family." Mrs. Wheaton was pained to think of the gossip occasioned by the suicide and blamed herself for not having dismissed Eliza earlier.[77] Some employers took the initiative in seeking institutionalization for disturbed domestics, but most probably just sent them packing. Ellen Dwyer has found that the women admitted to the New York State asylums for the insane at Utica and Willard between 1843 and 1890 included disproportionately large numbers of foreign-born young women who had worked in domestic service. They were commonly reported to have lapsed into depression or become erratic and violent.[78]

Lacking experience other than in housework, married women whose husbands had died or deserted them often turned to service, and some even struggled to keep their children with them. Perhaps a child might have been useful on a farm, but hiring a domestic with a child seemed an unwelcome burden to most prospective employers, who fell into calculations about schooling and supervision for the child.[79] In the life of a well-supervised domestic there could be little time for child care, even when employers meant well. Emerson witnessed a "little tragedy" in May 1842. "An Irish woman with a babe of seven weeks came to live with us as cook on Monday;" he wrote in a letter, "her babe seemed very ill from want of early attention, and though Lidian and indeed the whole house, chiefly Louisa [the chambermaid] gave it all care and watching it died on Saturday." The mother hurried the little body into a bandbox, he wrote, and took the afternoon coach to Boston in search of a priest and a Catholic burial.[80] The Rochester Home for the Friendless placed a Mrs. Chesney in a situation with her child in 1853 where "she was much prized by her employers, who said she did more work with the child than most girls without one." At her next job, her employers discovered how Mrs. Chesney managed this feat; they dismissed her for being cruel to the child.[81]

More commonly, women whose marriages had failed had to give up their children in order to enter domestic service, leaving them with relatives, boarding them, or binding them out. After Margaret Connally arrived at the Rochester Home for the Friendless in February 1856, she left her nine-year-old to board at the home for fifty cents a week while she went into service. In 1851 a Mrs. Hall arrived at the home with her sixteen-month-old daughter. The matron recorded that Mrs. Hall "calls herself a grass widow as her husband being a drinker and gambler had left her. She has three little boys in the Orphan Asylum." After several unsuccessful attempts at service while keeping the baby with her, Mrs. Hall finally left her daughter with a sister and, having lost all four of her children, took a place in service alone.[82] When Mary Stebbins called at the Springfield, Massachusetts Home for the Friendless in March 1873, her husband had left her and she was expecting a child. The managers of the home helped her find work in service and assured her they could place the child when the time came. Similarly, a woman named Libbie Reis wrote to Amy Kirby Post in fear that her employer would discover her past when he paid a call on the Posts: "He does not know that I am a married woman nor he does not know that I have got a baby and do not make him any the wiser if you please?" She wished the baby could be with her now: "I would give her some kissing. But that cannot be, no one would employ me with her. Oh how hard-hearted some people are."[83] Another woman in service, aged about twenty-eight, was described in a letter of recommendation as "somewhat old, has been married and had three children. Lost them all, husband dissipated has not seen him for four years and his character is such she don't desire to see him again."[84] Employers found that mothers made distracted domestics. The author of *Plain Talk and Friendly Advice to Domestics* (1855) referred to employing a domestic who was a married woman boarding her child in the neighborhood. The author eventually dismissed the woman because she was "sickly" and "willful about exposing herself to all kinds of weather," doubtless in visiting her child on her time off.[85] At the Anchorage, a home for unwed mothers in Elmira, New York, young women who bore out-of-wedlock babies were placed in service, while the Anchorage kept the infants and their mothers paid weekly board for their care. The institution did this precisely because employers did not want a domestic with a baby, feeling that the baby's care would drain the energy of the worker.[86]

Service also enlisted a number of aging widows who were thrust suddenly onto the job market and tried to convince employers that they were still strong enough to keep up with the work load. Those who still had a family home might do daywork or take in boarders, the proverbial resort of nineteenth-century widows, but women who were without property or children to depend on would likely be reduced to live-in service. In 1855 over 20 percent of the widows in New York's working-class Sixth Ward worked as domestic servants.[87] Some older women, like the Scottish housekeeper Mary Abigail Dodge hired in 1870, found service the final chapter in a lifetime of working-class hardship. "She was burnt out in the Portland fire," Dodge wrote. "Her husband died a week after, has lost four babies, and one son of twenty-five was stabbed in California. . . . When the mills were first started in Salem thirty years ago, she came on from Pawtucket to teach the operatives." The old woman soon found herself on the move again, as Dodge found her amiable, but hopelessly sloppy, and dismissed her.[88] Hannah Wright Gould discovered that her childbed nurse, Mrs. Kilbourne, could tell a similar story. She had been a widow for sixteen years, after her husband left her to go out west and look for a home and then died there of "the western fever." "She has had ten children," Gould wrote. "One fine lad of seventeen was drowned skating on the Hudson River, another went to sea and has never returned, several died in childhood, and in those who remain the poor woman seems to take little comfort." Mrs. Kilbourne had determined not to be a "burden to her children": "She will work while she can and when she can no longer, she will go to the Old Ladies Asylum near New York."[89] Mrs. E. W. Knapp described herself as "very poor and a sick daughter to support" in 1875, and she wrote to Freeman Clarke, "knowing that you employ many persons in your family." Though "hopeing you will not feel I mention these things in a wrong spirrit," she recalled how she had aided Clark's half-sister nearly thirty years before. She declared she was "very compitent in all domestic matters" and pleaded that she could "do better than your Irish servants."[90]

Single women who remained in service their whole lives found it a struggle to hang on in old age. Irish immigrants were more likely than southern-born blacks to become inmates of almshouses or workhouses in Massachusetts in the late nineteenth century, and one contemporary explained: "Among the Irish there was a large proportion of single immigrant women who come to this country when young and for years probably gain fair employment but small savings. As time passes, employment becomes more difficult to obtain, and having no one to care for them these women find their refuge in the almshouse."[91] The applicants for admission to the Home for Aged Women in Boston in the 1850s and '60s included large numbers of former servants and single women.[92] Aging domestics could seldom expect to be cared for by their employers even if they had given years of service. Kate Gannett Wells was urged by her children to pension off "Mary," but she refused. "Why she may live forty years and I don't love her $4000." In fact Wells did not love Mary at all, for the woman had become cranky and disagreeable—"nihilistic," as she put it. Rejecting the idea of a pension or of hiring a third servant to compensate for Mary's increasing incompetence, Mrs. Wells dismissed her, paying her through the end of the month and giving her fifteen dollars extra. Clearly hoping she might extract further benefits, Mary thanked the family "for kindnesses past, present, and *future*." On her last day Mary wandered upstairs and down, "carrying duds of thirty-seven years," and when she was gone Mrs. Wells exclaimed, "Hallelujah!"[93]

For women who were aged or widowed or handicapped, service must have been an especially hard life, for their particular difficulties left them vulnerable either to exploitation by unscrupulous employers or to dismissal and destitution. As their plight suggests, the meaning of the service experience depended not only upon conditions within service but also upon the situation of the individuals who served, especially upon what sociologists would term their "life course" context—that is, their age and family roles or relationships, including both past experiences and future prospects.

Exits: Changing Jobs, Getting Married, Crime and "Vice"

Not surprisingly, given the conditions of service, working women tended to look for avenues of escape. Employers were often forced to recognize that working women preferred almost any alternative to service, especially as the century wore on and other types of work began to open up to women. In Cohoes, New York in 1881 the local newspaper declared that obtaining competent servants was "next to impossibility," due to the employment available in the cotton mills.[94] In 1872 a housekeeper in Clinton, New York thought it a "remarkable providential blessing" to find a servant available in August when all the other young women wanted to go hop picking. Another matron reported in 1870 that her relatives in Sandusky had been "dreadfully troubled" for servants ever since some vineyards were planted and two big resort hotels built nearby: "Between the Hotels and vineyards, the servants are all taken up and private families suffer."[95] Servant employers in Maine at the turn of the century would report that they lost girls to mills, sardine factories, and summer resorts.[96] In her 1890 study, Lucy Maynard Salmon referred to girls leaving service for more popular seasonal work: resort waitressing, hop picking, berry and grape-picking; work in canning, pickle, and fruit-drying factories.[97]

Young women who entered domestic service regularly left it for marriage, so regularly that one employer referred to a domestic who "was married (of course)."[98] Despite the predictability of this outcome employers were often surprised; many domestics kept their private lives to themselves. "Is it possible that Margaret is going to be married!" exclaimed one employer. "What will not happen next. I don't know that I should be surprised now to hear that I was going to be married myself. I wish Mr. Hennessey joy."[99] Perhaps domestics were prone to hurry into marriage, the burdens of service making any offer seem attractive. Anny, who worked for Hannah Wright Gould, took two days off to see her family at Christmas and returned to announce she was married. "Her story is that Father, Mother, Brother and sister over persuaded her and so she had to."[100] Laura Porter of Philadelphia concluded that her "poor Bridget" had not done "as well by getting married as she expected." Mrs. Porter had made many inquiries in vain: "I am fearful she is somewhere in a retired part of the city and unwilling to acknowledge it."[101] The nature of service work could only have made marriage look like an attractive alternative, for service was economically precarious, socially isolating, and subject to harsh supervision and work discipline. If one was to do housework, how much better it must have seemed to do it for husband and children, in a role that at least promised emotional fulfillment and social authority and respectability. Leslie Tentler has argued that women's factory work in the early twentieth century carried powerful implicit social messages: low wages, long hours, lack of advancement possibilities, and humiliating supervision all tended to make the employment interval in young adulthood a time in which women learned to accept dependence upon male wage earners and a primary focus on domestic roles.[102] Perhaps this thesis is not perfectly convincing as regards twentieth-century factory work, but it certainly applies to nineteenth-century domestic service. And service lacked the one great advantage young women would find in the factories, social freedom and lively personal relations with their peers.[103]

Although service thus implicitly encouraged marriage and withdrawal from the labor force, the restrictions on their time and movement made it difficult for young women in service to meet eligible young men and find marriage partners. Some employers simply declared a "no followers" rule, with the predictable result that a girl had to meet her male friends at street corners or alley gates.[104] Others considered it their prerogative to pass judgment on the domestic's choice of companions. One writer on the subject favored allowing "Bridget" to receive "respectable" male visitors "under regulations of strict morality," but the separation of servants' quarters from the rest of the house made such surveillance difficult in practice and probably helped prompt blanket prohibitions.[105] One employer described the maid as "not inclined to marry" and added, "We have discouraged the set of followers which such a girl usually has in her train."[106] Some employers were pleased to employ "old maid" domestics, "old enough not to have beaux."[107] One maid met her husband, a grocery deliveryman, while in service, but few other male occupations would have entailed contact with domestics. Even without an employer's deliberate hindrance, the labor market could separate couples whose illiteracy made it hard to keep in touch. An employer in Newark, New Jersey found her new German girl crying: "Our beau that lives in New York don't write to us and tears are streaming etc."[108] Some evidence suggests that men discriminated against servant girls in social situations. In 1888 a group of working men in Terre Haute were reported to have "got up some dance parties and they drew a line—at servants! Sales ladies, overall ladies, all might be invited, but not cooks!"[109] Labor reformer Jennie Collins, who had worked in domestic service as well as mill and needle work, was impatient with those who could not appreciate why working women avoided service. At a meeting of the Boston Working-

Woman's Association in 1870 she dismissed the question with a reference to social opportunities: "If a girl goes into the kitchen she is sneered at and called the Bridget, but if she goes behind the counter she is escorted by gentlemen." [110]

Assuming they tended to look first for husbands among their fellow countrymen, the skewed sex ratios among most migrant groups favored a woman's chances to find a husband. In Seattle, for example, young Scandinavian women were heavily concentrated in domestic service, but young single Scandinavian men outnumbered their female counterparts by more than two to one. The major problem then was "where to meet eligible males," and the churches and ethnic clubs filled that function. [111] The Irish were one of the few groups of immigrants in which there was not a distinct excess of males over females. [112] Yet young Irish women apparently understood that migration would enhance their status and their marriage chances: the London *Times* referred to their going to America "in search of service and husbands." They had heard, or would discover, that in America a young woman did not need a dowry to attract a marriage offer. As one young Irish woman pointed out when she wrote home, "Over in Ireland people marry for riches, but here in America we marry for love and work for riches." [113] Some Irish women stayed too long in service sending remittances home to their parents; by their late twenties they were growing too old to find husbands but they could return to Ireland where their savings would enable them to "marry into a farm." [114]

The bleak conditions of life in service together with the unavailability of other "respectable" work prompted some young women to rebel or to make a "disreputable" choice. Numbers of domestics became involved in crime. One social investigator explained, "The opportunity it offers for larceny attracts to domestic service some professional thieves, especially in the larger cities." [115] Some young women gave in to petty theft after being exposed to so many fine things. Yet given the temptations they faced, dishonesty seems to have been unusual and relatively trivial. One servant, for example, stole a chemise and a pair of fine linen pillow cases.[116] More sensational charges linked domestic service and prostitution. The first annual report of the New York Magdalen Society in 1831 shocked New Yorkers with the claim that their city harbored ten thousand prostitutes, plus "hundreds" of private harlots who kept up a show of industry as domestics or seamstresses in respectable families and arranged to "throng the houses of assignation every night." The society claimed to have discovered abundant proof that "hundreds if not thousands of female domestics in this city, who serve in respectable families . . . visit the houses of assignation at convenient intervals, sometimes nightly, and by returning in tolerable season escape detection. . . . One of these who has forsaken her evil ways states that she met one man every Tuesday night, and another every Friday night, for months together without missing a single night, and without ever incurring suspicion."[117] Mrs. Trollope found a large audience for similar claims, declaring she had discovered that her apparently pious domestic was "the most abandoned woman" in Cincinnati on her evenings off.[118] Alarmist reports like these probably encouraged employers to enforce tighter restrictions on their domestics' time. The more likely pattern was not the combination of domestic service and prostitution but the movement from one into the other. Nineteenth-century investigators of prostitution found that former domestics constituted by far the largest group of recruits to prostitution, disproportionately outnumbering women who had worked as seamstresses, or clerks, or in any other line of work.[119]

Nineteenth-century observers tended to blame the connection between domestic service and prostitution on the intelligence office and the streets. George Ellington's The Women of New York (1869), a trashy, police-gazette style account of the New York demimonde, is heavily padded with descriptions of ordinary and respectable women, all of whom gain an unsavory air through

Ellington's leering prose. He dwells lovingly on detail, evidently inventing it where wanted, and much of this detail focuses on domestics looking for work. Ellington attacks the "Situations Wanted—Female" columns, saying that while many are bona fide, a large number of the advertising housekeepers and governesses are lascivious women who "solicit custom" under this guise: "The extent to which these women abound is perfectly enormous." [120] In his chapter on "Female 'Help' in New York," Ellington portrays a thicket of vice centering around the intelligence offices, whose swindling ways pale next to their facilities for recruiting young women "not only to service, but to sin." In this kind of vision, everything becomes subject to the worst assumptions, and working women are suspect simply by virtue of their looking for work. Such overripe imaginings aside, looking for work in service could indeed carry a young woman into dangerous paths, for a domestic out of work was also "out of place" and doubly vulnerable. One fictional domestic felt she was "luckier than lots, I had a place to go when I was out of work to my aunts." [121] Magdalen rescue groups fighting prostitution could point to specific cases where women had been sent to houses of ill fame from intelligence offices or through newspaper advertisements. [122] In servants' boardinghouses, domestics could become acquainted with degenerate habits. Mrs. Keys, who kept such a boarding house in Pacific Street in New York in the 1870s, was reported to be fond of drink, "like all the lodging women." [123]

Separated from her family, a domestic was vulnerable to men who practiced seduction under the promise of marriage and then moved on. When "Katie Burke left this PM under the *most trying circumstances*," Caroline Barrett White noted, "Katie should be ashamed of herself!" It was "the only case of the kind in all my housekeeping. Three months later Mrs. White journeyed into Boston to see Katie and her baby at Chardine Street House, a charitable home: "She does not know what she will do or where go." [124] Women in Katie's position sometimes gave up their babies and returned to service, but others turned to prostitution. The Rosine Society told of their rescue of a young woman who came from rural New Jersey to Philadelphia: "She lived some months in a family, conducting herself with perfect propriety, when in an unfortunate hour, she formed an acquaintance with one who, under a marriage engagement, planned and effected her ruin and then absconded." [125] The Anchorage in Elmira, New York attempted to rescue and rehabilitate such young women, and its case histories, though from a slightly later period, reveal how vulnerable young women in service could be. At seventeen, for example, her mother dead and her father an alcoholic, Isabelle Boltwood went to work as a housemaid and nurse in a family in Rochester, where she was "ruined" by a young man who worked in a hotel. She claimed he had committed rape, but no charges were filed because reports held Isabelle to have been "very immoral." This "willful and headstrong" girl was discovered to have contracted "syphilis in its worst form." [126]

Reformers who fretted about domestics turning to prostitution seldom paused to contemplate one group responsible—the men of the employing families. When Elizabeth Blackwell worked in the women's syphilitic ward in the Philadelphia almshouse in 1848, she recorded, "Most of the women are unmarried, a large proportion having lived at service and been seduced by their masters, though, on the whole, about as many seducers are unmarried as married." [127] In the privacy of their records, the Anchorage administrators recorded a number of cases when girls came to them from service pregnant and named a member of the employing family as the father. In one case of a girl sixteen years old, the police were notified and the man arrested. [128] Karen Kearns has noted that investigators of prostitution were often reluctant to take note of the connection between domestic service and prostitution that their own studies revealed, preferring to focus on the dangers of shop or factory work. [129] Sometimes, of course, the identity of the culprit could not be ignored, as in a choice piece of gossip retailed

by Elizabeth Sullivan Stuart in a letter to her daughter from Detroit in 1851. "She was Mrs. McCarthy's sister, a common, coarse,
uneducated Irish *servant* girl, old enough, and if I mistake not
smart enough to take care of herself. *She could not be urged to leave the
house before the event.*" No one but Edward K——, her employer's
son, suspected anything, as "these sacks are admirably calculated
for concealment." When her labor began, the domestic went upstairs to K——'s office and told him she would have her child
there. He "flew off and got a carriage to drive himself, no, she
'would not stir a step,'" and at last the baby was born. "Mrs.
K—— would not go near the scene and none to wash or do for the
child until the next morning when (so I am told) Mrs. Bingham
came to the relief and performed the office!" Two weeks later,
Edward K—— having gone to "parts unknown," Mrs. K——
insisted the woman take her child and depart; and when she refused, Mrs. K—— called the constable and had her carried off. "I
understand she has named the child Edward K——!" Mrs. Stuart
declared herself "astonished" at her daughter's remark that Edward
K—— should have married the woman: "I look upon her as one
bitten where she meant to bite. She was too cunning to have been
'seduced.'" [130]

This domestic's behavior in refusing to leave and naming her
son after her seducer, Kate Baker's remark, and even Mrs. Stuart's
imputed motive all indicate that it was at least an open possibility
that an employer might have to marry a domestic he had seduced.
This possibility, a contrast to European customs, may have tended
to reduce sexual contact between servants and their employers by
making employers more cautious. American employers had to be
careful of how they dealt with hired girls. William Avery Rockefeller, father of John D. Rockefeller, had to flee the family home in
Moravia, New York in 1849 after he was indicted for the rape of
Anne Vanderbeak, a hired girl in the family. [131] Other hired girls
pressed their cases in church proceedings or in civil cases; one

claiming in a breach of promise suit that she was seduced by her employer under promise of marriage, was awarded $3,000.[132] An employer was not able to elude responsibility as easily as could drifters and traveling-men. Even very wealthy families could not dismiss the possibility of marriage with a domestic, as many must have reflected with a shudder when they read the headlines, "Douglas Weds His Domestic: Aged Capitalist Fools His Relatives." Benjamin Douglas, a wealthy California social leader, was seventy-nine; Louise Kretzler, his bride and former servant, was thirty. The Douglas family was reportedly "crushed," especially since the bridegroom made a new will that left Louise $20,000.[133] Given these possibilities, perhaps sexual contact between employer and domestic was rather limited after all, or at least flourished more in imagination than in reality.[134]

Some observers thought that prostitution recruited many ex-servants because service was filled with "low" women. One group of reformers referred to the daughters of the poorer classes as growing up "without judicious systematic training to qualify them to fulfill their duties." "As they approach womanhood, they become dissatisfied and ungovernable, and are frequently hired by the week into families. But the idle careless habits generated at home usually prevent them from retaining their situations; and the frequent changes produce an unsettlement that is detrimental to the moral character."[135] The Philadelphia Society for the Encouragement of Faithful Domestic Servants also professed to detect a willful minority in domestic service, "the small number who are reckless of character and who bring undeserved discredit on the class."[136] Late nineteenth-century social investigators referred to service as drawing upon women among whom tenement-house life had produced "absolute shamelessness" and noted that "women can secure employment in it when they are of too low grade to be employed elsewhere."[137] Middle-class reformers' definitions of "character" were biased and self-serving, but institutional case records seem to confirm that domestic service was often the last stop for women whose family backgrounds included alcoholism, desertion, destitution, mental problems, or petty crime.

The connection between domestic service and prostitution reflected not only the background and situation of some service workers but also the conditions of the work itself. One investigator of prostitution, William Sanger, pointed a finger at employers who treated their domestics "in a manner which would bring a blush to the cheek of a southern slave-driver." "Is it any wonder that girls are driven to intoxication and disgrace by this conduct?" Sanger asked.[138] Ruth Rosen's work on prostitution in the Progressive era seems to confirm Sanger's implication that some women entered prostitution because they were simply unwilling to submit to the long hours, low pay, and degrading treatment dealt out in service. Rosen's Maimie Pinzer was too bright and able to consider service work. "Maimie saw nothing 'respectable' about poverty and menial labor," Rosen writes.[139] Beecher and Stowe remarked that some self-respecting and well-educated women seemed to "prefer either a miserable pittance or the career of vice" to service.[140] Perhaps, as Judith and Daniel Walkowitz have suggested, prostitution could seem "in many ways a rational choice, given the set of unpleasant alternatives" facing poor women.[141]

Once a woman had entered "the life," the drudgery of service stood as a barrier to prevent her leaving it, since the lowest forms of service were often the only work open to former prostitutes, and many charitable organizations explicitly pushed them into service work in the name of rehabilitation.[142] Dora Armstrong, for example, had been an illegitimate child, adopted when young into a good home but inclined to "immoral company, falsifying and theft." She left home and drifted to a house of ill repute. When her adoptive parents complained to the police, she was arrested and sent to the state reform school; after two years the authorities placed her in service.[143] In Philadelphia one "notorious character," repentant, was "placed in a worthy family" where she "won golden opinions from all around her." Though she had "never laid by a farthing" in all her years of dissipation, she now began a savings account.[144] The Lancaster Industrial School for Girls in Massachusetts, established in 1855 to reclaim female delinquents, included large numbers of former servants among its inmates, and concluded their rehabilitation with a two-year indenture in service.[145] Not until the twentieth century would reformers begin to notice that the road to rehabilitation was mapped across the same occupation through which so many women and girls moved in downward paths.[146]

Money and Mobility?

Employers often declared they were mystified at working women's reluctance to enter or remain in domestic service, since the work was so well-rewarded. They could compare service to other forms of women's work, most of which did not pay a living wage, and they wondered aloud at working women's failure to appreciate the "good" pay in service. In *The American Woman's Home* (1869), Beecher and Stowe summed up the prevalent view after midcentury: "Now what is the matter with domestic service?" they wrote. "One would think, on the face of it, that a calling which gives a settled home, a comfortable room, rent-free, with fire and lights, good board and lodging, and steady, well-paid wages, would certainly offer more attractions than the making of shirts for tenpence, with all the risks of providing one's own sustenance and shelter."[147] The problem with service, they went on to say, was not one of compensation but one of conditions, prejudice, and social stigma. Similarly, Robert Tomes declared in 1875 that the problem with service was definitely not one of wages: indeed, he declared, servants "thrive."[148] This view of domestics' wages may have been lent force by actual trends, since domestics earned higher cash wages than help, and many employers' memories spanned the transition from help to domestic service.[149] Beginning in the

1870s and in large numbers by the 1890s, social scientists tackled the subject of women's work. Some attempted to gather data about domestic service and compare it systematically and "scientifically" to other types of women's work. Most of these early surveyors concluded that service paid as well as or better than other lines of work open to women.[150] But the views of employers and surveyors were not objective, nor did they coincide with those of working women themselves.

Cash wages in service varied between local labor markets, depending on the presence of alternate forms of female employment, and perhaps on the availability of male employment, and within them depending on business cycle unemployment and even on seasonal hirings and layoffs.[151] Cash wages also varied because of the wide range of skill and experience among the workers; some domestics were adolescents who received little more than their room and board, while adult women earned wages several times as high.[152] The differing wealth of employers also created wide variations in servant wages.[153] These facts made it crucial for surveyors to employ representative sampling techniques, but none did so. The Vassar alumnae and club women polled by Salmon and Laughlin tended to be more urban, to enjoy higher incomes, and to employ larger staffs than would have been representative.[154] Surveyors also emphasized the lack of unemployment in domestic service compared with other women's jobs, which were often seasonal, but again they chose estimates that were excessively optimistic. Although unemployment was low in service, turnover was notoriously high, and it is difficult to change jobs without losing some time.[155]

More important than any other difficulty, the surveyors' findings routinely depended upon their estimates of the value of room and board. Cash wages for servants were lower than wages for other types of work, and it was only through the correction for room and board that they could be concluded to be competitive. Most surveyors chose to make this correction by adding on an estimate of what a working girl would pay for room and board in a boarding house. This procedure led to overestimation, as surveyors took their estimates from the charges at the "respectable" boarding houses where each boarder occupied a room of her own. [156] As other social investigators would discover, few working women could afford such places; instead they boarded in more modest circumstances where they had to share rooms; they set up "light housekeeping" in a room with a stove; or—most often of all—they lived at home. [157] The few surveyors who chose a different method of comparison, subtracting from other working women's wages the amounts those women actually reported spending on room and board, did not come to such rosy conclusions about the superior compensation of domestics. [158]

Domestics valued their room and board below the replacement cost of a good boarding house. The boarder paid to have someone else prepare and serve her meals, keep up the fires and lights, clean her room and provide fresh linen, perhaps even do her laundry, while the domestic did all the work associated with her food and shelter, or at best shared the work with other servants. In emphasizing the value of room and board, employers actually fastened upon one of the most objectionable aspects of service. As Bettina Berch argues, "From the servants' point of view, living in was a fringe benefit for the *employer*, rather than the *employee*." [159] Women who worked in factories told Ida Jackson that the family economy determined whether compensation in the form of room and board was desirable. "They quite failed to attach the importance to the board and lodging phase of the question which employers of domestic service are inclined to give it," she explained. "It was generally admitted that where a girl was without home or friends, housework would be more lucrative for her, but factory work at $3 a week was reckoned better than housework at the same figure, when the worker could live at home and contribute out of her earnings toward the rent, and out of her leisure towards the performance of home duties." [160] When a Detroit cook was asked why more women did not choose housework as a regular employment, she replied, "[For] girls who have homes in the City it is much nicer to be working where they can be under their own parents' roof." [161]

Service, though not well-paid, did offer a young woman certain remunerative advantages. Since she need not pay for room and board, and could avoid lengthy periods of unemployment, and perhaps too because long hours curtailed spending opportunities, a woman in service could accumulate savings. Domestics were the largest single occupational group among the depositors in ante-bellum savings banks. [162] Though service was not "well paid," young women who had reasons to save could grit their teeth for a few years, exploit its possibilities, and then move on. It was this ability to accumulate cash that recommended service to dutiful immigrant daughters who wanted to send remittances home. But it could not last forever, and women who failed to find marriage partners faced grim prospects as they grew older in service.

Even the value of the ability to accumulate savings depended upon the family economy and life course context within which working women approached service. No group illustrated this better than blacks in domestic service, for whom family context, future expectations, and wages were decisively different. In a society in which their race was presumed inherently menial, blacks were excluded or discouraged from nearly all other types of work except service. Discrimination pressed males into an otherwise female occupation: among all ethnic groups, only Chinese men were as prone to enter service work. [163] The presumption that free blacks of all ages and both sexes would naturally work in domestic service was dramatized in the early months of the Civil War when Emma Willard petitioned Congress with a tidy solution to the national crisis: black slaves would be placed in their "true" position, as a regulated caste of domestic servants of which the nation, and white women in particular, stood in need. [164] After emancipation, the Freedmen's Bureau played out the logic of such assumptions about

the place of free blacks, directing many newly freed slaves to service jobs in the North, but they soon discovered the contradictions
involved in trying to place a whole people in service work. Re-
quests flowed in from prospective employers until demand exceeded supply, but the employers wanted young single women or
girls, not families. [165]

Having suffered cruel separations under slavery, the former
slaves were loathe to break up their families in order to go into
domestic service. Josephine S. W. Griffing, employment agent for
the bureau, explained she could not "get the women to go without
the men" to service positions in the North and asked her Rochester
correspondents, "Can we send a man and wife and two children
who are young?" "Nearly all our applications say no young children," she wrote, "as though Black babies were twelve years old
when they were born." [166] Twelve was the age at which, presumably, they could go into service alone.

Young black women who worked as domestics struggled with
loneliness similar to or worse than that of immigrant girls. Mary
Ann Pitkin, looking for work as a domestic in Rochester, New
York in 1858, was prevailed upon to try a place in the country,
although her "sable friends" all advised her not to go for "she would
be so lonesome." And in less than two weeks Mary Ann confessed
she "could not stand it much longer," she was so lonely on Sundays. [167] Given the relatively small free black populations in the
North, those concentrated in urban areas, it was easy to be cut off,
and those blacks who migrated north after emancipation took a
lonely path. Judy Jackson, an ex-slave, migrated to Ithaca, New
York in 1867 and worked in service. She kept in touch with a
brother and a niece in Virginia, but remained in Ithaca and died
there in 1897. In 1871 Mary Ball went into service in Springfield,
Massachusetts. Mary had come north from Richmond, leaving her
father, mother, brother, and younger sisters behind. She did have
one aunt in the Springfield area. [168]

When white domestics objected to working alongside blacks,

they probably redoubled the isolation of black domestics and cut off already foreshortened lines of advancement within service, by confining blacks to live-out positions or to solitary maid-of-all-work assignments. Looking for work in service seems to have held greater perils for black women than for white: investigators claimed that intelligence offices for black domestics routinely sent applicants to "sporting houses" to work either as inmates or as menial employees.[169] And young black women found escape from service through marriage doubly difficult: cut off, as were all domestics, from opportunities to meet men, they were also, in the cities, part of a black population in which there were pronounced excesses of females over males. Nor could a black domestic fortunate enough to find a suitor confidently expect to retire from the work force upon marriage, as did other domestics, since employment discrimination so often made it difficult or impossible for black men to support their families. Married black women responded with unusually high rates of labor-force participation.[170]

Likely to continue working after marriage, black women in service compromised as best they could between work and family life by living out, that is, by living in their own homes rather than with their employers. Living out permitted them to combine marriage and family life with service, but at a fearful cost. The long hours employers demanded meant a live-out domestic saw her own children only briefly, in moments of fatigue. Even if she took some of her meals at her employers' house, living out meant she had to pay for housing and food. But her cash wages were no more than those paid to servants who lived in; the pecuniary advantages of service disappeared and she labored on in the most grinding poverty.[171]

One specific variety of live-out service, laundry work, had certain advantages: one could carry the clothing back to one's own home and do it there while keeping an eye on the children. In fact, the children could help, by running back and forth with laundry and fuel. Laundry work could prove a position of stability and even authority in the midst of desperate poverty. One washerwoman was described as always ready with a place on her stove for neighbors who could not afford the coal or wood to do their cooking. "In winter she always has warming at her fire some cold little body whose mother is off for a day's work, or some little chap who has nowhere to go after school, or some little working-boy who does errands, cuts wood and cleans sidewalks." Two or three poor neighbors "would hardly ever get their clothes washed for want of soap and warm water, only she makes them welcome to her suds after her washing is done." [172] But laundry was extremely heavy work and it involved exposure to dampness in all sorts of weather, so it was suited only to the fittest and strongest women. These few cruel occupational alternatives took a great human toll. It is probably significant that most of the black women admitted to New York State asylums for the insane, 80 percent of whom were domestic servants, presented medical histories of overwork, illness, financial disaster, family problems, and physical exhaustion. [173]

In the postemancipation South, some of the harshness of live-out domestic service may have been mitigated by particular southern conditions and traditions. Relatively integrated residential patterns made it possible to live out and yet return home easily, even for an hour at noon, to be with one's children. And traditions dating from slavery granted black domestics a considerable degree of autonomy in their work, discouraging the close supervision that became prevalent elsewhere. [174] Above all, the customary "service pan" or food basket augmented pathetically low wages: black domestics carried home the leftovers of the whites' meals. The service pan probably fulfilled a religiously based sense of obligation to assist the less fortunate, but it also fed racist assumptions about blacks' inability to support themselves, since, as David Katzman has pointed out, whites viewed it as "something unearned and given benevolently." [175] Like many aspects of racist society, the service pan enabled black people to survive but demanded they surrender a measure of dignity, the dignity of the worker, however lowly, who is presumed to earn his or her pay. Southern domestic service also seems to have carried greater dangers for black women in the risk of sexual exploitation by white employers; within the southern racial caste system such liaisons carried few risks or obligations for whites. [176]

Southern service, as formed in the heritage of a slave society, seems to have implied a kind of paternalistic care that was at once loyal and kindly, manipulative and debasing. In Henry Seidel Canby's memoir of Wilmington in the 1890s, he recalls the Negro "waiters" and their wives as "part of Us, moulded to our needs. . . . When they were sick or destitute we took care of them if they were our darkies, but of course what they thought, if they thought, and what they wanted, if they wanted more than we gave them, was not significant." Canby recalled that sometimes a black domestic "went mean." Young black women would chase a small white boy, spit on his hair and claw his cheeks: "We dreaded them like fire—but a few years later they would be good-natured and useful like the rest." [177] The young black women who "went mean" must have understood how trapped they were by race and sex, and a large part of that trap was domestic service. The material rewards of service, limited at best for white women, were simply nonexistent for blacks.

Nineteenth-century employers also liked to believe they exercised uplifting influence on their domestics, and they harped on the moral benefits of service work. "If servants but realized how much they gained in real culture and refinement by constantly associating, as they do, with those above them," one benevolent group editorialized, "they would appreciate the privilege of entering a lady's house." [178] In a modern echo of these claims, sociologists have called domestic service a "bridging" occupation, one that, by encouraging the acquisition of new skills, resources, and values, facilitates occupational mobility. Yet the original "bridging" theory described occupational mobility among male servants, and women were conceded to enjoy "fewer opportunities." [179] Because a woman's social status was affected most decisively not by her occupation but by that of her husband, historians have attempted to assess European servants' mobility out of service through the use of marriage records. Theresa McBride compared the servant's father's occupation with that of her bridegroom and concluded that one-fourth to one-third of all nineteenth-century French servants made upwardly-mobile marriages. Having examined marriage records, Cissie Fairchilds concluded that their accumulation of dowries helped late eighteenth-century French servants to make ambitious or at least adventuresome marriages. [180] In contrast to McBride, Fairchilds is careful to stress that the "upward" mobility of these marriages may be marginal or even illusory. The lack of comparable marriage records precludes a parallel study of American domestics, but because marriage in the United States did not require a dowry, the systematic relationship between savings in service and marriage chances seems to have been broken, or at least relaxed. [181] There is simply no evidence that domestics in America were, as a group, more upwardly mobile through marriage than other working women. Domestics' marriages could owe more to a desire to escape service than to skills and aspirations acquired there.

The attitudes and values a woman acquired in service were sometimes thought to have their effect after marriage, through influence on her family. Catharine Beecher advised the domestic that she was going through "exactly the best training possible to prepare her to conform her will and wishes to those of her husband, to train up her children well, and to become a neat, industrious, and economical housekeeper." Perhaps such influences seemed unlikely to assure upward mobility, for Beecher clinched the argument by declaring that domestic service prepared a woman for spiritual elevation, *"whatever* may be her future earthly lot," since it provided the best training to make her "a submissive, benevolent, and self-denying Christian." [182] As Beecher apparently realized, service work did not reliably train those who passed through it to imitate their social superiors. It could as easily imply the acquisition of qualities, like resignation, appropriate to staying on the bottom of the social ladder. In fact the notion of upward mobility draws the question too narrowly; it is more useful to think in terms of the influence of service work, including both the situation of the worker and her response to it.

As Herbert Gutman has pointed out, individuals respond to the powerlessness and dependency of wage work in different ways. Some do respond with a determination to "make it," to do whatever it takes to advance themselves as individuals or to make it possible for their children to succeed. Domestics were especially well-placed to appreciate the motives for such a struggle, having seen at close hand the sweetness of privilege. And they learned certain useful skills, most notably how to conform to a rigorous work discipline—to work hard, under supervision, and by the clock. [183] Some immigrants learned in service to speak English and to become accustomed to American ways, though others found that isolation impeded acculturation. [184] Some learned new ways of housekeeping—new standards of neatness, for example. Little Maria Willis astonished Susan Hooker with her "thoughtfulness and orderly ways," habits she had clearly acquired in her employers' homes, for "when one sees her mother's house one feels like exclaiming can any good thing come out of Nazareth." [185] Immigrants' memoirs suggest that seemingly small matters of dress or food or cleanliness often provided the occasions through which they were made to feel somehow wrong, inferior, un-American. One young girl, for example, understood her family was "shanty" rather than "lace curtain" Irish because of an incident in which the silverware was detected to be "greasy." [186] Domestic servants had some advantage in learning and passing on to their own families the small but crucial details of American housekeeping.

Other domestics acquired values and aspirations that would have to be realized, as Beecher implied, through husband or children. Marie Haggerty, who worked as a nursemaid and second girl in New England in the 1880s and 1890s, reminisced for a Works Progress Administration interviewer. "I like things nice, but there's no use pretending; I can't have them that way now." She spoke of having had a "nice" room and "the best of food," of going to Cape Cod every summer. "I was really next thing to a lady's maid, for when the children went to bed, often the mistress would let me hook her dress, or brush her hair, and all the time she'd be talking to me just like I was her equal." Her husband tried to advance himself as a grocer, but he suffered a breakdown from overwork and had to go to work in a machine shop. "Pa knowed I was used to better things, and he always tried hard to get them for me."

The children were Marie Haggerty's hope. "We always tried to give the children the best" and made them all finish high school "so they could have a chance to become high-class people." They disappointed her. Young Kitty, sent to a normal school, did not want to be a schoolteacher. And the boys teased and laughed so at their mother once when she had company and "kind of put things on a little fancy like rich people do," that she vowed never to do it again. "I don't know why," she sighed, "things never turn out the way you want them." [187]

Caroline Barrett White kept in touch with her former cook, Jane Blunt, after she married and continued to live in the Boston area. Jane Blunt Welsh did daywork for Mrs. White on occasion, washing or housecleaning. She also paid social calls on Mrs. White, although they were not exchanges between equals: "Mrs. Jane Welsh has been to see me this P.M. I think a good deal of her. She seems to appreciate kindness and has more sense than most in her station." [188] On one occasion Jane Welsh brought Caroline White a pot of ivy to put in the library window. Yet her continued attachment to the way of life she had seen at Cliffside did not make Mrs. Welsh happy: on the contrary. Even Mrs. White understood as much. When Mrs. Welsh paid her a visit at the Christmas holidays in 1870, she wrote, "The course of life does not run so smooth as she desires." Caroline Barrett White could only hope that "she will not make shipwreck of her happiness by impatience." [189]

One more bit of testimony on the influence of service came from a young factory worker quoted by Lucy Maynard Salmon. "I think shop or factory girls make the best wives," she declared. "The domestic after she gets married she gets careless. . . . She has lived in such fine houses that her small tenement has no beauty for her." Similarly, she was inclined to extravagance: "She has so much to do with before she is married and so little to do with after, she don't know how to manage." [190] Such examples suggest that influence on husbands and children could be ineffective or unhappy, and the styles and standards young women learned in service would likely prove inappropriate for working-class home life. Those who did take middle-class values to heart may have acquired little more than troublesome dreams.

There was another way of responding to wage work, in collective forms of resistance and mutual support. The structure of service, tiny house-by-house units, militated against such a response, yet domestics found ways to offer one another surprising amounts of mutual aid. They traded information about employer practices and so provided each other with community standards that could be invoked to refuse excessive demands or shame an employer into concessions. The author of *Plain Talk and Friendly Advice to Domestics* (1855) pictured a group of servants meeting regularly to talk shop. "I am sorry to say it is nothing uncommon for the hired girls of a village to have some special place of resort, where on certain evenings they run together, and hold a sort of club meeting, discussing their fancied grievances, boasting of their impertinences and faithlessness—to say nothing of more criminal practices— towards their respective employers, and encouraging each other in such conduct." [191] She pictured a Sunday evening gathering of Irish girls, where Elizabeth, Bridget, and Caty all lay plans to demand more time off, vowing, for example, not to stay home

from mass "if a busy day it is, or mistress is sick, or babby cries."
But Sarah, the author's model servant, refuses. "You must love
your mistress," she declares. "Live with her till she feels and you
feel that you belong to her. My mistress says she loves her faithful
and honest servants next to her children." At this Elizabeth snorts,
"Sarah preaches like a heretic parson. She's only a half-breed Irish
girl anyway." [192] Of course the author intends Elizabeth for the
villain of the piece, but it is easy to see how Sarah's sugary foolish-
ness could be rejected, with solidarity cemented by ethnic bonds
and violators read out of their heritage. The fictional Sarah wanted
to "belong to" her employer, but real women were probably more
likely to feel they belonged to a group of fellow workers. When all
five servants in one Chicago household quit in 1891, one of the
maids, Emma Siniger, wrote to the employer. "I was true to you I
did my work well. I was faithful to the girls as well," Emma wrote.
"I could not be unfaithful to the rest of the help and stay right in
with the lady of the house. I must choose my friends from working
girls—and it would never do for me to give them up for my
mistress." [193]

Mary Virginia Terhune complained that the bad influence of
fellow servants amounted to a de facto labor union. "Every consci-
entious, well-meaning housewife knows what a brake is this informal, but terrible 'Union' upon her endeavors to improve and
really benefit those under her direction. I have been amazed and
disgusted at the tyranny exercised by this irresponsible body over
the best servants I have ever seen." "We would be hooted at,
ma'am, if we didn't give in to them," one girl told her. "There's not
a girl in the town would speak to us if we didn't join in with the
rest. It's like a strike, you see—awful upon them as holds back."
Terhune does not reveal the issue on which servants showed so
much solidarity, except to say it involved an effort to "improve and
really benefit" domestics; obviously they saw things differently. [194]
Terhune's account of their methods suggests that domestics adopted tactics—such as ostracizing scabs—from more formal labor

struggles and organizations. Intelligence-office waiting rooms must have offered an ideal opportunity to exchange information and build camaraderie.

Mutual protection marked more informal occasions within the home itself. When, as a new young servant, Marie Haggerty reached for a "fancy cake" in the parlor, the cook gave her a crack on the hand. "She pulled me back into the kitchen and made me sit down and eat my fill of fancy cakes and told me never to take anything that was outside the kitchen, for it was always a trick to see how honest we was." [195] In 1862 Harriet Beecher Stowe overheard one domestic, Maggie, talking to a second, Joanna, "in a low, sly, continuous strain . . . and the subject seemed to be the regularity, ease and comfort with which the girls elsewhere get through their work, how they were never called off or called upon for anything and got through so early etc. etc." Deciding that her servant problems were due to Maggie's acting "the traitor in the camp," she sent word, "I want Mr. Stowe to pay her and see her out of the house." [196] Similarly, when Elizabeth Sullivan Stuart became convinced that some "snake in the grass" was "ruining" Margaret, a hitherto docile domestic, she determined to forbid the troublemaker entry into the house. [197]

Only on rare occasions did surreptitious and informal mutual aid give rise to trade-union struggles. During the great wave of strikes in 1877, the black washerwomen of Galveston, inspired by the success of a strike by black longshoremen, united to demand $1.50 a day. The Knights of Labor included several locals of black domestics in the 1880s, and in 1881 the black laundresses of Atlanta went on strike. But in Atlanta and elsewhere, the outcome was defeat. Unskilled and working separately in a high-turnover occupation, domestics found it difficult to build and maintain solidarity. [198]

Because the structure of their work made responding to powerlessness and dependency through collective action extraordinarily difficult, domestics often had to settle for asserting themselves in individualistic but negative fashion, not by climbing but by quitting. Many domestics agreed with Mehitable Goddard's cook who said she "meant to change [places] until she got one that entirely suited her." [199] Others rejected not just specific places but all they had seen in service, and employers might have been appalled to learn how thoroughly their notions of good influence could backfire. Touring the women's section of the Tombs in New York, Fredrika Bremer spoke to a young black woman who was a prisoner, asking if she were a Christian. The young woman replied that she could not become a Christian: "I have been servant with many Christians; I have seen many things; I cannot turn to a Christian." [200] During the New York City draft riots of 1863, a servant girl pointed out the home of abolitionist James S. Gibbons and told some of the mob that Horace Greeley lived there. The mob proceeded to loot, sack, and burn the house, while two daughters made a narrow escape over the rooftops. The servant's "error" may well have been a deliberate act by one who knew the Gibbonses well enough to know their politics and to nurse a grudge. [201]

Domestics reacted not just to the example of middle-class life but to their own work experience, to all the burdens and indignities of the service relationship. Mary Dempsey, a cook in the Glessner household in Chicago, drew the line in 1885 when Mrs. Glessner gave all the domestics the same Christmas gifts, including an umbrella and a fan. She refused them, laying them on the dining room table and telling the children she had an umbrella and had no use for a fan. When Frances Glessner reprimanded her, she threatened to leave. The break actually came two years later when Mrs. Glessner decided she wanted the servants to call the children Miss Fanny and Master George. She also asked Mary Dempsey to check up on the other servants, making sure the beds were made in their rooms before breakfast and the like. Having had enough of demeaning treatment and being unwilling to separate herself from the other servants by assuming a supervisory role, Mary was "very impertinent" and quit. [202] However momentarily satisfying, quitting was not a completely effective form of self-assertion; as long as domestic service remained a major sector of female employment, a woman either had to find a more tolerable employer or compete in more crowded lines of work.

The domestic service relationship contained as much antagonism as emulation. If some domestics learned middle-class values, others yearned to escape or acquired the ability to stand up for themselves—to demand, for example, prompt and regular payment. Domestics could and did use both the skills and the values they learned from their employers to reject them and the service relationship altogether. One family story tells of a grandmother who came to this country from Scandinavia and entered service without knowing any English. When her employer seized her slice of bread and butter and began to scrape off the butter because it was applied too thickly, she spoke her first words in the new language: "I quit!" [203] Julia Ward Howe took a stinging lesson in feminism from her cook, "who was furious when I took her to task, which I intended to do very moderately." "Her insolence left me no choice but to discharge her on the spot," wrote Howe. "She came to me with very deferential manners and leaves me a perfect demon, having given us literally nothing but discomfort. As she drove off in a drizzle, she laughed and said, 'Women's rights!'" [204] When some young women learned in service to rely upon themselves and one another, it was surely a benefit but not the kind of improvement that employers had in mind when they touted the work. Young women who helped could combine their work with school attendance and continue to make life at home with their parents their primary reference, but work as a domestic was a more demanding, total experience. Many young girls spent all or part of their adolescent years in service. In Buffalo in 1855, for example, over half of all Irish-born girls had gone into service before the age of seventeen. Girls entered service as young as eleven or twelve. [205] Employers who complained of the servant problem blamed it on ethnicity or urbanization or the intelligence office, but they were remarkably silent on the subject of age, failing to point to what has since become a standard explanation for socially disordered behavior, the fact of adolescence itself.

The long hours, the harsh work discipline, the need to stand up for oneself and negotiate the path from job to job, above all the loneliness—all these conditions of service work suggest that its most consistent influence may have been to put an early end to childishness, to encourage a toughness and maturity on the part of the women who spent their teenage years within it. The service relationship thus implied a trade in the ability to experience childhood. Middle-class children were the gainers, working-class girls the losers. The nature of the service experience depended upon the life course context of the women workers, but service work also had the power to affect, in turn, the fundamental patterns by which individuals moved through time. The young working-class women, largely immigrants, who had to grow up early in domestic service left behind one form of silent but eloquent testimony about their experience. They kept their own daughters out of service. Second-generation women were much less likely than their mothers to go into domestic service; they were in fact underrepresented in servant ranks for nearly all ethnic groups.[206] Their mothers knew, too well, that "girls" in service could not be girls in fact.

Conclusion

When Lucy Maynard Salmon undertook her study of domestic service in 1888, she drew upon Vassar alumnae, to whom she distributed her questionnaires. She asked them to contact other women who would be willing to complete and distribute more of the forms. Because her questionnaires failed to ask about many important particulars, and because she was in effect soliciting co-operation in the project from many former students, she received from them not only completed forms but also letters in which they described experiences with household service which the questionnaires seemed inadequate to convey. Salmon evidently destroyed the questionnaires, but the letters remain, offering a vivid picture of domestic service in the late 1880s.

Help had not yet disappeared in some areas, and western housekeepers wrote to complain that the questionnaire did not fit their situations. Sarah Glazier Bates, Vassar class of '68, wrote from Omaha that she had been married thirteen years, and in that time had moved into twelve houses, had five children, and "*needed* cooks, seamstresses, second girls, nurses beyond all human account—and except for times so short that they amount to *nothing*, have had none of them." "As for any of the 'help' to be obtained in this town," she declared, "deliver me! . . . In general you must remember you'll get no sympathy out of us, west of the Mississippi."[1] Lucie Isaacs wrote from Walla Walla, Washington with a similar message: "Please bear in mind that in all new countries (and this is new) the domestic is an unknown quantity. . . . the average housekeeper is happily fortunate if she [can] find *any one* willing to become a 'help' for a money consideration." Mrs. Isaacs went on to complain that such helpers were apt to prefer to work only during the forenoons and to take all their evenings and Sunday afternoons off as a matter of course. She thought their scarcity due to the fact that a girl of "any ability" usually married "quite early."[2] Another employer in Quincy, Michigan (population 1,250) was troubled with "girls who expect to sit at your table and share your sitting room," and who "do not desire continuous service."[3]

Though help still prevailed in rural and western areas, alumnae in more eastern and urban locales dismissed girls' pretension to be "one of the family" as "utter abomination" and wrote instead about the complications and contradictions of supervising domestics.[4] One correspondent from Syracuse provided little sketches of some of the ladies she knew, sketches that testified to the varied uses and styles of supervision. "Mrs. George Barnes. James Street, rich, stylish, *very* particular housekeeper, thinks of nothing else, pays high wages, has English help generally, is a slave to her possessions and ceremonies. Mrs. Patrick Lynah. 68 James Street, rich, economical, thrifty, orderly, exacting, pays high wages, changes servants frequently, seldom keeps one a year, has a hard name among servants."[5] Even in Des Moines, determination, backed up by a large budget, could create "a sort of 'palace' home with twelve house servants."[6] An employer in Germantown, Pennsylvania favored Salmon with the lessons of her experience: "It is a great encouragement to a good servant to have 25 cents per week added to her wages after years of efforts to please you—and it scarcely fails to secure her services for more years."[7]

Professor Salmon received testimony of the toll exacted by this kind of household regime, even though many domestics were unwilling to fill out the questionnaires meant for them. An employer in Andover, Massachusetts wrote to point out that she had "never had any girl who would not have looked with suspicion and distrust on any such queries," fearing they might be somehow used against her. "My Annie was disposed to treat the matter as a joke and fill out the blanks with nonsense but this I protested against. When I asked her for it a few days later she said she had put it in the fire, that only very ignorant persons would ask such questions or expect to get them answered. She for one never would answer them."[8] One young woman named Florence Wilcox wrote to explain herself. "Though brought up and educated for a lady, reverses came and I felt under the necessity of taking anything to earn my own living that came in my way. The opportunity came in the shape of housework in a minister's family in the central part of New York State." Although the "most cordial" relations prevailed between the family and herself, she wrote, "yet in many things it is very hard and I no longer wonder as I did in former days why so few are willing to go out to service."[9]

Professor Salmon must have written back asking what she meant by her last remark, for Florence Wilcox wrote a second time. "Ladies wonder how their girls can complain of loneliness in a house full of people but oh! it is the worst kind of loneliness, their share is but the work of the house, they do not share in the pleasures and delights of a *home*." "Real love exists between my employer and self," she wrote, "yet at times I grow almost desperate from the sense of being cut off from those pleasures to which I had always been accustomed." She belonged to her employer's church yet had no share in the social life of the church, and "reading and writing comprise my sole recreations."[10] Few young women in service could have been satisfied with such amusements or written such letters, but Florence Wilcox expressed some of the pain all domestics must have felt.

Salmon found many employers who were interested in the servant problem and eager to help in any way. Some individuals had made household service a major preoccupation in life. One correspondent referred Salmon to her aunt, who had worked out a plan for a training school for servants. "She has been more than twenty years elaborating its details, and she has them now all in good shape on paper."[11] But such individual efforts were by that time dwarfed by organized activity on the issue. From local women's clubs and women's exchanges to the Association of Collegiate Alumnae, the College Settlements Association and the YWCA, women in organized groups were beginning to make household service their focus. At a minimum they proposed to cooperate with academics like Salmon and others in the newly founded home economics field who were studying the problem for the first time. As Salmon's correspondence testifies, many became involved in ambitious local projects to regulate or displace the intelligence office, to found homes for unemployed women, to organize training schools for servants, and to educate employers. In 1904 all this activity would reach its highest point with the formation of the Inter-Municipal Committee on Household Research, through the combination of the Women's Educational and Industrial Union of Boston, the New York Association for Household Research, and the Philadelphia Civic Club and Housekeeper's Alliance. The committee announced the opening of offices in all three cities and declared its purposes: "to study impartially and thoroughly the conditions which attend household work, to place this information before employers, employees and students, and to encourage helpful movements for adjustment."[12] In the New York area its members included Lucy Salmon, Grace Dodge, Margaret Dreier, Frances Kellor, Lillian Wald, and Mrs. Russell Sage.

A new era had arrived. College-educated Progressives had begun to apply the methods of social science to the servant problem, subjecting hitherto private and family matters to investigation and expert analysis. In the process of doing so, many women carved out for themselves roles as experts, and they dealt with employer practices from a new standpoint of critical detachment. Their analyses of the servant problem were not always incisive; they harped on the "social stigma" attached to service but did not always understand that that stigma reflected poor wages, hours, and working conditions.[13] Their reform proposals emphasized putting service on a "business basis" and they recommended training schools, contracts, regulated placement services, the adaptation of profit-sharing, and increased use of live-out day labor.[14]

The irony of the work produced by Salmon and the other household service reformers was that their work was so ineffectual and even irrelevant. Service was indeed on the verge of great change but not because of reformers' efforts. Immigration restriction in the 1920s would cut off a major source of supply, and the migration of blacks out of the South began to supply northern cities with more and more service workers who worked after marriage and lived out. In the twentieth century live-in household service would be virtually eliminated from the middle-class American home. The live-out cleaning woman would take the place of the domestic. As alternative employments continued to open up to women, as the public school took in more and more working-class daughters and government-funded transfer payments eased the desperation of the poor, the numbers of household servants would fall drastically in relative and even in absolute terms.[15]

The transition from help to domestics reflected both economic and ideological change and was therefore indirectly but distinctly associated with the emergence and maturing of the industrial capitalist economy in nineteenth-century America, with its labor markets, its rising standards of living, its unequal rewards, and its created "needs." The change in service was hard on the young women who served: many who would have helped, refused to be domestics, and those who did enter service found it a "hard and lonely life," useful or even tolerable only if one had some realistic prospect of leaving it in a few years. For employers the change in service represented a gain in time, energy, and human possibilities. The transition from help to domestics meant that, for about seventy-five to one hundred years, a window opened for women of the middle class. Although low levels of household technology continued to make home life a great burden, these women could, on the strength of hiring domestics, realize new possibilities. Most elaborated a life within the private sphere according to the tenets of domesticity, for which purpose the supervision of domestics was admirably suited in both practical and psychological terms. Others forged the vast network of voluntary organizations known as the "benevolent empire," and devoted themselves to temperance, moral reform, Sabbatarianism, domestic and foreign missions, and aid to the poor. But a few middle-class women took advantage of household service to create and pursue the logic of the liberation of women. Few notable nineteenth-century feminists operated without the aid of domestic servants. For every woman like Lydia Maria Child or Abigail Scott Duniway, who had to struggle with few or none, there were many more feminists who matter-of-factly relied on domestics. Mary Livermore, for example, hired a housekeeper and a governess and then volunteered for the Sanitary Commission work that catapulted her into feminist activity.

Then, as now, feminism was very largely a middle-class movement. Some feminists, such as Julia Ward Howe, were perfectly capable of claiming rights for women yet always assuming that the only women who counted were white, middle-class, and native-born. They used other women to achieve their own freedom and could not see it as ironic that feminism was underwritten by the household labors of domestic servants. Few feminists could fully escape the biases of their background, though some, like Melusina Fay Peirce, learned to try. With characteristic penetration and eloquence, Elizabeth Cady Stanton acknowledged her debt to Amelia Willard, for thirty years her servant and housekeeper: "She was indeed a treasure, a friend and comforter, a second mother to my children, and understood all life's duties and gladly bore its burdens. . . . But for this noble, self-sacrificing woman, much of my public work would have been quite impossible. If by word or deed I have made the journey of life easier for any struggling soul, I must in justice share the need of praise accorded me with my little Quaker friend Amelia Willard." [16] This tribute sounds familiar because it is remarkably similar to the thanks that husbands have, more recently, been accustomed to pay to wives. In the nineteenth century some few women exercised privileges and won accomplishments on the strength of the hard work of other women. It was not always an exploitative, unhappy relationship. We need to remember Amelia Willard, or little Irish Winny sobbing over a tintype of her employer's daughter and sending back a letter "full of love." [17] But who would Winny's next employer be, and how would she fare? The odds were fearfully against her, for service was the death of many a young woman's youthful innocent enthusiasm. Ultimately it is not possible to calculate exactly the human costs and benefits of nineteenth-century household service. If it were, perhaps one might judge that the emergence of the idea of women's rights, universalist in theory however biased in practice, was worth the painful sacrifices of unnamed, unnumbered domestics. As it happened, no one asked the many serving women if they wished to sacrifice their youth to the goals of others, whether those goals be polished newel posts or women's rights. From this distance we can only try to understand, to cease forgetting what it meant to serve and to be served.

Notes

The following manuscript collections were used for this book. Chapter citations employ the abbreviations listed below for sources most frequently quoted.

Alcott, Abigail May Papers. Houghton Library, Harvard University, Cambridge, Massachusetts.

Beecher-Stowe Family Papers. Schlesinger Library, Radcliffe College, Cambridge, Massachusetts.

Beem, Eva C. Diary. Cornell University, Ithaca, New York.

Bliss Family Papers. State Historical Society of Wisconsin, Madison, Wisconsin.

Breese-Stevens-Roby Papers. University of Rochester, Rochester, New York. (hereafter, B-S-R)

Camp Family Papers. Cornell University, Ithaca, New York.

Camp Family Papers Additional. Cornell University, Ithaca, New York.

Clarke, Freeman Family Papers. University of Rochester, Rochester, New York.

Dodge, Augustus C. Papers. Iowa State Historical Society, Iowa City, Iowa.

Eastman, Phebe Orvis Diary. St. Lawrence County History Center, Canton, New York. (POE)

Forbes, Susan Parson Brown Diaries. American Antiquarian Society, Worcester, Massachusetts. (SBF)

Garrison Family Papers, Sophia Smith Collection. Smith College, Northampton, Massachusetts.

Goddard Family Correspondence. American Antiquarian Society, Worcester, Massachusetts.

Goodenough, Lizzie Wilson Diary. American Antiquarian Society, Worcester, Massachusetts.

Gordon, Elizabeth S. Correspondence. State Historical Society of Wisconsin, Madison, Wisconsin.

Gould, Hannah Wright Diary. Cornell University, Ithaca, New York.

The Home for Aged Women Records. Schlesinger Library, Radcliffe College, Cambridge, Massachusetts.

Howe, Julie Ward Diary. Houghton Library, Harvard University, Cambridge, Massachusetts.

Huntington-Hooker Papers. University of Rochester, Rochester, New York.

Kelly, Jane Bewel Diaries. State Historical Society of Wisconsin. (JBK)

Knox and Thompson Family Papers in possession of Mrs. Dorothea Ives, Historian of the Town of Salisbury, New York.

McCormick, Nettie Fowler Papers. State Historical Society of Wisconsin, Madison, Wisconsin.

McDonald, Almira D. Diary. The Margaret Woodbury Strong Museum, Rochester, New York.

May-Goddard Papers. Schlesinger Library, Radcliffe College, Cambridge, Massachusetts.

Munn-Pixley Family Papers. University of Rochester, Rochester, New York.

Pascoe, Mary Elizabeth Diary. State Historical Society of Wisconsin, Madison, Wisconsin.

Porter Family Papers. University of Rochester, Rochester, New York.

Post Family Papers. University of Rochester, Rochester, New York.

Proctor, Maria Williams Papers. Oneida County Historical Society, Utica, New York.

Proctor, Rachel Williams Papers. Oneida County Historical Society, Utica, New York.

Rochester Home for the Friendless Papers. University of Rochester, Rochester, New York.

Salmon, Lucy Maynard Papers. Vassar College Library. Poughkeepsie, New York. (LMS)

Seward Family Papers. University of Rochester, Rochester, New York.

Smith, Gerrit Family Papers. George Arents Research Library. Syracuse University, Syracuse, New York.

Stoughton, Sarah Josephine Diary. American Antiquarian Society, Worcester, Massachusetts.

Wells, Kate Gannett Papers. University of Rochester, Rochester, New York.

White, Caroline Barrett Diary. American Antiquarian Society, Worcester, Massachusetts. (CBW)

Williams, Helen Munson Papers. Oneida County Historical Society, Utica, New York.

Williams, Josiah Butler Family Papers. Cornell University, Ithaca, New York. (JBW)

Introduction

1. Mrs. A. J. Graves, *Woman in America* (New York: Harper & Bros., 1841), p. 79; Eliza Leslie, *The House Book* (Philadelphia: Carey & Hart, 1848), p. 3.

2. Grace Ellis, "Our Household Servants," *The Galaxy* 14 (September 1872): 352.

3. Catharine Beecher and Harriet Beecher Stowe, *The American Woman's Home; or, Principles of Domestic Science* (New York: J. B. Ford, 1869), pp. 307–312.

4. William Chauncey Fowler, *The English Language in Its Elements and Forms*, rev. ed. (New York: Harper & Bros., 1888), p. 120. See also references to help in: John Pickering, *A Vocabulary, or Collection of Words and Phrases Which Have Been Supposed to Be Peculiar to the United States of America* (Boston: Cummings and Hilliard, 1816), pp. 104–105; John Russell Bartlett, *Dictionary of Americanisms* (New York: Bartlett and Welford, 1849), p. 175; and the reprint of Robley Dunglison's "Glossary of Americanisms" from *The Virginia Literary Museum and Journal of Belles Lettres of 1829–1830* in A. W. Read, "Dunglison's Glossary," *Dialect Notes* vol. 5, pt. 10 (1927): 427.

5. Frances Trollope, *Domestic Manners of the Americans*, ed. Donald M. Smalley (New York: Alfred Knopf, 1949), pp. 47, 52, 157. Also the remarks of Elias Pym Fordham, who observed that north of the slave territories the want of domestic servants produced "sordid manners and semi-barbarism": Fordham, *Personal Narrative of Travels . . . 1817–1818*, ed. Frederic Austin Ogg (Cleveland: Arthur H. Clark Co., 1906), p. 229.

6. See, for example, Francis J. Grund, *The Americans in Their Moral, Social and Political Relations*, 2 vols. (1837, reprint ed., New York: Augustus M. Kelly, 1971), 2:66, 69.

7. Tocqueville explicitly connected the service of help with American democracy. See Alexis de Toqueville, *Democracy in America*, ed. Phillips Bradley, 2 vols. (New York: Alfred Knopf, 1945), 2: Chapter 5, "How Democracy Affects the Relations of Masters and Servants."

8. On household service within slavery, see Eugene D. Genovese, *Roll, Jordan, Roll: The World the Slaves Made* (New York: Pantheon, 1974), esp. pp. 327–365. On southern service after emancipation, the best source is David Katzman, *Seven Days a Week: Women and Domestic Service in Industrializing America* (New York: Oxford University Press, 1978), Chapter 5. My limited comments on free blacks in service reflect my conviction that the peculiar complexities of the subject warrant a separate study.

9. See Sharon V. Salinger, "Colonial Labor in Transition: The Decline of Indentured Servitude in Late Eighteenth-Century Philadelphia," *Labor History* 22 (Spring 1981): 165–191; Edgar J. McManus, *Black Bondage in the North* (Syracuse: Syracuse University Press, 1973). Relevant general discussions include Edmund Morgan, *The Puritan Family: Religion and Domestic Relations in Seventeenth-Century New England* (New York: Harper & Row, Harper Torchbooks, 1966), p. 185; idem, *American Slavery, American Freedom: The Ordeal of Colonial Virginia* (New York: W. W. Norton, 1975); Richard B. Morris, *Government and Labor in Early America* (New York: Columbia University Press, 1946); Abbot Emerson Smith, *Colonists in Bondage: White Servitude and Convict Labor in America, 1607–1776* (New York: W. W. Norton, 1971).

1. Hired Girls

1. Samuel Griswold Goodrich, *Recollections of a Lifetime*, 2 vols. (New York and Auburn, N.Y.: Orton & Mulligan, 1856), 1:84–85.

2. Psychoanalytic theory may suggest certain grounds for a general human tendency to mythologize in memories of early infancy as a "golden age," "when nothing was asked of us and all that we wanted was given." Bruno Bettelheim, *The Empty Fortress* (New York: The Free Press, 1967), pp. 13–14. Servants' roles in child care might contribute to a tendency to view them in this light.

Household Production

3. Goodrich, *Recollections of a Lifetime*, 1:71–72.

4. See Nancy Cott, *The Bonds of Womanhood: "Woman's Sphere" in New England, 1780–1835* (New Haven and London: Yale University Press, 1977), pp. 28–29; Laurel Thatcher Ulrich, "'A Friendly Neighbor': Social Dimensions of Daily Work in Northern Colonial New England," *Feminist Studies* 6, no. 2 (1980): 392–405. For a nineteenth-century example of spinning "on shares," see Roscoe Carlyle Buley, *The Old Northwest Pioneer Period, 1815–1840* (Indianapolis: Indiana Historical Society, 1950), p. 206. On "changing work," see Mary Beth Norton, *Liberty's Daughters: The Revolutionary Experience of American Women, 1750–1800* (Boston and Toronto: Little, Brown and Co., 1980), pp. 17–18. On the economic value of homespun, see Rolla Milton Tryon, *Household Manufactures in the United States, 1640–1860* (Chicago: University of Chicago Press, 1917).

5. See Schob, *Hired Hands and Plowboys*, pp. 199–201. New England men were more likely to milk than men of southern backgrounds, but in either case women did the churning. Paul Gates confirms that dairying and poultry raising were largely women's work. See his *The Farmer's Age: Agriculture, 1815–1860* (New York: Holt, Rinehart and Winston, 1960), pp. 244, 247.

6. See: Francois Alexandre duc de La Rochefoucauld-Liancourt, *Travels Through the United States* . . . *1795–1797*, 2 vols. (London: R. Phillips, 1799), 2:396; Mrs. M. C. J. F. Houstoun, *Hesperos; or, Travels in the West*, 2 vols. (London: John W. Parker, 1850), 1:96. Production of both milk and eggs tended to peak in the summer, a seasonal pattern that in itself contributed to marketable gluts at certain times. Few farmers tried to continue milking through the winter. See Gates, *Farmer's Age*, pp. 241–242 and chap. 11.

7. See Theodore C. Blegan, ed., *Land of Their Choice: The Immigrants Write Home* (St. Paul: University of Minnesota Press, 1955), pp. 429–430.

8. When crop failure left a family in eastern Kansas short of tax money, "Mother . . . got together about 200 pounds of butter and some eggs, and took them to Leavenworth, hoping to get the tax money with them." John Ise, *Sod and Stubble: The Story of a Kansas Homestead* (Lincoln: University of Nebraska Press, 1936), p. 62.

9. *Diary of Sarah Connell Ayer* (Portland, Maine: Lefavor-Tower, 1910), pp. 372–373, letter of 13 March 1810.

10. It may be helpful to consider Marx's reflections on the difference between hiring service workers to obtain a service and hiring other workers to realize a profit. Marx noted that the use-value of the service worker's service "immediately vanishes," and thus the transaction has the effect of injuring the self-esteem of the purchaser, since he hires the service not to realize gain but "as a result of his ordinary human frailty." Karl Marx. *Gründrisse, Foundation of the Critique of Political Economy*, trans. Martin Nicolaus (New York: Random House, 1973), pp. 272–273.

11. Diary of Phebe Orvis Eastman, 28 August 1827, St. Lawrence County History Center, Canton, New York (hereafter POE).

12. Ibid., 10 December 1827, 23 August 1826.

13. Ibid., 3 March 1826, 9 January 1827.

14. Ibid., 3 January 1828.

15. Ibid., 8 and 10 January, 22 and 26 February 1828.

16. On the decline of homespun, see Tryon, *Household Manufactures*, pp. 291–292, tables XVI and XVIII. I am indebted to Mrs. Dorothea Ives, historian of the town of Salisbury, New York, for sharing with me her privately-held manuscript materials on these two hired girls who made cheese for the market.

17. Phebe Eastman's diary is not very explicit about her husband's work or the farm's products. She never seemed to buy wool, and the 1835 New York State Census showed nearly 3,000 sheep in the town of Hopkinton, which had a population of 910. Hopkinton was heavily wooded and contained three sawmills and two asheries in 1835. See New York State Secretary of State, *Census of the State of New York for 1835* (Albany: Croswell, VanBenthuyson and Burt, 1836), "County of St. Lawrence," n.p.

18. The idea that early nineteenth-century farms were "subsistence" farms is a persistent misconception, often advanced to claim importance for women's work in that context. For a recent version of this argument, see Ann Douglas, *The Feminization of American Culture* (New York: Alfred Knopf, 1977), p. 50. Agricultural historians long ago abandoned the notion of absolute subsistence in nineteenth-century agriculture and began to talk about relative degrees of orientation to markets and to distinguish between the two aspects of that orientation—the sale of produce and the purchase of consumer goods. Late eighteenth-century farmers already sold substantial portions of their produce in the market. In the nineteenth century the pace and pattern of westward settlement and the great influence of developments in transportation both testify to farmers' need to market their crops. At the same time, farm families did contrive to purchase relatively few consumer goods. To the few items they could never produce at home—like coffee, salt, and spices— they added first textiles, then farm implements and stoves. One can argue for the importance of women's work on the family farm without citing subsistence. Even on market-oriented farms, women's work, by precluding the need to purchase many consumer goods, kept overhead costs down to levels that made the operation economically feasible. See: Rodney C. Loehr, "Self-Sufficiency on the Farm," *Agricultural History* 26 (April 1952): 37–41; James T. Lemon, "Household Consumption in Eighteenth-Century America and Its Relationship to Production and Trade: The Situation Among Farmers in Southeastern Pennsylvania," *Agricultural History* 41 (1967): 59–70; Clarence H. Danhof, *Changes in Agriculture: The Northern United States, 1820–1870* (Cambridge, Mass.: Harvard University Press, 1969), chaps. 1 and 2.

19. One traveler in the Northwest Territory in 1822 wrote, "A batchelor has no business in the Backwoods . . ." Cited in Stanley Lebergott, *Manpower in Economic Growth: The American Record Since 1800* (New York: McGraw-Hill, 1964), p. 278. See also letters from single and widowed farmers cited in Schob, *Hired Hands and Plowboys*, p. 194.

20. See examples from the *Ohio Cultivator*, the *Ohio Valley Farmer*, and the *Michigan Farmer* cited in Schob, *Hired Hands and Plowboys*, p. 191, n. 22; and similar remarks in the western Canadian press cited by Genevieve Leslie, "Domestic Service in Canada, 1880–1920," in Janice Acton et al., eds., *Women at Work: Ontario, 1850–1930* (Toronto: Canadian Women's Educational Press, 1974), p. 109.

21. Most studies of servants' wages argue that room and board were roughly equivalent to cash wages. See Katzman, *Seven Days a Week*, p. 174; Lebergott, *Manpower in Economic Growth*, pp. 283–284. Blaine McKinley suggests that room and board amounted to more than half of total compensation, but he relies on some sources, such as tracts addressed to servants, that we should suspect of upward bias. See his "'The Stranger in the Gates': Employer Reactions Toward Domestic Servants in America, 1825–1875" (Ph.D. diss., Michigan State University, 1969), p. 23. In fact, employers and social surveyors often overestimated the value of room and board. In any case, it seldom occurred to the employers of help to try to calculate the monetary value of room and board, an attitude that in itself reflects some lack of distinction between paid and unpaid work.

22. "She," *Scribner's Monthly* 3 (November 1871): 117. The editors thus sneer at rural ways, but the hit was palpable.

Family Relations

23. Lucy Larcom, *A New England Girlhood* (1889; reprint ed., New York: Corinth Books, 1961), pp. 188, 190.

24. POE, 1820–1822.

25. Catharine Maria Sedgwick, *Life and Letters of Catharine Maria Sedgwick*, ed. Mary E. Dewey (New York: Harper & Bros., 1871), p. 54.

26. For an excellent case study of the binding of orphans into domestic service, see Carol S. Lasser, "A 'Pleasingly Oppressive' Burden: The Transformation of Domestic Service and Female Charity in Salem, 1800–1840," *Essex Institute Historical Collections* 116 (1980): 156–175. On the eighteenth-century roots of this practice, see David J. Rothman, *The Discovery of the Asylum: Social Order and Disorder in the New Republic* (Boston: Little, Brown &

Co., 1971), pp. 35, 41. On the dual aims of binding out, see Susan L. Porter, "Mother/Mistress, Servant/Child: The Orphan as Indentured Servant in the Early Victorian Family" (Paper delivered at the Fourth Berkshire Conference of Women Historians, Mt. Holyoke College, Aug. 1978).

27. See Rothman, *Discovery of the Asylum*, chap. 9 and pp. 258–261; Lasser, "A 'Pleasingly Oppressive' burden," p. 157; Robert H. Bremmer, *From the Depths: The Discovery of Poverty in the United States* (New York: NYU Press, 1966), p. 47; Barbara Brenzel, "Lancaster Industrial School for Girls: A Social Portrait of a Nineteenth-Century Reform School for Girls," *Feminist Studies* 3 (Fall 1975): 40–53.

28. It is difficult to trace the history of orphan binding out because it was administered by localities and private charities under different state laws. Rothman indicates that rising concern with disorder prompted increasing concern with delinquent children. But they made poor candidates for binding out: it was too easy for them to run away, and few families wanted to take in young girls with "vicious habits." See James Leiby, *A History of Social Welfare and Social Work in the United States* (New York: Columbia University Press, 1978), pp. 54–55; Robert S. Pickett, *House of Refuge: Origins of Juvenile Reform in New York State, 1815–1857* (Syracuse, New York: Syracuse University Press, 1969). The Salem Female Charitable Society placed only 82 girls between 1801 and 1840, while the Boston Female Asylum placed 177 girls in about the same forty-year period. See Lasser, "A 'Pleasingly Oppressive' Burden," p. 157; and Porter, "Mother/Mistress, Servant/ Child."

29. Jane L. Hardy to Mary Hardy Williams, n.d., Josiah Butler Williams Family Papers, Cornell University, Ithaca, New York (hereafter JBW).

30. Siba Hand Smith to Henrietta Ward Clarke, 29 March 1837, Freeman Clarke Family Papers, University of Rochester, Rochester, New York. Mrs. Smith writes that the girl's mother "is willing you should take her upon trial, and if there is mutual satisfaction wish you to keep her until she is eighteen."

31. M. S. Beatty to Amy Kirby Post, 10 May 1850, Post Family Papers, University of Rochester, Rochester, New York.

32. Eliza K. Bacon to Helen Breese, 5 March 1834, Breese-Stevens-Roby Papers, University of Rochester, Rochester, New York (hereafter B-S-R).

33. Mary E. Forman to Kitty Breese Graves, 8 April 1846, B-S-R. This letter suggests, as do some of the examples above, that women who lived in cities and towns found girls for their friends who lived in the hinterlands.

34. The New York Children's Aid Society operated a modified form of binding out in the 1850s and 1860s in New York City. Their system was called "placing out," and it did not require employers to assume formal legal responsibilities for specified terms. The society faced strenuous opposition from local Catholic organizations and Catholic parents. See Charles Loring Brace, *The Dangerous Classes of New York and Twenty Years Work Among Them* (New York: Wynkoop and Hallenbeck, 1872); and Miriam Z. Langsam, *Children West: A History of the Placing-out System of the New York Children's Aid Society, 1852–1890* (Madison, Wisconsin: State Historical Society of Wisconsin, 1964). Brace and his Children's Aid Society pushed placing out as a solution to urban delinquency even though binding out was on the wane, and had never been notably successful with delinquents. In part this was due to the fact that institutionalization was by the 1850s already offering a ready target for criticism and alternative proposals. More important, Brace's modification of the legal requirements permitted placement with less prior investigation or initial commitment, and this in turn permitted shipping the children long distances to the rural West. He placed mostly boys on farms, and his program probably owed its "success" to the fact that there was little follow-up on the boys: those who did run off or turn to crime were at all events not in New York City when they did so. On the long-term mortality decline as it affected orphanhood, see: Peter R. Uhlenberg, "A Study of Cohort Life Cycles: Cohorts of Native-Born Massachusetts Women, 1830–1920," *Population Studies* 13 (1969): 414.

35. See Porter, "Mother/Mistress, Servant/Child"; and Lasser, "A 'Pleasingly Oppressive' Burden," pp. 164, 168.

36. Harriet Martineau, *Society in America*, 3 vols. (1837; reprint ed. New York: AMS Press, 1966), 3:137–138.

37. Catharine Maria Sedgwick, *Home*, 15th ed. (Boston: James Munroe, 1841), p. 72.

38. See Lasser, "A 'Pleasingly Oppressive' Burden," pp. 171–172.

39. The early looseness of the term *family* became anachronistically fixed in census usage, where "families" continued to be defined as those sharing a roof and a table long after common usage insisted on the presence of blood ties and emotional bonds. See Carroll D. Wright, *The History and Growth of the United States Census* (1900, reprint ed., Johnson Reprint Corp., 1966), pp. 156–157, 170–171, 186.

40. Mary P. Ryan, *Cradle of the Middle Class: The Family in Oneida County, New York, 1790–1865* (New York: Cambridge University Press, 1981), pp. 25, 36–39.

41. Eliza Farnham, *My Early Days* (New York: Thatcher and Hutchinson, 1859).

42. POE, 8, 11, and 30 March 1829.

43. Ibid, 12, 19, and 29 May 1829.

44. Ibid., 2, 4, 5, and 10 June 1829.

Recruitment and Hiring

45. Hezekiah Niles in *Niles' Weekly Register* 9 (2 December 1815): 238–239, cited in George Rogers Taylor, *The Transportation Revolution, 1815–1860* (New York: Holt, Rinehart and Winston, 1964), p. 4. See also examples cited in Schob, *Hired Hands and Plowboys*, pp. 202–203; and Frances Willard, *Glimpses of Fifty Years* (Chicago: Women's Temperance Publication Association, 1889), p. 70.

46. Thomas Low Nichols, *Forty Years of American Life*, 2 vols. (1864; reprint ed., New York: Negro Universities Press, 1968), 1:21.

47. Sedgwick, *Life and Letters*, p. 20.

48. Eunice Bullard Beecher, *From Dawn to Daylight; or, The Simple Story of a Western Home* (New York: Derby & Jackson, 1859), pp. 184–185. The names have been changed, but Mrs. Beecher betrays no desire to protect the guilty, whether servants, congregations, or husbands.

49. Caroline M. S. Kirkland, *A New Home—Who'll Follow? or, Glimpses of Western Life*, 4th ed. (New York: C. S. Francis, 1850), p. 63.

50. Caroline M. S. Kirkland, *Western Clearings* (New York: Wiley and Putnam, 1846), pp. 168–169.

51. Frances Wright D'Arusmont, *Views of Society and Manners in America* (Cambridge, Massachusetts: Harvard University Press, 1963), p. 283.

52. *Diary of Sarah Connell Ayer*, p. 246.

53. Mary Huggins to My Dear Friends, 29 January 1858–60?, Farmington, Illinois, cited in Schob, *Hired Hands and Plowboys*, p. 205, n. 75. For other examples of girls who helped and attended school, see: Susan Breese Snowdon to Brother, 29 September 1830, Sacketts Harbor, New York, BSR; and Susan Hooker to Mother, 4 March 1877, Rochester, New York, Huntington-Hooker Papers, University of Rochester.

54. POE, 8 August through 14 September 1826.

55. Diary of Ida M. Bliss, 6 March 1888, Bliss Family Papers, State Historical Society of Wisconsin, Madison, Wisconsin.

56. See, for example, Martha Williams to Mary Hardy Williams, 14 May 1845, and Mary Hardy Williams to Jane Hardy, 10 December 1846, JBW.

57. Niles cited in Taylor, *Transportation Revolution*, p. 4. The agricultural frontier was conducive to early marriages. See Richard A. Easterlin, "Factors in the Decline of Farm Family Fertility in the United States: Some Preliminary Research Results," in Michael Gordon, ed., *The American Family in Social-Historical Perspective*, 2nd ed. (New York: St. Martin's Press, 1978), table 1 and p. 538. The median age at first birth, a proxy for age at marriage, was almost a year and a half higher in long-settled areas than in newly settled western townships.

58. Diary of Ida M. Bliss, 7 March 1888. See also Diary of Mary Elizabeth Pascoe, State Historical Society of Wisconsin.

59. Susan Porter found that families tended to request girls from the Boston Female Asylum at two points in life, early in the marriage, when they had many small children, and again about twenty years later when the children were grown. See her "Mother/Mistress, Servant/Child."

60. Childbed nurses seem to have been hired despite the presence of regular servants and female relatives. For examples, see: POE, 7—16 April 1824 and 14—26 February 1826; Elizabeth Cady Stanton, *Eighty Years and More: Reminiscences, 1815—1897* (1898; reprint ed., New York: Schocken Books, 1971), pp. 115—121; Augustus Stevens to Parents, 13 July 1832, B-S-R; Diary of Mary Hardy Williams, 19 October 1843, JBW; Ann Fitzhugh Smith to Elizabeth Smith Miller, February 1845, Gerrit Smith Papers, Syracuse University. The most complete portrait of a childbed nurse I have found is that of Mrs. Kilbourne in the Diary of Hannah Wright Gould, 15 September to 14 October 1851, Cornell University (hereafter HWG).

61. See, for example, references to Maria in Robert Stuart, *The Stuart Letters of Robert and Elizabeth Sullivan Stuart and Their Children, 1819—1864*, ed. Helen Stuart Mackay-Smith Marlatt, 2 vols. (Washington?: Privately printed, 1961), pp. 602—603, 688, 692; and references to Jenny in the Munn-Pixley Family Papers, University of Rochester.

62. Mary Todd Lincoln to Mary Brayman, 17 June (1861), in Justin G. Turner and Linda Levitt Turner, *Mary Todd Lincoln: Her Life and Letters* (New York: Alfred Knopf, 1972), p. 90.

63. Mary Stuart Turner to Kate Stuart Baker, 25 July 1850, in Stuart, *The Stuart Letters*, pp. 110–111.

64. Diary of Jane Bewel Kelly, 3 June 1866, State Historical Society of Wisconsin (hereafter JBK). For another example of a farm family who engaged a hired girl only after illness, see: Anne Gertrude Sneller, *A Vanished World* (Syracuse, New York: Syracuse University Press, 1964), pp. 284–285.

65. William Andrus Alcott, *Ways of Living on Small Means* (Boston: Light and Stearns, 1837), p. 32. Compare the remarks of another critic of service, Thorstein Veblen, who excepted "servants employed to attend on the persons of the infirm and the feeble-minded." Thorstein Veblen, *The Theory of the Leisure Class* (New York: New American Library, Mentor Books, 1953), p. 59.

66. Diary of Sarah E. Beaulieu, 1–7 March 1865, cited in W. Elliot Brownlee and Mary M. Brownlee, *Women in the American Economy: A Documentary History, 1675–1929* (New Haven and London: Yale University Press, 1976), pp. 127–130.

67. A late survey of Wisconsin farmers documents this pattern. Among the 555 farmers who responded to a questionnaire circulated by the Wisconsin Bureau of Labor, Census and Industrial Statistics in 1895, 36 percent hired "female help" in the summer, while only 24 percent did so in the winter. Many of those who hired a girl year-round had to pay an extra twenty-five or fifty cents a week in the summer. See: Wisconsin Bureau of Labor, Census and Industrial Statistics, *Seventh Biennial Report, 1895–96* (Madison, Wisconsin: Democrat Printing Co., 1896), pp. 66–85, 107. See also Schob, *Hired Hands and Plowboys*, p. 191.

68. POE 1–3 November 1827.

69. Larcom, *A New England Girlhood*, p. 119. She notes that they were not called servants and that they had homes of their own.

70. Elizabeth Breese Stevens to Mother, 26 April 1832, B-S-R.

71. Diary of Sarah Christie Stevens, 1894, cited in Gerda Lerner, *The Female Experience: An American Documentary* (Indianapolis: Bobbs-Merrill, 1977), pp. 260–261. For other references to married women as temporary help, see JBK, 12 April 1871, 3 March 1882, and 8 July 1886.

72. For examples of such complaints, see Schob, *Hired Hands and Plowboys*, pp. 204–205; Editorial Correspondence, *Arthur's Home Magazine* 21 (March

1863): 199; Elizabeth Ellet, "Helps," *Godey's Lady's Book* 28 (April 1844): 194.

73. Diary of Eva C. Beem, 27 June and 19 August 1871, Cornell University.

74. See Thomas Dublin, *Women at Work: The Transformation of Work and Community in Lowell, Massachusetts, 1826–1860* (New York: Columbia University Press, 1979), pp. 33–37. Dublin refers to two young women, Mary Paul and Sally Rice, who both helped and worked in the mills.

75. JBK, 5 March 1871.

76. Hannah Kirby Post to Amy Kirby, 14 November 1824, Post Family Papers.

77. See Grund, *The Americans*, 2:320; and Charles Mackay, *Life and Liberty in America: Sketches of a Tour in the United States and Canada in 1857–1858* (New York: Harper & Bros., 1860), p. 243.

78. William P. Cutler and Julia P. Cutler, *Life, Journals and Correspondence of Rev. Manasseh Cutler*, 2 vols. (Cincinnati: Robert Clarke, 1888), 2:155.

79. See Sedgwick, *Life and Letters*, pp. 40–42, 73; references to Peter Crosby in Frances Seward to Lazette Warden, 18 January 1834, Seward Family Papers, University of Rochester; and Stanton, *Eighty Years and More*, pp. 5–7, 14–17. Such client-relationships may have reflected patterns of paternalistic obligation developed under slavery. The purchase of slaves for domestic servants showed relatively little attention to pecuniary considerations. See McManus, *Black Bondage*, pp. 37–38, 41. For references to such paternalistic relations, see Anne Grant, *Memoirs of an American Lady*, 2 vols. (New York: Dodd, Mead and Co., 1903), 1:80–83; Sidney George Fisher, *A Philadelphia Perspective: The Diary of Sidney George Fisher Covering the Years 1834–1871*, ed. Nicholas B. Wainwright (Philadelphia: Historical Society of Pennsylvania, 1967), p. 295.

Working Conditions and Hours

80. POE, 6 August 1826.

81. JBK, 16 June 1871.

82. John Bigelow, *Retrospections of an Active Life*, 5 vols. (New York: Baker and Taylor, 1909), 1:14.

83. Christiana Holmes Tillson, *A Woman's Story of Pioneer Illinois*, ed. M. M. Quaife (Chicago: R. R. Donnelly and Sons, The Lakeside Press, 1919), pp. 111, 147.

84. JBK, 1 July 1866.

85. Cited in Schob, *Hired Hands and Plowboys*, p. 202. La Rochefoucauld understood the advantages of participatory supervision. He noted a tone of resentment among the agricultural laborers on Samuel Elem's farm near Newport, Rhode Island: "As Mr. Elem is the only farmer in the island who does not labour with his own hands, so he often meets with a contradictory spirit in his working-people, who are apt to think that their toil must make them more skillful in husbandry than their idle master." See La Rochefoucauld-Liancourt, *Travels Through the United States*, 1:495.

86. Fredrika Bremer, *The Homes of the New World*, trans. Mary Howitt, 2 vols. (New York: Harper & Bros., 1853), 1:645.

87. For Trollope, the insistence on such eating arrangements was just another example of the ridiculous pride and want of refinement she discovered everywhere in American life. See her *Domestic Manners of the Americans*, pp. 53–54. As usual, some travelers confounded and others elucidated the differences between help and domestics. For an example of one who clarified the distinction, see: Alexander Mackay, *The Western World*, 2nd ed., 3 vols. (1849; reprint ed., New York: Negro University Press, 1969), 1:223. Mackay wrote: "The farmer, his sons and servants, work together and eat together, living as nearly in a state of equality with each other as can be . . . but to think that the same practice in its totality or even in a modified form enters all grades of society is erroneous."

88. Goodrich, *Recollections of a Lifetime*, 1:84.

89. Sedgwick, *Life and Letters*, p. 21. Julia Ward Howe was another woman from a prominent background, but because she came from New York City rather than western Massachusetts, she was less aware than Sedgwick of arrangements that differed from her own family's. When as a young matron she encountered a servant who wished to share her table, she declared that she had never seen such a thing, but had only read of it in Mrs. Trollope. Maud Howe Elliott and Laura E. Howe Richards, *Julia Ward Howe, 1819–1910*, 2 vols. (Boston: Houghton Mifflin and Co., 1916), 1:114.

90. Jonas Booth to Joseph Booth, 20 March 1829, cited in Charlotte Erickson, *Invisible Immigrants: The Adaptation of English and Scottish Immigrants in Nineteenth-Century America* (Coral Gables, Fla.: University of Miami Press, 1972), p. 255.

91. *Journals and Letters of Mother Theodore Guerin*, in Rosemary Radford Ruether and Rosemary Skinner Keller, eds., *Women and Religion in America*,

(New York: Harper and Row, 1981), vol. 1, *The Nineteenth Century*, p. 120. Mother Guerin had come to Indiana to establish her order. She wanted to banish the "miserably clad" young washerwoman from her table, but did not dare to do so when she saw the looks on the faces of her American postulants.

92. Grace Goddard to Grace Goddard Drury, 2 February 1828, Goddard Family Correspondence, American Antiquarian Society, Worcester, Massachusetts.

93. See Peter Farb and George Armelagos, *Consuming Passions: The Anthropology of Eating* (Boston: Houghton Mifflin, 1980).

94. Mary C. Hungerford, "Domestic Service," *Lippincott's Magazine* 59 (October 1895): 567.

95. See Schob, *Hired Hands and Plowboys*, p. 205.

96. See Carl Sandburg, *Abraham Lincoln: The Prairie Years*, 2 vols. (New York: Charles Scribner's Sons, 1940), 2:278. Mrs. Lincoln supposedly met him at the door and told him off in no uncertain terms. The uncle then went to Lincoln and told him his grievance. Lincoln listened carefully and finally asked, "If I have had to stand this every day for fifteen years, don't you think you can stand it for a few minutes one day?" The story may be apocryphal; even so, its incidental structure, including the uncle's behavior, must have been believable.

97. JBK, 4 March 1872.

98. Goodrich, *Recollections of a Lifetime* 1:84.

99. *Diary of Sarah Connell Ayer*, pp. 259, 271, 273.

100. See, for example, John McCall, "Remarks on the Diseases of Oneida County, New York, in 1854," *New York Journal of Medicine* 14 (1855): 265; and the Dr. Orin Shepard Campbell Account Books, cited in Schob, *Hired Hands and Plowboys*, p. 203, n. 64.

101. See Mary Williams to Elizabeth Breese Stevens, 28 November 1855, B-S-R. Here an ex-servant asks Mrs. Stevens to see the doctor and find out how much his bill is, so that she may save up the money.

102. Oliver E. Lyman, "The Legal Status of Servant Girls," *Popular Science Monthly* 22 (1883): 806. Although not bound to furnish medical attention or medicine, the hiring party was bound to furnish proper food and to support the servant during the illness so long as she remained in employ.

103. According to Paul Starr, demand for physicians' services was relatively low early in the nineteenth century, but it began to grow by mid-century due

to improvements in transport and communications. See Paul Starr, "Medicine, Economy and Society in Nineteenth-Century America," *Journal of Social History* 10 (Summer 1977): 589–595.

104. Caroline C. Briggs, *Reminiscences and Letters*, ed. George R. Merriam (Boston and New York: Houghton Mifflin and Co., 1897), pp. 31, 33.

105. Ibid.

106. Ibid, p. 31.

107. Thomas C. Grattan, *Civilized America*, 2 vols. (London: Bradbury and Evans, 1859), 1:250. See also Emily Faithfull, *Three Visits to America* (Edinburgh: D. Douglas, 1884), p. 278.

108. Michel Chevalier, *Society, Manners and Politics in the United States*, trans. from the 3rd Paris ed. (Boston: Weeks, Jordan and Co., 1839), p. 284.

109. Moritz Busch, *Travels Between the Hudson and the Mississippi, 1851–1852*, trans. Norman H. Binger (Lexington, Kentucky: University Press of Kentucky, 1971), pp. 256–257.

110. Médéric Moreau de Saint-Méry, who visited the United States in the 1790s, cited in Oscar Handlin, ed., *This Was America* (Cambridge, Massachusetts: Harvard University Press, 1949), p. 99.

111. Diary of Anna Bryant Smith, cited in Cott, *Bonds of Womanhood*, p. 29.

112. Nathaniel Hawthorne, *Passages from the American Note-Books* (Boston and New York: Houghton Mifflin, 1883), p. 74.

113. Kirkland, *Western Clearings*, p. 25. This was a fictionalized account of her own experiences.

114. JBK, 24 June 1872.

115. Dunlap Letterbook, 9 February 1853, cited in Schob, *Hired Hands and Plowboys*, p. 203.

116. Martineau, *Society in America*, 3:137.

117. Briggs, *Reminiscences*, p. 32.

118. Mary Robbins Post to Isaac Post, 185?, Post Family Papers. The author of one fictionalized reminiscence told of finding her cook entertaining the tailor's apprentice. She left them "in undisturbed possession of the settle," noting that "there is a tacit agreement in New England" to allow such kitchen company. Caroline Howard Gilman, *Recollections of a Housekeeper* (New York: Harper & Bros., 1834), p. 97.

119. Stanton, *Eighty Years and More*, p. 6.

120. Diary of Sarah Josephine Stoughton, 28 July 1869, American Antiquarian Society, Worcester, Massachusetts.

121. *Diary of Sarah Connell Ayer*, pp. 272–273, letter of 13 March 1810.

122. Diary of Sarah J. Stoughton, 28 July 1869, 12 August 1869, and 30 May 1870.

123. Gilman, *Recollections of a Housekeeper*, pp. 90–91; Briggs, *Reminiscences*, p. 93.

2. Domestics

Recruitment and Hiring in an Emerging Labor Market

1. See Louise Fargo Brown, *Apostle of Democracy: The Life of Lucy Maynard Salmon* (New York: Harper & Bros., 1943), p. 5. For a useful account of the triumph of a rationale for schooling women beyond basic literacy in the years between 1780 and 1835, see Cott, *Bonds of Womanhood*, chap. 3. The best summary of institutional development is still Thomas Woody, *A History of Women's Education in the United States*, 2 vols. (New York: Octagon Books, 1966).

2. Larcom, *A New England Girlhood*, p. 199.

3. On the sporadic and seasonal patterns of early nineteenth-century school sessions, see Joseph Kett, *Rites of Passage: Adolescence in America, 1790 to the Present* (New York: Basic Books, 1977), chap. 1. See also Richard M. Bernard and Maris A. Vinovskis, "The Female School Teacher in Antebellum Massachusetts," *Journal of Social History* 10 (March 1977): 332–345. Bernard and Vinovskis estimate that one out of five white women in pre-Civil War Massachusetts was a school teacher at some time in her life.

4. Cott, *Bonds of Womanhood*, p. 28.

5. See Gerda Lerner, "The Lady and the Mill Girl: Changes in the Status of Women in the Age of Jackson," *Midcontinent American Studies Journal* 10 (1969): 5–15. Joseph Kett has argued that class differences in the activities and occupations of young people became more marked as the nineteenth century progressed (Kett, *Rites of Passage*, pp. 30, 151–152). His point is based mostly on the lives of young men, but the choices facing young women might support the same contention. Helping had drawn on a relatively wide spectrum in the early farming communities, including girls who found a

money income temporarily desirable but not absolutely necessary; urban domestic service would be more a matter of sheer economic necessity.

6. See Paul E. Johnson, *A Shopkeeper's Millennium: Society and Revivals in Rochester, New York, 1815–1837* (New York: Hill and Wang, 1978); Ryan, *Cradle of the Middle Class*, p. xiii and chapter 4. For another brief account of this transformation, see Sam Bass Warner, Jr., on Philadelphia, where new middle classes of businessmen, retailers, factory owners, and mill supervisors lived in larger, more elaborate homes separated from the office, shop, or store in which the husband worked. *The Private City: Philadelphia in Three Periods of Its Growth* (Philadelphia: University of Pennsylvania Press, 1968), pp. 65–67. I use *middle classes* in plural form to denote the different situations of upper and lower middle class, groups that might be better denoted as *bourgeoisie* and *petite bourgeoisie* if only these terms sounded more appropriate to the American social landscape.

7. Cited in Cott, *Bonds of Womanhood*, p. 68. I have relied on the discussions of domesticity in Cott, *Bonds of Womanhood*, and Kathryn Kish Sklar, *Catharine Beecher: A Study in American Domesticity* (New York: W. W. Norton and Co., 1976). Cott and Sklar note the large volume of prescriptive literature on women's roles that appeared beginning in the 1830s and helped to crystallize the concept of domesticity. They both argue for its close relationship to the lives of middle-class women, Sklar by showing how the writing of influential advice literature grew out of one woman's experience, Cott by comparing its tenets with the experiences of ordinary middle-class women as shown in their diaries and letters.

8. See Kett, *Rites of Passage*, p. 138; Ryan, *Cradle of the Middle Class*, pp. 192–194; and Laurence A. Glasco, "Ethnicity and Social Structure: Irish, Germans, and Native-Born of Buffalo, New York, 1850–1860." (Ph.D. diss., SUNY Buffalo, 1973), pp. 201–205, re. the household status of native-born females.

9. See Beecher, *Letters to Persons Who Are Engaged in Domestic Service* (New York: Leavitt & Trow, 1842), pp. 87–89. Beecher noted that "even if domestics were ever so well-educated and well-bred, there are reasons why it would be more agreeable and convenient to have the family eat and sit by themselves, and domestics eat and sit in the kitchen." Among these were the fact that the father could often see his family only at mealtimes, and he needed the liberty to talk as he could not before "every stranger he hires." Beecher and Stowe acknowledged that separate tables reflected not so much the decline of servants as a group but the elevation, or at least the ambitions,

of servant employers. They refer to hired girls having shared the table and then note that "families increased in refinement and education so as to make these conditions of close intimacy with more uncultured neighbors disagreeable." *The American Woman's Home*, p. 319.

10. Lydia Maria Child, *The Frugal Housewife*, 3rd ed. (Boston: Carter & Hendee, 1830), p. 105. John Bigelow recalled hearing a talk in 1860 by Shaftesbury in which the earl remarked on the great transformation cheap travel and the penny post had caused in English domestic service: servants could change positions so easily that they did so merely from a desire to see more of the world. See Bigelow, *Retrospections of an Active Life*, 1 : 257–258.

11. Mehitable Goddard to Lucretia Dawes, 8 July 1831, May-Goddard Papers, Schlesinger Library, Radcliffe College, Cambridge, Massachusetts.

12. Oliver Wendell Holmes, *Life and Letters*, ed. John J. Morse, Jr., 2 vols. (Boston and New York: Houghton Mifflin, 1896), 1 : 34.

13. Martineau, *Society in America*, 2 : 33.

14. Eloise Miles Abbott, *Personal Sketches and Recollections* (Boston: A. Tompkins, 1861), pp. 113–114.

15. See Kett, *Rites of Passage*, pp. 95–96. Kett compares the 1830 sex ratios for fifteen- to nineteen-year-olds for rural Middlesex County, Massachusetts with the ratios for the cities of Charlestown and Lowell, to show that young women went to the cities as well as migrating in more noticeable fashion to the textile mill towns. Compare John Modell, "The Peopling of a Working Class Ward: Reading, Pennsylvania, 1850," *Journal of Social History* 5 (1971): 95, app. B. An exceptionally zealous census taker enables Modell to compile age-specific place-of-birth data for some residents of Reading in 1850. In the fifteen to nineteen age group there is a sudden jump in the percentage of females born in contiguous townships or in the rest of Berks County. In fact, the percentage of residents (aged fifteen to nineteen) who inmigrated from those areas is higher among females than males.

16. New York Society for the Encouragement of Faithful Domestic Servants (hereafter cited as NYSEFDS), *First Annual Report* (New York: D. Fanshaw, 1826), p. 3.

17. Leslie, *The House Book*, p. 336. On the elaboration of needs associated with the employment of domestics, see below, chapter 4.

18. Diary of Helen Munson Williams, 22 February 1854 and 28 June 1854, Helen Munson Williams Papers, Oneida County Historical Society, Utica, New York. For other references to the hiring of temporary dayworkers, see:

Susan Hooker to Mother, 21 March 1869 and 15 April 1877, Huntington-Hooker Papers; Jane L. Hardy to Mary Hardy Williams, n.d. (ca. 1850) and Diary of Mary Hardy Williams, 21 April 1849, JBW.

19. Mariette A. Chapin to Mother, 25 May 1862, Joseph and Mariette Armour Correspondence, Madison County Historical Society, Oneida, New York.

20. Lillian Pettengill, *Toilers of the Home: The Record of a College Woman's Experience as a Domestic Servant* (New York: Doubleday, Page and Co., 1903), chap. 6. Because Pettengill was a college woman who entered domestic service in order to investigate it, she is not a reliable source about servants' motives or reactions, but there is no reason to doubt her reports about employer practices.

21. Lydia Maria Child explained, "The law compels everybody who intends to move at all, to quit his premises before twelve o'clock, on May morning. . . . This regulation, handed down from old Dutch times, proves very convenient in arranging the Directory with promptness and accuracy." *Letters from New York* (New York: C. S. Francis, 1845), p. 286. Stuart Blumin found that the same custom prevailed in Kingston, New York. See his *The Urban Threshold: Growth and Change in a Nineteenth-Century American Community* (Chicago: University of Chicago Press, 1976), p. 109.

22. NYSEFDS, *First Annual Report*, p. 6.

23. When in 1863 the New York City draft rioters targeted the wealthy, they usually had to settle for looting their homes, since the vast majority of New York's wealthiest citizens were out of town in July. See Adrian Cook, *The Armies of the Streets: The New York City Draft Riots of 1863* (Lexington, Kentucky: University of Kentucky Press, 1974), pp. 66, 90–91, 99, 108. The June exodus could generate servant turnover even among those who did not leave. See Lucy A. Dunning to Mary Hardy Williams, 15 April 1845, JBW. Here a New York City acquaintance wants the Dunnings, presently boarding, to take his house for the summer while he and his family go into the country; the Dunnings will then require a servant in the kitchen, just for the summer. For reference to nurses accompanying their charges to Ballston Spa, New York, see Susan Porter to Husband, 31 July 1856, Porter Family Papers, University of Rochester. One piece of evidence from a later period may suggest the magnitude of seasonal turnover. When the Domestic Efficiency Association of Baltimore began to take applications from unemployed servants in the early 1920s, between one-fourth and one-third stated that they had left their previous employment because the house had been closed.

See Mary V. Robinson, "Domestic Workers and Their Employment Relations: A Study Based on the Records of the Domestic Efficiency Association of Baltimore, Maryland," U.S. Women's Bureau *Bulletin*, 39 (1924): 16.

24. See Katz, *People of Hamilton*, pp. 58, 158–159. Katz computes phi coefficients to show that acquisition or loss of a servant is the variable most strongly related to economic mobility, more so than changes in occupational title or property holdings. He concludes that "the acquisition or loss of servants may turn out to be the best quick index of mobility in the mid-nineteenth century" (p. 159).

25. See Louisa May Alcott, *Work: A Story of Experience*, intro. by Sarah Elbert (1873; reprint ed., New York: Schocken Books, 1977), pp. xxix–xxx.

26. Mehitable Goddard to Lucretia Dawes, 21 February 1830, May-Goddard Papers.

27. NYSEFDS, *First Annual Report*, p. 13.

28. Mathew Carey, "Essay on the Relations Between Masters and Mistresses, and Domestics," *American Ladies' Magazine* 10 (June 1835): 244. Carey noted stiffly, "This is a shameful practice, of which some of our citizens who hold their heads very high, are guilty. The writer of this has been a sufferer by this conduct."

29. Catharine Beecher, *A Treatise on Domestic Economy*, intro. by Kathryn Kish Sklar (1841; reprint ed., New York: Schocken Books, 1977), p. 203. For other complaints on this point, see Robert Tomes, "Your Humble Servant," *Harper's New Monthly Magazine* 29 (June 1864): 54; Hungerford, "Domestic Service," p. 568.

30. C. W. Porter to Lucy Maynard Salmon, 13 April 1889, Lucy Maynard Salmon Papers, Vassar College, Poughkeepsie, New York (hereafter LMS).

31. Lavinia Field Stuart to Kate Stuart Baker, 25 March 1852, in Stuart, *The Stuart Letters*, pp. 297–298.

32. Rev. H. Winslow, "Domestic Education of Females," *The Mother's Magazine* 22 (March 1854): 93.

33. H. E. Dodge to Elizabeth Breese Stevens, 26 June 1859, B-S-R.

34. See a collection of her columns: Eunice Bullard Beecher, *Motherly Talks with Young Housekeepers* (New York: J. B. Ford, 1873), pp. 112–116.

35. C. Beecher, *Treatise on Domestic Economy*, p. 198.

36. E. L. Godkin, "The Morals and Manners of the Kitchen," *The Nation* 16 (2 January 1873): 7.

37. Ellis, "Our Household Servants," p. 353.

38. Beecher and Stowe, *The American Woman's Home*, p. 324.

39. Charles Loring Brace, "The Servant Question," *The Nation* (26 October 1865), p. 528. Late in the nineteenth century, reformers hammered away on this line of explanation for servant problems, and offered a series of proposals, including training schools for servants and employer education in domestic science. Susan Strasser has discussed these reformers—including Lucy Maynard Salmon, Gail Laughlin, Jane Addams, and Henrietta Goodrich—in her "Mistress and Maid, Employer and Employee: Domestic Service Reform in the United States, 1897–1920," *Marxist Perspectives* vol. 1, no. 4 (Winter 1978): 52–67. Strasser argues that the view of the servant problem in terms of wage labor was a new development at the turn of the twentieth century. In fact, however, it developed gradually throughout the nineteenth century, along with the displacement of help by domestics. "Friendly advice" to servants, such as Strasser cites from the midnineteenth century, emphasized nonmarket behavior ("Never quit a place of your own accord."), but employers were moved to press such advice by contrary behavior, and some of them offered analyses that recognized servants' rights to marketplace behavior. What was new at the turn of the century was the institutional forms these ideas gave rise to—training schools for servants, investigative commissions, and the like—and the formation of a cadre of experts who defined the problems, did the investigating, and administered the institutions and programs.

40. For ample documentation of this theme, see McKinley, "Stranger in the Gates."

41. See Christopher Lasch, *Haven in a Heartless World: The Family Besieged* (New York: Basic Books, 1977), pp. 7–8, on the obscurity of classical economics' description of the market economy, an obscurity that lent itself to confusions and contradictions such as this.

Caroline Barrett White and Her Domestics

42. All references will be to the Diaries of Caroline Barrett White, 1855–1874, American Antiquarian Society, Worcester, Massachusetts (hereafter CBW).

43. Ibid., 17 April 1858. For other examples, see: 17 November 1860, 21 October 1861, 30 August 1864.

44. Ibid., 19 and 23 September 1857.

45. Ibid., 23 October 1865 and 9 April 1858.

46. Ibid., 13 May 1859 and 19 June 1856.

47. Ibid., 10 April 1858.

48. Ibid., 9 and 20 November 1872.

49. Ibid., 11 October 1867.

50. Ibid., 15 May 1874.

51. Ibid., 18 April 1858.

52. Ibid., 8 May 1858.

53. Ibid., 29 May 1859.

54. Ibid., 2 May 1858.

55. Ibid., 25 and 26 October 1865.

56. Ibid., 3 October 1865.

57. Ibid., 7 August 1863.

58. Ibid., 24 April 1858, 28 June 1859, 23 September 1857, 26 April 1858.

59. See, for example, ibid., 28 June 1859 or 3 July 1860.

60. Ibid., 13 April 1858.

Ethnicity and Race in the Market for Domestics

61. See for example, Kate Harrington, "Irish Blunders," *Godey's Lady's Book* 51 (September 1855): 247–248; or Virginia De Forest, "Biddy's Blunders," *Godey's Lady's Book* 50 (April 1855): 329–330.

62. NYSEFDS, *First Annual Report*, p. 8. See also Carol Groneman, "Working-Class Immigrant Women in Mid-Nineteenth-Century New York: The Irish Woman's Experience," *Journal of Urban History* 4 (May 1978): 255–273; and George Potter, *To the Golden Door: The Story of the Irish in Ireland and America* (Boston: Little, Brown & Co., 1960), pp. 133–134.

63. Groneman, "Working-Class Immigrant Women," p. 257; Robert E. Kennedy, *The Irish: Emigration, Marriage and Fertility* (Berkeley and Los Angeles: University of California Press, 1973), pp. 80–84; Brinley Thomas, *Migration and Economic Growth: A Study of Great Britain and the Atlantic Economy* (Cambridge: The University Press, 1954), p. 74, table 15.

64. Robert Ernst refers to immigrants from the Continent, especially Germans, as being "barred from American households because of ignorance of the English language" and asserts that those who did enter service usually turned to wealthier members of their own national group. See Robert Ernst,

Immigrant Life in New York City, 1825–1863 (New York: King's Crown Press of Columbia University, 1949), pp. 66, 175.

65. See Potter, *To the Golden Door*, pp. 119–121. Mathew Carey first publicized the extent of Irish remittances in a series of public letters to Bishop John Hughes of New York. For a characteristic sentimental tribute to the Irish woman's sacrifices, see John Francis Maguire, *The Irish in America* (1868; reprint ed., New York: Arno Press, 1969), pp. 314–332. Maguire observed that "in populous cities the women send home more money than the men" (p. 321).

66. Maguire, *The Irish in America*, p. 207.

67. See Katz, *People of Hamilton*, pp. 97–98.

68. See her "Working-Class Immigrant Women," p. 258.

69. Mary Frances Cusack (Sister Mary Frances Clare), *Advice to Irish Girls in America, By the Nun of Kenmare* (New York: McGee, 1872). Chapter 3, "The Honor of Being Servants," did not even mention other forms of employment for comparison's sake.

70. Blumin, *The Urban Threshold*, p. 89.

71. Katz, *People of Hamilton*, p. 288, table 5.21. In 1861 the respective percentages had dropped to 31 percent and 58 percent.

72. Laurence A. Glasco, "The Life Cycles and Household Structure of American Ethnic Groups: Irish, Germans and Native-Born Whites in Buffalo, New York, 1855," *Journal of Urban History* 1 (May 1975): 355. Glasco's article is marred by his apparent assumption that the Irish migrated in family units and then sent their daughters out to work. Data from the manuscript census do not reveal whether the foreign-born servant living in her employer's home had a family elsewhere in the city or country, or had come to this country without them. Glasco's dissertation is both fuller and more cautious as a source. See Glasco, "Ethnicity and Social Structure," pp. 210–211, 216–219.

73. See Glasco, "Ethnicity and Social Structure," pp. 217–218; and Carol Groneman Pernicone, "The 'Bloody Ould Sixth': A Social Analysis of a New York City Working-Class Community in the Mid-Nineteenth Century" (Ph.D. diss., University of Rochester, 1973), p. 167. Glasco indicates that German-born young women also worked as servants for shorter periods of time, marrying earlier than Irish-born women.

74. A study of the 1890 federal census found Scandinavian and German-born women, like the Irish, overrepresented in service. See: Edward P.

Hutchinson, *Immigrants and Their Children, 1850–1950* (New York: Wiley, 1956), table 29b, p. 129. Also Janice Reiff Webster, "Domestication and Americanization: Scandinavian Women in Seattle, 1888 to 1900," *Journal of Urban History* 4 (May 1978): 279; and data on the female occupational structure of Cleveland in 1890, in Kenneth L. Kusmer, *A Ghetto Takes Shape: Black Cleveland, 1870–1930* (Urbana, Illinois: University of Illinois Press, 1976), table 8, p. 72.

75. Katzman, *Seven Days a Week*, p. 70.

76. See William J. Bromwell, *History of Immigration to the United States* (New York: Redfield, 1856); and the discussion in Thomas, *Migration and Economic Growth*, pp. 42–47, to appreciate the limitations of the data. A few countries collected data on their out-migrants. See Kennedy, *The Irish*, pp. 80–84, re. data collected beginning in the 1870s; Ulf Beijbom, *Swedes in Chicago: A Demographic and Social Study of the 1846–1880 Immigration*, trans. Donald Brown (Sweden: Scandinavian University Books, 1971). The composition of given immigrant groups was not necessarily constant over time. Census data from local areas are potentially misleading because immigrants often ended up in an area according to the availability of jobs appropriate to the age, sex and skills of individuals or family members. For a discussion of some of the factors that affected immigrant women's entrance into domestic service and the work force in general, see Virginia Yans-McLaughlin, "Patterns of Work and Family Organization: Buffalo's Italians," in Michael Gordon, ed., *The American Family in Social-Historical Perspective* (New York: St. Martin's Press, 1973), pp. 136–151; and Louise A. Tilly, "Comment on the Yans-McLaughlin and Davidoff Papers," *Journal of Social History* 7 (1974): 452–455.

77. See Kennedy, *The Irish*, table 22 and chaps. 3 and 4. Also Suzanne Berger and Michael J. Piore, *Dualism and Discontinuity in Industrial Societies* (London and New York: Cambridge University Press, 1980); and Michael J. Piore, *Birds of Passage: Migrant Labor and Industrial Societies* (London and New York: Cambridge University Press, 1979). For a twentieth-century study, see Barbara Klaczynka, "Why Women Work: A Comparison of Various Groups—Philadelphia, 1910–1930," *Labor History* 17 (1976): 73–87.

78. It is possible to compare the change in service with the change that occurred in the Lowell mills, when the greater economic need of Irish immigrants made possible speed-ups and harsher conditions that would have aroused resistance among Yankee workers with rural homes to which they might return. See Dublin, *Women at Work*, chap. 9 and p. 156.

79. C. Beecher, *Treatise on Domestic Economy*, p. 17.

80. New York State Commissioners of Emigration, *Annual Report*, 1869 (New York: Douglas Taylor, 1870), p. 25. Other years for which statistics are available show comparable breakdowns.

81. See Ernst, *Immigrant Life*, pp. 213, 215, 32. Hershberg found that in Philadelphia in 1838 eight of ten black women worked as servants. Theodore Hershberg, "Free Blacks in Antebellum Philadelphia: A Study of Ex-Slaves, Freeborn and Socioeconomic Decline," in Theodore Hershberg, ed., *Philadelphia: Work, Space, Family and Group Experience in the Nineteenth Century* (New York: Oxford University Press, 1981), p. 382.

82. See Katzman, *Seven Days a Week*, pp. 89–93, 198–202.

83. Hershberg, "Free Blacks in Antebellum Philadelphia," in Hershberg, *Philadelphia*, p. 382. On a similar pattern in Buffalo in 1855, see Glasco, "Ethnicity and Social Structure," p. 159, n. 15.

84. See Leon F. Litwack, *Been in the Storm So Long: The Aftermath of Slavery* (New York: Random House Vintage Books, 1979), pp. 296, 312–313.

85. See Leon F. Litwack, *North of Slavery: The Negro in the Free States, 1790–1860* (Chicago: University of Chicago Press, 1961), pp. 153–168; Hershberg, "Free Blacks in Antebellum Philadelphia," in *Philadelphia*; and Carl D. Oblinger, "Alms for Oblivion: The Making of a Black Underclass in Southeastern Pennsylvania, 1780–1860," in John Bodnar, ed., *The Ethnic Experience in Pennsylvania* (Lewisburg: Bucknell University Press, 1973), pp. 94–117. See re. the southern case Ira Berlin, *Slaves Without Masters: The Free Negro in the Antebellum South* (New York: Random House Vintage Books, 1974), pp. 230–231.

86. See, for example, James Stuart, *Three Years in North America*, 2nd ed., 2 vols. (New York: J. & J. Harper, 1833) 1:323; Mrs. M. C. J. F. Houstoun, *Hesperos: or, Travel in the West*, 2 vols. (London: John W. Parker, 1850) 1:216; George Lewis, *Impressions of America and the American Churches* (1848; reprint ed., New York: Negro Universities Press, 1968), p. 69.

87. See Thomas Hamilton, *Men and Manners in America* (1833; reprint ed., New York: Russell & Russell, 1968), p. 63.

88. William Chambers, *Things As They Are in America* (1854; reprint ed., New York: Negro Universities Press, 1968), p. 189. See similar remarks in Frances Wright D'Arusmont, *Views of Society and Manners in America*, p. 238; Martineau, *Society in America*, 3:140; and summarized in Max Berger, *The*

British Traveller in America, 1836–1860 (New York: Columbia University Press, 1943), pp. 57, 170.

89. Fisher, *A Philadelphia Perspective*, 6 October 1862, p. 439. See also a reference to "the transition period between black servants and Irish," in Sedgwick, *Life and Letters*, p. 74.

90. L. M. Alcott, *Work*, p. 20.

The Irish "Biddy"

91. "The New York Labor Market: Female House Servants," *Harper's Weekly* 1 (July 4, 1857): 418–419.

92. *Plain Talk and Friendly Advice to Domestics*, pp. 68–69.

93. Elizabeth Ellet, *The Practical Housekeeper: A Cyclopedia of Domestic Economy* (New York: Stringer and Townsend, 1857), p. 42.

94. Elizabeth Sullivan Stuart to Kate Stuart Baker, 6 April 1852, in Stuart, *The Stuart Letters*, p. 304. An article in *Scribner's* compared Chinese servants to the Irish: "Having dared so much in coming to a foreign land for the sole purpose of money-getting, a spirit of unrest and greed takes possession of them" (Sarah E. Henshaw, "California Housekeepers and Chinese Servants," *Scribner's Monthly* 12 [September 1876]: 738).

95. Elizabeth Sullivan Stuart to Kate Stuart Baker, 3 October 1850, in Stuart, *The Stuart Letters*, p. 137.

96. Cited in Carl F. Wittke, *The Irish in America* (Baton Rouge: LSU Press, 1956), p. 44; see the description of the cottages in a Galway village quoted in Arnold Schrier, *Ireland and the American Emigration, 1850–1900* (Minneapolis: University of Minnesota Press, 1958), p. 140. There was neither range nor grate, only a peat fire and a kettle or cooking pot in which everything was boiled. It was impossible to fry or roast.

97. Tomes, "Your Humble Servant," pp. 53–54.

98. Elizabeth Sullivan Stuart to Kate Stuart Baker, 3 October 1850, in Stuart, *The Stuart Letters*, p. 138.

99. E. Elcourt, "The Persecuted Woman," *Lippincott's Magazine* 5 (January 1870): 27–32. Also published as "The Domestic Canker-Worm," in *The Ladies' Repository* 30 (December 1870): 444–447.

100. CBW, 28 March 1868.

101. Ibid., 14 October 1867.

102. Elizabeth Sullivan Stuart to Kate Stuart Baker, 14 April 1852, in Stuart, *The Stuart Letters*, p. 312.

103. William Ellery Channing, "Letter to the Editor of the *Christian Palladium*," *Christian Register* (Boston), 25 February 1837, p. 30. For an example of a servant who was incapacitated by excessive religious enthusiasm, see the semi-fictional "Hannah Sanders" in Gilman, *Recollections of a Housekeeper*, p. 119.

104. Susan M. Huntington, *Memoirs of the Late Mrs. Susan Huntington*, ed. Benjamin B. Wisner (Boston: Crocker & Brewster, 1826), p. 85.

105. Mary Grey Duncan, *America As I Found It* (London: James Nisbet & Co., 1953), p. 187.

106. For example, see Mary Robbins Post to Isaac & Amy Post, 19 February 1850, Post Family Papers; Jessie F. A. Bank to Lucy Maynard Salmon, 11 Jan. 1889, LMS.

107. *The Jeffersonian and Tompkins Times*, 30 March 1836, in *What They Wrote: Nineteenth Century Documents from Tompkins County, New York*, ed. Carol Kammen (Ithaca, N.Y.: Cornell University Department of Manuscripts and University Archives, 1978), p. 61.

108. Ray Allen Billington, *The Protestant Crusade, 1800–1860* (Chicago: Quadrangle Books, Quadrangle Paperbacks, 1964), p. 312.

109. "The Irish Nursemaid," *The Mother's Magazine and Family Monitor* 20 (October 1852): 318. For a short note on Hogan and an excerpt from his *Popery! As It Was and As It Is*, see David B. Davis, *The Fear of Conspiracy: Images of Un-American Subversion from the Revolution to the Present* (Ithaca and London: Cornell University Press, 1971), pp. 100–101.

110. HWG, 23 November 1851.

111. Syracuse *Journal*, 18 August 1876, cited in Mary E. Laird and Robert S. Pickett, "Women in 'Hard Times': An Analysis of an 1855 Birth Cohort of Women Undergoing Young Adulthood in the Depression of 1873" (Paper delivered at the Social Science History Association Meeting, Columbus, Ohio, 4 November 1978), p. 24. For examples from the New York City papers, see Ernst, *Immigrant Life*, p. 67. Caroline Barrett White commonly used "Irish" and "Protestant" as antonyms.

112. Cusack, *Advice to Irish Girls*, pp. 71–72, 160.

113. "Bridget's Comment," *Life and Light for Heathen Women* 1 (1869): 97.

114. See, for example, "The Family Circle: The Christian Mistress," *The Ladies' Repository* 28 (June 1868): 465–466. For other examples, see Alice B. Neal, "The Servant Question," *Godey's Lady's Book* 55 (October 1857): 325–330; Barbara Leigh Smith Bodichon, *Women and Work* (New York: C. S. Francis, 1859), p. 7.

115. See Joan Jacobs Brumberg, "'Zenanas and Girlless Villages': The Ethnology of American Evangelical Women, 1870–1910," *Journal of American History* 69 (Sept. 1982). On British conversion efforts in Ireland and the corresponding opinion that apostasy was "the greatest of crimes in the sight of the Irish peasantry," see Potter, *To the Golden Door*, p. 79.

116. Hannah Corcoran was an Irish servant in Charlestown, Massachusetts who had been converted to the Baptist faith of her employers. When she disappeared in 1853, rumors flew that she had been abducted by priests and mob violence threatened. She returned with a fanciful tale to tell, but her mother insisted she had merely gone to Philadelphia to look for work. See Billington, *Protestant Crusade*, pp. 312–313.

117. Elizabeth Sullivan Stuart to Kate Stuart Baker, 21 August 1852, in Stuart, *The Stuart Letters*, p. 395.

118. Billington, *Protestant Crusade*, p. 347.

3. Changing Patterns of Service

The Contemporary Record

1. C. W. Janson, *The Stranger in America* (1807), cited in Albert Matthews, "Hired Man and Help," *Publications of the Colonial Society of Massachusetts* 5 (March 1898): 250.

2. See New York Secretary of State, *Census of the State of New York for 1855* (Albany: Charles Van Benthuysen, 1857), pp. 191–192, 182–183. There is no listing for cities; I refer here to the listing for New York County and to the findings for the city of Buffalo prepared by Glasco.

3. See McKinley, "Stranger in the Gates," pp. 6, 61. Similarly David Katzman concludes that help had "little significance in the overall pattern of domestic servants, and nearly none on the market from the point of view of employer or employee." *Seven Days a Week*, p. 152.

4. U.S. Bureau of the Census, *Historical Statistics of the United States, Colonial Times to 1970*, Bicentennial ed., pt. 1 (Washington, D.C., 1975), p. 124.

5. Lillie Devereux Blake, "Women as Census Enumerators," *The National Citizen and Ballot Box*, v. 4, no. 10 (February 1880): 7.

6. See Massachusetts Bureau of Statistics of Labor, *A Compendium of the Census of Massachusetts: 1875* (Boston: A. J. Wright, 1877), pp. 10, 78, 577, 86.

7. For an explicit defense of the decision to rely on self-identification, see Lebergott, *Manpower in Economic Growth*, pp. 70–73. Lebergott argues that low labor-force participation rates for nineteenth-century women are plausible because the burden of child care and housework was too great for many women to be able to work for pay. Yet women entered the work force not because of free time but because of economic need—and the burden of nineteenth-century housework can also argue in favor of demand for a large sector of service workers.

8. *Census of the State of New York for 1855*, pp. 191–192.

9. Michigan Bureau of Labor and Industrial Statistics, *Twelfth Annual Report, 1895* (Lansing: Robert Smith, 1895), p. 422. The method of selecting the farmers in the sample is unknown, although the surveyors declare that they varied "from the smallest to the largest, the aim being to secure representative tillers of the soil."

10. Wisconsin Bureau of Labor, Census, and Industrial Statistics, *Seventh Biennial Report, 1895–1896* (Madison, Wisconsin: Democrat Printing Co., 1896), pp. 66–85, 107; Ohio Bureau of Labor Statistics, *Seventeenth Annual Report for the Year 1893* (Norwalk, Ohio: Laning Printing Co., 1894), pt. 1, table 6. A similar survey of wage labor in Nebraska in 1897 produced questionable data, but it incorporated into its research design the distinction between help and domestics. Compare Division G, "Farm Labor," with Division H, "Miscellaneous Labor," including "domestics, city," in Nebraska Bureau of Labor and Industrial Statistics, *Sixth Biennial Report for the Years 1897 and 1898* (Lincoln, Nebraska: Jacob North, 1898), tables 7 and 8.

11. Michigan Bureau of Labor and Industrial Statistics, *12th Annual Report, 1895*, p. 335. Also Nebraska Bureau of Labor and Industrial Statistics, *Sixth Biennial Report*, table 7, re. average number of days worked.

12. Sherwood Anderson, *Memoirs* (New York: Harcourt, Brace, 1942), p. 26.

13. Ann Banks, ed., *First-Person America* (New York: Alfred A. Knopf, 1980), p. 165.

14. Brown, *Apostle of Democracy*, p. 198.

15. Cornell Reading Course for Farmers' Wives in *The American Kitchen Magazine*, cited in Norton Juster, *So Sweet to Labor: Rural Women in America, 1865–1895* (New York: The Viking Press, 1979), pp. 101–102.

16. The standard surveys include: Alba M. Edwards, "Comparative Occupational Statistics for the United States, 1870 to 1940," in *Sixteenth U.S. Census, 1940, Population* (Washington, D.C., 1943); Joseph A. Hill, *Women in Gainful Occupations, 1870 to 1920*, Census Monographs 9 (Washington, D.C., 1929); Janet M. Hooks, "Women's Occupations Through Seven Decades," U.S. Women's Bureau *Bulletin*, no. 218 (1947); and Robert W. Smuts, *Women and Work in America* (New York: Columbia University Press, 1959). Many surveyors prefer 1880 as a starting point, yet even after that date labor force economists find sufficient problems with the data to fuel controversy, much of which revolves around the reporting of casual and part-time women's work. See Katzman, *Seven Days a Week*, chap. 2, for a thorough discussion of the twentieth-century decline of service. The 1870 census counted servants in a number of major cities. See *Ninth U.S. Census, 1870, Population* (Washington, D.C., 1872), table 32, pp. 775–804.

17. See: Lemuel Shattuck, *Census of Boston for the Year 1845* (Boston: J. H. Eastburn, 1846); Providence City Council Census Committee, *Census of the City of Providence Taken in July 1855* (Providence: Knowles, Anthony, 1856); Glasco, "Ethnicity and Social Structure;" Katz, *People of Hamilton*; and Kathleen Neils Conzen, *Immigrant Milwaukee, 1830–1860* (Cambridge, Mass.: Harvard University Press, 1976).

18. Katz, *People of Hamilton*, p. 57.

19. *Census of the City of Providence*, p. 5; Shattuck, *Census of Boston for the Year 1845*, p. 84.

20. Calculated from: Shattuck, *Census of Boston for the Year 1845*, p. 84; *Census of the City of Providence*, p. 5; Glasco, "Ethnicity and Social Structure," pp. 20, 142, 155. The figure for Buffalo is not exact.

21. Katz, *People of Hamilton*, p. 58. Since families were more likely to hire domestics at certain points in the family cycle, the percentage hiring servants in their lifetime would be even larger. Note, too, that if we assume the families whose daughters went out to service did not themselves employ servants, the percentage of families employing servants cannot approach 100 percent.

22. *Census of the City of Providence*, p. 5.

23. Glasco, "Ethnicity and Social Structure," pp. 203–219, 155, 158–159. Also Ryan, *Cradle of the Middle Class*, pp. 201 and 208. In Utica at midcentury fewer than one in five native-born households had live-in servants, as compared with one in 10 of all households. Utica's textile and garment industries probably tended to reduce the ranks of servants.

24. Claudia Goldin, "Family Strategies and the Family Economy in the Late Nineteenth Century: The Role of Secondary Workers," in Theodore Hershberg, ed., *Philadelphia: Work, Space, Family and Group Experiences in the Nineteenth Century* (New York: Oxford University Press, 1981), p. 282.

25. Conzen, *Immigrant Milwaukee*, p. 81. Foreign-born families in similar occupational groups were less than half as likely to employ domestics.

26. See Handlin, *Boston's Immigrants*, new ed. (New York: Atheneum, 1969), p. 61 and table 16. Such procedures leave a wide margin for error in confounding servants with resident kin of different last names and with boarders and lodgers. Since the proportions of these may vary among ethnic groups, it is no help to say, as Handlin does, that his totals of servants are minimal, "intended merely to show the relative proportion in each nativity group." See also a critique of Peter Laslett on the same grounds: Lutz Berkner, "The Use and Misuse of Census Data for the Historical Analysis of Family Structure," *Journal of Interdisciplinary History* 4 (1975): 721–738.

27. For the estimates, see Lebergott, *Manpower in Economic Growth*, table A–10. For an explanation of their bases, see Stanley Lebergott, "Labor Force and Employment, 1800–1960," in *Output, Employment and Productivity in the United States After 1800*, Studies in Income and Wealth, vol. 30 (New York: National Bureau of Economic Research, 1966), pp. 203–204.

The Intelligence Office

28. The earliest reference I have found to an intelligence office dates from the New York City Directory of 1786. Aeneas Lamont of 22 Water Street listed his business as "Intelligence office and broker." See *The New York Directory of 1786* (reprint ed., New York: F. B. Patterson, 1874), p. 37. The term *intelligence office* may have originally referred to the trade in indentured servants, handled by ship captains and brokers who dealt in "shipping intelligence," i.e., shipping information. In the 1820s intelligence offices are described as New York institutions of long standing. See NYSEFDS, *First Annual Report*, p. 5; and Stuart, *Three Years in North America*, 1 : 32. According to one source, British registry offices dated back to the mid-eighteenth century. See Ernest Sackville Turner, *What the Butler Saw: Two Hundred and*

Fifty Years of the Servant Problem (New York: St. Martin's Press, 1963) , pp. 76–77.

29. Diary of Susan Brown Forbes, 24 and 25 May 1867, American Antiquarian Society, Worcester, Massachusetts.

30. Diary of Nettie Fowler McCormick, 13–19 Feb. 1866, State Historical Society of Wisconsin, Madison, Wisconsin.

31. For references to such methods, see Mary G. Lundie Duncan, *America As I Found It* (London: James Nisbet, 1853), p. 191; Rosine Association of Philadelphia, *Reports and Realities from the Sketch-Book of a Manager* (Philadelphia: J. Duross, 1855), pp. 143, 370.

32. Virginia Penny, *How Women Can Make Money* (1870; reprint ed., New York: Arno Press, 1971), pp. 403–405. See also a later study, Frances A. Kellor, *Out of Work: A Study of Employement Agencies* (New York: G. P. Putnam's Sons, 1904), chap. 7, "Domestic Service and Intelligence Offices." Kellor found that two-thirds of the offices in New York, Boston, Philadelphia, and Chicago were run by women, usually in their own homes.

33. *Trow's New York City Directory*, vol. 79, for the year ending May 1, 1866, p. 70.

34. Chapter seven of Kellor's *Out of Work* is almost entirely devoted to documenting an astonishing variety of abuses. See also reference to an investigation of Boston intelligence offices in 1894 in Gail Laughlin, "Domestic Service," *Report of the Industrial Commission on Relations and Conditions of Capital and Labor*, vol. 14 (Washington, D.C., 1901), pp. 755–756. These investigations suggest that prospective servants were more often victimized because of their greater ignorance and credulity, although payment of fees in advance by either party invited abuses.

35. Fisher, *A Philadelphia Perspective*, pp. 539–558.

36. Mary Abigail Dodge ("Gail Hamilton"), *Woman's Worth and Worthlessness* (New York: Harper & Bros., 1872), pp. 73, 79, 74.

37. Patience Price, "The Revolt in the Kitchen: A Lesson for Housekeepers," *Godey's Lady's Book* 76 (February 1868): 142–144.

38. Ibid. Mrs. Y's solution to the servant problem was to get a "half-grown girl who was glad of a home and knew how to prize it." Soon she has three of them, and she surmounts any temporary difficulties by resort to the bakery, the restaurant, and temporary dayworkers. This "solution" combines new urban facilities and a romanticized version of the old practice of binding out.

39. Ellet, *The Practical Housekeeper*, p. 27.

40. CBW, 2, 3, 5, and 6 July 1860.

41. "House Servants," *Harper's Weekly* 1 (9 May 1857): 289–290.

42. Caroline Healey Dall, *Woman's Right to Labour; or, Low Wages and Hard Work* (Boston: Walker, Wise and Co., 1860), pp. 173–174.

43. NYSEFDS, *First Annual Report*, pp. 5, 7, 25–27.

44. "Report to the South End Friendly Society" (April 1850), p. 2, Abigail May Alcott Papers, Houghton Library, Harvard University.

45. Claudia L. Bushman, *"A Good Poor Man's Wife": Being a Chronicle of Harriet Hanson Robinson and Her Family in Nineteenth-Century New England* (Hanover and London: University Press of New England, 1981), p. 110. Harriet Robinson applied to her for a domestic.

46. Miss C. M. Cantine to Mary Hardy Williams, 19 September 1850 and 5 December 1851; J. C. Guldin to Mary Hardy Williams, 12 June 1852 and 14 June 1852, JBW. Mary Williams applied to Guldin for a servant.

47. Dall, *Woman's Right to Labor*, pp. 173–174.

48. For announcements and accounts of the association see: "The Industrial Women's Aid Association. A Good Work. Who Will Aid?" *Godey's Lady's Book* 56 (January 1858): 82; and "The Industrial Women's Aid Association," *Godey's Lady's Book* 56 (March 1858): 276–277. See also Isabelle Webb Entrikin, *Sarah Josepha Hale and Godey's Lady's Book* (Philadelphia: Lancaster Press, 1946), p. 119. Entrikin suggests that Hale may have been inspired by the activities of Eliza Farnham, who organized a society to aid immigrant women to go west as domestics in about 1856.

49. "The Industrial Women's Aid Association," *Godey's Lady's Book* 56 (March 1858): 277.

50. See "What is Done for the Poor: Female Servants," *The Five Points Monthly Record* (August 1854): 113–114.

51. Ibid., p. 113.

52. Herman Mellville, *The Confidence Man: His Masquerade*, ed. H. Bruce Franklin (Indianapolis: Bobbs-Merrill, 1967), p. 160.

53. He has had thirty-five boys in fifteen years, all bad. One was sent to him by the New York Commissioners of Emigration. Melville's readers would have been familiar with the likelihood of fraud when the employer paid the fee in advance and with the chance that a boy sent to fill a place might well hop off the train somewhere on the way west. The intelligence office here

provides a boy, although most, in fact, provided women and girls for domestic service.

54. Melville, *The Confidence Man*, pp. 160–161.

The Problem of Payment

55. See her "How I Went Out to Service," *The Independent* 26 (4 June 1874): 1–2.

56. Ibid., p. 2.

57. Catharine Maria Sedgwick, *Live and Let Live: or, Domestic Service Illustrated* (New York: Harper & Bros., 1837), pp. 41, 69.

58. See Schob, *Hired Hands and Plowboys*, pp. 205–206. In the Michigan survey questioning farmers about their hired girls, few reported paying on any fixed schedule. See Michigan Bureau of Labor and Industrial Statistics, *Twelfth Annual Report*, p. 336.

59. POE, 23 February 1828.

60. Diary of William Thompson, 1853–1857, in the possession of Mrs. Dorothea Ives, Historian of the Town of Salisbury, New York.

61. See, for example, Diary of Eva C. Beem, 1871.

62. Anthony Trollope, *North America*, 5th ed. (London: Chapman and Hall, 1866), p. 151.

63. Rosine Association of Philadelphia, *The Sketch-book of a Manager*, p. 333.

64. *Plain Talk and Friendly Advice to Domestics, with Counsel on Home Matters* (Boston: Phillip, Sampson & Co., 1855), p. 74.

65. Hungerford, "Domestic Service," p. 569.

66. CBW, 20 November 1860.

67. Diary of Almira D. McDonald, 23 February 1885, The Margaret Woodbury Strong Museum, Rochester, New York.

68. Lavina Field Stuart to Kate Stuart Baker, 11 April 1853, in R. Stuart, *The Stuart Letters*, p. 512.

69. Women's Educational and Industrial Union, Boston, *Annual Report for the Year Ending May 1892* (Boston: L. Barta & Co., 1893), pp. 14–16, "Historical Sketch."

70. Women's Educational and Industrial Union, Boston, *Annual Report for the Year Ending May 1887* (Boston, 1887), "Report of the Protective Com-

mittee," p. 38. Yearly reports named domestic service as "a large part of our business." In 1891, for example, the committee dealt with 128 claims, 82 of which were in domestic service, 14 in needlework, and the rest in smaller categories.

71. Women's Educational and Industrial Union, Boston, *Annual Report for the Year Ending May 1888* (Boston, 1888), p. 38; and *Annual Report for the Year Ending May 1889* (Boston, 1889), pp. 36–37.

72. See *Domestic Employment: A Handbook* (New York: The Legal Aid Society, 1908).

73. Oliver Lyman, "The Legal Status of Servant Girls," *Popular Science Monthly* 22 (1883): 811.

74. Kate Gannett Wells, "The Servant Girl of the Future," *North American Review* 157 (December 1893): 719.

From Country to City

75. Eliza W. Farrar, *The Young Lady's Friend* (Boston: American Stationers' Co., 1837), p. 250 and chap. 11.

76. *Plain Talk and Friendly Advice to Domestics*, pp. 101–102.

77. *Cortland* (N.Y.) *Democrat*, 15 May 1885.

78. Maud Nathan, *Once Upon a Time and Today* (New York: G. P. Putnam's Sons, 1933), p. 42.

79. See Jenny Lawrence, "Miriam Berry Whitcher Speaks Her Mind," *New York Historical Society Quarterly* 63 (January 1979): 24–53.

80. Marianne Finch, *An Englishwoman's Experience in America* (1853; reprint ed., New York: Negro Universities Press, 1969), pp. 105–106.

81. See, for example, Mary Hardy Williams's correspondence with Jane Hardy (n.d.) in which she reports that "Little Catharine" is going home to attend school, and she has engaged a new girl from Burdett named Elvira Himrod (JBW). Perhaps she was aided in this delicate combination by her considerable personal tact; then too, such a large family necessitated a division of household labor and may have helped to make measures such as separate tables seem merely logical. There seems to have been a division of labor in the Williams home in which immigrants and black women worked in cooking, cleaning, and laundry, while the local girls worked mostly in child care.

82. Elizabeth Sullivan Stuart to Kate Stuart Baker, 1 August 1850, in R. Stuart, *The Stuart Letters*, p. 116.

83. Elizabeth Sullivan Stuart to Kate Stuart Baker, 29 May 1851, ibid., p. 191.

84. Elizabeth Sullivan Stuart to Kate Stuart Baker, 28 April 1851, ibid., p. 177.

85. James Russell Lowell to C. F. Briggs, 18 February 1846, in *Letters of James Russell Lowell*, ed. Charles Eliot Norton, 2 vols. (New York: Harper & Bros., 1894), 1:105.

86. See David S. Kellog, *A Doctor at All Hours: The Private Journal of a Small Town Doctor's Varied Life, 1886-1909*, ed. Allan S. Everest (Brattleboro, Vt., 1970), p. 74.

87. "House Servants," *Harper's Weekly* 1 (1857): 289-290.

88. "My Chinese Cook," *The Ladies' Repository* 30 (April 1879): 301. The author's solution was to encourage Chinese immigration.

89. Harriet Beecher Stowe, *The Chimney-Corner* (Boston: Ticknor & Fields, 1868), p. 15.

90. Antoinette Adams to Mrs. Zephania Clarke, 13 March 1846, Freeman Clarke Papers.

91. Helen Williams Kathern to Helen Munson Williams, 23 July 1883, Helen Munson Williams Papers, Oneida County Historical Society, Utica, New York.

92. Mary Ann to Almira Porter, 14 December 1844, Porter Family Papers.

93. Editorial Correspondence, *Arthur's Home Magazine* 21 (March, May, and June 1863): 197-199, 304, 356.

94. Mary Ann Burr to Mary Hardy Williams, 1856? JBW.

95. Ibid. (Emphasis original.)

96. Diary of Lizzie Wilson Goodenough, 9 January and 20 February 1865, American Antiquarian Society, Worcester, Massachusetts.

97. Ibid., 20 January 1865.

98. Ibid., 20 February 1865.

99. Ibid., 23 March 1865.

100. Ibid., 27 March 1865; also 20 March 1865 and 29 April 1865.

101. Ibid., 19 August 1865.

102. Ibid., 27 July 1874. See also entries of 15 September, 22 September, and 3 October 1874, references to Ann Weberly and Jane Addams.

103. Clara Loring Bogart, *Emily: A Tale of the Empire State* (Ithaca, New York: Andrus & Church, 1894). Quotes that follow are from pp. 78–79, 131, 149, 121.

104. Mrs. Mary Travis to Susan B. Anthony, in *Elizabeth Cady Stanton and Susan B. Anthony: Correspondence, Writings, Speeches*, ed. Ellen Carol DuBois (New York: Schocken Books, 1981), p. 204.

105. Abigail Scott Duniway, *Path Breaking: An Autobiographical History of the Equal Suffrage Movement in Pacific Coast States* (1914, reprint ed., New York: Schocken Books, 1971), p. 16.

106. U.S. Department of Agriculture, *Social and Labor Needs of Farm Women*, Report no. 103. (Washington, D.C., 1914), excerpted in Rosalyn Baxandall, Linda Gordon, and Susan Reverby, eds., *America's Working Women: A Documentary History, 1600 to the Present* (New York: Random House Vintage Books, 1976), p. 154.

107. See Nell W. Kull, "'I Can Never Be Happy There in Among so Many Mountains'—The Letters of Sally Rice," *Vermont History* 38 (1970): 49–57.

108. Ibid., p. 52.

109. Ibid., pp. 54–55.

110. Jane Emeline Jacobs to Harriet Kimball Jewett, 16 April 1854, Harriet Kimball Jewett Papers, Oregon Historical Society.

4. The Elaboration of Needs and the Division of Household Labor

1. See Harriet C. Brown, *Grandmother Brown's Hundred Years, 1827–1927*, cited in Mary R. Beard, ed., *America Through Women's Eyes* (New York: Greenwood Press, 1933), p. 96; Seymour Cook, "Early Days in Homer," *Courtland County Chronicles* 2 (1958): 183.

2. POE, 4 January 1825. See Tillson, *A Woman's Story*, pp. 149–150. Mrs. Tillson considered candlemaking "the most tedious thing" in all the rigors of frontier life in Illinois in the 1820s. It took her three to four hours of constant dipping to do six candles at a time. See also Harold F. Williamson and Arnold R. Daum, *The American Petroleum Industry*, vol. 1, "The Age of Illumination," (Evanston, Illinois: Northwestern University Press, 1959), pp. 29–59.

3. See Buley, *The Old Northwest Pioneer Period*, p. 220; Gilman, *Recollections of a Housekeeper*, pp. 22–23; Eliot Wigginton, ed., *The Foxfire Book* (Garden City, N.Y.: Doubleday, 1972), pp. 159–164.

4. Isaac Weld, *Travels Through the States of North America* (London, 1799), cited in Richard Osborn Cummings, *The American and His Food*, rev. ed. (Chicago: University of Chicago Press, 1941), p. 26. See Jane Louise Mesick, *The English Traveller in America*, 1785–1835 (New York: Columbia University Press, 1922), pp. 59, 103–104.

5. Cummings compares the length of cookbooks. Lydia Maria Child's *The Frugal Housewife* of 1829 had 95 pages, while Eliza Putnam's *Receipt Book and Young Housekeeper's Assistant* of 1868 had 223 pages, and *The Boston Cooking School Cook Book* of 1896 ran to 567 pages (Cummings, *The American and His Food*, p. 42).

6. POE, 2 April 1827 and 25 March 1830.

7. Brown, *Grandmother Brown's Hundred Years*, cited in Beard, *America Through Women's Eyes*, p. 95. Buley wrote that dried fruit was frequently blackened by fly specks and babies slept with clusters of flies parading over their mouths. See his *The Old Northwest Pioneer Period*, pp. 233–234. For further reference to the difficulty of discouraging flies and vermin, see Bremer, *Homes of the New World*, 1:645.

8. POE, 28 December 1827, 7 July 1829.

9. Tillson, *A Woman's Story*, p. 147. One Norwegian immigrant, observing such procedures in Iowa in 1862, wrote home describing them and concluded, "So you see, there is a lot of extra work in washing clothes" (Gro Svendsen, 20 November 1862, cited in Blegan, *Land of Their Choice*, p. 394).

10. POE, 11 March 1823, 9 January 1828.

Status and Domestics

11. See Lance Davis et al., *American Economic Growth: An Economist's History of the United States* (New York: Harper & Row, 1972), p. 29 and chap. 3, "Consumption and the Style of Life." Theoretically, an increase in per capita product might reduce the number of servants by reducing the supply of those compelled to enter service work, but this did not occur in nineteenth-century America, thanks in part to regular infusions of Europe's poor.

12. On the growth in the size of the largest fortunes, see ibid., p. 29. Robert Gallman estimates that there were sixty millionaire families in the United States by 1840. See his "Trends in the Size Distribution of Wealth in the Nineteenth Century: Some Speculations," in Lee Soltow, ed., *Six Papers on the Size Distribution of Wealth and Income*, National Bureau of Economic Re-

282 NOTES TO PAGES 108–109

search Studies in Income and Wealth, vol. 33 (New York: National Bureau of Economic Research, 1969), p. 15.

13. See Edgar W. Martin, *The Standard of Living in 1860* (Chicago: University of Chicago Press, 1942); Warner, *The Private City*, pp. 66–67; Thomas C. Cochran and William Miller, *The Age of Enterprise: A Social History of Industrial America*, rev. ed. (New York: Harper & Row, Harper Torchbooks, 1961), pp. 256–261. On the development of advertising, see Frank Presbrey, *The History and Development of Advertising* (Garden City: Doubleday, Doran & Co., 1929), chaps. 22–27. Presbrey cites the 1830s as the beginning of significant growth in the advertising industry, with the rise of penny journalism and the instructive exploits of P. T. Barnum.

14. On the emotional tenor of the experience of antebellum economic growth, see Marvin Meyers, *The Jacksonian Persuasion: Politics and Belief* (Stanford, California: Stanford University Press, 1957), chaps. 3 and 6. Meyers writes that "the almost instantaneous conversion of economic gains into conspicuous improvements in living standards" in the Jacksonian era prompted many Americans to wring their hands in genuine alarm about "the really wicked personal extravagance" around them. Yet all the while these same individuals, "venturous conservatives," seldom neglected an opportunity to increase their own profits, incomes or living standards. Sam Bass Warner, Jr. describes rising standards of living in Philadelphia and notes that at the same time, "The theme of foolish wives and husbands consuming beyond their means abounded in the sentimental novels and household guides of the period." *The Private City*, p. 67, n. 8.

15. J. A. Banks, *Prosperity and Parenthood* (London: Routledge and Kegan Paul, 1954), pp. 74, 85, and chap. 5.

16. See T. B. Bottomore's *Sociology: A Guide to Problems and Literature* (New York: Random House Vintage Books, 1972), chap. 11, "Social Stratification," and esp. p. 195. And see Raymond Williams, *Keywords: A Vocabulary of Culture and Society* (New York: Oxford University Press, 1976), pp. 251–252. Even though Weber was concerned to distinguish status from class, which was to be defined by property ownership or "market situation," he conceded a close connection: "Property as such is not always recognized as a status qualification, but in the long run it is, and with extraordinary regularity." See H. H. Gerth and C. W. Mills, eds. and trans., *From Max Weber: Essays in Sociology* (New York: Oxford University Press, 1946), p. 187. Weber's definition of status is thus more subtle than the notion of status as it is often employed in sociology, either merely confounded with class, as in

W. Lloyd Warner's Yankee City studies, or else treated as a wholly separate "independent variable."

17. See Dixon Wecter, *The Saga of American Society: A Record of Social Aspiration, 1607–1937* (New York: Charles Scribners' Sons, 1937), p. 212. Wecter provides a rich record of anecdote and detail, including the language of "nob" and "swell," but he tends to exploit the inherent entertainment value of the social whirl without much analysis.

18. C. Wright Mills, *The Power Elite* (New York: Oxford University Press, 1956), p. 52.

19. Mills tends to underestimate the antebellum status struggle, which seemed like a placid affair only when Gilded Age socialites looked back on it. See ibid., pp. 48–49. Wecter makes this same error more markedly, taking the pell-mell public reception after Jackson's inauguration as the prototype of antebellum social style, in a chapter entitled, "Aristocracy in Retreat." *Saga of American Society*, pp. 91–92. For a useful corrective view of antebellum social customs, see Douglas T. Miller, *Jacksonian Aristocracy: Class and Democracy in New York, 1830–1860* (New York: Oxford University Press, 1967), pp. 159–178. Miller notes that N. P. Willis coined the term "upper ten thousand," a source that probably indicates an important connection between self-consciously high society and urban journalistic publicity. See Willis, *The Rag-Bag, A Collection of Ephemera* (New York, 1855); and Charles Astor Bristed, *The Upper Ten Thousand: Sketches of American Society* (New York: Stringer & Townsend, 1852).

20. Fisher, *A Philadelphia Perspective*, p. 233. He may have arrived at such specific figures not by unaided memory but by reading over old diary entries.

21. Working from different disciplines and to different purposes, both Douglas Miller and Leonore Davidoff have remarked on the characteristic stridency of American status claims. These claims were often marked by artificial attempts at closure based on religion, ethnicity, or even the number accommodated by Mrs. Astor's ballroom. See D. Miller, *Jacksonian Aristocracy*, p. 158. Miller argues that antebellum New Yorkers were probably more status-conscious than Europeans, since the absence of firm ranks led to competition and the lack of sanction for status in republican ideology prompted a continual need to assert it. See Leonore Davidoff, *The Best Circles: Women and Society in Victorian England* (Totowa, New Jersey: Rowman & Littlefield, 1973), p. 101.

22. For examples, see Edward Pessen, *Jacksonian America: Society, Personality and Politics* (Homewood, Ill.: The Dorsey Press, 1969), p. 31.

23. Ward McAllister, *Society As I Have Known It* (New York: Cassell Publishing Co., 1890), p. 114. McAllister served as social advisor to Mrs. William Astor, the premier hostess of the Gilded Age, and it was McAllister who actually composed the list of the 400. See Wecter, *Saga of American Society*, pp. 207–224, for an account of McAllister's role.

24. McAllister, *Society As I Have Known It*, p. 258.

25. Ibid., p. 161. McAllister in effect suggests that we can "brighten up and enliven" life by our manner of *spending* money.

26. See Blumin, *The Urban Threshold*, pp. 193–194, citing the diary of Nathaniel Booth.

27. See *Six Hundred Dollars a Year; or, A Wife's Effort at Low Living Under High Prices* (Boston: Ticknor & Fields, 1867), p. 6. This account purports to be a true story, although its characters suggest fictionalizing for the sake of the drama and the moral of the story. It includes detailed family budgets that do seem to reflect close knowledge of having to live on $600 a year.

28. Mark Twain and Charles Dudley Warner, *The Gilded Age: A Tale of Today* (1873; New York: The New American Library, Signet Classics, 1969), p. 55.

29. Caroline Cowles Richards Clarke, *Village Life in America, 1852–1872*, new ed. (New York: Henry Holt & Co., 1913), p. 156.

30. Harriet Beecher Stowe, *We and Our Neighbors; or, the Records of an Unfashionable Street* (New York: J. B. Ford, 1875), p. 35.

31. Fisher, *A Philadelphia Perspective*, p. 532, entry of 4 October 1867.

32. Leonore Davidoff, "Mastered for Life: Servant and Wife in Victorian and Edwardian England," *Journal of Social History* 7 (1974): 411–412.

33. Harriet Beecher Stowe, *House and Home Papers* (Boston: Ticknor and Fields, 1865), pp. 126–132.

34. Frances Miriam Berry Whitcher, *The Widow Bedott Papers* (New York: Albert Mason, 1876), pp. 222–223, 161.

35. Ibid., pp. 189, 205–206.

36. Ann Sophia Stephens, *High Life in New York* (Philadelphia: T. B. Peterson & Bros., 1854), pp. 4, 12, and chapter 2 in general.

The Work Behind the Status Struggle

37. See, for example, Tomes, *Bazar Book of the Household*, p. 142; Augusta H. Worthen, "Servants," *Godey's Lady's Book* 68 (March 1864): 284–287;

Mary E. W. Sherwood, *An Epistle to Posterity* (New York: Harper & Bros., 1897), p. 15.

38. Florence Hartley, *The Ladies' Book of Etiquette and Manual of Politeness* (Boston: G. W. Cottrell, 1860), p. 285; *Six Hundred Dollars a Year*, p. 89.

39. See Howard Mumford Jones, *The Age of Energy: Varieties of American Experience, 1865–1915* (New York: Viking Press, 1970), p. 131.

40. See Davidoff's analysis of the social functions of etiquette in *The Best Circles*.

41. On the call as the basic social unit of exchange, see Davidoff, *The Best Circles*, pp. 41–49. There is no account of American social customs comparable to Davidoff's work on English society, but the most useful work is Arthur M. Schlesinger, Sr., *Learning How to Behave: A Historical Study of American Etiquette Books* (New York: Macmillan, 1946). Schlesinger offers little analysis of the functions of social customs, but his summary of American etiquette advice helps to confirm the applicability of elements of Davidoff's analysis to American practices.

42. For a detailed exposition of the etiquette of calls, see Eliza Leslie, *Miss Leslie's Behaviour Book* (1859; reprint ed., New York: Arno Press, 1972), chaps. 1–5 and chap. 24. Nineteenth-century fiction often illustrates the mechanisms of calling and the use of servants in its management. The chapter entitled "Calls" in Alcott's *Little Women* shows the exchange of obligation, the sense of being debtor and creditor. Henry Adams's *Democracy* illustrates the assurance of privacy: Mrs. Lightfoot Lee's servants enable her to be "not at home" to anyone but Senator Ratcliffe in order that they may be alone for the final scene in which she rejects his marriage offer.

43. On the uses of cards, see Schlesinger, *Learning How to Behave*, pp. 40–41; and Caroline M. S. Kirkland, "The Mystery of Visiting," *Sartain's Union Magazine of Literature and Art* 6 (May 1850): 138–139. Schlesinger dates the introduction of cards after the Civil War, but this is certainly too late. One source recalled their use as an innovation of the 1820s. See Timothy Flint, *Recollections of the Last Ten Years in the Valley of the Mississippi* (1826: reprint ed., Carbondale, Ill.: Southern Illinois University Press, 1968), p. 279.

44. From the Philadelphia *Press*, reprinted in the Cortland *Democrat*, 23 April 1886.

45. CBW, 19 April 1858. Mrs. White was, of course, aided in summoning up good grace by the fact that her situation was so obviously a matter of temporary emergency.

46. Compare John Ise's memoir about his parents, *Sod and Stubble.* Despite the fact that a traveling preacher infested their house with bedbugs, and itinerants often practiced petty thievery on them, this family never felt that they could simply turn strangers away. In their newly settled area, there was nowhere else to send them.

47. This was most marked in cases where rural help were hired to fill what their employers hoped would be the role of an urban domestic. See the encounter cited in chap. 3, p. 73, in which a front-door inquiry as to whether the master is home prompts a colloquy on the hired girl's own social standing.

48. See Gilman, *Recollections of a Housekeeper*, pp. 34–35.

49. See for example, Kirkland, *A New Home—Who'll Follow?* or Tillson, *A Woman's Story.* Both of these women employed help.

50. Davidoff, *The Best Circles*, p. 46.

51. Mrs. S. T. Martyn, "One in a Thousand," *The Ladies' Wreath* 2 (1848): 25–29. The author forces her point by flatly asserting that Mrs. Morris is "one of the most lady-like and dignified of women . . . and either in the kitchen or parlor must command the respect of all who know her." But she thus undermines the moral of her own story, implying that individuals who lack such formidable personal attributes had better equip themselves with domestics after all.

52. See DeForest, "Biddy's Blunders," pp. 329–330; Harriet Beecher Stowe, "The Trials of a Housekeeper," *Godey's Lady's Book* 18 (January 1839): 5–6. The practices of an entry thief did not seem to be so novel as to require explanation.

53. See "Chambermaid. Her Work and How To Do It," Rachel Williams Proctor Papers.

54. Robert Tomes, "The Houses We Live In," *Harper's New Monthly Magazine* 30 (1865): 737. Davidoff remarks on this phenomenon in England: "In women's magazines, there is constant reference to the fact that the first appearance of the footman or parlourmaid at the door reflected the family's rank and quality" (*The Best Circles*, p. 88).

55. Hartley, *Ladies' Book of Etiquette*, p. 242.

56. See Erving Goffman, *The Presentation of Self in Everyday Life* (Garden City, N.J.: Doubleday and Co., 1959), chap. 3. On changes in domestic architecture, see McKinley, "Stranger in the Gates," chap. 6.

57. Fragment, ca. 1850, Proctor Family Papers.

58. See Caroline M. S. Kirkland, *The Evening Book; or, Fireside Talks on Morals and Manners* (New York: C. Scribner's, 1852), pp. 58–59; [Sarah Savage], *Advice to a Young Woman at Service: In a Letter from a Friend* (Boston: J. B. Russell, 1823), pp. 6, 21–25.

59. See Nichols, *Forty Years of American Life*, 2:73; *Ann Connover* (Philadelphia: American Sunday School Union, 1835), p. 99; Catharine Beecher, *Letters to Persons Who Are Engaged in Domestic Service* (New York: Leavitt & Trow, 1842), letters #12, 14.

60. C. Beecher, *Letters to Persons Who Are Engaged in Domestic Service*, pp. 147–148.

61. Sir Charles Lyell, *A Second Visit to the United States*, 2 vols. (London: John Murray, 1850), 1:93.

62. Frances Seward to William Henry Seward, 11 November 1832, Seward Family Papers.

63. "The Family Circle: How to Have a Good Servant," *The Ladies Repository* 26 (February 1866): 115. On the cap and apron, see Lucy Maynard Salmon, *Domestic Service*, rev. ed. (New York: Macmillan, 1911), pp. 209–210.

64. Elizabeth Smith Miller, *In the Kitchen* (Boston: Lee & Shepard, 1874), p. 22.

65. See R. Stuart, *The Stuart Letters* 1:99–100, Elizabeth Sullivan Stuart to Kate Stuart Baker, 6 July 1850.

66. See Stanton, *Eighty Years and More*, p. 138; and letter to Elizabeth Smith Miller on a different but apparently similar occasion in Theodore Stanton and Harriet Stanton Blatch, eds., *Elizabeth Cady Stanton as Revealed in Her Letters, Diary and Reminiscences*, 2 vols. (New York and London: Harper & Bros., 1922), 1:52, letter of 20 June 1853.

67. On tardiness as an embarrassment, see the short story by Kate Sutherland, "Cooks," *Godey's Lady Book* 47 (1852): 392–395.

68. Sarah Josepha Hale, *The New Household Receipt-Book* (New York: H. Long & Brother, 1853), p. 252.

69. *The House Book*, pp. 259–261.

70. Hartley, *Ladies' Book of Etiquette*, pp. 91, 95.

71. On the increasingly elaborate style of service, see Schlesinger, *Learning How to Behave*, chap. 4. He quotes the cited remark on p. 42.

72. The dinner party graced by swans is mentioned in Wecter, *Sage of American Society*, p. 180.

73. Hartley, *Ladies' Book of Etiquette*, pp. 90, 95.

74. E. Miller, *In the Kitchen*, p. 23.

75. Leslie, *The House Book*, p. 267.

76. "Home Management," *The Mother's Magazine* 24 (February 1856): 46. Also see Hartley, *Ladies' Book of Etiquette*, p. 290: "It is a great point to live, when alone, as if you expected company."

77. See Robert Sutcliffe, *Travels in Some Parts of North America in the Years 1804, 1805 and 1806* (London: C. Peacock, 1811), p. 64.

78. This had not always been the case. On the conflict resulting from the abolition of "vails," tipping by guests, in eighteenth-century England, see J. Jean Hecht, *The Domestic Servant Class in Eighteenth Century England* (London: Routledge & Kegan Paul, 1956), chap. 6. In the nineteenth century the presence of domestics underwrote the regular exchange of lengthy visits among family and friends. One woman referred to a visit as "no interruption to her, for she has two good girls." See Esther Titus to Amy Kirby Post, 186?, Post Family Papers. Eunice Beecher complained of the practice of "visiting for one's own convenience" for long periods, noting that among other things, servants would rebel at the extra work. Since Mrs. Beecher displayed so little solicitude for her domestics' convenience in other matters, her remarks may have been a veiled censure of her sister-in-law, Catharine. See Eunice Bullard Beecher, *Motherly Talks With Young Housekeepers* (New York: J. B. Ford, 1873), p. 144.

79. Jane Cunningham Croly, *For Better or Worse: A Book for Some Men and all Women* (Boston: Lee, Shepard & Dillingham, 1875), p. 229.

80. Elliott and Richards, *Julia Ward Howe*, 1:348. For a fictional treatment, see Margaret Hosmer, "Mary Ann and Chyng Loo," *Lippingcott's Magazine* 6 (October 1870): 354–361.

81. Daniel T. Rodgers, *The Work Ethic in Industrial America 1850–1920* (Chicago: University of Chicago Press, 1978).

82. See William McLoughlin, *The Meaning of Henry Ward Beecher* (New York: Alfred Knopf, 1970), pp. 25–27 and (quote) p. 112. Rodgers offers a

more subtle interpretation of Beecher, arguing that he successfully worked both sides of this question. See his *Work Ethic in Industrial America*, pp. 94–99.

83. See Marvin Meyers, *Jacksonian Persuasion*, chaps. 5 and 6. For the attack on fashion, see William R. Leach, *True Love and Perfect Union: The Feminist Reform of Sex and Society* (New York: Basic Books, 1980), chap. 9.

84. See William Andrus Alcott, *The Young Wife; or, Duties of the Woman in the Marriage Relation* (1837; reprint ed., New York: Arno Press, 1972), pp. 158–169 for Alcott's attack on the employment of domestics. For Alcott's dietary strictures, see *ibid.*, pp. 170–171, 174–176, and his *The Young Housekeeper; or, Thoughts on Food and Cookery* (Boston: G. W. Light, 1838).

85. See Mrs. H. C. Conant, "Notice of Useful Books," *Mother's Monthly Journal* (Utica, New York) 3 (1838): 78–79.

86. Graves, *Woman in America*, pp. 85–86, 72.

87. See Child, *The Frugal Housewife*, pp. 97 and 117.

88. Veblen, *Theory of the Leisure Class*, p. 59.

New Conveniences and Higher Standards

89. Anthony N. B. Garvan, "Effects of Technology on Domestic Life, 1830–1880," in *Technology in Western Civilization*, ed. Melvin Kranzberg and Carroll W. Pursell, 2 vols. (New York: Oxford University Press, 1967), 1:547; Siegfried Giedion, *Mechanization Takes Command* (New York: Oxford University Press, 1948); Elizabeth Mickle Bacon, "The Growth of Household Conveniences in the United States from 1865 to 1890" (Ph.D. dissertation, Radcliffe College, 1942), pp. 136, 252. Bacon contends that the greatest advances in labor saving occurred after 1880.

90. See Joann Vanek, "Time Spent in Housework," *Scientific American* (November, 1974), pp. 116–120; William F. Ogburn, "The Family and Its Functions," in President's Research Committee on Social Trends, *Recent Social Trends*, 2 vols. (New York: McGraw-Hill, 1933), 1:664–671; Ruth Schwartz Cowan, "Two Washes in the Morning and a Bridge Party at Night: The American Housewife Between the Wars," *Women's Studies* 3 (1976): 147–171, and "The 'Industrial Revolution' in the Home: Household Technology and Social Change in the Twentieth Century," *Technology and Culture* 17 (1976): 1–23; Barbara Ehrenreich and Deirdre English, "The Manufacture of Housework," *Socialist Revolution* 5 (1975): 5–40; Heidi Irmgard Hartmann, "Capitalism and Women's Work in the Home, 1900–1930"

(Ph.D. dissertation, Yale University, 1974); Bettina Berch, "The Development of Housework," *International Journal of Women's Studies* (1978): 336–347. See also Staffan Burenstam Linder, *The Harried Leisure Class* (New York: Columbia University Press, 1970), pp. 8, 42–44; and John Kenneth Galbraith, *Economics and the Public Purpose* (Boston: Houghton Mifflin, 1973), chap. 4.

There has been less work on the nineteenth century. William and Deborah Andrews chose to emphasize "the fact that the household *was* mechanized" in the nineteenth century but preferred to withhold judgment on whether mechanization actually reduced household labor. Susan Strasser pointed out that traditional historians were too optimistic, neglecting the gap between invention and diffusion, and she argued that most women enjoyed little benefit from the inventions of the nineteenth century. William D. Andrews and Deborah C. Andrews, "Technology and the Housewife in Nineteenth Century America," *Women's Studies* 2 (1974): 321–323; Susan Strasser, "Never Done: The Ideology and Technology of Household Work" (Ph.D. dissertation, State University of New York at Stony Brook, 1977), chap. 2; and Strasser, "An Enlarged Human Existence? Technology and Household Work in Nineteenth Century America," in *Women and Household Labor*, ed. Sarah Fenstermaker Berk (Beverly Hills and London: Sage Publications, 1980), pp. 29–51. Strasser's book, *Never Done: A History of American Housework* (New York: Pantheon, 1982), the first full account of household work throughout American history, is an admirable survey and fills a great need.

91. Hale, *New Household Receipt Book*, p. 252.

92. See Fisher, *A Philadelphia Perspective*, p. 314, entry of 10 January 1859. On the introduction of coal, see: Howard N. Eavenson, *Coal Through the Ages* (New York: American Institute of Mining and Metallurgical Engineers, 1939), pp. 55–57; Jeremiah Dwyer, "Stoves and Heating Apparatus," in *One Hundred Years of American Commerce*, ed. Chauncey Depew, 2 vols. (New York: D. O. Haynes & Co., 1895), 2:357–363.

93. In 1860 about one million stoves were manufactured, compared with 25,000 in 1830. See Edgar W. Martin, *The Standard of Living in 1860* (Chicago: University of Chicago Press, 1942), p. 92. For a comment on stoves' fuel economy, see Clara Dodge to Augustus C. Dodge, 11 January 1849, Augustus Dodge Papers, Iowa Historical Society, Iowa City, Iowa.

94. See McLoughlin, *The Meaning of Henry Ward Beecher*, p. 108. Caroline and Frank White had a furnace installed at "Cliffside" in 1858. See CBW, 9 August 1858.

95. See Sandford Salyer, *Marmee: The Mother of Little Women* (Norman, Oklahoma: University of Oklahoma Press, 1949), p. 188. By the 1870s furnaces were appearing in middle-income homes. See C. Cook, "Beds and Tables," pp. 86–88; and Frank R. Stockton and Marian Stockton, *The Home: Where It Should Be and What to Put in It* (New York: G. P. Putnam & Sons, 1873), p. 88.

96. C. Cook, "Beds and Tables," p. 86; Tomes, "The Houses We Live In," p. 739. A furnace also consumed less fuel than did several different stoves throughout a house, so that it could be more economical after the large initial installation cost.

97. See E. Beecher, *Motherly Talks*, p. 6; Fisher, *A Philadelphia Perspective*, pp. 314, 527; Nathan, *Once Upon a Time*, p. 81.

98. See Williamson and Daum, *American Petroleum Industry*, 1:38–39, 57. Gas lighting was not available in rural areas, nor was it extended into working-class neighborhoods in the cities. Gas lighting would not reach the height of its popularity until the 1880s and 1890s, when a new type of "water" gas and a new design for mantles gave gaslight much greater candlepower at significantly lower prices.

99. *The Diary of Ellen Birdseye Wheaton* (Boston: Privately printed, 1923), p. 106, entry of 9 January 1852.

100. Unless the kerosene lamp was allowed to cool for several hours, refueling, trimming wicks, and removing chimneys for cleaning were also hazardous. See Williamson and Daum, *American Petroleum Industry*, 1:312–314.

101. C. Beecher, *Treatise on Domestic Economy*, p. 304.

102. This account of the clothing industry is based on: Harry A. Corgin, *The Men's Clothing Industry: Colonial Through Modern Times* (New York: Fairchild Publications, 1970); Joel Seidman, *The Needle Trades* (New York: Farrar & Rinehart, 1942); Pauline Arnold and Percival White, *Clothes and Cloth: America's Apparel Business* (New York: Holiday House, 1961).

103. See, for example, Anna to Ella, 30 March 1873, Camp Family Papers Additional, Cornell University; Helen Breese to Catharine Breese, 28 October 1835, Breese-Stevens-Roby Papers.

104. See for examples: Mary Hardy Williams to Jane Hardy, 13 November 1846 and 5 October 1849, JBW; and Elizabeth Strong Worthington, *The Biddy Club* (Chicago: A. C. McClurg & Co., 1888), p. 80.

105. The Lymans were being conventional when they advised in 1867 that every housekeeper should make all the family clothing, except perhaps dress-coats and overcoats. This they reasoned would be feasible with "the present facilities for sewing," i.e., a sewing machine, and the savings achieved would "more than pay the wages of a domestic who will perform all the drudgery of a household, such as washing, cleaning, ironing, sweeping, etc." (Joseph B. Lyman and Laura E. Lyman, *The Philosophy of Housekeeping: A Scientific and a Practical Manual* (Hartford: Goodwin & Betts, 1867), p. 335.) One writer admitted that this was common practice, but she complained that it made for nice dresses and bad dinners. See Louise Palmer Smith, "Dinners Versus Ruffles and Tucks," *Putnam's Magazine* 15 (June 1870): 710.

106. The sewing machine, patented in 1846, came into wide use during the 1850s. As Singer and Howe carried on the "sewing machine war," improvements were incorporated in the machines, and prices fell. For an example, from this decade, of praise for the sewing machine as a liberator of women, see "Gleanings of Gossip," *The Home: A Fireside Monthly Companion* 2 (October 1856): 192. Misgivings soon followed. Observers complained that the sewing machine prompted women to expand their wardrobes, to add ruffling and tucking, and to pursue fashion more avidly. See: "My Friend's Sewing Machine Experience," *The Ladies Repository* 29 (January 1869): 48–50; L. Smith, "Dinner Versus Ruffles and Tucks," pp. 708–711. Tissue paper patterns introduced in the 1860s, had much the same effect. The patterns made it easier for a woman to cut a dress to fit herself, but an aggressive advertising campaign tried also to convince customers they needed to buy patterns regularly if they wished to stay in fashion. See Margaret Walsh, "The Democratization of Fashion: The Emergence of the Women's Dress Pattern Industry," *Journal of American History* 66 (September 1979): 309, 311.

107. Morris J. Vogel, "Patrons, Practitioners and Patients: The Voluntary Hospital in Mid-Victorian Boston," in *Victorian America*, ed. Daniel Walker Howe (Philadelphia: University of Pennsylvania Press, 1976), pp. 121–138; Charles Rosenberg, "And Heal the Sick: The Hospital and the Patient in Nineteenth Century America," *Journal of Social History* 10 (1977): 428–447.

108. Catharine Beecher, *Miss Beecher's Domestic Receipt-Book*, 5th ed. (New York: Harper & Bros., 1870), pp. 191–203, 209–216.

109. For an example of exhausting home nursing, see the family letters, February through May 1832, in the Breese-Stevens-Roby Papers. Margaret Breese Roby's baby was born in February 1832. She died, probably of puerperal fever, at the end of March, and her infant lingered until May. Her mother and sister nursed both Margaret Roby and the infant until their deaths. They did the same in 1844 when another sister, Helen Breese Graves, died in childbirth and the baby struggled along for several months before succumbing. In a better-known example: when diphtheria finally claimed four-year-old Eddy Lincoln in 1850, his parents had been nursing him for fifty-two days and nights. See Turner and Turner, *Mary Todd Lincoln*, p. 40.

110. "The New York Hospitals: A Boon Not Only to the Poor But to the Well-to-Do," *New York Times*, December 31, 1900, cited in Paul Starr, "Medicine, Economy and Society in Nineteenth Century America," *Journal of Social History* 10 (1977): 600.

111. See Buley, *The Old Northwest Pioneer Period*, pp. 220–221; Dwyer, "Stoves and Heating Apparatus"; and Douglas Branch, *The Sentimental Years, 1836–1860* (New York: D. Appleton Century, 1934), p. 57. Contemporary usage distinguished between the stove and the range, depending on the location of the oven in relation to the firebox, but I refer to both as cookstoves.

112. See Sutherland, "Cooks," pp. 392–395; Louise Palmer Smith, "Brevities," *Putnam's Magazine* 15 (January 1870): 114; De Forest, "Biddy's Blunders," pp. 329–330. To understand how difficult it was to start a coal fire using wood kindling in such a stove, see E. Miller, *In the Kitchen*, pp. 24–25.

113. In the 1870s Eunice Beecher recalled the rapid acceptance of the cookstove: "We well remember when cookstoves and ranges were first brought into common use, and how positive the good housekeepers were that nothing could be prepared with these strange contrivances. But only a few days were needed to work a complete conversion" (*Motherly Talks*, p. 205).

114. Caroline F. Corbin, "Enlightened Motherhood," in Association for the Advancement of Women, *Papers and Letters Presented to the First Women's Congress*, New York, October 1873 (New York: Mrs. William Ballard, 1874), p. 28.

115. Early in the century, all of Asher Benjamin's popular neoclassical plans, even for country houses, included a basement kitchen. Asher Benjamin, *The

American Builder's Companion, 6th ed. (1827; reprint ed., New York: Dover Publications, 1969). Twenty years later, Andrew Jackson Downing thought that the kitchen was gradually moving to the first floor, in a separate wing, and his own plans usually called for this location. Andrew Jackson Downing, *The Architecture of Country Houses* (1850; reprint ed., New York: Dover Publications, 1969), p. 272.

116. See Catharine Maria Sedgwick, *Home*, 15th ed. (Boston: James Munroe, 1847), p. 7; C. Beecher, *Treatise on Domestic Economy*, p. 270. James Richardson was still deploring its continued prevalence in New York City homes in the 1870s. See his "The Homes of New York," *Scribner's Monthly* 8 (May 1874): 67.

117. Beecher and Stowe's *The American Woman's Home* has been cited as a forerunner of modern domestic architecture for its labor-saving designs locating the kitchen in the center of the living area. See Andrews and Andrews, "Technology and the Housewife," pp. 321–323; and Giedion, *Mechanization Takes Command*, p. 515. These authors fail to consider the problems of summer weather. Beecher and Stowe dealt with these by proposing a large air vent to carry off cooking heat. They also had to include a dumbwaiter to lift fuel from the basement to the central kitchen.

118. Cited in Cummings, *The American and His Food*, p. 39.

119. In her *Treatise on Domestic Economy* of 1841, Catharine Beecher mentioned the refrigerator as a desirable article, and described it, as if her readers might not know what it was (p. 374). In her *Receipt Book* of 1846 she offered instructions on how to use an old barrel to make a homemade refrigerator. By the turn of the century only 19 percent of urban working-class families lacked iceboxes. See also Robert Coit Chapin, *The Standard of Living Among Workingmen's Families in New York City* (New York: Russell Sage Foundation Charities Publication Committee, 1909), p. 153.

120. See Thomas Farrington DeVoe, *The Market Book: A History of the Public Markets of the City of New York* (1862; reprint ed.: New York: Augustus M. Kelley, 1970), p. 485.

121. Cummings, *The American and His Food*, pp. 54–57, and chapter 5, "Health by Rail," in general.

122. Ibid., pp. 43–47. The best source on Graham's ideas is Stephen Nissenbaum, *Sex, Diet, and Debility in Jacksonian America: Sylvester Graham and Health Reform* (Westport, Connecticut, and London: Greenwood Press, 1980).

123. May Blake, "Letters to a Young Mother: The Baby's Food," *Scribner's Monthly* 13 (December 1876): 273.

124. C. Beecher, *Receipt-Book*, p. 227. For examples of the axiom that it was "shiftless" to buy baker's bread, see: Louise Palmer Smith, "Biddy Dethroned," *Putnam's Magazine* 15 (January 1870): 115; "My First Year of Housekeeping," *The Ladies' Repository* 29 (September 1869): 165–169.

125. Pauline Arnold and Percival White, *Food: America's Biggest Business* (Pound Ridge, N.Y.: White and Arnold, 1959), p. 67. At the time that Depew's *One Hundred Years of American Commerce* was published, in 1895, there was no baking industry established; Depew mentioned only the "biscuit" or cracker industry. One economist estimates that in 1900 the typical housewife used in baking nearly half a ton of flour per year (See Stanley Lebergott, *The American Economy* [Princeton: Princeton Univ. Press, 1976], pp. 104–105).

126. The 1870s saw the patenting of the autoclave and the development of machine-made tin cans. Commercial canning had existed since the 1820s but only as a minor luxury trade plagued by frequent spoilage. See Cummings, *The American and His Food*, pp. 67, 69; and James F. Collins, *The Story of Canned Foods* (New York: E. P. Dutton, 1924), pp. 20–22.

127. Mary Virginia Terhune, *Common Sense in the Household: A Manual of Practical Housewifery*, rev. ed. (New York: Charles Scribner's, 1882), p. 9.

128. Nathaniel Willis, "Lecture on Fashion Delivered Before the New York Lyceum," *Mirror Library*, cited in Cummings, *The American and His Food*, p. 33.

129. Pierre Blot, the Julia Child of his day, taught cooking-school courses in Boston and New York and advised the readers of *Harper's Bazar* on menus. See, for example, *Harper's Bazar* 6 (22 March 1873): 178; or 6 (19 July 1873): 450; *Professor Blot's Lectures on Cookery Delivered at Mercentile Hall* (New York: 1866). Juliet Corson opened her New York Cooking School in 1876. See F. E. Fryatt, "The New York Cooking School," *Harper's New Monthly Magazine* 60 (December 1879): 22–29.

130. Hale, *New Household Receipt-Book*, p. 254.

131. Edith Wharton, *A Backward Glance* (New York: D. Appleton-Century, 1934), p. 58.

132. Martineau, *Society in America*, 3:61.

133. This contrasts with the style of elaboration evident in other national cuisines, where protein was sufficiently scarce and expensive that elaboration in cooking reflected the need to extend and enhance it by combining it with spices, starches, and vegetables, in sauces, soups, stews, pasta, and rice dishes. See Farb and Armelagos, *Consuming Passions*, pp. 196, 199.

134. See Mesick, *The English Traveller in America*, pp. 59, 91, 103–104.

135. C. Beecher, *Receipt-Book*, p. 227. Also *Six Hundred Dollars A Year* (Boston: Ticknor and Fields, 1867), p. 55. Here an economizing wife deplores needless profusion at meals.

136. F. Trollope, *Domestic Manners of the Americans*, p. 85. She also mentioned that attendance at the market was a necessity, since there were no butchers, fishmongers, or other shops—except bakeries—for eatables in the town.

137. Martineau, *Society in America*, 3:139; Chevalier, *Society, Manners and Politics*, p. 430; Carl David Arfwedson, *The United States and Canada in 1832, 1833 and 1834*, 2 vols. (London: Richard Bentley, 1834), 1:137–138.

138. C. Beecher, *Receipt-Book*, pp. 26–36, 217–223.

139. "Wanted—A Healthy Wife," *The Home: A Fireside Monthly Companion and Guide* 2 (September 1856): 127–132.

140. E. Beecher, *Motherly Talks*, p. 91.

141. Eunice Beecher, *All Around the House; or, How to Make Homes Happy* (New York: D. Appleton & Co., 1885), p. 89.

142. Robert Tomes, *The Bazar Book of the Household* (New York: Harper & Bros., 1875), p. 152.

143. Fryatt, "The New York Cooking School," pp. 22–24.

144. DeVoe, *The Market Book*, pp. 411, 455, 563.

145. See Cummings, *The American and His Food*, p. 95.

146. Tenth U.S. Census, 1880, *Report on the Social Statistics of Cities*, comp. George E. Waring, Jr., pt. II (Washington, D.C., 1887), p. 371.

147. At least one comment cited by Thomas DeVoe suggests that middle-class men also began to feel that their time was too valuable to spend in this way (*The Market Book*, p. 394).

148. One native of upstate New York who moved to New York City in the 1850s remarked that city living required much more dusting and sweeping

and cleaning. See H. E. Dodge to Mrs. Stevens, 14 August 1859, B-S-R. For a good short description of New York City in 1863, with its privies and slaughterhouses and horse dung, see A. Cook, *Armies of the Streets*, chap. 1. He notes, "Mansions and fever nests, town houses and slaughterhouses stood side by side" (p. 17).

149. See "Summer Conveniences," *Harper's Bazar* 2 (1869): 533, cited in Bacon, "Growth of Household Conveniences," p. 46; see also JBK, 26 and 28 June 1873. Kelly refers to "mosquito frames" and "doors for flies."

150. See, for example, Mary Ann Porter to Almira Porter, 14 December 1844, Porter Family Papers; Elizabeth F. Camp to Jacob Camp, 23 May 1861, Camp Family Papers, Cornell University; Elizabeth Breese Stevens to Father and Mother, 1 May 1844, B-S-R.

151. See Nelson Blake, *Water for the Cities* (Syracuse, N.Y.: Syracuse University Press, 1956). By 1860 the sixteen largest cities in the nation, each with 50,000 or more inhabitants, had built waterworks of some kind, and many smaller towns had done the same. But within each city the working-class districts were apt to remain dependent upon scanty, sporadic supplies of water hauled by hand from pumps or faucets in the streets. See Susan J. Kleinberg, "Technology and Women's Work: The Lives of Working Class Women in Pittsburgh, 1870–1900," *Labor History* 17 (1976): 58–72.

152. The furniture industry grew during the 1840s and 1850s from small shops and individual artisans to moderate-sized factories equipped with rudimentary power tools. The invention of the jig saw and carving machines permitted an elaborate bric-a-brac style. The value of factory-built furniture jumped from $7 million in 1840 to $28 million in 1860. See Carl Bode, *Antebellum Culture* (1959; reprint ed., Carbondale, Ill.: Southern Illinois University Press, 1970), pp. 56–57. Also Giedion, *Mechanization Takes Command*, pp. 390–392.

153. See Bode, *Antebellum Culture*, pp. 89–91.

154. Jane Cunningham Croly, *Jennie Juneiana: Talks on Women's Topics* (Boston: Lee and Shepard, 1864), p. 100.

155. Dodge, *Woman's Worth and Worthlessness*, p. 55. See also her article, "That Best Room," *Harper's Bazar* 6 (22 February 1873): 114. For examples of attacks on the closed parlor, see: "Living Rooms and Back Stairs," *Arthur's Home Magazine* 44 (December 1876): 644–645; Richardson, "The Homes of New York"; "Best Rooms versus Happy Homes," *The Ladies' Repository* 25 (September 1865): 522–524.

156. "Servants and Housekeepers," *The Ladies' Repository* 21 (March 1861): 159. On eighteenth-century usage, see Mary Beth Norton, *Liberty's Daughters: The Revolutionary Experience of American Women, 1750–1800* (Boston and Toronto: Little, Brown & Co., 1980), p. 4. For other warnings against "famous" housekeepers, see: "Domestic Happiness," *The Ladies' Companion* 1 (August 1834): 158–159; "The Newly Married: or, A Good Lesson," *Godey's Lady's Book* 47 (October 1853): 346–347; and "Housekeeping and Homes," *The Ladies' Repository* 22 (October 1862): 609–614.

157. "Servants and Housekeepers," pp. 158, 160.

158. "Over-Busy Housekeepers," *Harper's Bazar* 7 (23 May 1874): 330.

159. "The Moral Influence of Good Housekeeping," *Mother's Monthly Journal* 4 (November 1839): 171.

160. "The Kitchen," *The Home: A Fireside Monthly Companion* 1 (May 1856): 233.

161. Croly, *Jennie Juneiana*, pp. 144–145.

162. See E. Beecher, *Motherly Talks*, pp. 10, 38, 161, 90, and (quoted) p. 330. The "tidy" was a cover designed to prevent soiling—a bedroom version of the antimacassar.

163. E. Beecher, *All Around the House*, p. 296.

164. W. Alcott, *Ways of Living on Small Means*, p. 56.

165. Mrs. F. D. Gage, "The Housekeeper's Millennium," *Lippincott's Magazine* 4 (July 1869): 78–81.

166. C. Beecher, *Treatise on Domestic Economy*, pp. 149, 311. On the "rub and boil" method, see Buley, *The Old Northwest Pioneer Period*, p. 223.

167. On the mechanical washer and the wringer, first patented in 1847, see Giedion, *Mechanization Takes Command*, pp. 561–563. In American cities, drainage and sewer systems closely followed the extension of the water systems. See Blake, *Water for the Cities*, pp. 268–271.

168. *Motherly Talks*, p. 22. Running hot water was possible if families who had tap water installed a "self-acting boiler" that filled automatically, but this convenience required vigilance in cold weather lest the pipes freeze and an explosion result. See Hale, *The New Household Receipt Book*, pp. 259–269; Lawrence Wright, *Clean and Decent: The Fascinating History of the Bathroom and the Water-Closet* (London: Routledge & Kegan Paul, 1960), pp. 188–192. This problem points out the maintenance difficulties involved in ex-

tending indoor plumbing before reliable automatic central heating was available. See Blake, *Water for the Cities*, p. 269.

169. Soap powders were not introduced until the early 1920s. See Ruth Schwartz Cowan, "The 'Industrial Revolution' in the Home: Household Technology and Social Change in the Twentieth Century," *Technology and Culture* 17 (1976): 5. The market for commercially-made soap expanded rapidly in the nineteenth century—securing the Colgate fortune—but it is difficult to measure the relative use of the commercial versus the homemade product. See Samuel Colgate, "American Soap Factories," in Depew, ed., *One Hundred Years of American Commerce* 2 : 422–428; and *Dictionary of American Biography*, s.v. "Colgate, William."

170. Cited in Elliott and Richards, *Julia Ward Howe*, 1 : 110. Rachel Williams Proctor instructed her cook to save the grease and exchange it for soft soap with "the man who calls for it" ("Cook. Her Work and How to Do It," Rachel Williams Proctor Papers).

171. See Hale, *The New Household Receipt Book*, p. 263.

172. *Treatise on Domestic Economy*, pp. 233–326.

173. Giedion, *Mechanization Takes Command*, pp. 562–563. One observer wrote of "extensive laundries" established in New York City in the 1850s and saw capital entering into competition with the washerwoman. See William Burns, *Female Life in New York City* (Philadelphia: T. B. Peterson, 185?), p. 94.

174. See Diary of Mary Hardy Williams, 16 June 1860, JBW; Elizabeth Breese Stevens to Mother and Father, February 1844, B-S-R; Harriet Beecher Stowe, *Life and Letters of Harriet Beecher Stowe*, ed. Annie Fields (Boston: Houghton Mifflin, 1897), pp. 13, 118, 175.

175. R. Stuart, *The Stuart Letters*, p. 152.

176. Ellet, *The Practical Housekeeper*, p. 44.

177. George Martin to Peter Martin, 9 February 1851, cited in Erickson, *Invisible Immigrants*, p. 295. For later evidence of working-class families paying to have the laundry done when the mother was ill, see Louise Bolard More, *Wage-Earners' Budgets: A Study of Standards and Costs of Living in New York City* (New York: Henry Holt, 1907), pp. 99, 103, 106.

178. Compare Blake, *Water for the Cities*; Charles E. Rosenberg, *The Cholera Years: The United States in 1832, 1849, and 1866* (Chicago: University of

Chicago Press, 1962); and Richard H. Shryock, *Medicine in America: Historical Essays* (Baltimore: Johns Hopkins Press, 1966).

179. Beecher and Stowe, *The American Woman's Home*, chap. 4, esp. pp. 52–53; Robert Tomes, *Bazar Book of the Household*, p. 118. Tomes also claimed that wallpaper could be unhealthful because it released its arsenic dye into the air.

180. See Charles F. Wingate, "The Unsanitary Homes of the Rich," *North American Review* 137 (1883): 172–184.

181. Catharine Beecher, *Miss Beecher's Housekeeper and Healthkeeper* (New York: Harper & Bros., 1876). For evidence in the popular women's press that the microscope revealed a world of unseen "filth" all around, see: Helen R. Cutler, "Journal of a Housekeeper," *The Ladies' Repository* 26 (February 1866): 666. An illustration was included in "Wonders of the Microscope," *Mother's Magazine* 27 (September 1859): 284–285.

182. Regina Morantz, "Making Women Modern: Middle Class Women and Health Reform in Nineteenth Century America," *Journal of Social History* 10 (Summer 1977): 490–507.

183. Clara Dodge to Augustus C. Dodge, 25 Jan 1849 and 24 Dec 1848, Augustus Dodge Papers.

184. "Chambermaid. Her Work and How to Do It," Rachel Williams Proctor Papers. The Proctors had no children and at least three servants.

185. Ellet, *The Practical Housekeeper*, pp. 44–45.

186. Ibid.

187. Susan Hooker to Mother, 2 Feb 1869, Huntington-Hooker Papers. See another description of the division of labor on a wash-day, when a woman in Flint, Michigan who employed only one domestic had a busy time of it: Elizabeth Breese Stevens to Parents, February 1844, B-S-R.

188. *Six Hundred Dollars a Year*, pp. 35, 49.

The Division of Middle-Class Mothering

189. Nancy Cott has written of how "child care revealed itself at the heart of women's domestic duties" between 1780 and 1835 (*Bonds of Womanhood*, pp. 46, 84–91). See also Bernard Wishy, *The Child and the Republic: The Dawn of Modern American Child Nurture* (Philadelphia: University of Pennsylvania Press, 1968); and Anne L. Kuhn, *The Mother's Role in Childhood Education: New England Concepts, 1830–1860* (New Haven: Yale University Press, 1974).

190. *Diary of Ellen Birdseye Wheaton*, entry of 20 March 1851.

191. See, for example, *Plain Talk and Friendly Advice to Domestics*, pp. 154–155; Julia McNair Wright, *The Complete Home: An Encyclopedia of Domestic Life and Affairs* (Philadelphia: J. C. McCurdy, 1879), p. 92; Helen E. Brown, *The Mother and Her Work* (Boston: American Tract Society, 1862), pp. 67–68; Elizabeth Sullivan Stuart to Kate Stuart Baker, 1 August 1850, in R. Stuart, *The Stuart Letters*, p. 116.

192. J. Wright, *The Complete Home*, p. 92. Oliver Wendell Holmes attributed his childhood fear of ghosts to contact with the "kitchen inmates." *Life and Letters of Oliver Wendell Holmes*, 2 vols. (Boston and New York: Houghton Mifflin, 1896), 1 : 32.

193. J. S. Tomlinson, "Our Female Influences," *The Ladies Repository* (March 1841): 77.

194. Lydia Huntley Sigourney, *Letters to Mothers*, 2nd ed. (New York: Harper & Bros., 1839), p. 42.

195. M. F. Tupper, "Household Training," *Mother's Magazine and Family Monitor* 20 (1852): 274.

196. Philadelphia Society for the Encouragement of Faithful Domestic Servants, *Address* (Philadelphia, 1829), p. 1.

197. R. Stuart, *The Stuart Letters*, Elizabeth Sullivan Stuart to Son, 26 April 1852, p. 327; and Elizabeth Sullivan Stuart to Kate Stuart Baker, 1 Aug 1850, p. 116.

198. Sigourney, *Letters to Mothers*, p. 86.

199. Ibid., pp. 86–91. Similarly, Julia McNair Wright detailed the ill doings of nursemaids but went on to recommend their hire (*The Complete Home*, p. 92).

200. Wright, *The Complete Home*, p. 94.

201. See, for example, Edwin Munn Pixley to John Pixley Munn, 13 February 1873, Munn-Pixley Family Papers.

202. CBW, 12 June 1856.

203. Ibid., 29 September 1858.

204. Stanton, *Eighty Years and More*, pp. 115–118.

205. Diary of Nettie Fowler McCormick, 20 April 1868. Also see entries of 5 November 1859 and 18 September 1867.

206. Mary Hardy Williams to Jane Hardy, 30 November 1846, JBW.

207. Elizabeth Breese Stevens to Mother and Sister, 17 October 1849, B-S-R.

208. Frances Seward to William Henry Seward, 23 June 1829, Seward Family Papers.

209. Robert Coles, *Privileged Ones: The Well-off and the Rich in America* (Boston: Little, Brown & Co. 1977).

210. Fisher, *A Philadelphia Perspective*, p. 259.

211. Ibid., p. 280, entry of 3 October 1857.

212. Stanton, *Eighty Years and More*, pp. 14–17.

213. Edith Wharton, *A Backward Glance*, p. 26. R. W. B. Lewis notes that as an adolescent Wharton was possessed of some "nameless terror" and could not sleep at night unless a light were on and a nursemaid in the room with her. See his *Edith Wharton: A Biography* (New York: Harper & Row, 1975), p. 25.

214. James H. Brossard, *The Sociology of Child Development* (New York: Harper, 1948), chap. 12, "Domestic Servants and Child Development."

215. Heinz Kohut, *The Restoration of the Self* (New York: International Universities Press, 1977), pp. 276–277.

216. Christopher Lasch, *The Culture of Narcissism* (New York: W. W. Norton, 1978).

217. HWG, 15 December 1851.

218. Ibid., 27 November 1851.

219. Ibid., 9 December 1851.

220. Ibid., 27 December 1831.

221. Ibid., 3 November 1852.

5. A Woman's Business: Supervision

1. Graves, *Woman in America*, p. 29.

A Flexible Balance Between Work and Leisure

2. See C. Beecher, *Treatise on Domestic Economy*, pp. 204–213; idem, *Receipt-Book*, 269–280; Sigourney, *Letters to Mothers*, p. 198; Sarah Josepha Hale, *The Good Housekeeper; or, The Way to Live Well While We Live* (Boston: Weeks, Jordan, 1839), p. 128; Ellet, "Helps," p. 194; Farrar, *Young Lady's Friend*, pp. 34, 237; Sedgwick, *Home*; and idem, *Live and Let Live*.

3. Sedgwick, *Live and Let Live*, preface.

4. Rev. Jesse T. Peck, "The Kitchen," *The Ladies Repository* 18 (January 1858): 33–35.

5. "Housekeeping and Homes," pp. 609–614.

6. Ellet, *The Practical Housekeeper*, pp. 15–16.

7. "Doing our Own Work," *Harper's Bazar* 6 (2 August 1873): 482. When domestic advice-givers were more alarmed by one form of excess than the other, they left themselves open to misreadings by recent scholars. Catharine Beecher, for example, did not propose in her *Treatise on Domestic Economy* "the first servantless household," as has been argued, nor did Beecher and Sarah Josepha Hale campaign for the abolition of servants. See Sklar, *Catharine Beecher*, p. 151; Dolores Hayden, *The Grand Domestic Revolution: A History of Feminist Designs for American Homes, Neighborhoods, and Cities* (Cambridge, Mass. and London: The MIT Press, 1981), pp. 56–57; Strasser, *Never Done*, pp. 166–167. If this were so, why did Beecher devote an entire chapter of the *Treatise* to the "care of domestics" and follow it with a volume of *Letters to Persons Who Are Engaged in Domestic Service* in the following year? Sklar has noted in her introduction to the 1977 reprint of Beecher's *Treatise on Domestic Economy* that Beecher's floor plans included room for "a servant or servants" (p. x). Beecher and Stowe's *American Woman's Home* (1869) lends itself to confusion because its text and floor plans are inconsistent, the book being a slightly reworked compendium of previous work by both authors.

8. CBW, vol. 14, 1874, inside back cover (emphasis original).

9. See Mrs. Beecher's semi-autobiographical novel, *From Dawn to Daylight*, pp. 40, 46–47, 100. For the press comments quoted, see Paxton Hibben, *Henry Ward Beecher: An American Portrait* (New York: George H. Doran, 1927), p. 207.

10. This view of her housekeeping standards is taken from her *Christian Union* columns, collected in *Motherly Talks* and *All Around the House*. She did on occasion announce that "the fewer servants the better the work is done," (*Motherly Talks*, p. 6) but this was a scornful criticism of servants' competence rather than a serious proposal about household staffing.

11. See *Motherly Talks*, pp. 248–249, 322.

12. Josiah Gilbert Holland, *Letters to the Joneses* (New York: Charles Scribner, 1863), p. 91.

13. Worthen, "Servants," p. 286.

14. Eunice Bullard Beecher, *The Law of the Household* (Boston: Privately printed, 1910), pp. 3–4.

15. Ibid., p. 3.

16. See Stella Virginia Roderick, *Nettie Fowler McCormick* (Rindge, New Hampshire: Richard R. Smith Publisher, 1956), and the Nettie Fowler McCormick Papers at the State Historical Society of Wisconsin, Madison, Wisconsin.

17. For an example of the "butterfly," see "Poor Little Lillie," *The Home: A Fireside Monthly Companion* 1 (January 1856): 20–21. For the contrasting case, see: Sophie May, "How the Sisters Kept House," *The Ladies' Repository* 27 (August 1867): 470–472; or Mrs. B. B. Hawkins, "The Discipline of Life," *The Ladies' Repository*, 24 (September 1864), 559–563.

18. Douglas, *Feminization of American Culture*, p. 65.

19. Harriet Beecher Stowe, *My Wife and I*, Riverside Edition of the Writings, vol. 12 (New York: AMS Press, 1967), p. 454. Douglas's contention that Eva has no "faculty" is contradicted.

20. Sarah Josepha Hale, *Keeping House and House Keeping: A Story of Domestic Life* (New York: Harper & Bros., 1845), p. 112.

21. Ibid., p. 139.

Entrepreneurial and Benevolent Models

22. See Barbara Welter, "The Cult of True Womanhood, 1820–1860," in Michael Gordon, ed., *The American Family in Social-Historical Perspective* (New York: St. Martin's Press, 1973), pp. 224–250. This influential piece shows little empathy for its subjects and carries the implicit message that women who failed to rebel against conventional female roles must have been either spineless or foolish.

23. *Ann Connover*, pp. 14–15, 17.

24. "Our Cook Book," *Peterson's Magazine* 36 (August 1859): 149.

25. Florence Hartley, *The Ladies Book of Etiquette and Manual of Politeness* (Boston: G. W. Cottrell, 1860), p. 241.

26. Abby Sage Richardson, "A Plea for Chinese Labor," *Scribner's Monthly* 2 (July 1871): 290.

27. "Maids of All Work," *Godey's Lady's Book* 54 (March 1857): 286.

28. "Servants and Housekeepers," *The Ladies' Repository* 21 (1861): 159.

29. "The Family Circle: An Educated Housekeeper's View, *The Ladies Repository* 25 (August 1865): 502.

30. "The Family Circle: Honor to the Housekeeper," *The Ladies Repository* 29 (April 1869): 313.

31. Diary of Nettie Fowler McCormick, 11 December 1858 and 7 April 1867; *Diary of Ellen Birdseye Wheaton*, 28 February 1852, p. 117.

32. "Servants and Housekeepers," p. 159.

33. Worthington, *The Biddy Club*, p. 39.

34. T. S. Arthur, "Sweethearts and Wives," *Godey's Lady's Book* 23 (December 1841): 268.

35. Cott, *Bonds of Womanhood*, p. 73. See also Mary Ryan's observation that "the home was infused with some semblance of the 'time and work-discipline' venerated by large-scale manufacturers" (*Cradle of the Middle Class*, p. 203).

36. K. Sutherland, "Cooks," pp. 392–395.

37. Sedgwick, *Live and Let Live*, p. 201.

38. Ibid.

39. Ibid., p. 214.

40. Stowe, *We and Our Neighbors*, p. 254. Also the explicit statement of this theme in Julia McNair Wright's *The Complete Home*. Our relation to our servants is, she writes, "of moment to society, to the state. In this relation, as in the rearing of our children, the home reaches beyond itself, and builds or destroys in other homes" (*The Complete Home*, p. 436).

41. "Requisites for carrying out the plan," holograph, n.p., n.d., Helen Munson Williams Papers. Perhaps Mrs. Williams's plan was inspired by Sedgwick's novel. We know that the book was present in the family home, for she refers to her father having read it with "approval and interest" (Helen Munson Williams to M. Bagg, 13 September 1877, Helen Munson Williams Papers).

42. Nineteenth-century feminists often chose to include domestic servants in their fiction: "It was in relation to women different from themselves that they developed a deeper understanding of their own position in society and of their need to unify among themselves for social, economic, and political action" (Leach, *True Love and Perfect Union*, p. 183).

43. "Aims of Our Institution," *Journal of the Rochester Home for the Friendless*, 1 February 1862, p. 44, and 1 October 1860, p. 13, Papers of the Rochester Home for the Friendless, University of Rochester, New York. The ladies of the home were soon troubled by the apparently unanticipated fact that numbers of friendless women proved unfit for service because they were too old or too feeble. Eventually the home had to start an "aged women's department" to provide them a more or less permanent lodging.

44. Beecher and Stowe, *The American Woman's Home*, pp. 327–332.

45. Worthington, *The Biddy Club*, pp. 53–54.

46. Anna O. Williams to Elizabeth Camp, 25 March 1864, Camp Family Papers.

47. Diary of Susan Parson Brown Forbes, 1 and 2 April 1865, American Antiquarian Society, Worcester, Massachusetts.

48. Ibid., 1–5 January 1866 re Ann Dury, 3 January and 17 September 1871, and 27 and 29 April 1872 re Mary Parker.

49. Ibid., 20 June 1865, 13 August 1867, 2 and 16 September 1867.

50. Ibid., 10 February 1872 and 1 April 1873.

51. Proctor Family Papers; R. Stuart, *The Stuart Letters*, pp. 321–322.

The Problems of Supervision in Practice

52. See George S. Gibb, *The Saco-Lowell Shops: Textile Machinery Building in New England, 1813–1949* (Cambridge, Massachusetts: Harvard University Press, 1950), pp. 10, 12, 50–62, 83, 90, 105, 176; Richard Lowitt, *William E. Dodge: A Merchant Prince of the Nineteenth Century* (New York: Columbia University Press, 1954), pp. 131, 133. Also Sidney Pollard, *The Genesis of Modern Management; A Study of the Industrial Revolution in Great Britain* (Cambridge, Massachusetts: Harvard University Press, 1965), pp. 266–270. Pollard refers to "the days when it was held to be axiomatic that control by salaried managers was the quickest way to ruin" (p. 270).

53. Gibb, *Saco-Lowell Shops*, p. 85.

54. Richard C. Edwards, *Contested Terrain: The Transformation of the Workplace in the Twentieth Century* (New York: Basic Books, 1979), pp. 54–55. Re the "foreman's empire," see Daniel Nelson, *Managers and Workers: Origins of the New Factory System in the United States, 1880–1920* (Madison: University of Wisconsin Press, 1975).

55. See the discussion of the principles and practice of scientific management in Harry Braverman, *Labor and Monopoly Capital* (New York: Monthly Review Press, 1974), chaps. 4 & 5; Edwards, *Contested Terrain*, pp. 97–104; David Montgomery, *Workers' Control in America: Studies in the History of Work, Technology and Labor Struggles* (Cambridge, Massachusetts: Cambridge University Press, 1979).

56. Beecher explained in the preface to the third edition of her *Treatise*: "The author of this work was led to attempt it, by discovering, in her extensive travels, the deplorable sufferings of multitudes of young wives and mothers, from the combined influence of *poor health, poor domestics, and a defective domestic education*" (emphasis original).

57. Beecher and Stowe, *The American Woman's Home*, p. 314.

58. Ibid., p. 315.

59. Kitty Breese Graves to Mother, 1847, B-S-R; Susan Hooker to Mother, 12 May 1876, Huntington-Hooker Papers.

60. C. Beecher, *Receipt-Book*, p. 230.

61. Jane Hardy to Mary Hardy Williams, n.d., JBW; Martha C. Wright to Ellen Wright Garrison, 12 January 1867, Garrison Family Papers, Sophia Smith Collection, Smith College.

62. C. Beecher, *Treatise on Domestic Economy*, p. 362.

63. Ibid., p. 367.

64. Beecher and Stowe, *The American Woman's Home*, p. 331.

65. Mary Virginia Terhune, *Marion Harland's Autobiography* (New York: Harper & Bros., 1910), p. 338.

66. Fannie Roper Feudge, "How I Kept House by Proxy," *Scribner's Monthly* 22 (September 1881): 681–687.

67. C. Beecher, *Receipt-Book*, p. 251; Mary Hooker Cornelius, *The Young Housekeeper's Friend; or, a Guide to Domestic Economy and Comfort* (Boston: C. Tappan, 1846), p. 14; Worthington, *The Biddy Club*, p. 53.

68. "Training School for Cooks," *The Woman's Journal* 10 (31 May 1879): 171.

69. C. Beecher, *Receipt-Book*, pp. 252, 247; "Chambermaid," and "Cook," Rachel Williams Proctor Papers. See also "Instructions to Chambermaid," "Instructions to Cook," Maria Williams Proctor Papers, Oneida County Historical Society.

70. See for example, E. Beecher, *Motherly Talks*, pp. 29–30.

71. Louisa May Alcott wrote a case of wrongful accusation into her novel *Work*. See Alice B. Neal, "Mrs. West's Experience," *Godey's Lady's Book* 47 (November 1853): 430–436.

72. Jane L. Hardy to Mary Hardy Williams, n.d., JBW.

73. D'Arusmont, *Views of Society and Manners*, p. 239.

74. "Cook," Rachel Williams Proctor Papers.

75. For evidence of this practice, see: "Our Little Beggar Girl," *Journal of the Rochester Home for the Friendless* 6 (2 February 1863), p. 47; R. Stuart, *The Stuart Letters*, p. 176; *Diary of Ellen Birdseye Wheaton*, p. 187.

76. "Servants in America," *All the Year Round* (3 October 1874), p. 585.

77. *Plain Talk and Friendly Advice to Domestics*, p. 59. On traditions of Irish charity, see Potter, *To the Golden Door*, pp. 52–53; Elizabeth Hafkin Pleck, *Black Migration and Poverty; Boston, 1865–1900* (New York: Academic Press, 1979), p. 188; or Wright, *The Complete Home*, p. 276.

78. C. Beecher, *Receipt-Book*, p. 272.

79. Elizabeth Breese Stevens to Sister, 25 March 1855, B-S-R.

80. E. Beecher, *Motherly Talks*, pp. 31–32; Harriet Prescott Spofford, *The Servant Girl Question* (Boston: Houghton Mifflin, 1881), pp. 72–81. These pieces first appeared in essay form in *Harper's Bazar* in 1873 to 1875.

81. For a good brief summary of these investigations, see Katzman, *Seven Days a Week*, pp. 111–115. Still useful in their own right are: Salmon, *Domestic Service*, and Gail Laughlin, "Domestic Service," pp. 743–767.

82. Ida Jackson, "The Factory Girl and Domestic Service," *Harper's Bazar* 37 (1903): 954. For similar complaints, see Helen Stuart Campbell, *Women Wage-Earners* (1893; reprint ed., New York: Arno Press, 1972), p. 241. Katzman states that servants' time off was increasing in the nineteenth century. He argues that prior to the 1870s servants had only one half-holiday per week, while by the turn of the century two was the rule. Katzman, *Seven Days a Week*, pp. 113–114. But this interpretation neglects the flexible, task-oriented schedule of the hired girl.

83. On the movement of dinner from noon to evening, see remarks from the *Utica Daily Gazette*, 1856, cited in Ryan, *Cradle of the Middle Class*, p. 203; and Croly, *Jennie Juneiana*, p. 46.

84. Graves, *Woman in America*, pp. 80–81; C. Beecher, *Letters to Persons Who Are Engaged in Domestic Service*, pp. 170–171.

85. "Maids of All Work," *Godey's Lady's Book* 54 (1857): 286.

86. Wells, "The Servant Girl of the Future," p. 718. For another reference to girls at service having no time they could call their own, see: Parker Pillsbury, "Domestic Service," *The Revolution* 4 (12 August 1869): 88.

87. *Plain Talk and Friendly Advice to Domestics*, p. 55. Despite its title, this book often seems addressed more to housekeepers than to servants; hence Elizabeth can be given these incendiary lines, arguments that might have seemed quite persuasive to domestics themselves.

88. Ibid., pp. 57–58.

89. "Domestic Service," *Harper's Bazar* 7 (2 May 1874): 284.

90. On women's "absorption of public welfare functions" in the mid-nineteenth century, see Ryan, *Cradle of the Middle Class*, pp. 213–215. Susan Porter Benson has pointed out that household management permitted Providence, Rhode Island matrons to develop skills they transferred into their voluntary associations. See her "Business Heads and Sympathizing Hearts: The Women of the Providence Employment Society, 1837–1858," *Journal of Social History* 12 (Winter 1978): 302–312. See also Barbara Berg's argument that middle-class women laid the foundations of feminism across class lines as their benevolent work led them to identify with the plight of less fortunate women. Berg lacks an appreciation of the ways in which sincere benevolent interest and even identification with the plight of poor women could find safe outlets well within women's conventional roles when supervision was interpreted as both improving and uplifting. See Berg, *The Remembered Gate: Origins of American Feminism* (New York: Oxford University Press, 1978).

Supervision's Problems Addressed: Cooperative Housekeeping

91. Eleanor Kirk, "From Life; or, a Broad Side from Maine," *The Revolution* 4 (2 September 1869), 130–131.

92. *Theodore Tilton versus Henry Ward Beecher*, 3 vols. (New York: McDivitt, Campbell, 1875), 2:467, 473.

93. See Hayden, *Grand Domestic Revolution*. Hayden discusses a broad tradition she calls "material feminism," which flourished between the end of the Civil War and the 1920s. I retain the narrower term "cooperative housekeeping," referring to specific efforts to collectivize household work to distinguish it from other strands of the "material feminist" tradition in which household work was to be collectivized incidentally, as in the "unitary households" of free-love advocates or in utopian socialist experiments. See also

discussions of cooperative housekeeping in Strasser, "Never Done," pp. 149–163, and Leach, *True Love and Perfect Union*, pp. 202–212.

94. Melusina Fay Peirce, "Cooperative Housekeeping," *Atlantic Monthly* 22–23 (November and December 1868 and January, February, and March 1869): 513–524, 682–697, 29–39, 161–171, 286–299.

95. See Cambridge Cooperative Housekeeping Society, *Prospectus* (Cambridge, Mass., 1869). The list of members appended to this appeal included Mrs. Horace Mann, Mrs. W. D. Howells, and Mrs. Alexander Agassiz.

96. "Modern Housekeeping," *The Woman's Journal* 1 (9 July 1870): 212.

97. Hayden, *Grand Domestic Revolution*, pp. 87–88; Corbin, "Enlightened Motherhood," p. 30; and Peirce, "Cooperation," in Association for the Advancement of Women, *Papers Read at the Fourth Congress of Women, Philadelphia, October 1876* (Washington, D.C.: Todd Bros., 1877), pp. 34–46.

98. See Hayden, *Grand Domestic Revolution*, chap. 9.

99. "Cooperative Housekeeping," *Arthur's Home Magazine* 33 (January 1869): 67–68,

100. "Woman's Work," *Harper's Bazar* 4 (19 August 1871): 514.

101. Cited in Hayden, *Grand Domestic Revolution*, p. 84.

102. See, for example, "Domestic Service," *Old and New* 6 (September 1872): 366; or Tomes, *Bazar Book of the Household*, 179–187. Also Hayden, *Grand Domestic Revolution*, appendix, for information on thirty-three associations Hayden was able to verify.

103. Peirce, "Cooperative Housekeeping," p. 683.

104. Ibid., pp. 161–170 and 286–294.

105. Ibid., p. 34.

106. Ibid., p. 685.

107. Ibid., p. 33. Peirce predicted that cooperation had the best chance in towns of 10,000–30,000 inhabitants, where "people are not all on a level as in country villages."

108. Melusina Fay Peirce to George Eliot, 21 August 1869, Sterling Library, Yale University.

109. "Modern Housekeeping," p. 212; see also Hayden, *Grand Domestic Revolution*, pp. 124–125.

110. Hayden, *Grand Domestic Revolution*, p. 218.

111. See, for example, Peirce's reference to the American economy as a "vast masculine realm of cooperative industries and activities" in the *Atlantic* article of February 1869, p. 166. The call to the initial meeting of the Cambridge group referred to adopting for housework the methods of "every other department of modern industry—the combination of Capital and the Division and Organization of Labor" (cited in Hayden, *Grand Domestic Revolution*, p. 80).

112. "Modern Housekeeping," p. 212.

113. See Peirce, "Cooperation," pp. 34-46. Her book, *Cooperative Housekeeping: How Not to Do It and How to Do It* (Boston: J. R. Osgood, 1884), reflects this revised view.

114. Ibid., p. 87.

115. See Hayden's discussion of the novels of utopian socialists who followed Bellamy, the cooperative housekeeping efforts of the Knights of Labor in New York, and Mary Kenney's "Jane Club" for working women in Chicago (*The Grand Domestic Revolution*, pp. 137-147, 155, 167-169).

116. Anna C. Garlin, "The Organization of Household Labor," in Association for the Advancement of Women, *Papers Read at the Fourth Congress of Women, Philadelphia, October 1876* (Washington, D.C.: Todd Brothers, 1877), pp. 32-34.

117. Helen Stuart Campbell, *Household Economics* (New York: G. P. Putnam's Sons, 1896), p. 243.

118. Charlotte Perkins Gilman, *What Diantha Did* (New York: Charlton Co., 1910), p. 114. The novel was serialized in *The Forerunner* in 1909-1910. According to Hayden, Gilman's emphatic rejection of genuinely cooperative as opposed to profit-making forms of associated housekeeping stemmed from a childhood experience in a cooperative household in Providence, Rhode Island. See *Grand Domestic Revolution*, pp. 196-197.

119. Hayden, *Grand Domestic Revolution*, p. 152.

120. See Heidi Irmgard Hartmann, "Capitalism and Women's Work in the Home," esp. chaps. 1 and 6.

6. A "Girl's" Life and Work

1. Diary of Eva Beem, 4 and 17 January, 11 February, 24 March, 11 April, and 17 September 1871.

2. See her Works Progress Administration interview in Banks, *First-Person America*, p. 165. Her helping was to be the unspoken quid pro quo if her uncle paid for her schooling.

3. Diary of Belle Rundlett Bliss, 6 July and 5 October 1867, Bliss Family Papers, State Historical Society of Wisconsin.

4. Grace Goddard to Aunt, 13 April 1848, Goddard Family Correspondence, American Antiquarian Society.

"A Hard and Lonely Life"

5. Jane L. Hardy to Mary Hardy Williams, 25 December 1872, JBW; Ruth Dugdale to Isaac and Amy Post, 25 April 1852, Post Family Papers. Also this comment from a working women's organization: "our middle-aged women are physically unfitted for domestic service" (The Working Women's Society of New York, *Annual Report, 1892* [New York: Freytag Printing Co., 1893], p. 10).

6. Worthington, *The Biddy Club*, p. 126.

7. Pillsbury, "Domestic Service," p. 88. Also, in the *Revolution*, Elizabeth Cady Stanton quoted the *Jamestown* (N.Y.) *Journal* on the severity of domestic service: "There is a large class that actually *cannot* do housework—they have not the necessary physical power and endurance." "Housework," *The Revolution* 2 (24 December 1868): 393.

8. Mathew Carey, "Female Labour," *American Ladies Magazine* 3 (November 1830): 497.

9. Selina to Sophia Clarke, 10 August 1872, Freeman Clarke Family Papers.

10. Mary Ann Porter to Mary Hardy Williams, 8 August 1848, JBW.

11. Pettengill, *Toilers of the Home*, pp. 113–114.

12. C. Beecher, *Letters to Persons Who Are Engaged in Domestic Service*, letter no. 11.

13. R. Proctor, "Cook."

14. See *Plain Talk and Friendly Advice to Domestics*, pp. 38–40; Tomes, "Your Humble Servant," p. 56; and *Six Hundred Dollars a Year*, pp. 51–52. See also a reference to a girl caught eating lump sugar in Mrs. E. M. Schroder to Lucy Maynard Salmon, [1889], LMS.

15. Pillsbury, "Domestic Service," p. 88.

16. Campbell, *Prisoners of Poverty*, p. 230.

17. Susan Hooker to Mother, 23 February 1876, Huntington-Hooker Papers.

18. Cited in Schrier, *Ireland and the American Emigration*, p. 30.

19. R. Proctor, "Chambermaid" and "Cook." See also Campbell, *Prisoners of Poverty*, p. 228.

20. Worthington, *The Biddy Club*, pp. 68, 71–72, 74.

21. Mary to Elizabeth Camp, 5 December 1869, Camp Family Papers. See also R. Proctor, "Cook"; Carrie Huntington Jessup to Alcesta Huntington, 15 January 1882, Huntington-Hooker Papers.

22. On backgrounds of dense sociability in poor Irish and black neighborhoods, and in working-class London and America, see: Pernicone, "The 'Bloody Ould Sixth'"; James Borchert, *Alley Life in Washington: Family, Community, Religion and Folklife in the City, 1850–1970* (Urbana: University of Illinois Press, 1980); Ellen Ross, "Survival Networks: Domestic Sharing in an East London Neighborhood, 1870–1914," (Paper delivered at the Fifth Berkshire Conference on the History of Women, Vassar College, 18 June 1981); Leslie Woodcock Tentler, *Wage-Earning Women: Industrial Work and Family Life in the United States, 1900–1930* (New York: Oxford University Press, 1979), pp. 176–177.

23. Clarke, *Village Life*, p. 6, a diary entry from 1852.

24. For references to sisters employed together, see Jane L. Hardy to Mary Hardy Williams, n.d., JBW; CBW, 22 November 1860 and 19 October 1861.

25. Campbell, *Prisoners of Poverty*, p. 225.

26. CBW, 16 May 1860 (and see 16 May 1866); HWG, 17 March 1852.

27. *Census of the City of Providence Taken in July 1855*, table VIII, p. 5; Shattuck, *Census of Boston for the Year 1845*, p. 84.

28. Catharine Breese Graves to Mother, 1847, B-S-R; Almira Porter to Mrs. Samuel Porter, 15 July 1840, Porter Family Papers.

29. Kitty Breese Graves to Mother, 24 July 1849, B-S-R.

30. See Elizabeth Breese Stevens to Sister, 25 March 1855, B-S-R; and Jane L. Hardy to Mary Hardy Williams, n.d., JBW, for references to these preferences. Carol Groneman Pernicone's study reveals the endurance and stability of family ties among the Irish in mid-century New York City ("'The Bloody Ould Sixth,'" chap. 3).

31. Reverend J. C. Guldin to Mary Hardy Williams, 12 June 1852 and 24 June 1852, JBW. See also Anna to Lizzie, 19 December 1853, Camp Family Papers Additional.

32. A. D. Adams to Lucy Maynard Salmon, 15 January 1889, LMS.

33. Harriet Prescott Spofford, *The Servant Girl Question* (Boston: Houghton Mifflin and Co., 1881), pp. 58–59, 67–68.

34. Jane L. Hardy to Mary Hardy Williams, n.d., JBW. On noise from the kitchen, see *Ann Connover*, p. 79; E. Miller, *In the Kitchen*, pp. 22–23.

35. Mary Robbins Post to Isaac and Amy Post, 1 July 1863, Post Family Papers.

36. N. S. Williams to Mary Hardy Williams, n.d., JBW.

37. R. Stuart, *The Stuart Letters*, p. 524, letter of 4 May 1853.

38. R. Proctor, "Cook." Rachel Proctor clucked that such behavior made it seem "as tho' all the time spent in the house was toilsome," apparently unaware that it must in fact have felt so.

39. See Theodore Hershberg, Harold E. Cox, Dale B. Light Jr., and Richard E. Greenfield, "The 'Journey-to-Work'; An Empirical Investigation of Work, Residence and Transportation, Philadelphia, 1850 and 1880," in Theodore Hershberg, ed. *Philadelphia: Work, Space, Family and Group Experience in the Nineteenth Century* (New York: Oxford University Press, 1981), pp. 128–173.

40. Susan Hooker to Mother, 4 April 1869, Huntington-Hooker Papers; See E. A. Wilkerson to Aunts, 19 June 1867, Camp Family Papers; *Diary of Ellen Birdseye Wheaton*, 1 and 4 April 1854; CBW, 30 August 1864. It is not clear that these "vacations" or "furloughs" were paid.

41. For examples of family emergencies, see Mary Louise Williams to Mary Hardy Williams, 15 February 1869. JBW; SBF, 15 July 1872.

42. *Diary of Ellen Birdseye Wheaton*, p. 262, 4 June 1854.

43. SBF, 13 June 1867.

44. Susan Hooker to Mother, 9 March 1879, Huntington-Hooker Papers.

45. See Mrs. George C. Ewing to Lucy Maynard Salmon, [1889], LMS, for reference to two such moves.

46. SBF, 30 June 1867, 12 July 1867.

47. Clara Dodge to Augustus C. Dodge, 25 January 1849, Augustus C. Dodge Papers.

48. SBF, 10, 11, and 13 September 1879. See CBW, 12 April 1858, re a domestic who quit saying she was sick, "but if she had said homesick I guess it would have been nearer the truth."

49. CBW, 17 and 18 June 1860.

50. Diary of Nettie Fowler McCormick, 12 February 1866; Susan Hooker to Mother, 9 March 1879, Huntington-Hooker Papers.

51. Cited in Schrier, *Ireland and the American Emigration*, p. 27.

52. *Theodore Tilton versus Henry Ward Beecher*, 1: 754.

53. Kitty Breese Graves to Mother, 3 July 1849, B-S-R.

54. Diary of Nettie Fowler McCormick, 31 December 1862.

55. CBW, 27 November 1862, 27 November 1873.

56. HWG, 25–27 December 1852; Helen Breese to Daughter, 26 December 1855, B-S-R; Mary Robbins Post to Isaac Post, 25 December 1861, Post Family Papers; CBW, 25 December 1873.

57. CBW, 25 December 1858.

58. CBW, 17 March 1873.

59. Schrier, *Ireland and the American Emigration*, p. 109.

60. *Diary of Ellen Birdseye Wheaton*, 25 December 1855; Aristeen Pixley Munn to John Pixley Munn, 4 July 1876, Munn-Pixley Family Papers.

61. Jay P. Dolan, *The Immigrant Church: New York's Irish and German Catholics, 1815–1865* (Baltimore and London: Johns Hopkins University Press, 1975), pp. 7, 56.

62. Susan Hooker to Mother, 21 February 1869 and 4 April 1869, Huntington-Hooker Papers.

63. Sarah E. Thayer to Amy Kirby Post, 1 December 1844, Post Family Papers. Also see Pillsbury, "Domestic Service," p. 88. Dolan notes that the Catholic churches of New York did not charge pew rents for early masses.

64. Sidney Stevens to Mother, 8 April 1858, B-S-R; R. Proctor, "Cook." Catholic services often included Sunday afternoon vespers and evening services, as was customary in Ireland, and Saturday afternoon and evening was the usual time to go to confession. See Dolan, *The Immigrant Church*, pp. 59–60, 62.

65. See Dolan, *The Immigrant Church*, p. 54.

66. Elizabeth Breese Stevens to Mother, 10 November 1851, B-S-R. See also CBW, 7 September 1862.

67. Catharine Breese Graves to Mother, 1847, B-S-R.

Vulnerable Workers

68. Quoted in Mary Conyngton, "Relation Between Occupation and Criminality of Women," in *Report on Condition of Women and Child Wage-Earners in the United States*, vol. 15 (Washington, D.C., Government Printing Office, 1911), p. 54.

69. Ida B. Ryan to Lucy Maynard Salmon, 5 February 1889, LMS.

70. Eliza Woodson Farnham, *Life in Prairie Land* (New York: Harper Bros., 1846), p. 15.

71. "The Doings and Goings-on of Hired Girls," *Lippincott's Magazine* 20 (1877): 589.

72. Mary Heaton Vorse, "Making or Marring, The Experiences of a Hired Girl," in Rosalyn Baxandall, Linda Gordon, and Susan Reverby, eds., *America's Working Women: A Documentary History, 1600 to the Present* (New York: Random House Vintage Books, 1976), p. 138.

73. Clarke, *Village Life*, p. 110.

74. Mehitable Goddard to Lucretia Dawes, 26 January 1829, May-Goddard Papers; Lavinia Field Stuart to Kate Stuart Baker, 25 March 1852, in R. Stuart, *The Stuart Letters*, p. 297. For a more ambiguous case, where the servant was perhaps merely inexperienced, see Martha Williams to Mary Hardy Williams, 18 August 1849, JBW. These reflections on the difficulties of service work for the developmentally disabled were suggested in part by a conversation with Karl Kabelac of the University of Rochester Library. Members of his family living in upstate New York early in the twentieth century employed a servant who could not tell time. She was, however, able to prepare meals punctually by noticing when the regularly scheduled trains passed on a nearby track.

75. SBF, 19 March 1874.

76. Martha Williams to Mary Hardy Williams, 26 August 1855, JBW; news items re Belle King in the *Cortland* (N.Y.) *Democrat*, 3 and 24 June 1887.

77. *Diary of Ellen Birdseye Wheaton*, p. 170.

78. Ellen Dwyer, "Female Insanity in Nineteenth-Century New York: An Analysis of Asylum Casebooks" (Paper delivered at the Quantitative History and Women's History Conference, Newberry Library, July 1979), pp. 7, 16.

79. Sarah Connell Ayer's family dismissed their hired girl not because she had a child but because she did not understand dairy work. See *Diary of Sarah Connell Ayer*, pp. 372–373. Also see Mehitable Goddard to Ann Goddard, 1 September 1828, May-Goddard Papers. Contemplating hiring a "Mrs. Gould" as a cook, Mehitable Goddard of Boston stipulated that she could bring her little daughter "provided however that the child has no *bad habits*, is kept under *proper discipline* and is tolerably bright." Mrs. Gould did not take the position. See Margaret Deland, *Golden Yesterdays* (New York: Harper & Bros, 1940), pp. 154–155, for the assumption, in the 1880s, that only those who hire help, as opposed to domestics, would be willing to take in a mother and child.

80. *Letters of Ralph Waldo Emerson*, Ralph L. Rusk, ed., 6 vols. (New York: Columbia University Press, 1939), 3:57.

81. Annals of the Home," p. 17, Papers of the Rochester Home for the Friendless, University of Rochester.

82. Ibid., pp. 20, 55.

83. On Mary Stebbins, see SBF, 14 March 1873. Libbie Reis [sp?] to Amy Kirby Post, 17 February 1863, Post Family Papers. See also Mary to Lizzie Camp, 30 April 1865, Camp Family Papers; Pleck, *Black Migration and Poverty*, pp. 192–193 re Lizzie Johnson, who left her illegitimate daughter with her aunts while she worked in service.

84. Chauncy Williams to Mary Hardy Williams, 11 November 1851, JBW.

85. *Plain Talk and Friendly Advice to Domestics*, pp. 106–107.

86. Information on the Anchorage is from research in progress by Joan Jacobs Brumberg based on the Records of the Anchorage at the Chemung County Historical Society, Elmira, New York.

87. See Pernicone, "The 'Bloody Ould Sixth,'" p. 164.

88. Mary Abigail Dodge, *Gail Hamilton's Life in Letters*, 2 vols. (Boston: Lee & Shepard, 1901), 2:660–661.

89. HWG, 15 September 1851.

90. Mrs. E. W. Knapp to Freeman Clarke, 31 March 1875, Freeman Clarke Papers.

91. Cited in Pleck, *Black Migration and Poverty*, p. 190.

92. Admissions records of the Home for Aged Women in Boston, 1858–1868, Schlesinger Library, Radcliffe College.

93. Kate Gannett Wells to Will and Mag, 10 August 1890, 18 June 1899?, Kate Gannett Wells Papers, University of Rochester.

Exits: Changing Jobs, Getting Married, Crime and "Vice"

94. *Cohoes Daily News*, 11 May 1881, cited in Daniel J. Walkowitz, "Working-Class Women in the Gilded Age: Factory, Community and Family Life Among Cohoes, New York Cotton Workers," *Journal of Social History* 5 (1972): 476.

95. Seline to Sophia Clarke, 10 August 1872, Freeman Clarke Family Papers; Anna O. Williams to Aunt Nancy, 4 September 1870, Camp Family Papers.

96. Maine Department of Labor and Industry, *Annual Report, 1910* (Augusta, Maine: Kennebec Journal Printing, 1910), p. 336.

97. Salmon, *Domestic Service*, p. 109.

98. Martha Williams to Mary Hardy Williams, 17 November 1856, JBW. See also Libby Gordon to Sarah Fairchild Dean, 15 August 1852, Elizabeth S. Gordon Correspondence, State Historical Society of Wisconsin.

99. Jane L. Hardy to Mary Hardy Williams, 20 November 1855, JBW; also Clarke, *Village Life*, p. 110: "Much to our surprise Bridget Flynn, who has lived with us so long, is married. We didn't know she thought of such a thing, but she is gone."

100. HWG, 27 December 1852. See a remark cited in Caroline Manning, *The Immigrant Woman and Her Job*, p. 148, by a girl from Hungary who entered domestic service in 1905: "I was sorry I took that job. Too hard work, that's why I get married."

101. Laura Porter to Maria Porter, 21 March 1830, Porter Family Papers.

102. Tentler, *Wage-Earning Women: Industrial Work and Family Life in the United States, 1900–1930* (New York: Oxford University Press, 1979).

103. See ibid., chapter 3.

104. See "Domestic Service," *Old and New* 6 (September 1872): 365; R. R. Bowker, "In Re Bridget: The Defense," *Old and New* 4 (October 1871): 500; "Bridget's Beau," *Journal of the Rochester Home for the Friendless* (1 May 1861), p. 72, reprinted from *The Presbyterian*; and Joseph W. Post to Isaac and Amy Post, 9 October 1854, Post Family Papers, referring to relatives having "discharged their girl two or three days ago because she had a lover come to see her." In Philadelphia in 1889 the New Century Guild of Working

Women held a discussion on why the "better sort" of girl avoided housework, and they mentioned "no place but the kitchen in which to receive her friends" and "the odious 'No Followers.'" See E. S. Turner to Miss Wood, 1 April 1889, LMS.

105. "Bridget's Beau," p. 72.

106. B. V. French to Lucy Maynard Salmon, 5 April 1890, LMS.

107. Sidney Stevens to Mother, 8 April 1858, B-S-R; Mehitable Goddard to Ann Goddard, 16 February 1820, May-Goddard Papers.

108. Mary Stevens to Mother, 14 February 1859, B-S-R. Re the maid who met a grocery delivery man, see Marie Haggerty's interview in Banks, *First-Person America*, pp. 171–172.

109. E. C. R. to Lucy Maynard Salmon, 16 January 1889, LMS.

110. "Domestic Service for Women," *The Revolution* 5 (10 February 1870): 86.

111. Webster, "Domestication and Americanization," pp. 275–290.

112. Thomas, *Migration and Economic Growth*, p. 74; Kennedy, *The Irish*, pp. 76–80.

113. See Schrier, *Ireland and the American Emigration*, pp. 25, 75. For evidence that marriage was both earlier and more likely for migrants to America, see John Modell and Lynn H. Lees, "The Irish Countryman Urbanized: A Comparative Perspective on the Famine Migration," in Theodore Hershberg, ed., *Philadelphia: Work, Space, Family and Group Experience in the Nineteenth Century* (New York: Oxford University Press, 1981), pp. 352–354.

114. Schrier, *Ireland and the American Emigration*, pp. 130–131.

115. See Conyngton, "Occupation and Criminality" pp. 73–74.

116. R. Stuart, *The Stuart Letters*, p. 384. See an apparently similar case in Diary of Mary Hardy Williams, 15 September 1843, JBW. When serious crimes did occur, they were treated with sensational publicity that put all employers on their guard. See for example the case described in "A Female Thief," the *Cortland* (N.Y.) *Democrat*, 8 May 1885. A domestic engaged at a New York City intelligence office worked briefly in an upstate home and carried off a diamond ring when she left. The whole town could savor the story as the local constable attempted to track her down.

117. New York Magadalen Society, *First Annual Report of the Executive Committee* (New York, 1831), p. 6.

118. F. Trollope, *Domestic Manners of the Americans*, p. 56.

119. See William W. Sanger, *The History of Prostitution* (1859; reprint ed., New York: Arno Press, 1972); Coynington, "Occupation and Criminality;" and other research summarized in Estelle B. Freedman, *Their Sisters' Keepers: Women's Prison Reform in America, 1830–1930* (Ann Arbor, Michigan: University of Michigan Press, 1981), pp. 121–125.

120. George Ellington, *The Women of New York* (1869; reprint ed., New York: Arno Press, 1972), p. 181.

121. Vorse, "Making or Marring," in Baxandell, Gordon and Reverby, *America's Working Women*, p. 138.

122. See Rosine Association of Philadelphia, *Reports and Realities*, p. 61, report for 1848; Dall, *Woman's Right to Labor*, pp. 173–174.

123. *Theodore Tilton versus Henry Ward Beecher*, 1:754, testimony of Kate Carey.

124. CBW, 16 April and 6 July 1874.

125. Rosine Association of Philadelphia, *Reports and Realities*, pp. 211–212.

126. Records of The Anchorage, Chemung County Historical Society, Elmira, New York.

127. Elizabeth Blackwell, *Pioneer Work in Opening the Medical Profession to Women* (1895, reprint ed., New York: Schocken Books, 1977), p. 79.

128. Mary Grace Ketchum file, Records of The Anchorage. But there were twice as many cases in which pregnant ex-servants either named men not of the employing family or else the identity of their seducers was not recorded or described as "unknown." The number of cases seems too small to support any conclusions from this breakdown.

129. See Karen Kearns, unpublished seminar paper on domestic service, History Department, City University of New York.

130. Elizabeth Sullivan Stuart to Kate Stuart Baker, 9 November 1851, R. Stuart, *The Stuart Letters*, p. 221.

131. Allan Nevins, *Study in Power: John D. Rockefeller, Industrialist and Philanthropist* (New York: Charles Scribners' Sons, 1953), 1:4.

132. See *Cortland* (N.Y.) *Democrat*, 4 November 1887, re Mary V. Mulvihill vs. J. Lawrence Brink; and cases brought before the Oneida conference of the Methodist Church referred to in Ryan, *Cradle of the Middle Class*, p. 36.

133. Nettie Fowler McCormick to Anita McCormick Blaine, 31 August and 8 September 1897, and enclosed clippings from the *San Francisco Chronicle*, Nettie Fowler McCormick Papers. See also "Married His Housemaid," The *Cortland* (N.Y.) *Standard* 16 July 1897, re the marriage of Dr. G. F. Cadwalader to Bridget Mary Ryan. The marriage was reported to have caused "quite a sensation in society circles" in Philadelphia.

134. Brossard suggests that it may have been common for small boys to experience "the first awakening of the romantic urge" through their awareness of servants as desirable women. Brossard, *Sociology of Child Development*, p. 272.

135. Rosine Association of Philadelphia, *Reports and Realities*, pp. 361–362.

136. Philadelphia Society for the Encouragement of Faithful Domestic Servants, *Address* (Philadelphia, 1829), p. 2.

137. Campbell, *Prisoners of Poverty*, pp. 234–235; Conyngton, "Occupation and Criminality," p. 74.

138. Sanger, *History of Prostitution*, pp. 535, 527.

139. See Ruth Rosen and Sue Davidson, eds., *The Maimie Papers* (New York: The Feminist Press, 1977), p. xviii.

140. Beecher and Stowe, *The American Woman's Home*, p. 466.

141. See their "'We Are Not Beasts of the Field': Prostitution and the Poor in Plymouth and Southampton Under the Contagious Diseases Acts," in Mary S. Hartman and Lois Banner, eds., *Clio's Consciousness Raised: New Perspectives on the History of Women* (New York: Harper & Row, Harper Torchbooks, 1974), p. 193.

142. For references to service as the refuge of ex-prostitutes, see La Rochefoucauld-Liancourt, *Travels Through the United States*, 2:678; Caroline Healey Dall, ed., *A Practical Illustration of Woman's Right to Labor; or, A Letter from Marie E. Zakrewska, M.D.* (Boston: Walker, Wise & Co., 1860), p. 12; A. Cook, *Armies of the Streets*, p. 135. On charitable organizations that attempted to channel ex-prostitutes into service, see Pickett, *House of Refuge*, pp. 3, 70–71, 78; and Henry J. Common and Hugh N. Camp, *The Charities of New York* (New York: Hard & Houghton, 1868), pp. 415–419, 459–462.

143. The Dora Armstrong file, 1893, Records of the Anchorage, and Joan Jacobs Brumberg's unpublished research on the institution.

144. Rosine Association of Philadelphia, *Reports and Realities*, p. 136.

145. See Brenzel, "Lancaster Industrial School," pp. 40–53. Of those girls who had been employed before coming to the school, more than half had been in service; forty-eight percent of the inmates were successfully indentured.

146. See Michael W. Sedlak, "Young Women in the City: Adolescent Deviance and the Transformation of Educational Policy, 1870–1960," *History of Education Quarterly* (in press).

Money and Mobility?

147. Beecher and Stowe, *The American Woman's Home*, p. 322.

148. Tomes, *Bazar Book of the Household*, p. 131.

149. Employers and servants alike routinely remarked that higher wages were available in the cities. See, for example, Mary Ann Burr to Mary Hardy Williams, 1856?, JBW; Clara Loring Bogart's *Emily*, discussed above, chapter 3; Lillian Krueger, "Motherhood on the Wisconsin Frontier," *Wisconsin, A Magazine of History* 29 (December 1945): 170–171; Rosine Association of Philadelphia, *Reports and Realities*, pp. 110, 211–212. See the wages Michigan farmers reported paying to their hired girls in Michigan Bureau of Labor and Industrial Statistics, *Twelfth Annual Report*, pp. 240–339. They were significantly lower than the wages reported for national and state samples of domestics at about the same time.

150. The most influential such conclusion was that of Salmon in *Domestic Service*, p. 165. Other surveys under discussion include: Laughlin, "Domestic Service"; Mary E. Trueblood, "Social Statistics of Working-women," *Massachusetts Labor Bulletin*, no. 18 (May 1901): 38–40; Mary E. Trueblood, "Housework Versus Shop and Factories," *The Independent* 54 (13 November 1902): 2691–2693; Massachusetts Bureau of Statistics of Labor, *Annual Report 1872* (Boston: Wright and Potter, 1872), pp. 59–67; Maine Department of Labor and Industry, *Annual Report, 1910*, pp. 311–343; Kansas Bureau of Labor and Industry, *Annual Report, 1894* (Topeka, Kansas: Hamilton Printing Co., 1895), pp. 198–203. David Katzman summarizes the surveys to conclude that earnings in service were "competitive" with earnings in other unskilled and semi-skilled female occupations: "When the equivalent cost of room and board are added to the annual earnings of domestic servants, their wages were at the same level or exceeded those of women in shops or in un- and semi-skilled factory jobs." *Seven Days a Week*, p. 313; also see appendix 3.

151. On the effects of male employment, see Krueger, "Motherhood on the Wisconsin Frontier," p. 170. Krueger reports that servants' wages were higher in the area of the lead mines in Wisconsin. Since it seems unlikely that women were employed in the mines, this is probably accounted for by higher male wages, which made it unnecessary for daughters to go out to work. On business cycle variation, see: Mehitable Goddard to Lucretia Dawes, 21 February 1830, May-Goddard Papers; "The Housekeeper's Millennium," *Lippincott's Magazine* 4 (July 1869): 78; "House Servants," p. 289; and New York State Commissioners of Emigration *Annual Reports* for the years 1869 and 1874. The Commissioners of Emigration reported wage rates for the women they placed in service that were consistently higher (11–25 percent higher) in the summer months than in the winter. The seasonal variation may reflect the availability of summer employment for working-class men in outdoor laboring jobs as well as alternative women's work in commercial agriculture—hop-picking, vineyards, and the like—or in resorts.

152. According to Susan Kleinberg, adolescents received fifty cents a week in Pennsylvania in the 1870s, while adult women earned two dollars. Cited in Katzman, *Seven Days a Week*, p. 305. In the spring of 1879 in Rochester a girl of fourteen could be hired for seventy-five cents per week, while two dollars a week was a low wage for an experienced adult. Susan Hooker to Mother, 9 March and 13 April 1879, Huntington-Hooker Papers.

153. In the 1930s George Stigler found that servants in high income families received wages 70 to 200 percent higher than those received by servants in middle-income families. He presents a Lorenz curve showing the unusual dispersion of servants' cash wages. See his *Domestic Servants in the United States, 1900–1940*, National Bureau of Economic Research, Occasional Paper 24 (New York, National Bureau of Economic Research, 1946), pp. 17–18 and chart 4. Similar differentials seem to have been common in the nineteenth century.

154. See Stigler, *Domestic Servants in the United States*, appendix B for a discussion of the biases of Salmon's and Laughlin's samples.

155. See, for example, two surveys that assume domestics worked a full fifty-two weeks a year: Massachusetts Bureau of Statistics of Labor, *Annual Report, 1872*, pp. 66–67; Salmon, *Domestic Service*, p. 98.

156. The 1872 Massachusetts survey pegged the value of room and board at $4.50. Salmon estimated $5.50 a week. Both figures were almost certainly too high.

157. See descriptions of working women's housing in Bessie McGinnis Van Vorst and Marie Van Vorst, *The Woman Who Toils* (New York: Doubleday, Page & Co., 1903); Dorothy Richardson, *The Long Day: The True Story of a New York Working Girl as Told by Herself* (New York: Century Co., 1905). Pernicone, "The 'Bloody Ould Sixth,'" pp. 67, 144; Carroll D. Wright, *The Working Girls of Boston* (1889; reprint ed., New York: Arno Press, 1969), pp. 127, 114.

158. See the Kansas survey, summarized in Katzman, *Seven Days a Week*, table A-21, p. 309; and Trueblood, "Housework Versus Shops and Factories."

159. Bettina Berch, "The 'Servant Crisis' and that Matter of Wages: Smokescreen or Lightning Rod?" (Paper delivered at the Social Science History Association Annual Meeting, October 23, 1981, Nashville, Tennessee), p. 13.

160. Ida Jackson, "The Factory Girl and Domestic Service," *Harper's Bazar* 37 (1903): 956.

161. Responses of C. A. Richardson to Schedule 2 Questionnaire, 1 December 1889, LMS.

162. See Weldon Welfling, *Mutual Savings Banks: The Evolution of a Financial Intermediary* (Cleveland: The Press of Case Western Reserve University, 1968), pp. 21–22; Alan L. Olmstead, "New York City Mutual Savings Banks in the Antebellum Years, 1819–1861" (Ph.D. dissertation, University of Wisconsin, 1970), pp. 90–91. Between 1819 and 1847 domestics comprised an average of 20 percent of the new customers of the New York Bank for Savings. They were an especially high percentage of new depositors between 1837 and 1844, reflecting the relative steadiness of service work in hard times. See Salmon, *Domestic Service*, p. 103; Laughlin, "Domestic Service," p. 751.

163. In Cleveland in 1870, for example, fifteen percent of all black male workers were domestic servants, compared to less than one percent of all male workers. See Kusmer, *A Ghetto Takes Shape*, p. 20. Also see Katzman, *Before the Ghetto*, pp. 110–111; Theodore Hershberg, "Free Blacks in Antebellum Philadelphia: A Study of Ex-slaves, Freeborn, and Socioeconomic Decline," in Hershberg, ed., *Philadelphia: Work, Space, Family and Group Experience in the Nineteenth Century* (New York: Oxford University Press, 1981), pp. 382–383. For a comparison with the Chinese, see Niles Carpenter, *Immigrants and Their Children, 1920*, census monograph, vol. 7 (Washington, D.C.: U.S. Government Printing Office, 1927), table 124. The

following remarks on the experience of blacks in domestic service are brief and tentative, meant to point out certain contrasts that seem evident when viewing service in general. The subject warrants treatment on its own; for a study that appeared too late to be consulted here, see Trudier Harris, *From Mammies to Militants: Domestics in Black American Literature* (Philadelphia: Temple University Press, 1982).

164. Emma Willard, *Via Media: A Peaceful and Permanent Settlement of the Slavery Question* (Washington, D.C.: C. H. Anderson, 1862).

165. On the bureau's placement efforts in Boston, see Pleck, *Black Migration and Poverty*, pp. 25–28. Sojourner Truth was associated with the bureau's placement efforts in Rochester, New York. See the letters to her from prospective employers, spring 1867, contained in the Post Family Papers. Re demand exceeding supply, see P. Glennan to Sojourner Truth, 25 March 1867, Post Family Papers.

166. Josephine Sophie White Griffing to Sojourner Truth and Amy Kirby Post, 26 March 1867, Post Family Papers.

167. Jacob Kirby Post to Amy Kirby Post, 25 April 1858; Jacob Kirby Post to Parents, 12 May 1858, Post Family Papers.

168. See Diary of Mary Hardy Williams 1867, and Mary Louise Williams to Mother, 5 April 1869, JBW; SBF, 1, 7, and 14 September 1872.

169. See Kellor, *Out of Work*, pp. 227–230.

170. See Hershberg, "Free Blacks in Antebellum Philadelphia," in Hershberg, *Philadelphia*, p. 190; Pleck, *Black Migration and Poverty*, pp. 168–169; Elizabeth Pleck, "A Mother's Wages: Income Earning Among Married Italian and Black Women, 1896–1911," in Michael Gordon, ed., *The American Family in Social-Historical Prespective*, 2nd ed. (New York: St. Martins Press, 1978), pp. 490–510; Claudia Goldin, "Female Labor Force Participation: The Origin of Black and White Differences, 1870 to 1980," *Journal of Economic History* 37 (March 1977).

171. For evidence that the cash wages of live-in and live-out servants were comparable, see: Robinson, "Domestic Workers and Their Employment Relations," pp. 30–31; and Katzman, *Seven Days a Week*, p. 263. Employers naturally resisted paying higher wages to domestics who were, in their view, less valuable because not always on call. It is not true, then, that the discrimination confining blacks to domestic service resulted in their being "pushed into an occupation with earnings higher than most other comparable occupations" (Katzman, *Seven Days a Week*, p. 273). On the contrary.

172. J. Wright, *The Complete Home*, p. 276. See also Carter G. Woodson, "The Negro Washerwoman, A Vanishing Figure," *The Journal of Negro History* 15 (July 1930): 269–277.

173. See Ellen Dwyer, "Categories of Female Insanity: A Case Study of Nineteenth-Century Black Women," (Unpublished paper, Department of Forensic Studies, University of Indiana), pp. 11–13.

174. Re residential patterns, see Berlin, *Slaves Without Masters*, pp. 253–257; Pleck, *Black Migration and Poverty*, p. 32. Re traditions of autonomy, see Katzman, *Seven Days a Week*, p. 197; and Terhune, *Marion Harland's Autobiography*, pp. 340–344, for an incident in which a southern cook "got her hand out" and refused to make bread.

175. Some employers expected or tolerated "totin'," while others considered it theft but could not effectively prevent it. See "More Slavery at the South" by a Negro Nurse, from *The Independent* (January 25, 1912), in Gerda Lerner, ed., *Black Women in White America: A Documentary History* (New York: Random House Vintage Books, 1973), p. 229; Evelyn W. Ordway to Lucy Maynard Salmon, 18 March 1889, [New Orleans], LMS; Katzman, *Seven Days a Week*, p. 198.

176. See Katzman, *Seven Days a Week*, pp. 216–218, and testimony excerpted in Lerner, *Black Women in White America*, pp. 275, 292.

177. Henry Seidel Canby, *The Age of Confidence: Life in the Nineties* (London: Constable & Co., 1935), pp. 26–27.

178. "Domestic Service," *Journal of the Rochester Home for the Friendless*, 5 (1 August 1862): 1.

179. See L. Broom and J. H. Smith, "Bridging Occupations," *British Journal of Sociology* 14 (1963): 321–334.

180. See Theresa McBride, *The Domestic Revolution: The Modernization of Household Service in England and France, 1820–1920* (New York: Holmes & Meier, 1976), pp. 82–99; and her "Social Mobility for the Lower Classes: Domestic Servants in France," *Journal of Social History* 8 (Fall 1974): 63–78; also Cissie Fairchilds, "Masters and Servants in Eighteenth-Century Toulouse," *Journal of Social History* 12 (Spring 1979): 368–393.

181. Carol Lasser traced young girls who were bound to service by the Salem Female Charitable Society and found that about one-fourth later received some form of public assistance. But it was not typical of servants to have been bound out. See Lasser, "A 'Pleasingly Oppressive' Burden"; pp. 173–174.

David Katzman's declaration that opportunities for upward mobility in service were more limited in the United States than in Europe seems weakly supported except as regards blacks. In the McBride study male servants constituted one of the largest groups of "upwardly mobile" bridegrooms for female servants. Such mobility seems marginal or debatable, and since in the United States the lack of male servants reflected greater labor market opportunities for men, it is hard to believe that American servants were worse off in their marriages. We know little about the relationship between savings and marriage chances. Many of the early Lowell mill girls were concerned to "lay up" money, but others did not. Did a working woman's savings actually make her a more desirable marriage partner, or did it merely permit a couple to marry without delay once they had decided on their intentions or to set up housekeeping promptly rather than board or live with in-laws for a time?

182. C. Beecher, *Letters to Persons Who Are Engaged in Domestic Service*, p. 75.

183. Irish immigrants writing home emphasized the heightened work discipline in America: "This is a driving country." See Schrier, *Ireland and the American Emigration*, pp. 27–28.

184. Frances Willard recalled that her mother taught English to many servants, especially Germans and Norwegians, on their farm in Wisconsin. See her *Glimpses of Fifty Years*, p. 49. For an example of one young Norwegian woman who went into service explicitly to learn English, see Krueger, "Motherhood on the Wisconsin Frontier," p. 171. See also remarks by Ole Raeder cited in Handlin, *This Was America*, p. 210. Caroline Manning's interviews with early twentieth-century immigrant women revealed contradictory views on this point. "Housework is best for greenhorns," one woman declared. "They learn how to do everything and get used to the country." But a Czech woman's knowledge of America was described as limited before her marriage, "chiefly on account of her confining work as a domestic." Another girl had gone into domestic service "thinking she would learn more English in a home than in a factory," "but she quit after six months because she "didn't understand the lady, she talked so strange." See Caroline Manning, "The Immigrant Woman and Her Job," pp. 109, 29, 148.

185. Susan Hooker to Mother, 4 March 1877, Huntington-Hooker Papers.

186. Mary Doyle Curran, *The Parish and The Hill*, excerpted in Maxine Schwartz Seller, ed., *Immigrant Women* (Philadelphia: Temple University Press, 1981), pp. 298–302.

187. Banks, *First-Person America*, pp. 170–174.

188. CBW, 17 July 1868. For references to daywork, see 18 December 1865 and 10 April 1867.

189. Ibid., 30 December 1870. For references to the pot of ivy, see 25 March 1867.

190. Salmon, *Domestic Service*, pp. 149–150.

191. *Plain Talk and Friendly Advice to Domestics*, p. 54.

192. Ibid., pp. 64–65. Note the similarity between this gathering and the one pictured by Spofford in *The Servant Girl Question*, pp. 58–59.

193. Emma Siniger to Frances Glessner, 28 September 1891, cited in Helen C. Callahan, "Upstairs-Downstairs in Chicago, 1870–1907: The Glessner Household," *Chicago History* 6 (1977–78): 208. My understanding of the ways in which "powerless" people can shape the circumstances of their lives even when they cannot directly challenge them owes a very great deal to Genovese's *Roll, Jordan, Roll*.

194. See Terhune, *Common Sense in the Household*, p. 367. First published in 1871, *Common Sense* was a very popular book, selling nearly 100,000 copies in the first edition.

195. See Banks, *First-Person America*, p. 171.

196. Harriet Beecher Stowe to Hatty, 9 June 1862, Beecher-Stowe Family Papers.

197. R. Stuart, *The Stuart Letters*, p. 192.

198. See Philip S. Foner, *Women and the American Labor Movement*, 2 vols. (New York: The Free Press, 1979) 1 : 176; Katzman, *Seven Days a Week*, pp. 195–197, 234–235. It is probably significant that these first organizing efforts arose among workers who all lived out and were of the same race. The Progressive era would see a number of short-lived attempts at forming servants' "unions," many of which were initiated by reform-minded employers to boost morale. A Chicago experiment sponsored by the Women's International Union Label League is described in Sutherland, *Americans and Their Servants*, pp. 133–137. By 1923 it would be possible to cite more than a dozen cities in which locals of domestic workers had been affiliated with the American Federation of Labor. See Elizabeth Ross Haynes, "Negroes in Domestic Service in the United States," *Journal of Negro History* 8 (1923): 435–436.

199. Mehitable Goddard to Lucretia Dawes, 8 July 1831, May-Goddard Papers.

200. Bremer, *Homes of the New World*, 2:607.

201. A. Cook, *Armies of the Streets*, 123.

202. Frances M. Glessner Journals, cited in Callahan, "Upstairs-Downstairs in Chicago," p. 207.

203. This family story, perhaps apocryphal, was told me by a participant in the Seneca Falls Women's History Conference, June 1979.

204. Diary of Julia Ward Howe, 29 July 1874, Houghton Library, Harvard University. Despite her support for reform causes, Julia Ward Howe maintained a haughtiness that must have made her a terror to work for. Anne Sullivan Macy clashed with her while still a young student at the Perkins School for the Blind and years later still nursed the grudge. "Mrs. Julia Ward Howe had the air of one who confers a favor by acknowledging one's existence," she recalled. See Joseph P. Lash, *Helen and Teacher: The Story of Helen Keller and Anne Sullivan Macy* (New York: Delacorte Press, 1980), pp. 34–35.

205. Glasco, "Life Cycles and Household Structure of American Ethnic Groups," p. 355.

206. My understanding of how the occupational choices of working-class children can be understood as reflections upon their parents' work experiences owes much to Richard Sennett and Jonathan Cobb, *The Hidden Injuries of Class* (New York: Random House Vintage Books, 1973). For data on the occupations of second generation immigrant women, see Hutchinson, *Immigrants and Their Children*, tables 29b, 33 and 35b. Also see Webster, "Domestication and Americanization," p. 286. This generational change for white ethnics again highlights the particularly deplorable conditions of blacks, who could not begin to effect such an escape from service until well into the twentieth century.

Conclusion

1. Sarah Glazier Bates to Lucy Maynard Salmon, 21 December 1889, LMS. (emphasis original).

2. Lucie Isaacs to Lucy Maynard Salmon, 26 December 1889, LMS.

3. M. A. O. Sutton to Lucy Maynard Salmon, 12 February 1889, LMS.

4. Mrs. George C. Ewing to Lucy Maynard Salmon (Enfield, Massachusetts) [1889], LMS.

5. Mary E. Bagg to Lucy Maynard Salmon, 4 September 1889, LMS.

6. Maria S. Oswig to Lucy Maynard Salmon, 27 February 1889, LMS.

7. Mary J. Strawbridge to Lucy Maynard Salmon, [1889], LMS.

8. L. W. Gould to Lucy Maynard Salmon, 12 February [1889], LMS.

9. Florence Wilcox to Lucy Maynard Salmon, 6 February [1889], LMS.

10. Florence Wilcox to Lucy Maynard Salmon, 11 February [1889], LMS.

11. C. W. Porter to Lucy Maynard Salmon, 13 April 1889, LMS.

12. *Bulletin* of the Inter-Municipal Committee on Household Research, vol. 1, no. 1 (November 1904), p. 1.

13. See I. M. Rubinow, "The Problem of Domestic Service," *Journal of Political Economy* 14 (1906): 502–519.

14. Strasser, "Mistress and Maid," pp. 52–67.

15. The best treatment of the twentieth-century decline of live-in domestic service is Katzman, *Seven Days a Week*, especially chapter two. The students in public high schools around the turn of the century were disproportionately female and seemed to include increasing numbers whose parents were "plain people," though the gender-differentiated effects of the rise of the high schools have not yet been studied. See: Edward A. Krug, *The Shaping of the American High School, 1880–1920* (Madison and London: University of Wisconsin Press, 1969).

16. Stanton, *Eighty Years and More*, p. 204.

17. HWG, 3 November 1852.

Index